CW00970208

'I wish it would last forever but as long as I am able to sit with a guitar on me lap, not even to sing to people but just to sing to myself, then I'll be all right.

''Cos sometimes when I'm in a bad mood I just go and lock myself into a room and just sing, just let off. So long as I've got that power then I'm the luckiest man in the world, because some people go out and shoot people 'cos they feel that way. But not me. I pick up my guitar and sing, "Dirty Old Town".'

Noel Gallagher, 25 May 1996

'It'll last as long as people keep their heads together. After six albums, which is what the deal was, once we do six albums – well, if we do six albums we're lucky – but as soon as six albums is up, then I'm off.'

Liam Gallagher, 12 August 1996

The Adventures of OASIS

Paolo Hewitt

GETTING HIGH

BOXTREE

First published 1997 by Boxtree

an imprint of Macmillan Publishers Ltd
25 Eccleston Place, London, SW1W 9NF
and Basingstoke

Associated companies throughout the world

ISBN 0 7522 0395 9

1 3 5 7 9 8 6 4 2

A CIP catalogue record for this book is available
from the British Library.

Cover design by Push, London
Photography Jill Furmanovsky

Typeset by SX Composing DTP, Rayieigh, Essex
Printed and bound by The Bath Press, Bath

This book is dedicated to
my mother Maria Supino (1921–1995),
and to battered and suffering children everywhere.
May music one day help to let you
see the light.

Acknowledgements

First and foremost my eternal thanks and praise go to Noel Gallagher, Liam Gallagher, Paul McGuigan, Paul Arthurs and Alan White. These are the members of Oasis who kindly invited me into their homes to talk about their past and present. They proved to be exactly the kind of people that their records said they would be. And then more.

I'd just like to add that many years ago I demonstrated to Noel a Roberto Baggio free kick using the last beer can in his house. The can swerved round a post, smashed against a wall and then spilt itself all over his carpet. Many thanks then for passing this ball back to me a year ago.

Special thanks also to Peggy Gallagher for taking the time to talk so candidly with me, a stranger in her house. This book would have been so much more poorer without her contribution. Major thanks also to Meg Matthews and the Oasis manager, Marcus Russell. Their contributions proved invaluable.

To all the other people connected to this amazing story and who graciously took time out to talk, I owe a real debt. They are Alan McGee, Owen Morris, Tim and Chris Abbot, Tony Griffiths, Graham Lambert and Johnny Hopkins.

Information also came from a series of informal chats that I found myself having with, Bobby Gillespie, Jeff Barrett, Bob Stanley, Johnny Marr, Martin and Paul Kelly, Andres Lokko, Tony Meehan, Miranda Sawyer, Tony Hedley, Marc Riley and the incorrigible Gareth Crowley. Again, a big yo and many thanks for your comments and insights.

In terms of research, I couldn't have asked for a more professional approach than that given to me by Beatrice Venturini. Her approach and dedication was, in the parlance of the group, double top. Similarly, Debbie Hicks at Go Discs

Acknowledgements

Records transcribed my interview tapes with a thoroughness that helped ease much of the weight from my shoulders. I am indebted to both women for their encouragement and hard work. My thanks also to Professor Mervyn Busteed for his more than helpful contribution to the history of Manchester section, and to Andy Spinoza for his help in detailing Manchester's club scene.

In terms of the band's radio and TV appearances I was greatly helped by Simon Kelly, who supplied me with three tapes filled with every Oasis TV appearance from start to early 1996. Many thanks. Also, seconds out and big thanks to Dean Powell whose procurement of certain CDs was just as valuable.

Thanks also to the eternal Mod, Eugene Manzi at London Records, daddy Nick White at Island, Iona at EMI's Premier label, and Matteo Sedazzi for supplying me with music that was absent from my collection but helped me no end in understanding Noel's writing and the subsequent Oasis sound.

Big thanks also to two guys and two gals at Anglo Plugging. They are head honcho Garry Blackburn, head of radio Dylan White, head of T.V. Karen Williams, and Ms. Bally Cheena.

Thanks also to the work put in by the band's photographer, Jill Furmanovsky, and her assistant Merle. Great gals, happy snappers. Another shout across town to Alec and Chris at Ignition Management for their patience in taking all my calls and answering all my questions.

I would also like to thank the following people for their help down the line. They are Stephanie Fertardo, Mark McNulty, Dean Marsh, Johnny Chandler, Mark Coyle, Phil Smith, David Irving, Andrew Whitelegg, Johnny and Kate, Fran and Charlotte Cutler, Digsy and all in Smaller, Pete Johnson, Len Brown, Brian Cannon, Irvine Welsh and Anne, all those connected to the Primal Scream, Real People and Ocean Colour Scene brigades, Andy MacDonald, Mike Heneghan, Michelle Potts, Fergus and Pete, Pippa Hall, Tony Crean, Naomi for the Bobby pic, Pete and Claire Barrett, George and Jenny, John and Anne Weller, Kenny Wheeler, Pete Garland and his beautiful family, the Woking boys and gals, Jim Le Hat, Mark Lewisohn, BBC2 for re-running *The Phil Silvers Show*, my two sisters Frankie and Nina, plus their husbands Pete and Alan, my three nieces Katy, Tanya Susannah, and the ever supportive Ms. Jess of Fulham's Cars and Bars, and Dean Kavanagh.

Acknowledgements

Top marks as ever to my daughter, Sarah Jane Bacchuss, plus the three geezers who go by the names of Paul Weller, Sir Simon Halfon and Marco Nelson. They are HEAVYWEIGHTS! Thanks also to Travis and Tash, who live in the nearest faraway place, to Dr. Eyal Lederman for sorting the movement on my shoulder so quickly, ('It's okay, I'll fix that'), and a special yo to my NHS physician, Dr. Le Roi Griffiths for his indispensable dispensary of medications. Last but never least, many big thanks to Ruth, Patsy, Kate and her daughter Lucy.

All the tour reports to be found in this book were helped no end by the Oasis road crew who went out of their way to make my 'holidays' with the band so enjoyable. For their care and general piss-taking, big thanks to Maggie, Jason, Scotty, Hugh, PK, Bear, Frank, Roger (Bradford football in the shops) and Trigger.

My thanks also to Jake Lingwood at Boxtree for his editorial input, general encouragement, impossible demands and for steering this book through the rocky waters to its graceful conclusion. Thanks to Jenny Parrott for her immense copy-editing skills.

Contents

Intro

Always at it. Always. The pair of them. Noel and Liam, Liam and Noel. The Gallagher brothers. Will it ever stop, this struggle for control? Probably not. Probably never. Tonight, of course, is no exception.

It is Friday 8 September 1995, and the whole country is still sweating on an inordinately hot summer. The days of late have been sticky, unbearable even, but the nights bring a warm calming breeze.

As London slowly cools down that evening, Noel Gallagher sits in the reception room of the Maison Rouge Studios in Fulham. Stamford Bridge, Chelsea's football ground, is a few hundred yards down the road.

On the table in front of him is a plate of Chinese food that he is eagerly digging into. The clock on the wall reads eight-thirty and there are three women sitting with Noel. They are his girlfriend, Meg Matthews, and her friends, Fran and Jess, and they too are eating.

Noel has known them all for about a year, ever since, in fact, he moved down to London and started seeing Meg. Above them the TV is on but the sound is down.

In the studio nearby, the producer, Owen Morris, is busy, mixing two new Oasis songs. They are called 'Round Are Way' and 'The Masterplan'. Noel has written the latter just two weeks ago and he plans to present both songs on Oasis's forthcoming single, 'Wonderwall'.

Noel is the band's leader, the songwriter. Nothing happens to Oasis without his say-so. His nickname within Oasis is 'The Chief', and his grip on the group is hard, tight, unshakeable.

Suddenly, literally out of nowhere, the man who has claim to the title of most charismatic frontman of the decade is looming over everyone at the table. His entrance has been so swift, so unconsciously dramatic, that everyone is taken by surprise. But before they can react, Liam Gallagher has kicked off.

'What the fuck do you think you're doing?'

The singer knows everyone at the table but he doesn't acknowledge any of them. He just stands there his eyes burning into Noel's face.

'I said, what the fuck do you think you're doing?'

Liam is wearing a bulky red and blue Adidas coat, tightly zipped up, as usual, to his neck. Beneath that are pale blue baggy jeans that bunch up by his ankles, and white trainers that halt their progress.

His brown hair is brushed forward and his eyes challenge his brother for a satisfactory answer. There is sweat on his forehead.

Behind Liam, uncomfortably lurking by the doorway, there is a girl. She is tall, skinny with long, shiny black hair and a pale thin sexy face. She stands staring at the ground, ignoring everybody.

Noel looks up, holding his fork. His face is slightly rounder than Liam's and his eyes are not as big. It means that his look is not as adaptable as Liam's, who one minute can look like a football hooligan, and the next boyishly desirable.

Noel's face is harder, less chameleon-like, craggy even. There are wrinkles round his eyes that shouldn't scar a twenty-eight-year-old face and his nose tilts a little to the right. Even so, he possesses a strange handsome look.

Tonight he is wearing a button-down white shirt, jeans that reach his ankles and a pair of black laceless shoes.

'What the fuck do you mean?' he demands. When Noel confronts his brother it is noticeable that his voice tends to go up a register.

'The vocals, man. That's what I'm talking about.'

'What about them?'

'They're wrong.'

'What do you mean, they're wrong?'

'They're wrong.'

'Look,' Noel states, 'if you don't tell me what's up with them, how the fuck am I meant to know what you're on about?'

He looks to his companions for confirmation of the truth in his statement but all three women concentrate on their food. Heads down, they stay silent, stay out of it.

'They're mixed all wrong,' Liam snaps back.

'No, they're not.'

'Yes they are.'

'Are they fuck,' Noel dismissively says before turning his attention back to the food in front of them.

The song Liam is talking about is 'Round Are Way', a stomping brass-driven song that Noel refers to, when he plays it to people, as 'the Oasis tribute to Northern Soul'.

'You can't fucking hear me properly,' Liam then says. Noel ignores him, carries on eating.

'It's a top song,' Liam adds, 'and you've fucked it right up.'

He looks at the girl near the doorway and jerks his head back. He is saying, let's split.

As they walk out, Noel looks up and shouts after him, 'I do know something about mixing a record, you know. I've been doing it the past two years in case you hadn't noticed, you dickhead.'

Noel resumes eating but the incident is bugging him so badly now, he can't enjoy his food. He drops his fork on to the table, pushes his plate aside, stands, and without a word heads for the studio.

He walks determinedly down the corridor, gold discs hanging on the walls, and pushes through the studio's heavy, sound-proofed doors. The first thing he sees as he enters is Owen at the mixing desk.

Scattered around the producer are half-empty silver cartons of takeaway food, beer cans and cigarette packets. Owen, a well-built man with short hair and an oval face, is sitting on a chair that has wheels. He is pushing himself along the desk, hitting various coloured buttons.

Blasts of music come firing out of the speakers above him. Owen pushes a button and it stops. The whine of a tape rewinding can be heard in the far corner. Owen then hits another button and the music starts again. The studio is half-lit, darkish.

Liam and the girl are sitting on a sofa behind Owen. They are not looking at each other or touching. Nobody is saying a word.

'Dickhead thinks the vocals aren't mixed up enough,' Noel announces to Owen. 'Dickhead thinks we don't know what we're doing.'

Owen briefly smiles and carries on pushing buttons, wheeling his chair along the desk. It is obvious that he too doesn't want to get involved. He has already spent many hours in the studio with the brothers and he knows this scene back to front.

'I didn't say that you didn't know how to mix fucking records,' Liam retorts, 'I said the vocals are not mixed up enough. You can't hear them.'

'You can't hear the vocals?' Noel replies.

'No, I can't hear my vocals and I think that ruins the song.' Liam enunciates the sentence as if he is talking to a dumb kid.

'Everybody else can hear the vocals but you can't?' Noel asks, using the same tone of voice as his brother.

The girl next to Liam looks uneasy but he laughs loudly. 'Who's everyone else?' he asks.

'Well, everybody else in this room to begin with,' Noel says.

'Well, I'm not everybody else. And who else are you talking about? Bonehead? Guigsy?'

'Oh yeah, Guigsy,' Noel says, picking up his cigarette box. 'How is Guigsy these days?' he asks of the Oasis bass-player.

'He's doing double fine.'

'Is he?'

'Yeah he is. Fucking double top, Guigsy is.'

'That's not what I heard. I heard different to that.'

'Did you?' Liam sardonically asks. 'Well, I haven't.'

'Well, I have,' Noel throws back, real irritation in his voice.

Owen stops pushing buttons and stops to stare at his desk. The girl next to Liam crosses her long legs.

'Marcus says he's in a bit of a state,' Noel continues. 'And it's funny, isn't it? Guigsy's fine and then off you all go to France while I stay here trying to learn how to mix a record and, surprise, surprise, he comes home early and he's not very well. Funny that, isn't it?'

'Yeah, double funny.'

'That's what you think, is it? That it's all double funny.'

'Look, it's got fuck all to do with me, mate. I told you what happened. Told you enough times.'

'Oh yeah? Well let's hear it again.'

Noel extracts a cigarette from his box and lights it. Strangely, he holds the ciggy between the second and third finger of his right hand and he shakes it accusingly at Liam. 'Because I know,

I just know you had something to do with it. I fucking know you did.'

'I didn't,' Liam protests. 'All I did . . .'

'All you did was to fuck things right up.'

'Hang on, hang on, you haven't heard what I've got to say, have you?'

Now the words are getting heated, the voices are being raised. No one else really knows where to look; all they know is that they don't want to get involved. But right now all Noel and Liam are aware of is each other. All they can see is each other. All they can hear is each other.

'Come on then,' Noel says, 'let's hear what you've got to say. This should be good, this.'

'I've told you once.'

'Well, fucking tell me again.'

Liam snorts defensively and begins his tale. 'We go to Paris and we're in this hotel, blathering to the press and all this shit, and suddenly, where's Guigsy? Nowhere to be seen. So we go up to his room, bang on the door and tell the mad cunt to get out of bed.'

'All you did was bang on the door.'

'That's all we did. Bang on his door. So the mad cunt is in there puffing up and we go in . . .'

'Hang on a sec,' Noel demands. 'You bang on his door and then go in even though the door is locked.'

'No, you mad fucker,' Liam replies, 'Guigsy let us in. Okay?'

Noel nods his head. Liam continues, 'So we said, "What you doing?" He goes, "I'm staying in bed." So we get him up . . .'

'How did you get him up?'

'Fuck sakes,' Liam says, 'we didn't beat him up or anything.' He shakes his head in amazement that his brother should think like that.

'We just told him to come out with us, right? So we go to this bar and there's some dickhead there and Guigsy goes, "I'm going to whack that guy."'

'And you said?'

'All I said was, "Well, hit him," 'cos to be honest, I'm sick and tired of people in this band saying they're going to hit someone and they don't. You're going to whack someone, whack them. If not, shut up.'

7

'And that's all you said to him?'

'That's all I said to him.'

'You're a fucking liar, mate. You said more than that to him. I know you did. I know you. I know what you're like.'

'I'm not a liar, dickhead. I said . . .'

'Oh for fuck's sake!' Owen has had enough and now he's snapped. He swivels round in his chair and says, 'For fuck's sake you two, you always get into one, don't you?'

'Well fucking tell him,' Liam shouts, pointing at Noel who is now smirking back at him, happy to see Liam riled. 'Don't fucking tell me. I'm telling the truth. That dickhead won't believe me.'

Noel again shakes his cigarette accusingly at his brother and says, 'There's more to this. I know it and I'm going to get to the bottom of it.'

'Look,' Owen interjects, raising his hands like a boxing referee who wants to stop a fight, 'can we please just listen to the mix.'

Before either Noel or Liam can say a word, Owen turns back to the desk, pushes a large button and the sound of a gentle acoustic guitar drifts in, its melody counterpointed by soft notes from a shimmering electric guitar. The guitars are joined by some slow swooping orchestral strings which add another melody before Noel's voice enters, plaintive but strong. This is 'The Masterplan'.

He sings, 'Take the time to make some sense/ Of what you want to say/ And cast your words away upon the waves/ And sail them home with acquiesce upon a ship of hope today/ And as they land upon the shore/ Tell them not to fear no more.'

Now the orchestra gets louder as Noel's voice changes from its gentle mode into one of hopeful determination.

'Say it loud and sing it proud today,' he urges before reaching the contagious chorus line, 'Dance if you want to dance/ Please brother take a chance,' and a horn section is introduced, adding to the majesty of the music as the song reaches its first climax.

Unexpectedly, a distorted electric guitar, like John Lennon's on 'I'm Only Sleeping' now butts in, rubbing against the strings, taking us up to the bridge. Then as Noel again urges, 'Say it loud and sing it proud today,' the song dips into its second chorus, propelled by chugging strings.

After the second verse, which contains the lines, 'Because everything that's been has passed/ The answer's in the looking glass/ There's four and twenty million doors on life's endless corridor,' the song goes back into its triumphant chorus before reaching its zenith, Noel's electric guitar solo put with backing vocals, strings, horns, all of them climbing together before an acoustic guitar enters to take us back to earth, back to ground. Its a masterpiece. The song ends with Noel's reverberating guitar sending out silver shivers of notes and chords.

In the studio there is a momentary silence and then Liam stands up, goes over to Noel and says, 'That is as good as any Beatles' song, I'm telling you man, it is. You don't know how fucking good you are.'

Noel looks shyly at the floor, drags on his cigarette.

Liam turns excitedly to Owen and the girl, a huge smile on his lips. Once again the music has healed the Gallagher brothers.

'And it's a B-side,' Liam excitedly exclaims. 'How fucking top is that?'

PART ONE

One

Tomorrow, she starts work. Proper work, that is. Her schooling is over now, finished for good. So is her youth. Now she is an adult with a job and responsibilities.

The year is 1956 and the place is County Mayo, situated in West Ireland. Her name is Peggy Sweeney and one day she will marry and bear the surname Gallagher. She is just thirteen years old.

Right now she is not thinking about school. Her thoughts are on the house in Charlestown where tomorrow she will get on her knees and clean and scrub, cook and dust. It is a big house, an imposing house that she will walk to in the cold dawn mist, a house stocked with objects and valuables that she has heard about but never ever seen. She hopes that these rich people, the O'Haras, will be nice.

To be sure, she can hardly imagine such wealth. Yet one day, incredible and staggering amounts of money will be sitting at her very fingertips, hers to keep if she so chooses. The sons that she is to bear will become world-famous. They will make millions and then they will bring those riches to her. But all she will ask for is a bigger colour TV.

Today, there is no work. Today Peggy will sit by the small stream that passes by the bottom of her garden and stare at her watery reflection. She is dressed in a grubby cotton dress and her feet are bare. She has sea-shell eyes and dark brown hair. Above her the sky is an azure blue and the sun is a yellow snooker-ball.

Around her are the fields and the open spaces that she knows so well; she has played here, laughed, cried and fallen upon this land.

Behind Peggy, stands her mother's home, a tiny two-up, two-down house that has ten children and one adult under its roof. Cows, chickens, hens and pigs surround it. Through their intermittent cacophony, the sound of her mother singing can be heard through the open window. The melody is Irish, the words are Gaelic.

Her ma has a rich, deep voice, a resonant voice that always brings pleasure. In the village the people say, 'Ah, that Sweeney woman, have you heard her sing? Such a happy woman, such a happy sound.' When Peggy hears those words about her mother it makes her feel so proud.

A light wind comes up and passes through Peggy's hair. She gives a slight shiver and looks down at the water to try to get a glimpse of her future. Occasionally she has sensed what is to happen next. But today, all she can see is work and tiny piles of worn-out pennies.

From an early age, she has known that life would never be easy. It is the way of the world, the way of her people who say that in life there are two realities: there are your dreams and then there are the facts – you are allowed one but you must obey the other.

In Peggy's dreams she would have liked to have stayed on at school. She loved reading and learning about Irish language and culture. But the luck was against her.

The family turns to Peggy. There are eleven of them now. If Peggy stays at school and lives in her dreams, how will they eat?

Her brother Paddy had already gone and now he is in Yorkshire. Each day he descends into the earth to wrench out coal, hour after hour after painful hour. When his paypacket arrives, his grimy hands rip open the flimsy envelope and his blistered fingers carefully extract a certain amount. Then he slowly walks to the post office and sends the money to his mother, his brothers and sisters. He does this every week. He is a good man, her brother, a great man. Unlike her father he hasn't deserted them.

Now it is Peggy's turn to help. She doesn't question this fact or allow herself any regrets. It is the way of the world and she can't change it.

You get on with things the best you can. Life is hard but it is simple if, like Peggy and all the villagers, you are not given the chance to make it complex. Plus, her ma calls her the most responsible of her children, and that must stand for something.

Peggy gazes down at the stream again. She studies the passing clean water for signs but there are none. How could she know that her mother's voice, so strong and so clear, would actually echo down the years? That it would never die. That it would, in fact, be immortalised.

Through Peggy that voice will travel to Manchester and there be passed on to her sons. And they, years later, will take that voice all around the world, and people everywhere will be hypnotised and inspired by its sound; their heads filled with colour and hope.

How could Peggy know such a fantastic thing at age thirteen? On the day before she began proper work?

Such possibilities hadn't even been invented.

So Peggy Sweeney, still mesmerised by the endless water that passes by her feet, gazes down into the river and looks upon the reflection of her face. It is glimmering, shimmering, and although today there is no sign, it really doesn't matter, because she has never felt happier to be sitting there, a proud and happy child, a tiny real piece of God's work.

Hard people, the Irish: hard workers, hard thinkers, hard players. God had made them so because theirs was a land of extremes, a country of hope washed in suffering. Famine, invasion, war and poverty had all, like vengeful banshees, ridden the Irish land, cutting down all before them. Yet still, in the face of such atrocities, the people sang, and still they endured.

'The Irish sing the saddest songs in the universe and then they get on with it,' Sex Pistol frontman John Lydon once wrote. Later on, in a more pertinent phrase, he noted, 'The Irish don't give a fuck.' This was also true, and between those two quotes would stand Noel and Liam Gallagher.

The Irish paused, not for self-pity but to find a way out of their desperate predicaments. They cast their eyes northwards and they saw the promised land that would deliver them. Its name: America.

Over the years, millions upon millions travelled there, to become policemen, labourers and politicians. Those that climbed the ladder and realised the dream had to be well versed in survival techniques.

The outside is a cold and useless place to be. Being on the outside, it kills. Literally. Ireland and capitalism, poverty and discrimination, taught them that. They learnt their lessons quickly. By the turn of this century, Tammany Hall, New York's centre of political power, was run by the Irish.

Yet America wasn't within everyone's grasp. There were other havens nearer to home for those wishing to escape but who had neither the strength nor the financial means to cross the Atlantic. Much nearer to home there lay Great Britain.

The British, insular and suspicious of everyone but their own, didn't take too well to the Irish. As early as 1413 the Crown was drawing up deportation laws to remove 'Irish vagrants' from their soil.

In the 16th and 17th centuries English troops were routinely sent over to campaign against the Irish. Many of the soldiers on these missions hailed from Manchester, although later on a more peaceful link between the Mancunians and the Irish would be established. Naturally, money would be the peacebroker.

Ireland's ability to provide raw wool and linen, and then livestock, dairy produce and fish to the English, set up a strong economic and cultural link between Ireland and Manchester which persists to this day.

Yet the image of the Irish person that was forged in the minds of the English, etched there by a media only too willing to act on behalf of the day's government, was not good, not good at all.

One potent source of derision was through humour; the major newspapers often carried anti-Irish cartoons. They depicted the Irish as yobs on the scrounge, uncivilised, stupid, incapable of anything but fraud and deceit. 'Did you hear the one about the Irishman . . .' isn't a new phrase.

In 1780 the winds of 'luck' changed. The Irish were suddenly in demand: to assist their rapidly expanding cotton industry, Manchester turned to Ireland's skilful hand-loom weavers, promising them significantly higher wages and better living-conditions.

It wasn't a hard choice to make. In Ireland even the farmers have it tough. In many areas the soil isn't particularly fertile; in County Mayo, for example, the spartan land is too exposed to the elements, especially rain, and only grass, oats and potatoes will grow. And, like the land they tilled, the Irish culture was also conservative, based as it is around the restrictive teachings of the Roman Catholic Church.

The first great wave of Irish migration to protestant Great Britain was in 1780. For those early travellers a huge culture-shock was awaiting them. They landed as the Industrial Revolution was starting to take shape.

It was bad timing on their behalf. New developments in machinery were about to cause the biggest upheaval that English society had ever known, and the Irish would bear the brunt of these turbulent times, pushed into extremes of poverty that would shock the world.

Manchester was about to become the first-ever modern industrial centre. And that kind of change doesn't come easy.

Paddy was the first born. Then came John, and Bridie. On 30 January 1943 Margaret Sweeney gave birth to her second daughter. She was christened Peggy and brought back to Margaret and her husband William's tiny house in Mayo. Over the next few years, there would be more brothers and sisters, namely Kathleen, Helen, Ann, Una, Pauline, Billy and Den.

The house the Sweeneys lived in stood on flat bog-land amid a beautiful but harsh landscape. It had been bequeathed to Margaret by John and Mary, her aunt and uncle. Margaret herself came from a family of eleven. As a little child, she had been sent to her aunt's to live. They had no family, so they welcomed her arrival.

When they died, the house was bequeathed to her. Margaret then married William and settled down to do what all women of her area did, which was to bring life into the world, and then nurture it as best she could. William worked as a labourer but sadly he wouldn't always stand by his wife's side.

Margaret would endure her husband abandoning her, not once, but twice. The first time occurred after the birth of Una; the second time after the eleventh child, Den, was born. Like most of Mayo's inhabitants, the Sweeneys were poor, desperately poor. Life was a tough struggle, further exacerbated by the elements. When harsh winter came and the land refused to yield food, well, that was the worst of it. Not to mention the lack of heating.

Each day, Peggy and her family would rise early from the beds they had crammed into, bruised somewhat by their unconscious kicking of each other as they slept. With hours of disturbed sleep behind them, and violently shivering against the cold, they would put on yesterday's clothes and wonder if today, at least, there might be enough food for breakfast. On some mornings, there would be nothing to fill their stomachs for the walk to school.

Each child had his or her own job to do round the small house, although its cramped size meant there was little to do. Even so, the boys would be allotted the manual work while the girls would wash, sew, clean and cook. One of the first lessons that Peggy learnt was that women tended to the house and the men went out into the world to do the tough work.

It was a way of life that was enthusiastically backed up by the Catholic Church. God had put women on this earth to give birth and raise children. Catholic children. Good Catholic children. This tenet was so sternly ingrained in them, they never once dared question its wisdom.

With breakfast finished, they would pull on their coats and, as morning light started to break, walk the one and a half miles to their school. It was named Chorton. In Ireland, at the time, there was no separation between the ages, and no primary or secondary schools.

Chorton was a National School: you stayed there until your circumstances forced you to leave. Most left early. At school Peggy loved reading. She especially liked girl's comics with titles such as *Secrets*. When she was engrossed in these magazines or if she had her nose in a book, it was as if the world and all its hardships magically fell away.

Reading suited Peggy. She wasn't a boisterous girl and she never drew attention to herself. She was quiet, withdrawn, a little bit of a dreamer, but with a strong sense of responsibility.

The lessons that captivated her mind the most were the Gaelic class (although today she would be hard pressed to remember a sentence), and English where she could indulge her love of reading. She wasn't good at sports but loved knitting and needlework at which she excelled. Again, it was another activity which allowed her to slip free from herself.

At the end of school, she would walk home again. On a lot of these occasions her stomach would ache with the pain of not eating all day. When she arrived home there would be a meal, usually made of milk and potatoes, awaiting her.

If Peggy was deprived financially, the same couldn't be said of her emotionally. The Sweeney children belonged to a tight, loved family, never starved of love. For sure the sisters tended to band together against the boys, and that was only natural. But there was no cruelty, no violence. Their parents gave them love and discipline, fully preparing them for the world by not allowing them any illusions. William and Margaret knew how tough things were, and weren't about to fool their children.

When Peggy was seven years old she received her first Communion. From then on the weekend belonged to her church: confession on Saturdays, Mass on Sundays. This small church, Bushfield was its name, lay to the West of the village and it was here, as well as school that Peggy was indoctrinated into the ways of a religion obsessed with sexual purity and strict moral behaviour.

In Catholicism priests do not marry, and boys born illegitimate can never enter the priesthood. To lose your virginity before marriage was a sin and, to this day, the use of contraception is strictly forbidden. Homosexuality was viewed as absolute proof of the Devil's work.

The Catholic Church instilled everlasting sexual and moral guilt in all its children, and Peggy was no different. She learnt about good and bad, heaven and hell. She was taught that one of the worst things that could ever happen to her was to be excommunicated from the Church. It would mean eternal damnation.

When Peggy thought about her God she imagined a vengeful and wrathful God, precisely what the Church wanted. Complete social control. The Church took the young and stole their minds. It taught that all people are born in sin and must spend their lives in penance. It said no one is without evil.

When Peggy went out into the world and married, she had to bear children and she must never, never, ever divorce; to part from your husband would mean severance from the Church. The Vatican would never sanction divorce, and therefore it was considered a terrible sin for which there could be no forgiveness. Such powerful ideas invade an impressionable young mind. At an early age Peggy vowed she would stick by her eventual husband, good or bad.

No one missed Mass in Mayo. It was unthinkable. Everyone went. In rain, sleet, snow and cold winds that howled across the bleak landscape in winter, Peggy and her family walked up their *bordeen* (country lane) and through the fields to church every weekend.

And still the babies kept arriving, one every year. Eventually there were too many children to house. Peggy, along with Kathleen, Una, Helen, Ann and Bridie were placed in the hands of a convent school in Ballaghaderren where they stayed for the next six and a half years and were further exposed to the scriptures and strictures of Catholocism. Yet Margaret knew that out of all her brood Peggy was the most reliable and the hardest worker. More than that, Peggy had a natural affinity for child rearing. Many times, with her baby sister Pauline in her hands, she would dream of the day when it would be her child that she would be tending to. It was the only dream that she would ever be encouraged to follow.

It was the twin forces of human invention and rugged determination that lay at the core of Manchester's dramatic rise.

Water power, the first steam-engines, the spinning jenny, the mule and the power loom, all of these revolutionised Manchester's cotton industry; made it, in fact, the first British industry to be fully mechanised.

To achieve such a vision, the people behind these changes had to be a dynamic breed. They had to be strong-willed and utterly single-minded in their pursuit of the New World that they had visualised, a new age which they, and only they, could define and make their own.

The architects of this vision were young, powerful Mancunian businessmen, determined to build Jerusalem on England's green and pleasant land, and so be acknowledged as the saviours of the country.

Their first move was to sweep away the old feudal system. Under this arrangement a Lord would give his workers land to farm, dwellings to live in and a wage, which was swiftly returned to him through rent charges.

In Manchester's case, the ruling power was the Moseley family. Their power was supposedly absolute, but to the new Mancunian it was spurious. The Moseleys were perceived as weak masters, ditherers who had no firm grip or vision. Manchester had no municipal infrastructure and very little in the way of administrative organisation. It laid the way open for change. In other words, if you wanted to build a factory and you had the money, power and vision, then it was yours to build. No one could stand in your way.

Unfettered by local laws or government, the new Mancunians zealously went to work, building huge factories and filling them with all the new machinery. They deliberately began a campaign to create a climate of enterprises, an 'every man for himself' ethos which rivalled Thatcherism in its brazen fanaticism.

As a speaker put it at the Manchester Mechanics organisation, 'Man must be the architect of his own fame.' The message was clear: it was everyone for themselves.

For many of the newly arrived Irish hand-loom weavers this was an unexpected development. By the time they had settled in, they literally had been displaced by machines and forced into factories. For these country dwellers who had fought and loved nature all their lives, it was hell on earth.

First of all, their rural lifestyle hadn't prepared them for city life. It was noted that many of them walked the streets barefooted, while their obvious Catholic fervour did little to impress their new Protestant neighbours. Furthermore, their willingness to accept such small wages (yet double their pay-packet back home) intensely annoyed those organisations that had sprung up in an attempt to reform the city's work conditions. For these concerned cabals, run by middle-class liberals, the factories symbolised all that was evil in this brave new world. It wasn't hard to see why.

Ugly, filthy and dangerous, these factories had no ventilation, no heat in the winter. The workers were forced to work nineteen-hour shifts for wages of just four shillings a week. And most of that went on rent and food.

Furthermore, their accommodation provided no respite from these conditions. The Irish squeezed into minute cottages, most of which had walls which were only one brick thick. In wintertime they huddled together against the biting winds that would howl through their small rooms and extinguish their fires. There was no ventilation and few sanitary amenities.

The Irish and their children were being crushed and, by severe poverty and disease, sacrificed to the new Mancunian's greed and inhumanity. Many children, some as young as seven years old, worked in factories; often they died before their years reached double figures. Many babies died through the administration of sleeping medicines, given to them by desperate mothers who simply didn't have the time to tend to them. These mothers were forced into the factories and away from their babies' side; the alternative meant they would all starve to death.

Cholera festered in the water and indiscriminately struck down whole families. So too did the cyclical nature of capitalism, where a boom-time is always followed by a slump.

As Manchester expanded, so it became a schizophrenic city with two strikingly different realities. The first was the one the businessmen were keen to promote: that is, Manchester as the world's first industrialised city. Its fame was worldwide, and observers came from many continents to study this civic success. Unfortunately, often they returned home depressed and shocked by the second reality, the atrocious living conditions from which they couldn't avert their eyes.

Henry Coleman, a visiting American, described the poor of Manchester as 'wretched, defrauded, oppressed, crushed human nature, lying in bleeding fragments all over the face of society'.

Frederick Engels arrived from Germany. He had been sent over by his rich industrial father to look after the family interests in some local cotton mills. Engels spent the next twenty-three years in the city and in 1845 he published his famous treatise, *The Condition Of The Working Class In England*. In it he devoted a whole chapter to Manchester, using the experiences of Mary and Liazzie Burns, two daughters of Irish immigrants with whom he lived for many years.

He described the city's poor as 'A physically degenerate race robbed of all humanity'. Engels and Coleman weren't alone in their disgust.

Yet the new Mancunian proved impervious to such conditions or the pleas for compassion that they were eliciting. Of far more concern to them were the issues of the day; and none more so than the introduction of the Corn Laws, first passed by Parliament in 1815, and which were met with first incredulity and then anger. Effectively the Corn Laws imposed a heavy tariff on foreign corn, which kept the price of bread, a staple element in the workers' diet, artificially high, and also pushed up the workers' wages.

Manchester and other Northern towns saw this law as a deliberate attempt by the government to protect the big Southern grain farmers, a jealous South stifling the new Mancunians' progress.

The Manchester man fervently believed that by his city's example so England could prosper. He believed that while the rulers in the South, with their dandy clothes and fineries, flounced around passing stupid laws, it was his kind of person, the real man, who made up the backbone of the country, whose vision and graft was the future.

'What London does with one sovereign, Manchester does with none,' was a favoured saying among Manchester's business community.

And now, with the Corn Laws, London had moved the goalposts, out of sheer envy. Well, fuck them, we'll show them. And they did.

Firstly they let their contempt be known by stealing some of London's most famous names, Piccadilly and Oxford Street, and planting them in their own city. Then they formed the Anti-Corn-Law League. For the next thirty-one years they vigorously campaigned against this restrictive law, and in doing so they set the tone for a North–South divide that has never been satisfactorily resolved. When, in 1846, the Corn Law was repealed, victory had never tasted sweeter. Through their own political muscle, the Mancunian had humiliated the South, and broken the government, forcing it to back down. They had rebelled and they had won.

Now they would go further in realising their destiny, now they would show the South a bit of real class. As they toasted their success, one of them might well have said, 'You see? Has-beens should never take on the Going-to-be's.'

In 1846 Ireland was struck by a famine that was so unforgiving in its nature the repercussions linger even to this day. The famine persisted for five years by which time a million people had emigrated and a million people had died.

Many of the Irish headed either for Liverpool or Manchester. When this second wave of Irish arrived they found in Manchester a city now taking note of some of the stinging criticisms levelled at it about its overriding obsession with money.

To counter these accusations, a small group of businessmen travelled to France in 1850. There, they asked the Charles Halle Orchestra to decamp from Paris and settle in Manchester. Halle agreed, no doubt swayed by the large amounts of money placed before him. Manchester now had its own orchestra. Just like London.

In 1853 the completion of the Cathedral gave Manchester permanent and official status as a city. In 1856 the Free Trade Hall was opened, built on the site of the infamous Peterloo massacre, where eleven people were killed and 400 injured, demanding the right to vote. The new building was a snub for the proles, but the message was clear – the new Mancunian was coming into his own.

The following year saw the opening of a huge arts exhibition, the largest display yet of private arts treasures. Such was its prestige that Queen Victoria, her Prince Consort and the Prince of Wales made the journey up to visit.

The exhibition was also opened to the public, another step towards giving the city a refined cultural depth, another way of attacking the perceived image of Manchester as a city built on slum dwellings and factory exploitation.

Certainly, this activity seemed to work. The *Illustrated London News* wrote that the exhibition 'now hurls back upon her detractors the charge that she [Manchester] is too deeply absorbed in the pursuit of material wealth to devote her energies to the finer arts'.

Other improvements came along. Better sanitary conditions, the creation of the city's own police force, the designing and creation of parks, and the building of Manchester Victoria University, which still stands today.

In 1894, the Manchester Ship Canal was opened, a major development in establishing once and for all a system of transport which avoided harbour fees at Liverpool, and which closely linked Manchester to its overseas suppliers and customers.

In the same year a significant football match took place. It was in Division Two of the Football League, and Manchester City, then known as Ardwick FC, played Newton Heath, later to become Manchester United.

In their first-ever derby, Ardwick FC lost 5-2 at home to

Newton Heath. Later the first derby game at their new ground, Maine Road, in 1923 would end in a 1-1 draw. One loss, one draw. Already a pattern was being set by City.

Yet, across the water in Europe darker clouds were gathering on the horizon. In the first half of the 20th century, Western Europe would be embroiled in two world wars. Millions of people would lose their lives and whole countries would be decimated.

But these wars would actually sustain Manchester economically. They were good for business, wars. And Manchester's new metal and engineering economy saw a brisk trade in weapons, ammunition and aircraft.

She walks into the small coffee shop in Mayo and, as she sits down, she lets out a sigh. It is seven in the evening and her bones ache and her mind is tired. It has been another long day cleaning and tending to the children of the O'Hara house, and Peggy Sweeney is now waiting for her mother to arrive.

When she does, Peggy will hand over her week's wages: one pound. Depending on the family's needs that week, Peggy will receive a tiny sum of it back. Maybe half-a-crown if she is lucky.

By her side is the small transistor radio that she has been able to save up for. Peggy loves the radio because it gives her music and sometimes listening to music is just like reading; you can disappear from yourself. More crucially, it allows you to lose for a while that cruel inner-voice which taunts every son and daughter of the Catholic Church.

Peggy's inner-voice will not stay quiet. Strict religions always produce major worries. Believers fret all their lives. And no one is harder on Catholics than themselves. It isn't a happy religion nor is it shaped to fill you with confidence and huge self-esteem. Rather it threatens you with damnation, tries to cut you down to size.

How can you not worry when hell is just a sin away, and every day you fight yourself over impulses, desires and thoughts that appear from nowhere to tease and torment you?

You go to confession on Saturday and for that night your soul feels cleansed. You can sense purity. By Monday afternoon, you are at war with yourself again. But music, this Irish music that Peggy listens to, talks to her, it sets her free.

Sometimes the radio plays the saddest song in the universe. Then, the fiddles and the guitars and the penny-whistles start up, and there will be a rousing song to help you on your way. The Dubliners, Big Tom, Dicky Rock, The Miami Show Band, Peggy knew the names and music of all the major performers and she was always thrilled when the disc jockey announced one of their tunes.

The door of the café opens and Peggy expectantly looks up. But it isn't her mum. It is the local policeman. She instinctively looks away, hoping she hasn't been noticed, not because she has anything to hide but because she is fearfully shy.

She hates crowds, her temperament is ill-suited to them. Instead, she loves quiet, peace and quiet. A lot of the time, all she wants is to be on her own. Even in company, when relatives visit or she is with friends, there are always the moments when she drifts away.

It's why she doesn't mind her job so much. The O'Haras, who run a successful confectionery business, are good to her. A lot of the time, it is just Peggy and the O'Hara children in the house, and that suits her fine. The rest of the time she is at home. There's not a lot to do in County Mayo and even if there were, local dances and the like, Peggy would rather stay indoors, reading or listening to her beloved radio.

Near where she works there is a cinema but films don't really interest her. Plus it would mean spending money that could be better used elsewhere.

Her life is one of routine and ritual, hard work, and solitude when she can grab it. She wouldn't really have it any other way.

After the First World War, the Americans arrived and cars and clothes took over as Manchester's main products. By the 1930s there were over 200 American firms in the city. The famous Ford Motor Car Company opened its first plant at Trafford Park. It was there that the Model-T car, the cheapest in Britain, was mass manufactured.

In the clothes sector there was a similar upsurge. Charles Macintosh had started his raincoat business in 1824 and 110 years later, thanks to a proliferation of sweatshops, the rainwear business now flourished.

The advent of the Second World War suspended normal

business activities. Once more Manchester found out that wars are great for trade.

For a time the textile and engineering industries flourished. Thousands of Mancunian men joined the forces, while thousands of women took their places in the factories. But in 1940 the city, severely blitzed by German bombers, lost many of its historic buildings.

In the 1950s, the food and chemical industries moved in as Manchester became the North's major distribution centre for supplies, aided by its railway and canal system.

The post-War British government also became major employers. It sent out notices to the Caribbean to entice workers over to rebuild Britain. The same offer was extended to the Irish. Soon thousands upon thousands of immigrants were arriving to experience the British way of life.

Yet by the 1960s, despite all efforts, another cycle was ending. Manchester's population began to fall. And fall. And fall. The city couldn't halt its decline, and the reason was simple. Work was becoming increasingly hard to find. The Manchester Ship Canal was too small to hold the new container ships, and the advent of motorways signalled the end of canals and railways as a major means of transportation. And crucially, Manchester's manufacturing industry was hit badly by the local economy shifting into the service sector. From 1961 to 1983 over 150,000 manufacturing jobs would be lost.

The print industry also went into decline, its end symbolised by the *Manchester Guardian* moving South to the city that Manchester had grown to despise and which would grab all the attention in the 1960s. The capital would become Swinging London and no one would speak of Manchester. The new Mancunian turned in his grave. And his sons and daughters planned their revenge.

At the hospital, they assured Peggy that her mum would be fine. All she had to do was rest, get some peace and quiet.

It had been like this for a few months now and Peggy was starting to realise that her mum was getting old, and that the years of hardship, both physically and within the mind, were starting to take their toll.

Because of Margaret's frequent illnesses, Peggy had been

forced to quit her job with the O'Haras to look after her brothers and sisters. Paddy, John and Bridie would be looked upon to supply money for food. Soon her mum would return and Peggy knew that when that happened, the day she had been dreading all her life would arrive.

It was time, her mum would tell her, for Peggy to leave County Mayo. There really was nothing to hold on for.

'You have to go, Peggy,' Margaret Sweeney said, 'and there's the end of it.' But where, and with whom? Nearby, the MacIntyre family lived, near enough to be considered neighbours.

Peggy had become friendly with their daughter Angela, and they hung out together. Peggy didn't have many friends but Angela she could count on.

Loyalty was very important to Peggy. It took her a long time to trust anyone bar her family. One day over coffee Peggy told Angela of her mum's wishes.

Angela had just returned from her holidays in Manchester, staying with her older sister, Teresa. Pretty soon Angela would be returning to Manchester for good, so why didn't Peggy come along? She was sure her sister wouldn't mind putting up Peggy until she settled in.

There was work aplenty there. Why, Angela enthused, you could start a job in the morning, quit it at lunchtime and be in work again by eventide. And getting a place to live in shouldn't be a problem. Come on now, Peggy, what do you say?

Margaret approved of the plan. She trusted the MacIntyres. But, as she spoke to her mother, Peggy's heart was breaking inside her. I don't want to go, she kept telling her mum, I don't want to leave you; I know there's nothing here but it doesn't matter, I'll stay.

But Margaret, toughened by life and all its terrible blows, would have none of it. It would be better in the long run for her to leave, of that she hadn't one doubt. Then Margaret would walk into the kitchen, and pretend to bake some bread and sing loudly to hide her own tears.

Peggy reluctantly arrived in England in 1961. She was eighteen, nervous and frightened, with tears that were always bubbling under her eyelids. She spent her first night at Teresa MacIntyre's flat and when the lights went out and everyone had said goodnight, she buried her face in the pillow and cried her eyes out. The next night, too. In fact, she cried for what seemed like an eternity, until one day she woke up and found that a feeling, something inside, had been lost. Now there was just day-to-day life to get on with. So get on with it.

Teresa was married, ironically to a Thomas Gallagher. They had a daughter, Patricia, who was near Peggy's age and it was she who took Peggy out and showed her around. The first priority was to get Peggy a job and somewhere to live, as the MacIntyre place was too small for her to stay there long.

By Central Station there was a block of flats. It was here that Peggy was first housed due to her employment at the train station as a waitress-cum-cleaner. She was paid three pounds a week.

'And I'd put a pound in an envelope and send it home,' she says, 'because me mum would be waiting for the pound to come over.'

Peggy spent a year at Central Station. In that time, she located an old school friend of hers in Manchester, Mary, and they started hanging out together.

Once Peggy made a happy trip back to Ireland to visit her family and on her return to Manchester, her sister Kathleen accompanied her. Together, with Mary, they moved into the Plymouth Grove area.

A new job came along, this time at a cardboard factory where the hours were better than those at the Central Station.

But just as Peggy was adjusting to a new life, some serious and alarming news broke: her mother was seriously ill and was back in hospital. Peggy instantly quit her job and went back to Ireland, where she took over the family, making sure that her younger brothers and sisters (all aged ten years and under) were properly tended to. A lot of the time her brothers would skip school and Peggy would tell them off. But she understood their disinterest. Who wouldn't?

After dropping off the children at school, Peggy would walk over to a seminary where she was employed washing, cooking and cleaning for the five priests who lived there. One day, 22 November 1963, Peggy heard a commotion in the TV room.

Intrigued, she went in to find out that the US President John Kennedy had been assassinated. Peggy couldn't believe it. Kennedy represented hope to her generation. He was going to change the world, make a better future. And he was of Irish stock.

And to kill a President? It was unheard of. Incomprehensible. It signalled something so evil and so dark that it frightened Peggy to her very soul. As she walked home that night, she truly believed that the world was about to end. In reality, the world was changing at an enormous pace.

The dull 1950s were over and so was the idea of a society administered by men of unimpeachable reputation. The Profumo affair the same year, in which a minister of the Crown lied to Parliament and brought down the Tory prime minister Harold Macmillan, signalled the end of the supposed sanctity of public figures. Only the Royal Family remained sacrosanct and even they, in time, would be exposed. The white heat of the 1960s was spreading quickly.

After nearly twelve months in hospital, Margaret came out to resume her familial duties and Peggy returned to Manchester. She soon found a new job, carrying out light clerical work for a mail-order business located in the centre of Manchester.

At night-time she rarely ventured out. She preferred to stay indoors, either watching TV or writing letters to her family back home. Again, all three of these occupations allowed her to lose herself.

Of course, going to a club and getting blitzed on booze was another way of losing yourself, but then Peggy would rather have died than indulge in alcohol or dancing.

Yet around her a thriving club scene had opened up in Manchester. It was just as well. Over the following years, Manchester would lose many manufacturing jobs and the city's focus would slowly switch to the musicians, the club runners, the hustlers and the footballers.

Noel Gallagher would one day tell an interviewer, 'In Manchester you either became a musician, a footballer, a drugs dealer or work in a factory. And there aren't a lot of factories left, y'know.'

In London, during the late 1950s, there had been a skiffle craze. Its centre was a club on old Compton Street in London's Soho area, called The Two I's, where later on, more sophisticated British pop acts, such as Adam Faith and Tommy Steele, took over from the Lonnie Donegans of this world and attracted a younger audience.

The atmosphere was smoky, the drink was coffee. In nearby

Notting Hill Gate, a more alluring form of night-clubbing could be experienced with the blues parties that the West Indians were secretly holding. Christine Keeler, the call-girl involved in the Profumo scandal, favoured such affairs.

In Manchester on 15 July 1960 Jack Johnson, the owner of the Mogambo Coffee Bar, and John Collier, a local builder, opened up The Two J's. The star attraction on the opening night was Ray Ellington, supported by Dave Wilson and his Original Dixieland Band.

The club, situated in Lloyd Street, was formerly a textile warehouse and its musical policy only extended to jazz. But in August of that year, Jackson decided to use local pop acts to attract a bigger clientele. His first pop booking was Johnny Martin And The Paiges, who made their début on 4 October 1960.

A few days later Jackson put on the club's first all-nighter. For those youngsters who were looking to jive the night away, this was a godsend. The night was hugely successful and it put the writing on the wall.

Still operating as a jazz venue, the club now put on weekend afternoon jiving sessions to cater for the demand, but soon rock 'n' roll had taken over. It was a musical slaying that had occurred all over Great Britain; thousands of teenagers dropped skiffle and trad jazz to give their souls to rock 'n' roll.

The Two J's was then bought by three businessmen, John Orr, Rick Dixon and Hugh Goodwin. They closed the club down, undertook major renovations and re-opened for business on 4 November 1961.

Goodwin had recently been to London. Sitting in the Beachcomber restaurant in Mayfair, with its South Seas setting, the palm trees depicted on the wall gave him an idea for the club's name. He put forward the idea to his partners. They agreed.

Which is how, The Oasis, 'Manchester's Most Fab Club For Young People', opened for business. Just three months later, Friday 2 February 1962, The Beatles made their Manchester début there. The Oasis, The Beatles. It was the first known linking of the two names.

Nineteen sixty-two was a significant year for The Beatles. It was the year they were turned down by Decca and signed by EMI, the year that the tailor, Beno Dorn of Birkenhead, was asked to supply four brushed-tweed suits to replace the group's leather jackets, jeans and plimsolls, and the year that they would have their first Top Twenty hit with 'Love Me Do/P.S. I Love You'. It was a year for laying the seeds of success.

Within twelve months The Beatles would become the biggest group in the world. Thousands of teenage girls would scream and faint when they heard their records or saw them play. But Peggy Sweeney had no idea what was going on.

She was totally bemused by pop hysteria of this kind. What were these girls playing at? she would think to herself. She never understood it. It all seemed so . . . silly, to be throwing yourself around in public like that.

That said, Peggy liked watching *Top Of The Pops*. She had an instinctive love of music and pop music was busy inventing itself. How could she not be attracted to the show that had started transmission on 1 January 1964 from a church in Manchester? The acts featured that day included The Rolling Stones, The Hollies and Dusty Springfield. All great acts. Yes, *Top Of The Pops*, she liked the show. And to think that it was being made just down the road.

The reason for the show's original Manchester location was simple; the majority of groups enjoying chart success hailed from the North. Liverpool had The Beatles, The Searchers, Gerry And The Pacemakers, Billy J. Kramer, the Merseybeat sound. Manchester was home to The Hollies, Freddie And The Dreamers, Herman's Hermits, Wayne Fontana And The Mindbenders, the last three names going on to score spectacular success in the US a year later.

But if Peggy was honest, when she wanted a night out, she much preferred to see one of the Irish bands play the Saturday-night slot at the Astoria club.

And it was there in January 1964 that Peggy, sitting quietly at her table, was introduced to a quiet, unassuming young man. He didn't drink, didn't say much.

He was a builder, but to Peggy he seemed exactly like her: quiet and contained. He told her his name was Thomas, Thomas Gallagher, and that his family hailed from County Meath. It was much nearer to Dublin than Mayo. He had left home when he was seventeen, leaving behind a family of five brothers and one sister. He was now twenty years old.

For the next nine months they courted. And then on 27 March 1965 at the Holy Name Church in Chorlton on Medlock, Peggy Sweeney married Thomas Gallagher.

The Beatles were just about to release their first single of the year, 'Ticket To Ride', which the second son that Peggy would bear would one day nominate as the greatest single ever released.

That day, the sun briefly shone and later on Peggy and Thomas held a reception party at the Plymouth Hotel in Plymouth Grove.

Three weeks later Peggy realised she had made the biggest mistake of her life.

Two

Somehow, Sunday 1 October 1995 became the first day of Oasis's week-long British tour in support of their second album, *(What's The Story) Morning Glory?* True, there was no gig to play – that would occur the next night in Blackpool – and true, the band weren't even all in the same town, as Guigsy and Bonehead were in Manchester, with Noel, Liam and Alan White in London.

But there was a party to launch the album. And it was here, at the Pavilion, a swank gentlemen's club in Knightsbridge, that Alan White and the Gallagher brothers, not to mention their record company, publishers and immediate friends, got seriously into tour mode.

The party, which had been organised by Meg Matthews, Noel's girlfriend of the past year and a half, was due to start at midday, but she had arrived early at the venue, by nine that morning in fact, anxious to make sure that everything was in place.

Meg wanted the party to be special. Not only for Noel and the band but to show her new employers, Creation Records, that they had been right to take her on.

She knew when she accepted Creation's job offer that people would bitch behind her back; they would say that she had only come in on the back of Noel. That kind of backbiting was inevitable. Meg accepted that. But, understandably, she wanted to prove her detractors wrong.

Noel arrived just after noon. He walked into the spacious hall and was guided upstairs to the party. He was wearing a dark brown suede jacket, jeans and trainers. The first thing he saw when he walked in the room was a huge ice block that spelt the band's name.

In the adjoining room there was a big buffet and a four-piece string quartet playing classical versions of the new album. All the rooms had tasteful paintings on the walls. The chairs were chintzy, there were long sofas and everywhere was painted pastel. The waiters spoke with public-school accents, and there were Sunday's newspapers strewn everywhere. It was a strange setting for Oasis. You didn't associate them with such a rarefied and polite environment.

Creation Records had spared no expense on the bash, but then they had heard the new album and, well, no one wanted to tempt fate but it was pretty obvious to all that they had something really special on their hands. *Morning Glory* had outstripped all their expectations. The word 'classic', kept springing to mind.

If Oasis didn't fuck it up, if everyone concerned in selling this album kept their nerves steady, there was a real chance that it was going to beat sales of *Definitely Maybe*, the band's début album which had now sold three million copies worldwide.

There was a real sense of expectation in the air. Everyone smelt glamour, success and money. These seemed permanently to be attached to the band, despite the relatively bad summer they had experienced, a time which had seen them receive a couple of unexpected dents to their armour.

The first such occasion was their summer appearance at the Glastonbury festival.

Oasis had been invited to headline on the Friday night. It was the festival's twenty-fifth anniversary and something special was required.

But the gig didn't really take off. A combination of sound problems and fraught nerves frustrated the band.

At one point, Liam offered the open-air crowd a fight. He also invited Robbie Williams, then a member of the UK teenybop sensation Take That, on-stage for a minute or so. Within two weeks of that appearance, Robbie would leave Take That.

The second incident occurred two months later when Oasis found themselves embroiled in their historic fight with Blur for the number-one spot in the singles chart.

Blur won. They pulled out all the stops, outmarketed and outmanoeuvred Oasis, giving them a smack to the chin the band wouldn't easily forget.

Oasis instantly retaliated by announcing two shows at Earls

Court. They would be the biggest indoor gigs ever seen in Europe. Tickets for both shows had sold out in hours.

Earls Court acted as a real booster for the band. It kicked Blur, but it also reminded the music press of the band's huge popularity. For the press, too, had stung the band. The overall tone of the reviews for *Morning Glory* hadn't been encouraging, especially when all concerned had actually *looked forward* to the reviews. Words such as 'lazy' or 'tired' had been used by some writers.

It was the first time press and band had failed to see eye to eye. The press saw Oasis as The Sex Pistols. Noel didn't. That was just one element of the band, and that's why he had moved away from the first album's dominant mood.

Many of the new songs had been written using acoustic guitar. Some he had even dared to fully orchestrate. Others, such as 'Don't Look Back In Anger', were classics as far as he was concerned; and that wasn't being arrogant, that was stating facts.

The critics disagreed, especially when they heard lines such as, 'And please don't put your life in the hands/ Of a rock 'n' roll band/ Throw it all away'. That really was heresy. That kind of talk totally demolished rock mythology. Band and press now dramatically differed over what Oasis should sound like and stand for.

'Would sir care for a drink?' The waiter looked at Noel.

'Nah mate,' he replied, 'I know exactly what's going to happen here. I need to line my stomach first.'

He made his way to the buffet and started spooning cereal and milk down his neck. Shortly afterwards, Liam arrived. He wore shades and an immaculate white three-quarter-length mac. With him was the singer Lisa M. Yet despite even Liam's boisterous presence, the atmosphere remained sedate.

The talk was polite, the level of conversation never higher than the sober and gentle sound of 'Wonderwall', 'Cast No Shadow', 'Don't Look Back In Anger', and other songs from *Morning Glory* that the four-piece quartet played.

The free booze was still only being sipped at and the toilets were, at this stage, being used for their designated purpose.

By one o'clock, the party had started to fill up. The band's manager Marcus Russell arrived with his then girlfriend, Dinny. Alan White, the band's drummer, showed with Kass, his long-time and now ex-girlfriend. Tim and Chris Abbott, former

Creation employees and the men behind Better Records (they had signed Smaller, a band fronted by Digsy, who had been immortalised on the song 'Digsy's Dinner' from the first Oasis album) showed up, as did the *Melody Maker* writer Paul Mathur, an early champion of Oasis. He and Tim Abbot would both publish books on the band.

Also present was Creation boss Alan McGee, who had signed the group just two years previously; the band's press officer, Johnny Hopkins; and with other Creation personnel, including Jane, the company's accountant who is depicted on the sleeve of 'Cigarettes And Alcohol'.

There were Sony people, and the photographer, Tom Sheehan, to take happy snaps of the occasion. But there was also one surprise guest. Peggy Gallagher, Noel and Liam's mother had been invited.

Meg had secretly arranged for her to be there. It was Peggy's first-ever visit to London. Later on that day, Meg and Lisa M. would take her sightseeing.

The first time Noel saw her, walking through the crowd, he thought to himself, God, that looks like my mum. The next minute he was hugging her, proudly introducing her to all his friends. Throughout the whole party, he and Liam would linger protectively by her side.

Two hours after Peggy's arrival, the party finally got into full swing. The champagne was starting to hit home and the waiters were getting busier. Then people started to gather around the four-piece string quartet. Half-pissed, now they wanted to hear more music.

'Here, go on,' Liam shouted, 'Give us, "Champagne Super-nova".'

'"Eleanor Rigby",' shouted another guest.

'"Live Forever",' said another.

Unable to play any song without the sheet music in front of them, the four-piece started to put a bit more effort into their playing, as if they too had been at the booze. The more the guests encouraged them, the harder they played. There were shouts of encouragement, request after request and good-natured banter all the way.

'Let's get them right at it,' Liam said to no one in particular.

'What do you think of them?' Meg asked Noel, above the din.

It had been her idea to have them there.

'Fucking top,' he enthusiastically replied, as Liam started singing 'Wonderwall'. 'I've told Marcus we should get them recorded, put out an instrumental version of the album. That'd be ace.'

At three the party finished, and taxis arrived to take everyone to a bar in Camden's Parkway. Sky TV were showing an important football match, Manchester United versus Liverpool, Eric Cantona's comeback game since his infamous Kung-Fu kick on a Crystal Palace supporter.

The bar was packed and the band's presence didn't go unnoticed. A couple of guys tried unsuccessfully to needle Liam. Meg's friend Fran and Lisa M. argued at the bar. Drink after drink arrived. Everyone got seriously smashed. The football match ended in a 2–2 draw. Cantona scored a penalty. Robbie Fowler hit two goals. Peggy kept ordering more drinks. Her first day in London was going extremely well.

Meg, Noel, Alan White, Kass, Liam, Jess, Peggy and Lisa M. then took a short walk to Noel's basement flat on Albert Street.

More drinking, more beer, more Jack Daniels and coke. Then Meg, Lisa and Peggy headed out for a sightseeing tour of London, leaving Liam and Jess to get into a discussion in the small kitchen. Liam had met Jess through Noel. She was a close friend of Meg's and made her living working for Kate Moss. She and Liam weren't arguing, but the alcohol had made their voices loud.

'You see, you're lucky,' Jess announced.

'How am I lucky?' Liam automatically shot back. He always resisted any notion other than skill and hard work accounted for his success.

'Because you knew what you wanted to do from day one.'

'Yeah, I wanted to be a singer.'

'And a lot of people don't have that, you see.'

'Don't have what?'

'The knowledge of what they want to do from an early age.'

'Why not? Don't you know what you want to be?'

Before Jess could reply, Noel was standing in the doorway. He looked furious.

'Will you lot shut up before I kick you out. I can fucking hear you from the sitting-room.'

'What, you kicking us out?' Liam challenged.

'Yeah, I fucking am. Get out of my flat.'

'It's not your flat. Half of it's mine.'

'No, it fucking ain't. Now get out. The lot of you. I'm fucking serious. Get out.'

For a second, everyone tried to figure out through their drunken minds if Noel was winding them up. But Noel's expression was deadly serious.

'Right, if that's the way you want it, dickhead,' Liam said.

'Yeah, it is,' Noel said, turning on his heels and walking off down the thin corridor that led into his sitting-room.

'Then fuck you,' Liam shouted. 'Come on, let's split from this moaning twat.'

And he and Jess left, leaving Noel with Alan White and Kass who sat apprehensively on his sofa.

'Right then.'

Noel looked around to make sure they were gone.

Then, with a triumphant tone, he said, 'That's them out of the way.' And he removed a small wrap of cocaine from his pocket. Alan and Kass weren't users. Never had been, never would be.

'Fucking hell,' Noel cried when he realised, 'even more for me.'

An hour later, Noel and Meg arrived at Jeff Barrett's Sunday Social club which had now moved to Farringdon from its original site, the Albany pub opposite Great Portland Street tube. The club was one of the best in London. Right from the start it had played music right across the board by utilising a wide range of DJs.

One week it might be a Northern Soul set, the next a hip-hop session. By adopting such a policy, the club had caught the spirit of the times. The only regular DJs were The Chemical Brothers who closed each session. By its second week, hundreds of people were clambering to get in.

After more imbibing, the party moved on to the Virgin Megastore at the end of Oxford Street. It was here that Noel, backed only by Alan White, had agreed to perform songs from *Morning Glory* which would go on sale at midnight. Noel would play acoustic guitar, Alan White some light percussion.

There were about 500 people present when they arrived, hundreds more locked outside.

Backstage, Liam insisted that he should introduce Noel and

Alan to the crowd. That, they agreed on.

Still wearing his white mac, he stumbled up on-stage as Noel positioned himself on a stool with an acoustic guitar and Alan stood behind him with some congas. But instead of introducing the pair of them, Liam sprang a surprise.

'Here, come on, I'll sing a few.'

'No,' Noel said.

'Why the fuck not?'

'Because then we can't do any of the new songs.'

'Why the fuck not?' Liam repeated. Both brothers were swigging on Becks beer bottles. But Liam's eyes were starting to roll.

'Because you won't remember the words to the new songs.'

'Yeah, I fucking will.'

'No, you won't.'

'Name a song then.'

'I'll bet you fifty quid that if I name a song you won't be able to sing it in front of this lot.' The crowd cheered, enjoying the banter tremendously.

'Okay, go on then, go on. Any tune. I'll sing it. Bet ya.' Both brothers dipped into their pockets and pulled out £50 notes.

'Right, "Rockin' Chair".'

This was one of two excellent songs that formed the B-side of 'Roll With It', the other being 'It's Better People'. When Noel first wrote 'Rockin' Chair' the whole band performed it. But somehow it didn't sound right. Noel then switched the instrumentation to acoustic guitars and now the song breathed properly.

'Okay,' Liam agreed. '"Rockin' Chair" it is.'

Noel played the opening chords, a knowing grin spreading across his face as he stared at Liam.

Liam turned to the mike and started singing. 'I'm older than I wish to be/ This town holds . . . nah, nah na . . .'

His voice trailed away and Noel stopped playing.

'Thank you very much,' Noel said and reached over and whipped the money out of Liam's hands. The crowd loudly cheered, called out for more.

'Here are, here are,' Liam said. 'Here's a song I remember.' He turned to the crowd. 'You know this one. Sing along.' Then, conducting the crowd with his hands, he sang, 'Kumbaya my Lord, kumbaya. Kumbaya my Lord, kumbaya.'

The crowd started singing back with great gusto, and Liam turned to his brother as if to say 'See'.

Noel played 'Wonderwall', 'Don't Look Back In Anger', and 'Cast No Shadow'. It was over. The time now was midnight. They had been drinking for twelve hours.

At ten-thirty the following morning, Noel arrived at the offices of Ignition, his manager's office in London's West End. It was from here that all Oasis's plans were made and executed.

Waiting for him was Marcus Russell and Alan White. Russell had agreed to drive them both to Heathrow. There they would catch a plane to Manchester and meet the tour coach. Then it was on to Blackpool for the first show of the tour.

Noel had something of a hangover. 'What time's the flight?' he sourly asked.

'One-thirty,' Marcus absently replied, sitting at his desk and studying some documents.

'Then why the fuck are we here so early? I could have stayed in bed.'

'Because you have to be there at least an hour before the flight,' Marcus patiently replied. 'I know I'm your manager and that I can do many things, but changing the way airlines and airports have operated for years and years isn't one of them.'

'Why not?' Noel cheekily replied. 'You get 20%. You should work harder. Make them transport us quicker instead of all this fucking around in airports.'

'I wish I could,' Marcus replied, standing up and pulling on his coat.

'Actually,' Noel said to no one in particular, 'I used to think about time travel when I was six years old.'

'Where the fuck is Liam?' Marcus asked Chris, one of his assistants.

'We're going to be late.'

'State he was in last night there's no way he's going to be here,' Noel pointed out.

'Well, we'll have to go soon.'

'There's no answer from the hotel room,' Chris said.

'Well, what shall we do?' Marcus asked, looking at Noel.

'Ah, don't worry about it,' Noel replied. 'We don't need a singer anyway. I'll sing them all. Have done before.'

'Okay,' Marcus said, glancing at his watch again, 'if he shows up then put him in a taxi to the airport straightaway. If not, I'll deal with it when I get back.'

'Marcus, don't worry about it,' Noel put in. 'He'll be at the gig tonight.' He said it with an absolute certainty in his voice.

Marcus, Alan and Noel drove to Heathrow. Marcus sorted out their tickets, then said goodbye. He was due to join the tour in Stoke the next night.

The plane journey was uneventful. Noel slept for most of it, Alan read the papers. It only took an hour. At the airport, Noel and Alan waited by the baggage carousel for their stuff to come through. Noel had checked in his guitar, but it refused to show. Eventually, he went over to an information desk to find that it had been put on the next flight from London. The company agreed to transport it to Blackpool as soon as it arrived.

Noel and Alan ambled outside where Maggie, the tour manager, Bonehead, and Scott Mcleod, the temporary bassist for Guigsy, were patiently waiting for them.

'How do,' nodded Bonehead.

'Lost my guitar,' Noel stated. 'They'd better find it the cunts. How's it going, Maggie?'

'Yeah, good,' she said, smiling sweetly.

They walked to the coach, a couple of people recognising them as they did so.

Bonehead was in good spirits. 'Ah,' he said to Alan White, as they approached the coach, 'breathe in that air, that good Northern air. Eh. Fill your lungs up.'

'Why? Is it good for me?'

''Course it is, son. Go on, Whitey. Get some of that Northern air in your lungs, get rid of all that cockney shit you have to breathe.' Bonehead took a great gulp of air. 'Do you the world of good.'

Whitey mimicked Bonehead.

'Mmmm,' he said, 'I can smell the black pudding.'

The coach was long, with beds in the middle and a back lounge with a video, TV and stereo. Everyone headed straight there. Once settled, Bonehead asked Noel, 'Are you going to do your acoustic set tonight?'

'Too right I am. I didn't get a fucking chance yesterday because of dickhead.'

'Why, what happened?'

Noel related the preceding night's story of the fifty-quid bet, Bonehead smirking all the way through it.

'God,' said Noel, concluding the story and stretching his body, 'I'm really looking forward to having a bath. It's one of the best things about touring.'

'You haven't got one at home?' Bonehead asked.

'No.'

'Why not?'

'Because the bathroom is too fucking small. I've only got a poxy shower. I like a bath. You can sit in there for ages doing absolutely nothing.'

'You should do what Jason did,' Bonehead said, lighting up a cigarette and offering the packet round.

'Why, what's he done?'

'He bought this huge cast-iron bath and him and his mate couldn't get it up the stairs. So he said, "Fuck it," and plumbed it in in his sitting-room. He's got his bath in the sitting-room, he has. He's got a tray put across it and he sits there, eating his dinner, watching TV and having a bath. His wife went mad. Can you imagine it? She's sitting there having a bath and his mates come round. Don't worry lads, it's only the missus. He's off his tits.'

All the time, Scott sat silently at the back. As the coach pulled up outside the hotel, situated along the Blackpool sea front, the growing nerves inside him, reminded him that he had about four hours to go before his live début as bass player with the biggest band in the country.

Outside the Empress Ballroom, there were a few fans waiting, and inside Liam still hadn't arrived.

As soon as Noel walked into the venue, the first thing he did was to run on-stage, plug in his guitar and start playing. Bonehead, Whitey and Scott followed.

After the soundcheck was finished, the four of them went for a meal downstairs. Now that they had money behind them and the gigs were getting bigger and bigger, Oasis could afford to take a catering company on the road. They used the firm, Cat And Mouse, whose staff was mainly women.

As they finished their meal, Liam walked in. He had driven up with Les, a Mancunian who works for a promoter and also acts as part-time driver for the band.

'Fucking hell,' Liam said, walking in, 'you should see Les's motor. Big fuck-off Rolls-Royce. Just drove up in it. Fucking ace. What's for dinner?'

'You got a Rolls then?' Noel asked. 'We're paying you too much fucking money, mate.'

Les sheepishly grinned. 'I got it cheap,' he offered.

At seven the doors opened and a stream of kids came running in, straight to the front of the stage. That's where they would stay until the band came on. By seven-thirty the place was packed. Outside the touts were offering tickets for £50.

The first group on was Smaller, who the crowd received politely. 'Buy me single,' Digsy said to the crowd, 'I've got a wife and three kids to feed.'

Records filled the spaces between Smaller and Oasis. Noel was the first on-stage, followed by Bonehead, Whitey and Scott. The crowd reacted like supporters who have just seen the winner scored in the last minute of the game. It was a sound that Oasis were going to hear for the indefinite future, the sound of people ecstatic just to see them, to be there.

They launched into 'Swamp Song', and halfway through Liam made his entrance, swaggering in time to the tambourine he banged against his leg. Again, a crowd eruption.

For the rest of the gig, indeed for the rest of their tour, the crowd would jump up and down, up and down, up and down, a relentless, seething mass of people fuelled by joy, alcohol, drugs and the pleasure of pure abandonment in Oasis's music.

The set list was the one that Oasis would stick to for nearly a year. The first half was upbeat and anthemic: 'Swamp Song', 'Acquiesce', 'Supersonic', 'Hello', 'Some Might Say', 'Roll With It', 'Shakermaker', 'Round Are Way', 'Cigarettes And Alcohol' and 'Champagne Supernova'.

Five hit singles, five coruscating B-sides and album tracks.

Then the band exited the stage leaving Noel sitting on the stool that Jason, his roadie, had placed on-stage. He picked up his acoustic guitar and launched into 'Wonderwall', 'Talk Tonight' and 'Cast No Shadow'.

This was the day of *Morning Glory*'s proper release and already most of the crowd knew the songs. They had obviously taken the day off to learn their lines, do some real homework.

With the conclusion of 'Cast No Shadow', the rest of the band walked back on except for Liam. Noel had now decided to follow his solo set by singing another song but this time on electric guitar.

Thus 'Don't Look Back In Anger' rang out before Liam returned for 'Live Forever', and then their finale, the Oasis rendition of John Lennon's 'I Am The Walrus'.

There was no encore. There rarely was. The crowd moved out, bubbling still with excitement. Backstage Alex Higgins, the ex-world champion snooker player, was talking to Bonehead in the dressing-room. He was telling him that they should cover the Troggs' 'I Can't Control Myself'.

'You'd do it well, you boys,' he said in his thick Irish brogue. 'Reg Presley's a great guy,' as if that was another compelling reason, 'he's really into crop circles.'

'Yeah, Noel likes a drop of that as well,' Bonehead replied.

Liam came over and shook Higgins's hand. 'What you up to, like?' he asked. 'What you been doing?'

'Still playing. Next game is on the 15th.'

'Who against?'

'Exhibition game. Come and see us.'

'If I'm around I will,' Liam replied. 'I'd do anything for you.' Higgins beamed.

He had once lived in Burnage, and Noel could remember singing Christmas carols outside his house which he had had fitted with triangle-shaped windows.

'No doubt he told you,' Noel said, '"yes, I remember Noel singing. I said then, "He'd be a great star. I could see it then, really I could."'

Noel was now talking to Johnny Hopkins, his press officer.

'Why didn't you play "Morning Glory"?' Hopkins asked.

'Liam can't get the notes, they're too high,' Noel laconically replied. Then he was out of the dressing-room and into the production office.

Noel Gallagher loves to control his own space, who enters and who doesn't. After show dressing-rooms are an anathema to him. Too many friends, too many people.

He far prefers to wind down in places such as the production office. There he'll talk to tour manager Maggie or Marcus or maybe the baleful-looking Trigger, the then road manager, or roadies such as Jason or Jacko.

The band, once they've cooled down, differ. They often meet people. It's mainly for Liam. He's the one who loves to entertain, to talk, flirt, have a laugh. Silence is deadly for him. So is not being at the centre of things. He can't stand it when his mind is going ten to a dozen, his ears are ringing and there's no one to vibe off. Silence becomes his enemy then. He wants life and noise around him. Noel just wants his space.

Back at the hotel, the bar was full and drinks ordered, but there was little for the hotel to complain about. No fights, no trashing of tables or chairs, no insulting other guests.

At one point, Alex Higgins approached Noel.

'When I get out of it, Noel,' he asked, 'can you get me a room?'

A friend of Noel's butted in and asked Alex whether he was still playing.

'Yes, I am. On the 15th. In King's Cross.'

'Whereabouts in King's Cross?'

Higgins looked at him incredulously.

'In the fucking snooker hall. Where else?'

Noel fell about laughing. Over to the right of him, some guy nudged him and started showing off his facial scars.

'This one was from 1981, razor fight I had. This one was at football . . .'

Noel nodded in all the right places. Then he announced he was going to get a drink. He wasn't seen for the rest of the night.

The next morning on the coach, Noel explained his disappearance.

'I had to get away from the guy with the scars. Doing me fucking head in,' Noel told Bonehead.

'What about that Alex Higgins?' Liam said. 'He's off his tits. All that money and fame and shit and he's blown the lot. What a fucking way to go. I hope that happens to me. One big fucking blowout. Top.'

'You did well last night,' Bonehead said to Scott. There was a general murmur of agreement.

'It was only when we got there that I realised what I had got myself into,' he revealed. 'Didn't think about it before, like.'

He returned to gazing out of the window.

The coach was heading for Stoke. At the hotel Robbie Williams was waiting in the foyer for the band to arrive. This was his hometown and now, since quitting Take That (or Take That quitting him, whatever), he had money in the bank and time on his hands.

He greeted the band, arranged to take them for a drink in a pub around the corner. On the way there the locals recognised Williams. There were admiring glances from the girls, who-the-fuck-do-you-think-you-are? looks from the boys.

But everyone who checked Oasis gave them a smile, a thumbs-up.

In the pub, a quarter full, Robbie used the word irony.

Bonehead said, 'Don't know what that means, mate.'

'It's Jamaican,' Liam said. 'They say it when they're pressing their trousers. Iron the knee.'

Noel interrupted. 'No, no, it's Irie – knee,' The brothers laughed. The band smiled. The mood was good. Expectant.

A pint later and the band went back to the hotel and then on to the coach for the trip to Trentham Gardens.

It was there that a TV crew from BBC2's *The O Zone* were waiting for the group. They were shooting a half-hour documentary on the band. Again, as soon as he reached the hall, Noel rushed on-stage, grabbed his guitar and started hammering out loud chords. Lost once more to the world.

In contrast, Liam loathed soundchecks. He would come up and sing one song, maybe two, and then leave it at that. Soundchecking was boring. As long as his mike and monitor (the on-stage amp that allows the band to hear themselves) were in order, then fine. The others could sort out the rest.

Sometimes, Liam would walk round the hall checking out the sound. He did this at prestigious gigs. Other times he just seemed to disappear.

Tonight catering had been placed in the upstairs part of the hall. It was a huge room where *The O Zone* people had taken over a corner and were busy setting up their lights and cameras.

This was a TV special in which Liam and Noel would be interviewed separately by the presenter Jayne Middlemiss, and Bonehead, Whitey and Scott together.

Noel was the first to be interviewed but every time they went to ask a question, the soundman stopped them. He kept picking up Liam's voice from right across the hall.

'Can you keep it quiet?' the producer asked, half-heartedly

shouting to the singer. Liam, as if still at school, kicked a chair.

'Not getting enough attention, then?' Noel bitterly shouted over to him. Liam giggled, pretended to kick the chair again.

'I'm warning you,' Noel threatened.

Finally, they were ready. Noel wore his dark brown suede jacket and gave a lively performance. When asked who his heroes were, he instantly named the four Beatles, his mam and Paul Weller, the former frontman of The Jam and The Style Council. He denied having an argument with Liam about the recording of 'Don't Look Back In Anger'. And then, to prove it, he shouted across to Liam, 'Did we have an argument about "Don't Look Back In Anger"? We didn't, did we?'

'Yeah, we did,' came the sullen reply.

Turning back to the interviewer, Noel said, 'Yeah, we did.' He paused. 'That's going to start an argument now.'

Noel talked about how he shouldered the responsibility ('Someone's got to carry the can'), and then made a telling observation about his work. 'I don't write songs because I want to or I need to,' he firmly stated, 'I write songs because I have to.'

Noel asked to be remembered as someone who did daft things, supported a crappy football team, wore great shoes, 'and did it'.

Now it was Liam's turn and he looked suitably nonchalant and disinterested. He wore shades, a dark blue top and incessantly swigged on a bottle of water. His voice was gruff and curt.

'Don't you ever feel like dancing on-stage?' the interviewer asked.

'I didn't join a band to dance. If I'd have wanted that I'd have joined Take That.' Of Blur, Liam said, 'I won't play the game with students. They're not worthy of being mentioned in the same breath as us.' And on being a 'sex symbol', he snorted, 'Not interested, I'm a singer, me.'

Naturally, the casually bitter way he said those words would send a million hearts fluttering when the show was broadcast.

Out of the other three, Bonehead spoke the most. He blamed the press for the Blur/Oasis spat, and for hyping up the argumentative side of Liam and Noel's relationship.

'People going mental, that's the buzz,' he said of live work. 'That's what it's all about.'

Yet the most telling part of the afternoon's filming was not to be found in any answers. It occurred during Noel's interview. As he spoke, one of the crew tripped over a wire that had somehow got entangled around a heavy light stand. The wire tightened and the stand toppled right on to the presenter's head with a sickening thump.

'Oh my God,' someone shouted as the lamp then lazily thundered on to the ground, leaving the woman clutching her head in shock and agony.

As people rushed towards her, Noel burst out laughing at her misfortune. 'I'm sorry . . .' he spluttered between laughs, 'but it's . . .' It was as if he had had an attack of the giggles.

One of the crew, kneeling down and tending to the woman shot him an accusing look.

'Well, you would have laughed if it had been me,' Noel pleaded. 'Wouldn't you?' He looked in all innocence at the TV crew and no one there had any idea how to answer him.

The Stoke gig was tighter and better than Blackpool. And for the first time, when Noel came on-stage, he walked to his guitar with his palms turned upwards, asking the crowd, like a footballer who's just scored, to give him even more applause.

The band and audience had a ball. No one was disappointed that night. Watching from the balcony, halfway through 'Supersonic', a young lad came up to congratulate Digsy on Smaller's support performance that night.

'Really liked a few of the songs,' the fan said, 'you're a good songwriter.'

Immediately, Digsy pointed to Noel on-stage and said in his loud scouse accent, 'Nah mate, that's a songwriter down there. I'm a songteller. He's a songwriter.'

An hour after the last note had died away, Oasis, minus Noel, were in their dressing-room. Robbie Williams was also present.

Bonehead had a copy of the *New Musical Express* with him. That week, Britain's largest-selling music weekly had published a letter from an Oasis fan complaining about having to queue up hours for Earls Court tickets 'only to find out that one-note-never-moves-on-stage-Guigsy is not playing because he is exhausted. Well, what about me who got to Earls Court at six in the morning.'

'The geezer's not far wrong,' Liam said with a cheeky grin.

'When that went down,' Robbie said of Guigsy having to temporarily leave the band due to severe exhaustion, 'I knew exactly how he felt. Been there myself.'

Outside, as the roadies trundled down gangways pushing huge boxes, Marcus Russell and Noel stood surveying the hall.

'Bloody hell,' Marcus said, looking at the fifty-strong road crew and local workers hired on the day to help out rushing around, 'I remember when we played gigs where there weren't this many people in the audience.'

It had, of course, all changed now. Marcus had come up bearing astounding news, and it was this; *(What's The Story) Morning Glory?* was outselling even their high expectations.

Three hundred thousand copies had gone to the shops on Monday and by the afternoon there were re-orders for 17,000 more. Today, that number was up to 48,000. It looked like being the fastest-selling album in the UK, ever. Another poke in the eye for the disbelievers.

'So I've spoken to Johnny Hopkins,' Marcus said, 'And I really think you should only be talking to the big dailies now and maybe a big Sunday paper, *The Times* or something.'

'Yeah, whatever,' Noel said. Then he spotted Digsy walking across the hall. Noel called him over, told him the news about the LP's sales.

'Can I swop bands?' Digsy asked.

'You can't swop tunes,' Noel replied.

'Ah, that's when you find out who your mates are.'

'How about swopping brothers?' Noel offered.

'Nah, swop instruments, mate.'

The pair laughed easily, much time already between them.

On the bus, Noel picked up the *Sun* and shouted, 'Liam, come here.'

'What?'

'Look at this.'

Noel turned to the gossip page where they had run a picture of Liam from the Megastore gig. His eyeballs were right at the top of his eyelids. He looked half-blind.

'Yeah, so? I was fucking E'd up. What do you expect?'

'I expect pop singers to look better than that,' Noel said with obvious glee.

At the hotel, everyone went down to the bar, except Noel. He stood by the lift, his white Adidas bag in hand. A friend of his then approached him.

'What are you doing, Noel?'

'Going to my room.'

'Do you want a line?'

'Nah, not for me.'

'You sure?' The friend had obviously never heard Noel turn down the offer of cocaine before.

'I've got to get up early and drive back to London,' Noel explained. 'I'm doing some XFM [an independent radio] show on acoustic guitar and I don't want to fuck it up. You going to the Bournemouth gig? I'll see ya there.'

Meanwhile, in the bar, Liam had Digsy on his shoulders and Scott was chatting to a woman. It was about five a.m. before the last person straggled out.

The next day was travel day. Noel had left the hotel with Marcus, around ten. Two hours later the band got on the coach with Maggie. Liam had a copy of the film *Head* starring The Monkees. It is a wilfully psychedelic film from 1968 that had been written by Hollywood actor Jack Nicholson in an attempt to smash The Monkees' clean-cut image.

As giant hoovers dispersed The Monkees into caves or they inexplicably spoke with Italian soldiers in the desert, Liam said, 'This is the kind of shit we should get into. Do a mad fucking film that will mess with everyone's heads. Be fucking top.'

He said it like a threat.

At a service station, Liam, Alan and Bonehead discovered a machine that gave the illusion you were being photographed with a celebrity. Liam, surprisingly, posed with Eric Cantona. So did Alan White. Bonehead had his head imposed on a Take That picture.

'I'll get the office to do a press release, then I'll send it to the *NME*,' he joked. 'Tell them I've taken Robbie Williams's place in Take That. Imagine, Bonehead Joins Take That.'

'Don't do that,' Liam said. 'The cunts will only believe you.'

Bonehead turned to Scott. 'How did you get on with that girl last night?'

Scott shook his head. 'Not at all. She said a few daft things. I thought, she's a spunker, so I went to bed.'

'Did you have a wank?'

Scott's face turned a slight red, his voice a little defensive.

'No.'

'Listen mate,' Bonehead said, adopting the tone of a sergeant major advising a private, 'in this band you're either shagging or having a wank. Got to be done, innit?' He looked round for confirmation, and everyone solemnly nodded their heads. 'Got to be done,' he repeated.

The coach finally pulled into Bournemouth at about seven. It had been a long drive. Jason, Noel's guitar roadie, wandered into the lobby as everyone booked themselves in.

'A very good evening to everyone,' he announced in his mock toff's accent. 'Not a lot doing here, boys.' The crew had travelled over night and already been round town.

'There's some bar which is meant to be good. If you would care to assemble in the hotel bar in about an hour, we can take things from there.'

'Rightio,' Bonehead said.

An hour later, Oasis's road crew and band members sat in the bar. There were three Birmingham girls sitting close by. They had planned a week's holiday around the Bournemouth gig.

Two of them were good-looking. They were the ones getting a lot of attention. Their other friend, having sussed out the situation, had opted to play mother, and look after them. She thought this advisable because Liam was the obvious attraction, and he had just discovered a potent cocktail. In twenty minutes, he had downed three of them and the spirit was with him.

'Have you ever noticed,' he said to Bonehead, 'how letters can become words?'

'How do you mean?'

'Well, check this. U.R.A.Q.T.'

'Fuck me, so they can.' Bonehead thought for a moment, and Liam looked pleased with himself. Words weren't his thing. He hated signing his name, for example. School had done that to him. Made him afraid of pen and paper.

He could stand in front of 20,000 people and front them out, big time. No problem there. But his achilles heel was words. Words frightened him. Words told him that there were two kinds of people in this world. There were those who could spell music and then there were those who could play it. Liam was the latter.

Instinctive, no thought.

'Liam?'

'What?'

'U.R.O.K.' Bonehead said.

Soon after, everyone left the bar. Some went in search of food. Liam and co. stayed with the girls who knew of a bar where the drinks were cheap. When Liam entered, people stopped to stare. But few approached him. Half an hour later, he disappeared into the toilet with Paul, a roadie.

They had just snorted up some cocaine when they were surprised by a banging on the door. It was the bouncer. He had spotted them going into the gents together.

'Fuck!'

Liam and Paul stared at each other. 'What?' Liam shouted to the bouncer.

'There better not be two of you in there.'

Paul reacted first. He undid the lock and the pair of them stepped out.

'Look,' he remonstrated. 'I know what you're thinking but it's not that. He's just split up with his girlfriend and I was talking to him about it, in private, you know what I mean. I mean, he can't get any peace out there and he is very upset.'

Paul and the bouncer looked at Liam. Particles of cocaine were falling out of his nostril. Paul knew then that it was useless to argue.

'I don't believe you,' the bouncer said.

'Okay, then mate, here's the crack,' Liam said. 'Me and him are gay and we were in there doing it.'

'Right, you two, out,' The bouncer went to take Liam's arm. Liam stepped back an inch and fixed him with a cold stare.

'Look mate, we'll fuck off from your poxy joint but don't you dare touch my fucking coat. That's all. Don't touch my coat.'

The bouncer considered the situation, stepped back and let Liam walk past him and out into the cold October air.

Back at the hotel there was football on the TV. Manchester City were playing in the Coca-Cola cup. Paul, Liam and the three girls retired to a room to watch it. The room had two single beds. Liam sat with the two pretty ones. Paul spoke to 'mum'.

But despite all Liam's subtle suggestions, there was to be no action tonight. The 'mum' of the party wasn't going to leave without her brood. They were keen to stay. No doubt there. They said so every time their friend went to the bathroom. But 'mum' was adamant. She wasn't budging without them.

Finally, reluctantly, they left for the house they were staying in. Liam promised to put them all on the guest-list.

'But I'm not putting the ugly one on,' he viciously stated after they had gone. 'She can fuck right off.'

Liam was now at a loose end. And he was pissed and wired. No way was he going to bed. Not in this state, not at this time. He grabbed the phone and ordered up some drinks, produced the coke he had left over, started chopping it out, started talking. Of all things, he spoke about his name first.

He hated William. Too long. Far too long. But he did have John and Paul to go in between William and Gallagher, and as they were the best songwriters ever, it was a good sign.

His brother's name then came up. Inevitably.

'Look at him kicking me out of his flat,' Liam said with mild disgust, like you would about someone who hadn't washed for days. 'Half of that flat is mine. I'm his brother, half of it's mine.' This was Liam logic.

Yet the main grievance wasn't about house evictions. No. It was about money. The way it worked was simple; Oasis members all got the same cut from records and gigs, and were given weekly wages. Apart from Noel, whose songwriting royalties and publishing money saw to that. That slice of the cake wasn't shared. To Liam, this was wrong.

'If I was the songwriter – I'm not, but if I was – I would divvy up that money as well. Spread it out among everyone. Not keep it to myself.'

After all, why were the band successful? Was it just the songs? Or was it other things? Like Liam's contribution. Or them working their arses off on the road. He didn't like it when Noel got involved on the money side of things. It changed him.

It was like in 1994 when they first went to New York. The record company took them out for a meal and this dickhead from Epic called them 'lucky'. Lucky? Lucky to be signing to their label. Fucking lucky? Us?

Liam rounded on him, 'You're fucking lucky to have us, not the other way round.' And Noel sat there and said nish, acted all business-like. Liam got annoyed and had a go at Noel as well.

Liam loved his brother, obvious innit? But sometimes he felt that Noel never gave anything back.

He bobbed his head and began talking about the Newcastle gig, the one where Noel got smacked on-stage. Here, Liam became indignant, the new Mancunian in him flaring up as his thoughts about the gig tumbled out.

The band's early attitude towards audiences was basically, 'You are lucky to be getting all these songs. And then you get up on-stage and hit the geezer who wrote them? Nah mate, that is wrong. So wrong.

'So I fucking grabbed the guy and pushed him in the pit. Kicked the cunt right in the head.' Liam stands up and mimes a vicious, silver-quick kick.

'Bosh! Noel wanted to carry on. I said, "Nah, we're off." Noel said, "I'm fine, we'll do him." I said, "Nah, that's it, we're off." So we left and then I thought, "Nah, I'm not having that."

'So I went back on-stage, stood by the mike and said, "Right, I'll take you all on. Not fucking thirty of you at once but one after the other. And I'll kick your fucking heads in. So who's having it?"'

Liam's voice dropped a register. 'Not one of them came up. "Come on, who's having it?" Not one.'

Bitterness, tinged with disappointment, crept into his mouth. 'And they call themselves our fans.'

Liam sat down and shook his head. It jogged another memory. Like that time at the video for 'Some Might Say', and all the shit he got for that. That was fucking murder.

They get back from New York and go to the hotel they've been booked in and it's there that he first sees the video storyline.

'And it's poxy. It's me in the passenger seat of a car singing. Then it cuts to me in a café eating beans and eggs. Shit, right? So I read it and I said, "Fuck off, I'm not doing it."

'This record, "Some Might Say", it's too important. To me, it's like "Imagine", this song.' And Liam sings, '"Some might say they don't believe in Heaven / Go and tell it to the man who lives in Hell." The song is too important.'

So on the day of the shoot, Liam says fuck off and refuses to go to the set. Stays in his hotel room. It costs the band twenty grand. But fuck it. Liam says he'll pay it. Guigsy and Bonehead talk to him. They don't like the treatment either.

'But it's all right for you,' Liam points out. 'You only have to stand there and play guitar. I have to fucking *sing* it. So I walk and I tell them, this song will get to number one anyway. We don't need a piss-poor video.'

According to Liam, for the next two weeks band and management blank him. Then the single goes straight in at number one. Marcus calls Liam the day it happens.

'Congratulations,' his manager says.

'Told you so,' Liam replies.

It's incidents like these that make Liam sure of his spiritual affinity with John Lennon. They share the same rebel spirit.

Liam obeys it without question and, without doubt, it certainly accounts for some of Oasis's success. But it's also the spirit which constantly threatens to break Oasis.

Not that Liam wants to meet the remaining Beatles. Fuck that. If he ever met Paul McCartney, he'd say, 'All right', and that would be it. Respect, like, but not arsed, not really.

As for The Rolling Stones, after what they did to Brian Jones, kicking him out of the group when he *was* the group, and then doing an interview, a fucking interview on the day he died, shameful, fucking shameful.

Nah, Oasis would never get like that. It's the most open band ever and the next album, that'll be the one. That album will blow minds. Literally. No fucking around. Spend six months on the fucker and get everything right, every note.

And then? And then one day, an Oasis record is going to come out and at the bottom, where the songwriting credit is, it will say, Gallagher and Gallagher, because that's Liam's main ambition. That's the mission. To write a song and have it released. So he's going to learn guitar.

'It might take four months, might take ten years, but one day I'm going to show them. I'm going to turn up and go, "Here you are, have that."'

Liam mimes throwing something on the floor, says, 'Ah, fuck it,' and he leaves the room to see if the girls are still hanging around and, if not, to try and kip. For Liam, the night wasn't yet over. It never would be.

George Michael, Keren Woodward and Sarah Dallin, ex-Wham frontman and Bananarama girls, stand in the Bournemouth International Centre watching Oasis. The 1980s view the 1990s.

One Oasis fan recognises George. The rest of the crowd are fixated on the band.

Oasis have just gone into 'Champagne Supernova', and then it happens.

Someone lobs a whole pint of beer over Liam. The alcohol drenches his blue paisley shirt, and everyone in the building feels the same question light up in their head: what is he going to do? How's he going to react? Consider it. There are two main options: one, walk off; two, dive into the crowd and sort the bastard out.

Liam does neither. He starts to walk round in circles. Round and round and round, circling, like a vulture. The band keep playing, one eye on him. Round and round and round.

The tension of the moment seeps right through the whole audience who are riveted. Round and round. And then Liam makes his move.

He goes up to the mike and he starts singing as if nothing has happened. The crowd loudly cheer him. It is the best moment of the gig.

In the hotel bar, a fan wants to read Bonehead his stars.

'What sign are you?' she asks.

'Saggy hairy arse,' he replies.

Behind him the ex-Wham star sits with Keren and Sarah. Liam comes in and sits with them. He's already met Keren and Sarah in Japan. It was at a party in the hotel when they crashed the swimming pool, and had managers and waiters screaming at them to stop.

After drinks have been ordered, greetings made, Liam says to George, 'Here, have you ever wondered how letters can make words on their own, like?'

'What do you mean?' George says.

'Well, U.R.A. . . .'

Noel enters and nods to George. He's already spoken with him at the gig. Not because he is a fan of the man's music but because anyone he perceives to be *trying* in the field of songwriting he believes is worth at least a chat.

Noel respects most people in his field. He figures if they go through half of what he does, they are worth acknowledging.

It was only with the songwriters whose music had actually

inspired Noel that he wanted more than just a quick drink and a chat from. Those people – the Marrs, the Wellers – he wanted to figure out. Then he might start getting some answers about himself.

Having acknowledged George, Noel makes his way to the bar. The room is packed and noisy. Some fans have sneaked in and soon Noel is talking to a few of them. They look at him with total admiration.

George Michael now leaves and soon after two girls suddenly throw up in front of everyone. They had each just swallowed an Ecstasy pill. After finishing their convulsions, they then bend down and extract the pills that lie in their mess. Then they swallow them again.

'That should do it,' one of them cheerfully says.

'Oasis fans,' the barman mutters in disgust.

A few minutes later Digsy approaches Noel. 'Hey Noel, do you want a drink, la?'

Noel smiles. He's heard this one before. 'Yeah, I'll have a pint of lager, Digsy.' Then he turns to the fan he has been talking to. 'And now he says, "Great, I'll have one too."'

'No,' Digsy protests, 'no wind up, la. I'll get the bevvies in. Sorted, mate.'

'What with?' Noel asks. 'You're always skint.'

'Don't you worry about that.'

Digsy goes to the bar and returns with a handful of drinks. He sets a pint in front of Noel.

'There you go. See . . .' Then he sits down and whispers conspiratorially. 'I've just nicked George Michael's roomkey. I'm getting the drinks on it.'

'But George Michael isn't staying here, Digsy,' Noel says. 'He's just gone home.'

'Well, whose key is this, then?'

It's then that one of the burly road crew on the table opposite loudly questions, 'Here, has anyone seen my roomkey?'

'Oh fuck,' says Digsy.

Noel Gallagher wakes up on his coach bed, yawns and pulls back the curtain. It is two in the afternoon and he is five minutes away from the week's final gig, the Leisure Centre, Gloucester.

In the back of the coach the talk is of a report in one of the music papers that claims receipts from one of the Earls Court shows will go to the Terence Higgins Trust to atone for Noel's publicly-stated wish that Damon and Alex from Blur catch AIDS and die.

In truth, contact had been made between Oasis and the Trust with a view to the band making a donation, but only if it was kept secret. Now the story has been leaked. It would be a surprise if the deal took place.

'Don't give a fuck,' Bonehead states. 'No one is having my money.'

As Noel sits there rubbing his eyes, the rain hammering on the roof now stopped, Liam walks past Noel to get his stuff from the back of the coach.

'My voice is fucked,' he says.

'What do you want me to do about it?' Noel retorts.

'You're just jealous because it's better than yours.'

'Not at the moment it ain't. You should stop fucking around and be a professional.'

Liam picks up his bag and starts walking back down the aisle to the exit door.

'You know all about that, do you?' he shouts back.

'Yeah, I do,' Noel replies. 'You know your problem?'

Liam stops, looks back at his brother.

'Yeah, come on then. What's my problem?' he demands.

'You should stop walking round going, Look at me, Look at me, I want all the attention. That's what you should do.'

Liam says, 'Ah, sack it,' and walks off. Even he is too knackered to argue. Noel jumps on to the coach floor, collects his bag and wearily walks up the coach aisle.

Like the others, the week has caught up with him.

Too many late nights, not enough sleep.

Worse than that, Meg is due to arrive tonight and to be honest Noel just isn't in the mood. Not because he doesn't want to see her but because this is what touring does. It puts you in a bubble and demands a state of mind which is very hard for people outside to penetrate, no matter how close to you they are.

Noel just wants to play the gig and then go home and rest. The next stop is America. They fly there on Monday. It's an important visit. There are signs that the band is gaining ground there. Everything has to be right.

At the soundcheck in Gloucester, Alan McGee stands

watching at the back of the hall with his girlfriend. Liam ignores the group and kicks a ball around as they play, and then they all go for something to eat.

At the table, Alan White orders beans on toast. When it arrives, he smothers the food in brown sauce.

'You can't do that,' Liam cries. 'That's disgusting.'

'You fucking watch me, mate,' Alan retorts.

At first, the band weren't sure about Alan, so obviously London, so obviously their idea of a cockney. But he was from the.same class, the same side of the street and now there was just friendship and respect. Not only for his drumming skills, which had brought an obvious new dimension to Noel's songs, but because he was someone who stood his ground.

'We were in Japan,' Liam had said in Bournemouth, 'And I couldn't sleep. So I was banging on everyone's door, going come on you cunts, let's go out.

'I'm banging on Whitey's door and he opens it and he goes, "I don't know about you but I've got a fucking gig to play tomorrow night for which I'm being paid and if I don't get any kip I ain't going to be able to play it, so will you kindly fuck right off."'

Liam loved that kind of shit. In your face. The fuck-off attitude. The attitude the band was built on.

The most amusing thing about tonight's gig, as far as Noel is concerned, is that the ex-Jam bassist, Bruce Foxton, who hasn't enjoyed a convivial relationship with the group's leader Paul Weller since the band split, was on the guest-list. Apparently, Bruce had also let it be known that he was up for taking Guigsy's place in the band.

'Can you imagine that?' Noel said, smiling. 'My mate Paul Weller comes to see us. Oh Paul, do you know our new bass player . . .'

The gig was fine. The crowd went mad. The band played well. Afterwards, they didn't stick around for too long. They were too tired. The coach made the short journey back to the hotel, and not long after, Noel and Meg got into an argument.

Meg had arrived with Fran, Fran's sister Charlotte, plus Amanda from Creation, the girl on the sleeve of 'Wonderwall'. Meg was in good spirits, happy to be seeing Noel, happy to be with her friends.

Others had also made the journey from London, such as Jess and Noel's mate, Sean Rowley, whose picture was now all over the country. Sean, better known as Travis, is one of the two guys on the *Morning Glory* album cover.

Meg was up for a party. She was with Noel, she was with close friends. She was in a good mood so she drank a lot and Noel started getting increasingly annoyed. Finally, he turned on her and told her that he hated it when she got pissed.

'Why?'

'Because you always repeat yourself. You say the same thing about five times.'

'Well, how long are you going to be pissed off with me for?' Meg demanded, her piercing blue eyes narrowing as she awaited his answer.

'Until I get off tour,' Noel snapped. That was in two weeks time. Meg just stared at him. Soon after, he went to bed. Liam followed. For everyone on the tour it was that kind of night, where the body finally says enough is enough, I don't care what you put into me, I'm closing down.

Meg let Noel go and then stayed up all night in the bar, catching the crew bus home. Later that day, the band travelled back to London.

Noel and Alan went to their homes and the other three booked into a Kensington hotel. On Monday they would re-group and fly to America.

On Sunday, it was revealed that over 350,000 copies of *(What's The Story) Morning Glory?* had passed over the counter.

Three

Father and eleven-year-old son sit in their small sitting-room watching TV. Son sits on the sofa, dad in his usual chair.

The gas fire is burning and there are photos of the family on the wall. These suggest a family harmony but that is thoroughly misleading. Father is not liked. His anger and domineering ways are too much to bear.

Father and son sit in silence. But Thomas Gallagher is smoking a cigarette and the way he draws on his cigarette is starting to bug the life out of his son, Noel.

Every time Thomas takes a drag on his non-filtered cigarette he spits out a small residue of tobacco. *Phut, phut, phut.* The noise is so aggravating.

'Here Dad, what you doing?'

'I'm spitting out the tobacco.'

'Why don't you smoke bifters with a filter?' Noel asks. 'That way you won't get so much tobacco in your mouth.'

There is a momentary silence.

'And how would you know that, then? What do you know about cigarettes?' Thomas slyly asks. His voice is quiet but menacing. 'Come on, Noel. Tell me. How do you know about filters if you're not smoking them yourself.'

Shit, Noel thinks to himself, furiously trying to figure out how to escape the trap he has set himself.

'No,' Noel replies as calm as he can. 'I don't smoke.'

'So how do you know about the filters?' his dad demands.

'I don't.' Noel keeps his gaze on the TV. He won't look at his father. But he can feel his face turning red. Then his father erupts.

'You've been smoking, haven't you!' Thomas shouts at him. 'I know you have.' The blood has gone to Thomas's brain now, the anger spilling out, fierce and uncontainable. 'What did I tell you about smoking? Ah! What did I tell you?'

The commotion is such that it attracts Peggy from the kitchen.

'For God's sake,' she says, entering the room, 'what's the noise about?'

'This one,' Thomas screams, 'smoking cigarettes, he is.'

'I don't smoke, do I Mam? Tell him.'

'Noel doesn't smoke,' Peggy says firmly. 'I know that for a fact.'

'Ah, that's it, cover up for him. Let him get away with it. You always do.'

'But, I don't smoke, Dad.'

'We'll see about that.' The father reaches over and roughly grabs Noel's hands. He turns them over, looking for nicotine stains on his son's fingers. Luckily, there are none.

'You see,' Peggy says. Noel glowers at his father.

'That proves nothing,' Thomas shouts at him. His eyes are full of fury. 'You smoke them with the gloves on, don't you?' Thomas sudenly announces. 'Say it, go on. I smoke them with the gloves on.' Thomas's face is bright red, the veins starting to bulge.

'I don't smoke,' Noel says defiantly. Father and son lock eyes for twenty seconds. Father breaks the terrifying silence.

'If I catch you at it, when I do, God help you.'

He turns to Peggy. 'I'm going out.'

'But where are you going at this time?'

'I'm going out.' He stares at his wife, defying her to make a move. Peggy says nothing.

And with that he pushes past her, leaves the house. When the door slams Noel looks at his distraught mum and then he quietly pushes past her and goes up to his room.

It hadn't always been like this. After their marriage, Peggy and Thomas moved into a small council house at 2 Sandycroft Street in the Longsite area of Manchester. Peggy was now seven months' pregnant.

The house had four rooms. There were two bedrooms upstairs, steep stairs took you down to a small sitting-room and kitchen, and outside was the toilet and a coal cellar. The street at the front was cobbled.

In the sitting-room was a sofa, a chair, a radiogram and a TV. Everything had been acquired on hire-purchase, the system by which you paid for your goods on a weekly basis. In the 1960s consumer boom, HP was the only way the working-class could gain access to such luxuries.

In the kitchen there were Formica chairs and tables, an oven and a sink. There was no fridge and Peggy did all the washing by hand. By the time they had moved into these surroundings, Peggy knew only too well her husband's temper and violence.

It was a fury so fearsome it shook her. But what was she to do?

'Thirty-odd years ago,' she explains, 'you never really heard of divorce. Thirty-odd years ago you never heard of the pill or birth control. You just thought you were married and that was your job, just get on with it.

'Like my mum used to say, you made your bed, now lie in it. I was in it then so I plodded along and made the most of it.'

On 11 January 1966 Peggy gave birth to her first son, Paul Anthony Gallagher. Fourteen months later, on 29 May 1967, a second son followed. He was proudly named Noel Thomas Gallagher. The Beatles' revolutionary album *Sergeant Pepper's Lonely Hearts Club Band* was released three days later on 1 June.

Peggy didn't go to hospital for either birth and both babies were delivered by a midwife in the house. Despite Thomas's threatening behaviour, Peggy could hardly contain her joy.

'That was a happy time and all,' she says. 'It was great when I had them, the two of them together. I was wanting two boys together 'cos I thought, they'd grow up and play football together and they'd be great friends for each other.

'They used to get along great. Paul and Noel went everywhere together up until they were teenagers. They'd half-kill each other but then you'd see them walking out of the gate together. They were always together.'

Their father worked on a building site and Peggy stayed at home to tend to her precious babies. When Noel was eighteen months old Peggy took an evening cleaning job. It was a real necessity. Bringing up two sons was expensive and their father wasn't that forthcoming with his wages.

The problem of what to do with the children while Peggy worked was solved when Peggy's sister Una agreed to come and babysit them.

The arrangement was that she would stay until Thomas returned from work, but more often than not, it was Peggy who would be home first. Thomas would roll in much later. He hadn't started drinking then, but he'd curtly inform his wife he had been playing cards. End of discussion.

'I used to do a lot of cooking myself,' she recalls. 'I'd always make me own bread, you see. I'd spend Sundays in the kitchen making apple-pies, making my own jam, my own bread. My life revolved around the boys. I'd spend my time washing, cooking or cleaning, and wherever I went they were with me. If I left the house, they were always with me.

'If I'd go out of a night-time visiting, they'd go with me. Even from an early age they wouldn't stay in the house with their dad because they never got any attention from him. He wanted to sit and watch television and that was it. Everything else was switched off. They wanted to watch cartoons and he'd say, "They're a load of rubbish." And he'd put on what he wanted to watch. So when I went out, they went out.'

Some children choose their football teams, others have them thrust upon them. Noel was the latter. The team given to him was Manchester City. At the age of four, he says, his dad would take him and his brother to Maine Road, Manchester City's football ground.

This choice of team reflected Thomas's contrary nature. Most Manchester Irish supported Manchester United. The brilliant Northern Ireland winger, George Best, played for them.

But Thomas Gallagher picked the Sky Blues. That said, City weren't a bad team, dominated at the time by class players like Mike Summerbee, Colin Bell and Francis Lee.

In 1969 they had won the FA cup at Wembley, beating Leicester City 1–0. The following year they bought home the European Cup Winners' cup, after beating Gornik Zabrze of Vienna 2–1. Lee and Young scored.

In 1971 it was Manchester City's policy to let people in for nothing after half-time. Thomas would take advantage of the scheme, getting to the ground at around a quarter to four and then locating himself and his sons in the ground's Kippax Stand.

'It was a big stand,' Noel recalls, 'and down the side, where the perspex screen was, there's a big slope with this ledge type thing. It was just big enough to get a kid on so all the dads would put their kids on there. It was like 2,000 kids all sat in a canoe and each dad knew exactly where his son was. He'd leave you there with a flask of Oxo and a bag of crisps and fuck off to the bar.

'All you could see was this big wall of little kids with big bobble hats and scarves on. Then me dad would come back at full time and pick you up and that would be it.'

To a four-year-old it must have been an amazing experience, to be sat there amidst a sea of grown men, taking in this deafening spectacle of noise, colour, songs and, when City scored, witnessing for the first time an eruption of unbridled mass joy, everyone jumping up and down, noise everywhere.

Then the songs would start, a community of working-class men joined together in one voice. The impression it made on Noel's mind was indelible. To see everyone so happy warmed his spirit and gave an inner glow. That feeling and how to produce it would form an integral part of his musical vision. It's why Maine Road became as important to Noel as the church would be to a thousand soul vocalists. It was his public place of inspiration.

When Noel, Paul and his dad entered the ground at half-time, the hit records of the day would be played through the speakers as everyone awaited the second half. The number one records that Noel might have heard that year, 1971, included The New Seekers' 'I'd Like To Teach The World To Sing', T-Rex's 'Telegram Sam' and 'Metal Guru', 'Son Of My Father', by Chicory Tip, 'Take Me Bak 'Ome' and 'Mama Weer All Crazee Now', by Slade, and 'You Wear It Well' by Rod Stewart.

The same tunes would be played at full-time as they left the ground to travel home to Longsite.

But soon the Gallaghers would leave the area. The family had received a letter from their landlords, the local council, informing them that their house had been marked for demolition. They were being rehoused across town in the area of Burnage.

Their new premises were at 14 Ashbourne Avenue, situated in a cul de sac. There were three bedrooms upstairs, a sitting-room, kitchen and, luxury of luxuries, a toilet inside the house.

The move meant new primary schools for the boys. Paul and Noel were currently attending classes at St. Roberts. Now, they were placed in St. Bernard's, a Catholic school where they would stay until secondary school age. Noel says that the best thing he can remember about primary school was being allowed to watch TV programmes such as *Stop, Look And Listen*, *Rainbow* and *Me*

And You, whose theme tune Noel loved singing: 'Me and you/ You and me/ There's lots and lots for us to see.'

By all accounts, Paul was the easiest of the two brothers to teach. He, like his mum, loved reading and writing. Noel was bright as well, but prone to laziness. It was only when something interested him that he would apply himself.

For instance, the books that most caught his fancy were mainly about football. He, as well as Paul, would often be found in the Burnage Lane library, poring over football annuals. Noel also had a leaning towards books that featured colourful, funny characters such as Tin Tin, Asterix and Doctor Seuss.

At this stage in Noel's life, music was on a par with everything else bar his fierce interest in football or his other hobby: the study of aeroplanes flown in the Second World War.

'I've still not been able to work that one out to this day,' he says. 'But I can tell you your Spitfires from your Hurricanes from your Lancaster Bombers. I used to get those Airfix models and we'd make them ourselves. I can never remember why I got into it.'

At night-time, after watching *Blue Peter* or *Vision On*, Noel and the local children would go outside on the street and play kick-can. This game involved one of them having to guard a ball while simultaneously trying to find where the others had hidden themselves.

It was always a treat when they persuaded some of the local girls to play; they were never as good as the boys and you got to touch them.

Peggy had no problems with her children playing on the streets at night. There was nowhere else to go and they were all within hearing distance. Plus this really was an era when you didn't have to worry too much about your child's safety. Their dad, as ever, took another view. He seemed to hate his children enjoying themselves.

'Where have you been?' he'd snarl at his sons when they returned home, exhausted but happy after running around for hours. 'Get to bed and don't go out there again.'

In summertime, the boys and their mum were freed from Thomas. In the long school holidays, Peggy and her sons would go back to Ireland, back to County Mayo to visit their gran, uncles and cousins. It was an idyllic and important time for Noel.

Manchester was grey concrete, motorways and high-rise flats. County Mayo was breathtaking scenery where you could run for miles. The country air was sweet, the way of life totally different from what Noel knew.

'We used to go out in the country,' Noel fondly recalls, 'picking blackberries to make jam. And my gran didn't have any running water so you used to have to go over to the well to get water. And then we used to go fishing with our uncle to get fish to eat.

'And then they used to have these big, massive, enormous barns. So my uncle and all the rest of my uncles and aunties would all be out and they'd have pitchforks, throwing hay into the back of the trailer.

'My uncle would then drive it into the barn and me and our kid and all my cousins used to get up on a ladder and go right into the rafters. Then we'd jump down on all this hay. All of us jumping together, all of us on our arses. Then we'd start scrapping. It was fucking ace.

'We used to love getting up in the morning. Chase cows around the field and that, throw stones at them 'cos we were from Manchester. And bringing in the cows to get milked. We used to love doing that because it used to take about six of us to get one cow through a gate.

'We used to pull a big stick off the hedges or somewhere and stand there like one man and his dog, only it was one man, his seven fucking nephews and a dog. It was ace.'

Sunday mornings were a particular treat.

'I've got so many memories of the local church in Charlestown,' Noel enthusiastically recalls. 'There was one Mass and it was like at ten in the morning and that was it, everyone was there.

'The first person to leave two minutes before anybody else was the landlord of the pub across the road because he used to have to go and open up. He'd be at the front somewhere and the priest would give him a nod, because the priest was mad for the ale as well, so as soon as you'd see him leave, it was like a two-minute warning. You knew you'd be straight across to the boozer.

'So we'd go over to the pub. I wasn't allowed to drink but you were allowed into the pub. Everyone was there, police, everyone. Top.'

On some occasions, when Noel accompanied Peggy into town, he would inadvertently witness the IRA at work. Towns such as Charlestown are easy prey. Totally isolated and with a police force of two men, such towns were the perfect spots for the IRA to stage robberies to replenish their funds. Who would dare stop them?

The same principle applied to the town's younger citizens. Young men, after a long session at the pub, would drive their motorbikes at high speeds and without helmets. Motorists would get behind the wheels of their cars, smashed on alcohol. No one seemed to care.

'Nobody had driving licences,' Noel states. 'Everybody was drink-driving all over the place. There was like two police officers, and these geezers from the IRA used to bowl into town, walk into the bank, loads of people around, and go, "How you doing? You all right? How's your mum? Give us the money. How you doing? Put the money in the bag. Thank you." Off they go.

'There's only Dublin which has the high-up police, the superintendents. The rest are like kids from the village. It's like the Wild West.'

This sense of freedom aligned with a drinking culture made an impact on Noel. Later on, his music and band would stand precisely for that principle, for freedom, total and absolute freedom.

Another element of Irish culture that would also seriously affect the young Noel Gallagher was to be found at night-time. His relatives couldn't afford a television, nor, one suspects, would they want one. There was far more fun to be had when they gathered together at night.

These get-togethers occurred at one of the family houses. Everybody would crowd in, young and old, and, in Noel's words, 'Talk all night. I remember sitting there crying with laughter. They all used to start taking the piss out of each other. And then me gran used to start going off at them, saying, "I remember when you did this when you were a lad." And they'd all be blaming things on each other.'

A radio would be on in the corner, playing Irish music, inspiring one of the family to pick up an instrument and lead the rest into a sing-song. The songs would always be melodic, with a great emphasis put upon the choruses.

Many of the adults there would be encouraged to take solo turns, as would the children. It was a good training ground for a prospective entertainer, an Irish education that would serve as the perfect antidote to the stuffy English culture that Noel was also exposed to.

(This was the England, remember, whose national radio station only five years previously had refused to continue its coverage of the 1966 World Cup Final between England and Germany, preferring instead to switch to the news as the players went into extra time.)

Growing up, Noel heard and was struck by certain Irish songs. To this day he cites The Wolfe Tones' version of Ewan MacColl's 'Dirty Old Town' as one of the greatest recordings ever made.

'There's no drums in it, no bass guitar,' Noel enthuses, 'it's just traditional Irish instruments and it's mind-blowing.'

Songs such as this, or other standards such as 'Four Green Fields', would have as much impact on Noel's later songwriting as Burt Bacharach, Lennon and McCartney, Paul Weller, Johnny Marr [ex of The Smiths] and U2.

Neither would it have escaped Noel's attention how the humour, the wordplay and the art of story-telling practised by his relatives, all played a vital part in entertaining those assembled.

Much of this rubbed off on Noel. He soon became a great story-teller, never adverse to changing a few facts to heighten the drama. From an early age people would always be drawn to him. He exuded a warmth and a humour that people found irresistible.

'Noel was always a happy-go-lucky type,' says Peggy, 'always had loads of friends, Noel would be growing up and he'd always have loads of girls, every one that knocked at the door was for Noel.

'Everyone loved Noel. Paul was more on the quiet side but they always had loads of friends. They were always well-liked as they were growing up and they were always happy-go-lucky.

'I'd play Irish records to them as well,' Peggy explains. 'They would be quite interested in them and they'd sit and listen to them. Big Tom and all these Irish bands. Later on, of course, they got their own type of music. All mine have done the paper-rounds. They'd get three or four pounds and that would go on buying their records.'

It was Peggy who bought Noel his first record player, a high-fidelity machine with a glass top. It was bought on hire purchase. Peggy also bought her two sons their first guitars. Noel and Paul were obviously attracted to music, and anything her sons showed an interest in, Peggy would do her utmost to encourage.

It was her way of making up for their father's seeming lack of interest in his children, as well as expressing the sheer joy and pride she felt for them. She also covered for their father when their birthdays or Christmas arrived.

'He wouldn't give a damn,' she recalls bitterly. 'They woke up Christmas morning and there wasn't a thing for them. It was all me that done it for them. I always made sure they had loads of presents. He'd go out Christmas Eve and you wouldn't see him again until Christmas night.

'And as the kids were growing up, he didn't give a damn as to whether there was a thing there for them or not.

'Then he'd say, "Why are you buying all these things for them? They've got more than enough." I'd say, "It's Christmas time." But he never bought them a thing.

'To be quite honest with you, I thought he was peculiar. I've never seen anything like it because he'd go out and spend money on others but his own never got anything. I always said that to him, his own never got nothing but everyone else did.'

Noel easily adapted to the tight monetary situation. He instinctively understood the pressure on his mum.

'You know,' Peggy remembers, 'as he was growing up, he'd say, "Will you do me a favour, Mam? Have you got a pound?" I'd say, "No, I haven't got it." And he'd say, "Okay, it doesn't matter," and he wouldn't bother.

'He wouldn't ask for much because he knew I didn't have it. And, then later on, when he was working, he would always come in and give you his keep. I remember when he was growing up, he was about sixteen or seventeen, and he'd see his father going out, and there would be all this shouting, and Noel would come down and say, "Here you are, there's a fiver for you, you go and get your hair done or you go out as well. Don't sit there and watch him go out, you go out as well." Mind you, I always brought them up to realise that if you can't afford something, you can't have it.

'If the money isn't there, you can't have it. They knew they couldn't have the dead-expensive trainers. I'd say, "I don't care what your mates have, they've probably got a dad in the house who must be giving them money." See, their father wouldn't entertain them with trainers.

'"They don't want them," he'd say. "The trainers are bad for their feet." It was just because he didn't want to part with his money. God, he was tight with them as they were growing up. He wouldn't give them a penny, not a penny would he give them.'

On 21 September 1972 there was a new addition to the family. Peggy gave birth to a third son, William John Paul Gallagher. He would be her last child.

Thomas Gallagher now found extra employment as a country and western DJ at the Holy Name Social club in Chorlton. For this, he earned £10 a night. Momentarily, Peggy was happy. She thought it might mean more money for the family. She was mistaken.

According to her, Thomas had now started drinking.

'I don't know whether that is when things went wrong,' muses Peggy, 'but I could never think the way he does. I'd think, you're out there doing a job, why not do it, get paid for it and come home? He felt he was getting paid and he should put all that money behind the bar for drink. That's when I guess his life turned around.'

As the father further alienated himself from the family, Peggy had to balance her life around work and her children. She was forced now to earn her own money, which she did by finding a job at the McVitie's biscuit factory.

'That wasn't a very happy time,' she recalls, 'because I had to go to work, I had no other choice. I had to feed them and clothe them. I'd leave for McVitie's at four o'clock in the afternoon and I'd work from four forty-five to nine-fifteen. I'd bring Liam into the sitting-room and I'd say, "Watch *Playschool*, Liam."

'He'd sit there, I'd draw the curtains, turn out the lights and he'd be quite happy, even though he was about six years old.'

Peggy would then rush to work. Every five minutes she would call Liam and ask if his brothers had returned home from school. She felt so guilty leaving her six-year-old on his own but there was no alternative.

'I'd spend my time on the phone ringing again and again until

I knew the others were in. I'd ring every hour and say, 'Liam, is your dad home yet?" He'd say, "No, he's not back and I want you to come home, Mam, I don't like being here on my own."

'I would say to his father, before he would go out, "Liam will be here on his own, I have to go to work." He'd say, "I'll be back, I'll definitely be back," but he didn't come back until the next day. Liam would come down the road to meet me, crying and looking to see where I was because there was nobody in the house. So you can imagine the condition I was in, as well as Liam. And there was the father, out with other women and expecting me to give him money as well.

'I was earning £40 a week but he'd always ask me, many times, if he could lend a fiver. He was going out with other women while I was trying to keep the three of them fed, clothed and put to school.'

In summertime, Thomas would force Noel and Paul to go raspberry picking with him. Thomas had discovered a patch of the fruit growing wild by an old disused railway line.

'Of course, the jam-making fetish all Irish people have came out in him,' Noel recalls, 'so after school in the summer I used to have to say to my mates, "I can't go out with you, I've gotta pick some berries, make some jam." All my mates would say, "Why don't you buy some?"

'Hey, that's not a bad idea. "Oi! Dad! Why don't you buy some jam like everybody else?" "I'm not fucking paying twelve pence for a jar of jam," he'd say. I'd think, what, a full twelve pence?

'And we used to have an allotment where they used to grow cabbage and all this shit. And he used to take us to the allotment and we used to fucking hate going there. All our mates would be playing football in the park. They didn't have that make-your-own-food nonsense. They went to a supermarket to buy it.'

Noel also remembers helping his father load up the car with his records for his night's DJing. But, however hard Noel tried to gain his father's love, it was all a waste of time. Out of his three children, Thomas seems to have hated Noel most. It was he who bore the brunt of his father's frustrations and anger.

'He didn't particularly like me for some reason,' Noel softly muses. 'I suppose I was a sarcastic little tyke and he could see right through it. I was always answering back, I was always asking, "What are you doing that for?" Or, "What's all that about?"'

'He gave Noel a bad time,' Peggy confirms. 'I don't know why. Maybe it was because Noel was that much closer to me. Noel got the worst of it but then again, Paul got a fair share of it as well, and Liam. Liam would be the most likely one to retaliate. Liam would stand there and you could see it in his face, Don't you dare touch my mam.

'But Noel got . . . he really didn't treat Noel well and I can't understand why he would just pick on one. Maybe it was because Noel was that much closer to me.

'I'll always remember Noel saying to me, "Soon as I can beat him, Mam, I'm going to kill him." He had beaten him [Noel] that bad one night.

'Maybe it was because Noel had gone out one night and he had said to him, "You be back by nine." But Noel would be stubborn. Noel would come in at nine-fifteen or maybe he would wait for him to go out and then come in. But if Noel got in five minutes after nine and he was there, then Noel got it.

'And it wasn't just a slap,' Peggy reveals, 'it was proper, you know, they'd get it in the face, in the mouth, he didn't care. And he'd kick them with his walking-boots and he wouldn't bat an eyelid. But I put it down to his conscience.

'He had a guilty conscience for what he was doing outside. He was coming back in and taking it out on us. I used to say to him over the years, "Why don't you walk out?" I swear if he had walked out, they probably would have had a bit of respect for him. But he didn't do that, he terrorised them.'

Peggy did her utmost to protect her sons but she was weak in the face of such a physical onslaught. Worse still, young Liam, who was constantly by her side, witnessed everything, engendering in him a pain he carries to this day.

'Wherever I went Liam went, so Liam saw more of his father hitting me. Noel would come in and say, "What happened to you, Mam? Where did you get that black eye?" "Oh, never mind that," I'd say, "I walked into the door." I'd cover up, you see. But of course, Noel knew and so did Paul. They'd seen it all before.'

It's impossible to fully calculate the affect upon Noel of his father's violence. Would he have pursued his career if things had been different? Did his father's lack of love mould him into the quality songwriter he is today? Or what about the reverse? Would unconditional love alone have propelled him into musicianship? Peggy certainly provided that.

One thing is for sure. Noel Gallagher's happy-go-lucky side was slowly being eroded. By the time he was fourteen, major depressions had set in. He became withdrawn and moody, as though there was a dark shadow constantly hanging over him.

Noel now suffered from a mild form of dyslexia and spent four years having a stutter in his voice seen to by a specialist.

Emotionally, his barriers went up. He wouldn't let anyone in. It's the standard response in all people, the only form of self-protection against unmitigated cruelty. Instinctively you learn to trust nobody but yourself. Your heart turns to ice.

And for many that will be their condition for ever.

Noel expressed his unhappiness in many ways. He became a thief, a football hooligan, and he found refuge from his miserable existence in drugs of many kinds. Later on in life he would find true lasting salvation in music.

And late at night as he lay in bed listening in abject terror to his father raging downstairs, waiting in terror for his steps to be heard on the stairs, the bedroom door flying open and himself being dragged out of bed to be hit for absolutely no reason, Noel imagined inflicting huge physical pain on his dad.

'I can't remember who said this,' he now says, 'but somebody said to me that Irish Catholic sons always turn out to be the antithesis of their fathers. They always grow up promising themselves they'll never be like their dad. The way he used to beat my mam and all that, that's why I'd never do that to a girl, like abuse them or take the piss out of them. I've seen me mam crying too many times to put anyone else through that.

'The effect it had on me was also to distrust figures of authority, like people, such as my dad, telling me what to do when they were no better than me. Like, he was giving me a hard time for not going to school and robbing shops, and he's just beaten me mam up. Hello? Is there anybody in there?'

Obviously, and sadly, there wasn't.

'Bad news, Noel.'
'What?'
'Your mum's the new dinner lady.'
Noel Gallagher entered St. Mark's secondary school in September 1978, and he ran straight into a nightmare.

First off, a lot of his friends had gone to St. Bernard's school. Then, much to his horror, he discovered that the school had now adopted a boys-only policy. There would be no girls in attendance.

On top of that, he was somehow placed in the wrong class.

'This is a true story,' he states. 'There were five classes in the year which went M, A, R, K, S. M, A and R were the top three classes. I gloriously failed my eleven-plus but my results got mixed up with a geezer called David Gallagher. I got put in the top bracket in the first year. So I'm with all these fucking nobs and I can't get my fucking head around it. I hated everyone in the class.

'They all had glasses, fucking briefcases and all this shit. I remember in the first assembly the teacher calling out the names and all my mates, who were in the divvies class, were going, "Where the fuck are you going? You must have passed your fucking exam, you swot bastard."

'Meanwhile, this poor bastard, David, was with all my mates and they used to kick his fucking head in, take his dinner tickets off him, his butties and all that. His mam and dad used to come to the school to complain. And they never sussed it out until a year later. Then, I swapped with him. I remember a symbolic thing at assembly when he walked passed me and gave me a dirty look as I was going to join my mates. I was like, you fucking twat, I'll do you. I think that's where I got all my hate of school from. I hated everyone.'

Especially so the bright kids, the ones who would always hand their homework in on time, who never got into trouble and looked down on people such as Noel. It's a snobbery that is never overt but Noel could sense it every time they watched him walking towards the headmaster's office for another rollicking.

Students, he hated students. And when, later on in life, his band would be pitched against a student band, his venom would come pouring out.

In the same month that Noel was starting school, Johnny Rotten's new group, Public Image Ltd., released their eponymous début single. Rotten had quit the Pistols while on their ill-advised American tour and was now embarked on a new musical journey. But for Noel The Sex Pistols were one of the most thrilling bands ever. They had tunes, disaffected but glorious anthems most of them, and they single-handedly re-kindled rock's rebellious nature before gloriously self-destructing.

Noel connected heavily with their don't-give-a-fuck attitude and the Pistols became a major influence. But at that time, there was little else to inspire him.

The Bee Gees soundtrack album for the film *Saturday Night Fever*, starring John Travolta, was number one for the tenth week running, while 'Summer Nights' by Travolta and Olivia Newton John had replaced 10 C.C.'s 'Dreadlock Holiday' as the UK's number one single. It would stay there for what seemed for ever.

Tragically, Keith Moon, The Who's drummer, would die in September, and The Jam would later pay tribute to him by covering The Who's 'So Sad About Us', placing it on the B-side of their next single, 'Down In The Tube Station At Midnight'. Records such as these aside, not a good time for music.

Punk was now dead and buried and New Wave acts, such as The Police or Elvis Costello, had taken its place. But for Noel punk was the business.

Yet there was still some way to go before he started taking a musical instrument seriously. Incidents such as briefly trying out guitar lessons in the last year of his primary school hadn't helped.

'I kicked it on the head because the teacher was trying to make me play left-handed because I'm left-handed,' he explains. 'And I couldn't get it. Then, when I got a right-handed one, it all made sense.'

Surprisingly, this guitar had been given to him by his father.

'Well, me dad, and I remember it to this day, he went out to buy me mam an eternity ring and he came back with an acoustic guitar. It's true. I remember him going off to get this ring and he came back and said, "Well, I was just passing the shop and I seen this guitar so I thought, fuck it, I'll get one of these." And he couldn't play a fucking crotchet on it so it ends up just lying around the house.'

Again Noel would take guitar lessons, this time at St. Marks. Again he would know only disinterest from his teacher.

'Somebody should have taken the time to say, fucking hell, this kid's got talent, he's actually left-handed but he's persevering to play it right-handed, there must be something here. But they never did.'

It was a slight that Noel would never forget.

'Noel won't forgive and forget,' Peggy says. 'If you cross him then that's it, and I'm like that as well.'

Faced with an unhappy homelife and filled with contempt for his school and classmates, Noel Gallagher started to isolate himself. He recalls his first two years at school as 'days filled with just staring out of the window'.

At home, he found himself writing poems, scraps of lyrics. And out in the street he fully involved himself in illegal activities.

Near his house lay a parade of shops. One of them, Mr. Sifter's, was where Noel would buy all his records. Later on, he would immortalise it in 'Shakermaker'.

Nearby, on Shorebrook Road, was a confectioner's run by two old women. At lunchtime, they would shut up shop but fail to secure the front door.

'And we hated them,' Noel says, 'because they looked like Hinge and Bracket. So me and two geezers bowl in at about half-past one while these old biddies sat in the back room having tea and biscuits.

'One of the geezers got to the door that leads to the back of the shop and he placed a chair underneath the handle and we proceed to take cigarettes. We couldn't open the till 'cos it was one of those electronic tills and they were a new-fangled thing in them days. We were pressing all these buttons and they didn't do a fucking thing.

'Anyway, as we were bowling out of the shop, full of cigarettes, tins of salmon and coffee, because they were the most expensive things, a delivery man shows up and sees us. So we get chased away and recognised.'

Noel appeared in juvenile court and was fined £2, a fee his mam had to pay.

Later on, another escapade. Bunking off school, Noel and his friends would often end up in a café in Levenshulme where, at the time, stolen goods were handled. It was here that Noel got talking with two guys one day. They asked him to accompany them on a job. Noel agreed finally and they entered a house, taking a digital watch and a Walkman, one of the first-ever models to appear on the market. The next day Noel sold them in the café.

'We actually got away with that for about six weeks, until one of the geezers we burgled this house with got caught doing another burglary. See, when you get caught,' Noel explains, 'the cops say to you, "If you admit to everything you've done, we'll let you off".

'So he told them that he had burgled the house with me. I was sat in the launderette doing me mam's washing and this fucking CID man walks in.

'"Are you Noel Gallagher? Does this address ring any bells?" Me mam's going, "How dare you? That's my son. He hasn't done anything wrong." Eh, sorry, Mam. So I went to court and got fined again.'

It was rapidly becoming apparent that Noel wasn't cut out for a successful criminal career. He had to face the facts: twice he had been caught now, but that wasn't really surprising as every time he committed a crime he sniffed glue beforehand to work up his courage. In other words, he was glued-up, not clued-up.

For many kids, sniffing glue is their first drug experience. It's legal and cheap, but the thrills are rich. Noel reckons he was about twelve years old when he first imbibed.

'How we ever actually managed to do any burgling I don't know,' he exclaims. 'We were all off our tits on drugs. We'd be hopeless, killing ourselves laughing, walking round a house, giggling like fuck. I mean, the people could have been there for all we knew.'

It didn't matter. Noel had found temporary relief from the pain in his life, discovered an instant solution to his problems. Glue, spliff, magic mushrooms, these would all now be consumed in great quantities. And then the world would look great again and the misery would magically disappear. There was just laughter and good times then. No more guilt, no more pain. How could he resist? He couldn't. Not even when robbing the local milkman.

'There was this public toilet where we used to get the bus to school,' Noel recalls, 'and the milkman used to pull up, buy a paper from the newsagent and go and have a shit in the toilets.

'Well, one day, we sussed that on a Monday morning, that's when he had the most money. So we hatched this plot which was that we were gonna lock the geezer in the bog and take the money which we had been told was under the guy's seat.'

The plan seemed foolproof. The boys met at the arranged time. They let the school bus go by and then surreptitiously sniffed some glue to chase away their nerves. As planned, the milkman arrived and entered the toilets.

'So my mate goes into the bog and comes out laughing, the geezer has got his kecks round his ankles. Into the milk float the three of us go, and then someone comes out the bog. Fuck this. Let's nick the milk float.

'This would be about half-ten in the morning. Glued-up. In a milk float. School uniforms on. Blazer, school ties and Adidas bags. We drive straight past our houses, up the main street on to the golf course. Then comes the realisation.

'What are we gonna do with a milk float and like 20,000 bottles of milk? Don't know. What have we nicked it for? Don't know. Isn't that a police siren I've just heard? Fuck me. So it is. We'd better get out and run.

'But you can't run because you're that caned off your tits. It must have been the easiest collar that policeman ever had. You think you're running dead fast with this big bag of fifty-pence pieces, but really we were just falling about laughing.

'Anyway, we get taken down the fucking police station. The coppers were like, "What do you think you're doing?" Don't know. Fuck knows. Mam turns up. Headmaster turns up. Then they got a fucking social worker.

'He starts going, "Why are you doing all these things?" 'Cos me mates do it. "So tell me about your childhood." Don't know. Then he was like, "I want to come round and speak to your dad." I was like, don't come round to my house, you don't want to speak to me dad. In fact, wait a minute, yes come round to my house. In fact, come on let's go. 'Cos I hated this cunt.

'He walks in and me dad's like, "You fuck off. You're telling me I'm a bad parent? It's that cunt there." And I'm standing there going, I told ya so.'

In Noel's third year, his mum left McVitie's biscuit factory and joined St. Mark's as a dinner lady. Exam question A. In not more than 100 words, describe how best to bunk off school, take drugs and hang out with your mates when your mum is the dinner lady and expecting to see you every day.

Answer. Go to school. Register. Then leave. But always ensure you are back at school by lunchtime. Walk into dinner hall. Make a point of saying 'Hello mum', preferably in front of teacher on lunch-duty. Eat dinner. Leave school for the afternoon and then return home at normal times. Full marks, Noel Gallagher.

'Me mam was flabbergasted at the military precision of how I managed to blag a whole term of school when she thought I was in every single day,' Noel proudly says. 'I think she admired me for that.'

Noel spent his days at his friend's houses, playing records, sniffing glue. At home, he practised the guitar and at age thirteen he attended his first concert, The Damned at the Manchester Apollo. He recalls being dazzled by the lights, the huge sound, the spectacle. He also remembers being bemused by the wild po-going that the band's fans erupted into throughout the band's performance.

Noel stayed at the back, coolly watching.

This po-going lark looked a little bit too energetic for his liking, plus he couldn't rid himself of the thought, the same one Peggy had experienced when she first saw screaming Beatles' fans, that somehow it all looked a bit silly. There must be something a bit more serious. And there was.

One Saturday evening, Noel found himself watching the Granada music show *So It Goes*. The show was hosted by Tony Wilson who was also head of Factory Records, based in Manchester.

Factory courted controversy. Their first major signing, Joy Division, took their name from the phrase used by the Nazis to refer to Jewish women incarcerated in concentration camps who were regularly raped. A Joy Division EP, 'An Ideal For Living', used as its front cover a photo of a Nazi stormtrooper, a Jewish boy and a member of the Hitler Youth. When their lead singer, Ian Curtis, committed suicide in May 1980, the band reformed under the name of New Order, the term used by the Nazis to describe their vision of the future.

Tony Wilson once said that his whole philosophy was contained in a Sid Vicious quote. 'I've met the man in the street,' the now-deceased Sex Pistols bassist had said, 'and he's a cunt.' Wilson liked that.

Yet in Manchester, the label was revered by many, especially students, the angst-ridden, middle-class teenagers who heavily related to Joy Division's Gothic music and elliptical lyrics. Plus, Joy Division weren't signed to a big company.

Punk had initiated a move away from major record companies. CBS, EMI and co. were all seen as the enemy, money-grabbing Conservatives who were out to stifle all innovation, all rebellion.

Taking advantage of the mood, several small record labels sprung up in the wake of punk. But many of them, Stiff Records being the prime example, were London-based.

Factory Records started in Manchester, signing local bands, and became a significant part of Manchester's cultural history before collapsing in the early 1990s. They would also have the distinction of being the only record company to turn down Oasis.

Tony Wilson's background in TV included presenting several music programmes for Granada. But *So It Goes* gained the highest ratings. As he explained once, 'We got all the best bands because the BBC wouldn't touch them.'

Noel saw a lot of punk groups on that show as well as more contemporary acts such as Joy Division or The Jam. Sub-sequently, he bought himself a pair of bondage trousers ('black ones with red tartan'), a black leather jacket, and 'huge Dr. Marten boots' which he strolled around town in. It was the sentiment behind punk, the energy, the fuck-you attitude, which riveted Noel so. He was young and isolated, and punk was the perfect vehicle with which to vent his frustrations.

In 1967, Paul McCartney read in the *Melody Maker* that The Who's new single, 'I Can See For Miles', was the loudest ever made. Determined to outstrip them, McCartney then wrote 'Helter Skelter'. The sound and attitude behind that song directly inspired The MC5 and The Stooges, who in turn inspired The Sex Pistols.

Which is why Noel Gallagher believes that Paul McCartney invented punk rock.

In contrast, it was Paul Gallagher who bought modernism into the Gallagher household. Paul was a fan of The Jam and the second wave of mod bands that had surfaced in 1979. Noel dismissed it all at the time. Mod carried none of punk's *frisson* and frankly most of the records from the likes of Secret Affair, The Merton Parkas et al. were lame. It was only much later on that Paul Weller would capture Noel's imagination.

'He was pissed off about something,' Noel enthusiastically relates about Weller. 'He was angry at the world and questioning everything, politics, ways of life, family life. To be honest, I didn't have a clue what he was going on about; it was the overall thing.'

All the groups that Noel would cherish (later on it would be The Smiths and then The Stone Roses), started from the street ('not some art concept'), and played for the people. It was the direction he would take his own group in, although at this point music still hadn't consumed his life. Football held more importance.

A regular now at Maine Road, Manchester City had performed well in the early 1970s. They gained respectable league positions (starting from the 70–71 season: eleventh, fourth, eleventh, fourteenth and eighth respectively), lost a League Cup final against Wolverhampton Wanderers in 1974, but beat Newcastle two years later to win the cup.

In the FA Cup, their progress was only so-so, but in the crucial local derbies, they often outplayed United, their greatest triumph coming in 1974 when Dennis Law, formerly of United, scored City's only goal with a backheel kick that pushed United into the Second Division. To see a former United legend such as Law dispose of his former teammates with a cheeky backheel, that was class.

There was another strain of football in Noel's life, but its only connection with Manchester City was that it was played on Huff End playing fields where the away-fans' coaches park.

Gaelic football is a mix of football and rugby. The goals are rugby posts but have a net strung beneath the bar. You kick the ball but you can also handle it.

Thomas Gallagher played, and he would take Noel and Paul along and they too would end up in a game. Eventually, Noel joined the Oisian's Gaelic Football Club and won many trophies with his team.

'It's a tough game,' Noel states. 'Physical contact is allowed and the Irish don't give a fuck. The referee's pissed anyway 'cos it's someone from the pub and all the dads are there, pissed up, watching their sons, going, "Go on, have him."

'We used to travel to Liverpool and Leeds and we used to win the league. We went on a trip to Ireland and played at Crow Park, which is the National Stadium in Dublin. It holds about 92,000 people and there were about four people when we played.'

If anywhere, this is where Noel would have gained his strength from, developing a strong constitution that would be constantly tested by drink and drugs in the coming years. But what always caught Noel's and some of the other boys' attention when they played in Manchester was a house that they could see from the field, situated on Mauldeth Road West. The number of the house was 388 and it always had this smart 1960s Zephyr car parked outside which the boys became fascinated by.

Another place to head for was Erwood Park. This was a huge park that divides Burnage from Levenshulme. By now, though, Noel was taking more of an interest in the guitar. He could play the bassline from songs such as 'Anarchy In The UK', if only on one string. And this impressed him so much that rock-star aspirations started to form in his mind. Soon after, he moved on to simple blues licks and the dream started to harden.

Eventually Noel learnt a song, the perennial classic for all aspiring guitarists, 'House Of The Rising Sun' by The Animals. Interestingly, many of Noel's later compositions would follow its style by incorporating a descending chord structure as an intro.

'I remember playing that song for, could have been two years, until I could do it flowingly,' he recalls. 'It used to take me about an hour to go from one chord to another but I persevered. This guitar I had, the strings were far off the fret board so you'd have to push the strings down really hard and it really hurt me fingers.'

Help came from an unlikely source. Quite often, Noel and his friends would play football matches against the boys from Levenshulme in Erwood Park. The outcome was always the same. As soon as the first foul was made, they would pile in and try to beat the shit out of each other.

Before or after these games, Noel would always spot a group of older guys in the distance, rolling around the grass in fits of laughter. Noel figured they were on glue. After all, that was the effect he and his friends got from the substance. But somehow their behaviour seemed different.

These boys were hippies ('smellies, that's what we called

them'). They wore kaftans, smelt of patchouli oil and their hair was long. One guy in particular interested Noel. He always brought an acoustic guitar to the park. His name was Flo and the local people thought him, well, weird.

'And me and him became really good mates,' Noel reveals.

'He used to sit in the park with his hippie mates, drinking cider, listening to Led Zeppelin's "Stairway To Heaven", and when we were playing football, it would be like, look at all those hippies. We were like little punk-rock kids, never trust a hippie and all that.

'But they were good guys. They were smoking all these weird cigarettes. We'd say, "Have you got a cold, mate? Your eyes are all red." And they had these tiny little tape recorders and sat there smoking pot.

'So I said, "I've got a guitar." They were like, "What, *you* can play?"

'I'd say, "I can do 'House Of The Rising Sun'," and me and him [Flo] became great mates 'cos I used to sit there for hours watching him play guitar. He could play "Rising Sun", but also things like "While My Guitar Gently Weeps" by The Beatles, which I thought was fucking phenomenal.

'That he could play a song and sing it all the way through. Everyone else would be laughing, going, "You fucking dickhead," but I thought it was fucking great.

'This was before I started taking drugs with him. 'Cos we were always proud of glue sniffing for ages and ages, but he was like, "That's just chemicals, man, you're fucking your inner-self. Take these mushrooms, they're natural, man." So he gave me some in a cup. Fucking ace.

'Mushrooms were just fucking brilliant. I have never laughed so much in my life, but in pain laughing – I couldn't stop laughing. And he had a ferret. He used to bring it for walks on a lead. It was golden coloured and it had red eyes and when we were on mushrooms, it wasn't a ferret then, it was some bizarre monster. We'd be hiding behind the trees on mushrooms thinking this monster was going to eat us. Top time.'

Another boy who played football in the park was a kid from Levenshulme. Everyone agreed that he was one of the ace footballers. By contrast, Noel was too lazy. He would stand in the middle of the park and never run. Just receive the ball and make long passes. But this guy was something else. He had balance, ball control and a footballing brain that allowed him to see moves before anybody else did.

'And at the end of every game,' says that kid, 'you would see all these dead cigarette butts where Noel had been standing.'

For Paul McGuigan, or Guigsy as he was better known, it was an image that would endure.

Four

They hadn't played here for just over a year. The last time was 18 December 1994 at the Academy. Now they were headlining the huge NYNEX arena in central Manchester, and close to 20,000 people had bought tickets. The first-ever Oasis gig took place on 18 August 1991 down the road, at the Boardwalk. No more than fifty people showed up. Tonight would be their 218th gig.

The last time Noel had been here was as a roadie for The Inspiral Carpets and nobody noticed him when he walked by. Now all eyes were on him.

The capacity for this venue was 19,300, but Marcus said, 'We've gone for 15,000 tickets. We calculated under so there should be tickets left at the office. That's the idea.'

He was standing in the venue's vast dressing-room. He jerked his head towards the exit door behind him and his Welsh accent became far more prominent. 'But the bloody touts are already out there. Fuck knows how they do it. After Brighton [29 December gig at the Conference centre] I set up a ticket-line to try and stop all that. I made it so that fans can ring up. If they haven't got a Barclaycard, then they go into town to pick them up.

'But most of them have got Delta or Switch cards. They can only buy four maximum. If I want to I can call up all the addresses of everyone who has ordered. But these touts have a network of people. They call up ten people who then order four and that's forty tickets in their hands already. And how are we supposed to know who's in on it?'

'At Earls Court,' he continued, the frustration rising in his voice, 'some were charging £100. The average was £40. Fuck, I wouldn't pay a hundred quid to see anyone. And then you've got the bootlegs. But you've got to hand it to them, some of them are brilliant, the covers especially.

'There's one just come out using the *Mojo* session we did. It's a better pic than the magazine used. In fact,' his voice dropped down a register, 'the cover's better than *Morning Glory*.'

From behind Marcus, the sound of the band soundchecking could be heard. It was a new song they were running through. It had no title as yet but it did have a memorable couple of lines that Noel was singing: 'Where angels fly/ You can't tread/ That's what you get for sleeping with the *NME*.'

Liam now enters the arena. Rather, he swaggers in, his long legs bent outwards, his long arms swinging, his whole demeanour that of 'who wants it?' One of the roadies kicks a ball to him.

Liam is wearing a Lennon-style cap, a large green jacket, jeans and trainers. He starts playing football with the roadie until he miskicks it and the ball rolls under the stage.

'Can't be arsed,' he shouts to his playing partner and then he runs to the stage and clambers on to it just as the band hit 'Round Are Way'. Liam saunters to the mike and starts to sing. At the song's ending, Noel wastes no time and immediately strikes up the chords to his new song.

By doing this, you may suspect that Noel wants Liam to disappear as his brother doesn't yet know the words. More likely is that due to their relentless touring programme, soundchecks are now the only place where Noel can try out new songs and new ideas with the band.

The way it happens is simplicity itself. Noel will start up a chord sequence that has been buzzing around his head of late. Bonehead and Guigsy will walk over to him, study the chords and then join in.

Alan White will then gauge the song's correct tempo, and bring his drums in. In this manner, a new song can be firing through the speakers within two minutes of Noel first playing it. Or they may play a Beatles' cover just to get them in the mood.

This afternoon, the four of them play 'Free As A Bird'. It is ragged but strangely touching, especially to hear Noel singing the line that Macca wrote to John Lennon: 'Whatever happened to/ The world that we once knew.'

Certainly, everybody's life in and around Oasis had changed irrevocably. They would never know again the world as they once did. There would never be any going back. They had pulled it off, escaped into their dreams and then made them a reality. How top was that?

A four-piece horn section, especially brought in for the gig, arrives and sets up at the back of the stage as the band troop off. They play their instruments without Oasis. Echoes of The Beatles again; 'Got To Get You Into My Life' to be precise.

Then Liam walks back on-stage clutching a Manchester City football shirt. It is a present, the actual top that Willie Donachie wore in the 1976 League cup final when Manchester City played Newcastle.

'Yeah, but who won the game?' asks Scotty, one of the road crew.

'Fuck knows, not arsed,' Liam replies, proudly holding it up. A minute later Noel walks back on-stage. Scotty asks him the same question. Noel, with a little bit of irritation in his voice, immediately says, 'We did, of course, 2–1. Barnes and Tueart scored.'

He straps on his guitar, and band and horn section swing through 'Round Are Way'. Then comes a thunderous 'I Am The Walrus', the song that has ended their set for years.

With horns now added, playing wayward, deliberately off-key and slightly off-time, the song gains so much more. Meanwhile, Trigger, the road-crew manager, the man responsible for ensuring that all the gear is set up on time, sits in the Oasis dressing-room. His baleful face looks exhausted.

'We got in here at two this morning to set the stuff up and we won't be out till five tomorrow I shouldn't reckon,' he explains. 'There was some classical thing on here last night and they [the venue] didn't tell us until two weeks ago. I keep telling them [the Oasis organisation] that one day there's going to be a disaster. There really will. We've nearly put as much gear up as we did at Earls Court in a day, and soon . . .' He shook his head, not wanting to contemplate such a scenario.

'All I know,' he said, standing up and stretching, 'is that I need a week in bed. That's all I need. One week. Do you think they'll give it to me?' And he ruefully smiled.

With the soundcheck now over, Noel had hopped into a car and was driven to a local radio station to be interviewed.

'The last time I was on it,' Noel said before departing, 'the DJ said, "And now we have Oasis, one of the biggest bands to come out of Manchester this year." I said, "Us and who else pal? Come on, who else?" This was live on air. I'm amazed they're having me back on.'

That night's support group, The Chemical Brothers, come on-stage round about seven forty-five. Tom and Ed stand behind a bewildering amount of machinery and fill the arena with huge drumbeats, sampled voices and analogue synths. Their music is derived from hip-hop and house, funk and rock, and, like Oasis's music, it could only have been made in the 1990s. The genuinely warm reception they receive, is a testament to this decade's musical stance.

In the 1980s, music had been divided. People spoke about it like they would their football team. Who do you support? Indie music. Fuck off mate, hip-hop is going to win the league.

Now that is over. In the 1990s there is only good music or bad music, good bands or bad bands, good people, bad people. The Berlin Wall went down in 1989, and so did a lot of other things.

At eight forty-five the lights darken, Steve Winwood's voice trails away from the speakers, and Noel Gallagher, Alan White, Guigsy and Bonehead walk on-stage to be drenched in the applause of nearly 20,000 people. Oasis are home, sweet and bitter home.

The four of them wave to the crowd, and a lone scouser shouts, 'Flash bastards!'

Noel pulls on his guitar, a red Epiphone Riviera, looks at Alan White and hits the opening chords to 'Swamp Song'. As his fingers pick out the riff that sounds like Marc Bolan misplaying Norman Greenbaum's 'Spirit In The Sky', Noel nods his head, Alan White plays a loud drum-fill and all the band come in. Bonehead takes over the rhythm and Noel begins to make his guitar screech. Already it's a juggernaut of sound, crushing all in its way.

Halfway through this instrumental, Liam walks on-stage, banging his tambourine. The crowd erupt again. Liam nods his head in recognition and then walks right to the front of the stage. He deliberately does this at every gig, goes up and stares the audience out, all the time menacingly hitting the tambourine he holds against his hand.

In a street fight it is always the one who doesn't back down that has the better of it. Fronting your opponent instils real fear in them. As Liam's nature dictates that he never backs away from anything, even in the face of huge odds, this was his way of psyching out the opponent and killing his own nerves.

The rest of the band take no notice of him. They either concentrate on their instruments or stare out the crowd.

After confronting the audience, Liam walks back towards his mike and shouts, 'Mad for it.'

Noel again looks over at Alan, a signal that the song is about to end. As Noel hits the final notes, Alan finishes with a huge flourish of his cymbals. Noel slowly walks back to his amp to extract howls of feedback from his guitar.

'Manchester,' Liam says amidst the noise and then Noel hits the jagged opening chords to 'Acquiesce'. The crowd roar in approval. Noel stands absolutely still as Alan's drums come thundering in and Liam places his hands behind his back and starts singing, 'I don't know what it is that makes me feel this way.'

And the whole crowd sing the lines with him, instantly turning into a seething mass, a swarming creature that jumps together and shouts together. Oasis have in their music, words and deeds, inherently always promised a good time. Tonight, Manchester will make sure that their word is good.

Oasis are so well loved and respected, no one comes to their shows with a cynical frame of mind or a 'prove it' attitude. People come to celebrate, to renew their faith. This is their music, their songs, their band, their chance to lose themselves.

Noel taps his feet a few times but soon desists as he turns to the mike and, in unison with his younger brother, starts singing the chorus. 'But we need each other/ We believe in each other.'

The line is pregnant with meaning, but more than that the strength of their singing adds a new dimension to the Oasis sound, a level that has only briefly been caught on record. Noel and Liam, in perfect harmony.

'Acquiesce' shows Noel's voice to be more powerful than say Keith Richards's, but not as rounded as Rod Stewart's in his prime. It is far more effective when heard in a sparser musical situation. In a live-band situation it tends to get drowned out a little, lacking the sheer strength of his brother's vocal.

The song finishes to rapturous applause. The girl by the barrier in the orange T-shirt holds her hand to her mouth as if she is witnessing a miracle.

'Cheers,' Liam says. '"Supersonic".' It is a sucker punch opening. Two B-sides to go and then a major hit single to raise the stakes even further. The heavy opening guitar lines of the song kick in.

Up each side of the arena, everyone is standing, everyone moving. Some have their hands in the air, some dance, others are simply transfixed. Oasis themselves hardly move. There is a reason for this. Oasis aren't natural dancers. They find it hard to express themselves physically.

Other performers get lost in their music and that feeling is dynamically transmitted to the audience through their vivid body movements. But not this band. They are well aware that they are loved for their forthright honesty. To move in a manner that even faintly whiffed of calculation would be to cripple the music.

Of course, what they found along the way was that the tension between their stasis and the huge music that erupts from themselves, actually adds to the audience's fascination with them. It gives their shows a tension that is an elixir to the band. Noel had first witnessed this when he saw Public Enemy live.

For the audience Liam is the central focus of this tension. They know only too well about his impulsive nature, are aware of his unpredictable behaviour. They know also of the tempestuous nature of his and Noel's relationship. Any communication between the brothers simply adds to the gig's frisson.

For Oasis, this tense mood reminds them of different things, reminds them of that minute when you are standing on the terraces and the word has gone out and now you're just waiting for the violence around you to kick off. You're as scared as shit but high as a kite, as that weird mix of adrenalin laced with fear courses through your veins.

When they walk on-stage that's precisely what Oasis are feeling.

On the third line of 'Supersonic' Liam muffles the line but quickly gains his composure. Noel hits stinging guitar riffs and Bonehead and Guigsy stare impassively ahead. Alan White, now drumming through a frenzy of sweat and facial contortions, can only see his cymbals.

The song finishes, Liam says something but the feedback that Noel is wrenching from his amp drowns him out. And then Noel hits the opening chords to 'Hello', and its back on again, no let up until the heights have been reached.

The band play it way too fast, but give a shit, this is live, this is excitement. 'Hello,' shout both brothers when it comes to the Gary Glitter chant that Noel so brazenly lifted, 'It's good to be back, good to be back.'

Noel's guitar now has a funky rock edge to it as his foot effortlessly pumps the wah-wah pedal on the song's finale.

The lights dim, Noel goes to his amp, fiddles with a few switches and then before you know it he is hitting the riff to 'Some Might Say'. The riff has been nicked to fuck but NYNEX should care. The audience hurl themselves at the band now and hurl themselves against each other.

From its first line, the song instantly grabs people. It's one of Noel's irresistible songs, anthemic and charged with meaning. Because of that, Liam makes sure that the song's best line is measured and audible: 'Some might say they don't believe in Heaven/ Go and tell it to the man who lives in Hell.'

Again, the brothers' voices come together, trade off each other, move with each other. For many people, this is the best Oasis single ever, a fact strengthened by the rapturous applause and cheers and shouts that erupt on the song's closing notes.

'Cheers,' Noel says, his first words of the gig. He sports a stripy jumper and his usual jeans and trainers. This band don't look flash, even if their clothes have high price-tags.

The lighting they use is similarly unobtrusive. Compared to some, the lighting is minimal, simple. Noel, of course, had a hand in its design. The finished effect ensures the audience's focus is kept on the music.

'This is called "Roll With It",' Liam announces, 'la la la.' Again his hands clasp themselves behind his back and his head is bent upwards to the microphone. They play a thunderous version and as the crowd's energy levels are once again lifted, the horn players now gather behind the stage.

Maggie, the tour manager, stands with them, her lighted torch dangling by her side. One of the trumpet players offers her his trumpet. She smiles, briefly and professionally.

As the band finish the song, the horn players troop up on to the riser. They stand above Oasis as Noel stands by his amp twiddling knobs, looking for all the world as if he is casually buying a packet of fags from a machine rather than standing on stage with 20,000 pairs of eyes on him and 20,000 voices cheering at him.

Liam gulps at a bottle of water, Guigsy and Whitey wipe themselves down with towels and Bonehead stares straight at the crowd, no reaction in his eyes.

Noel then looks up at the horn players, counts them in. 'Round Are Way' starts up, an intoxicating mix of blaring horns, ragged guitars and Alan White's basic soul stomp. Again, it's another contagious chorus that the crowd sing with abandonment and gusto, the song's title, a specifically Northern expression, taking on even more meaning in this part of the world.

Towards the end of the song, Noel starts singing another one of his songs, 'Up In The Sky'. He does this often, Noel. Throws in a couplet from another song as if to say, 'See how easy this music lark is?'

In truth, it's just another smokescreen. Noel knows more than most the price of it all.

'Hey you up in the sky / Flying so high . . .' Liam joins in, Noel steps away from his mike and the band end at precisely the same time.

Liam then says, 'I'm trying to think of something to say to you . . .' The crowd cheer. 'I'll just sing a song for you.'

Noel's guitar then starts churning out *that* riff to 'Cigarettes And Alcohol'. It is the sign for girls to start climbing on to their boys' shoulders, for the whole of the NYNEX to sing in unison, the words to this quintessential 1990s song: 'Is it my imagination / Or have I suddenly found something worth living for.'

The riff from this song came from the blues. Marc Bolan took it and wrote a song called 'Get It On' around it. But when he wasn't looking, Noel Gallagher stole in and lifted it out of Bolan's possession. Now whenever the people hear *that* riff they automatically think of 'Cigarettes And Alcohol'.

The song is also one of the most sexual in Oasis's arsenal.

The music, tough, menacing notes backed up by a primal beat, reeks of decadence and wild times. The lyrics, with their images of cocaine and of drunkenness, add to the fire. Yet there is a much wider meaning behind this song, a typical Gallagher message: seize the day, seize the moment.

In a country divided by wealth and opportunity, it's the youth of the poor, the ones who live in the wastelands where the local shop is barricaded up and there is day after numbing day to kill, who know only too well that it's not 'worth the aggravation/ To find yourself a job when there's nothing worth working for'. So you must be the architect of your own fame. It's up to you. Make it happen. Oasis have. They're the living proof.

Plus the song contains one great moment; this occurs on the second verse when Liam takes the word sunshine and transforms it into 'Suun-shii-ine!', in precisely the way Lennon did on The Beatles' 'Tomorrow Never Knows'. But now the phrasing belongs to Liam Gallagher.

'This is for a girl called Katy,' Liam then announces, '"Live Forever".' He moves back from the mike and starts circling the stage. Round and round.

The band ready themselves to play one of Noel Gallagher's finest moments, the song where everything dramatically comes together. In 'Live Forever' the words and the music are so intertwined, it often feels that they couldn't exist without the other.

Other Oasis songs with non-specific lyrics, create a distance between band and audience, a space created by words. Catchy as they may be, lines such a 'I've been driving in my car/ With my friend Mr. Soft/ Mr. Clean and Mr. Ben are living in my loft' are throwaway words. They have none of the resonant power of 'Live Forever'.

But when Liam steps to the mike and sings, 'Maybe I will never be/ All the things that I want to be/ But now is not the time to cry/ Now's the time to find out why/ I think you're the same as me/ We see things they'll never see/ You and I are gonna live forever', then you are talking about music and words that transcend all the barriers and fully join together, as punk had intended, band and audience. Manchester is no exception. They soar, the song soars. No wonder Noel thinks it the first 'proper' song he wrote. It finishes in a scream of guitars, drums and bass.

Liam says something which causes Noel to throw his brother a withering look, and say, 'No, it's not, it's "Champagne Supernova".'

The crowd momentarily stop, a little confused. Is it going to go off? No, it's not. The faithful who follow Oasis know the score when they see a disturbed sun light up behind Whitey's kit.

Noel opens with the song's delicate chords and the crowd turn to look at him, but he is deep into his playing, totally unreachable. Liam starts singing and the band join in. Of course, they play it too fast, but then they always do.

Live, they have little chance of repeating the subtleties this song achieves on record. Instead, they concentrate on finding its unstoppable momentum and turning that fully on to the audience. It is a majestic song, brilliantly arranged with different melodies and riffs piled upon each other and a set of lyrics that are ambiguous but good enough for everyone to read their own meaning into them.

In a decade where drugs are the norm and the authorities helpless to stop them, never has a crowd been more delighted than when they get to sing the 'Where were you while we were getting high?' refrain.

As the band head into the last third of the song and the crowd hold up their lighters, Noel now escapes into his playing. This is the nearest Oasis get to jazz, in that Noel now truly uses his guitar and not his pen to communicate with people. His guitar sounds angry, determined, focused yet utterly loose. Again, he brings forth that remarkable tension as you wonder where he's going with these notes, how he is going to pull it off.

It's a tension further heightened by his on-stage demeanour, which is totally motionless. There is no emotion on his face. Nor any sweat. He is still, yet his music is wild, urgent.

Then he brings the mood down and Alan White kicks in the soft military beat that ends the song in such a wistful manner. Noel hits the last chord and turns away. The lights dim to thousands cheering, and the rest of the band take off their instruments and walk off.

You would be forgiven for thinking that the gig has ended. No way. Now we are into phase two, the place where Noel displays his other sides, other moods. He calmly goes over to the stool Jason has just placed on-stage and sits down.

Noel adjusts the mike and says, 'This one's for a mate of mine. His name is Johnny and this is "Wonderwall".' After the radio show, Noel had met up with Johnny Marr, the former guitarist with The Smiths who had truly inspired him.

Noel hits those distinctive chords and opens his mouth to sing. He needn't have bothered. The whole of Manchester beats him to it.

'Today is gonna be the day that they're gonna throw it back at you/ By now you should have somehow/ Realised what you gotta do/ I don't believe that anybody feels the way I do/ About you now.' And everyone in the arena sings the last two lines to Noel and to Oasis. This is true community music, a binding together of people through words and sound that somehow mix to touch all the right nerves, tug all the right strings, inside of us all.

Years ago, across town, Noel heard a similar sound every time he went to Maine Road. He stood amongst the people as they sang together, united as one. Now, through his own music, he had repeated the magic.

In this part of the show, Noel is not the hard, cool rock star but the town healer. It's here that his voice comes into its own. Strong, plaintive and soulful.

At the song's conclusion, Noel says, 'Thanks for sticking by us this year,' and as they thank him back, he goes into 'Cast No Shadow', his elegy to songwriters.

Again, the crowd take the burden off him, and buoyed by their reaction, he changes the final wording to 'They can take *our* souls/ But they can't take *our* pride'.

The lights extinguish and when they come up again Noel says, 'This is a song about being young and having it large every night, the way you do. This is "Morning Glory".'

Played slower on acoustic, and bereft now of its almost thrash-like treatment on record, the song takes on greater depths of meaning.

Noel always wrings more meaning from his songs when he plays them acoustically, his sad-tinged voice throwing a different light on lines such as 'All your dreams are made/ When they're chained to the mirror and the razor blade'. On record those words sound like a celebration. Here, they sound like a lament.

The song ends, the lights dim and Noel Gallagher, with only his guitar by his side, becomes a silhouette, briefly trapped in his own isolation. The lights rise and the band, minus Liam, walk back on as Jason takes away the stool and Noel pulls on his electric guitar.

'Anyone here called Sally?' Noel asks. There's a shout from the front row. Noel peers over at the people. 'You're not Sally, you're a geezer.'

He kicks up the ringing chords to 'Don't Look Back In Anger'. Again, he changes the words: 'Take me to Maine Road/ Where the Blues play,' he sings, a line of deliberate provocation. There are many United supporters and some players here tonight.

The crowd miss the reference. They're too busy in their own rapture to notice.

'I Am The Walrus' is next but the horn section have missed their cue, they're late coming on-stage.

As Maggie desperately runs to locate them, Noel has to improvise. 'See City are doing well,' he tells the crowd. There are some cheers but many jeers. 'So are United,' he concedes. He looks behind him as the horn players finally arrive.

'I've been waiting for you lot,' he half shouts. 'Where the fuck you been?'

In compensation, they play their hearts out as Oasis deliver a gigantic version of 'Walrus'. Bolstered by the horns, the band's playing here is manic, mesmerising and relentless.

As on the opener, 'Swamp Song', Noel attacks his guitar, wrenching out all kinds of feedback and howling distortion to counteract the rhythm section's circular dynamics.

Liam stalks the stage. Noel goes and kneels by his amp, lost in music once more. At its fiery conclusion, Manchester stands in appreciation, their noise reverberating around the arena. The enthusiasm is such you believe the applause will never stop.

Oasis rarely encore. But tonight they clear the stage of the horn players and then the five of them tear into 'Rock 'n' Roll Star', the song that, according to its writer, says everything he ever wanted to say in a song. And, of course, Liam gets to sing the word 'Suun-shii-ine' again. The gig ends now, with Liam sauntering off-stage and being spat at by United fans. He should care. There are 20,000 people here and the music has swept them away, allowed them to taste freedom.

Freedom. This decade is about freedom. Freedom to take drugs, hold raves, protect the environment. Freedom to think differently from those before and those above, freedom to live how you see fit. Freedom is in short supply these days. But not at Oasis concerts. Their words are about freedom, their music breathes it.

An exhausted Noel Gallagher sits once more in the production office. 'I've escaped,' he says.

Five

It had to happen. Just had to.

In truth, there could be no other way. For the last few years, the Gallagher boys had remonstrated with their mother. Leave him, they'd say. He's no good to you or to us. Fuck it, let's go, come on. Of course, Peggy wanted to leave but one thing held her in check: her Catholic religion.

For Peggy to divorce or leave her husband would mean excommunication from the Church and, ultimately, that would lead her into hell. It was unthinkable for her to even consider placing her very soul in peril.

But Ma, the boys would argue, what kind of church is it that allows this to happen? I can't do it, she would reply, and for evermore the Gallagher boys would despise the church, and music would become their religion. Placed in this impossible situation, Peggy often tried to remonstrate with her husband.

'Why do you do such terrible things?' she would desperately ask of her husband.

'Because everyone else does,' he would chillingly reply.

'I don't care what everybody else is doing,' she would sadly say. But her words were no use. Now, only action was the answer.

She went to the council and she begged them to move her and her sons. She would sit in grey offices, tears streaming down her face, pleading for a new house so that the family could escape. Finally, the council relented.

Typically, Liam was against moving house. They should throw Dad out. Why should they have *their* lives disrupted? He was the one who should move. Why should they have to start from scratch again?

The stress got to Liam. Peggy recalls watching him in the dinner queue at school, nervous, biting his nails, so unhappy.

But move they did. One night, with Thomas out, Peggy Gallagher and her sons packed their bags and moved to a new council house in Burnage.

On the night they arrived, the boys chose their bedrooms – Liam and Noel sharing, Paul in another room – and then they finally slept.

In the early hours of the morning Peggy, who now weighed just seven and a half stone, sat down in the empty sitting-room and looked at the bare walls and uncarpeted floor. Then she asked herself, How on earth will this family survive? They had nothing to their name except the clothes on their backs. There was little money coming in. What on earth were they to do?

It was then that the uncontrollable tears burst through and Peggy wept like she had never wept before. Yet even in the midst of her weeping, she was careful not to wake her sons. It would never do for her boys to see her like this. For them she would always be strong.

Of course, Peggy's family pitched in. Her brothers and sisters gave her items to help make the house liveable. Soon, Thomas tracked them down. But he wouldn't come in. He'd stand at the front-door shouting, but that was the extent of it. No longer could he beat them. Noel was now the head of the family.

A few weeks after moving in, the local priest came to visit Peggy. He had heard what had happened. Peggy invited him in and gave him a cup of tea.

But when the priest started insinuating that she should perhaps consider returning to her husband, Peggy put down her cup and firmly told him to leave.

'Which is one of the reasons why I love her so much,' Noel proudly says.

Noel's violent side also manifested itself outside the home. The main example was at football matches. He never instigated fights and, as is so often the case, there was a lot of shouting and running down streets with very few punches thrown. But if it did kick off, Noel could more than handle himself. Guigsy remembers him once battering someone in a Nottingham pub, 'giving him a proper seeing-to'.

Noel actively enjoyed travelling away to matches. There

would be hundreds of them and their sheer number precluded the police enforcing the law in any kind of meaningful way. Noel and all his mates, defiant to the last, would be shepherded on to trains, for which they never bought a ticket. They would openly take drugs, get drunk, and then Noel and a few others would get off a stop early, walk into town and shoplift whatever they could.

The fights they had, Noel says, were usually sparked off by the opposing fans. Even when languishing in the Second Division, Manchester City still commanded a formidable following. The City fans' massive presence alone always ensured that there was immediate tension upon their arrival.

'We called ourselves the Young Guvnors,' Noel recalls, 'and then it got changed to the Cool Cats which was a really stupid name because we weren't cool and we certainly weren't cats. It was mainly two years spent just running up and down the streets. It was like those scenes from *Quadrophenia*. You'd go up a street and then the cops would come.

'Someone would launch a brick through a window and then they would chase us. It was a good laugh, but then I started getting more into music and that was the end of it.'

The music Noel refers to centred mainly around The Smiths. If anything, he has played down a little their appeal for him.

The band's melodic instincts, hewn from Johnny Marr's love of 1960s girl groups and quality pop, the fact that a major British band now hailed from Manchester (so starting a line that exists to this day with the later arrival of The Stone Roses and then Oasis), Morrissey's undoubted skill as a lyricist (especially in his song titles), all struck a major chord with Noel.

Later on, when working with The Inspiral Carpets, Noel sported a quiff in honour of Johnny Marr whose guitar playing and songwriting he so admired.

The haircut made his hirsute eyebrows even more prominent and the Inspirals were quick to nickname him Monobrow. They also nicknamed their manager, Antony Bodgiano, Binsy Smith after a character in a children's TV show, and on the spine of the sleeve for their single 'Find Out Why' they wrote 'Binsy Smith meets Monobrow'.

Another major influence on Noel was U2, especially, says Graham Lambert, The Inspiral Carpets' guitarist who Noel would roadie for, the album *Achtung Baby*, which Noel repeatedly listened to while on tour.

At home, Liam also recalls some Billy Bragg records in Noel's collection. Certainly, his older brother had a distinct penchant for guitar music, although it was somewhat after the event, Liam asserts, that Noel fell for The Jam.

This passion for music not only started to shape Noel's future, but it began to alienate him from his hooligan friends. They simply weren't interested in music. But for Noel, with anything that interested him he fully committed himself to it, a direct result of his Irish blood and a Catholic upbringing which demands full and utter dedication.

Music was now a major passion and, as ever, it was all or nothing.

Take Noel's twenty-first birthday, one of the few significant birthdays in any person's life.

'What are you doing?' his mates asked.

'Well, I wouldn't mind going to see The Stone Roses and James at the International Two.'

'Ah, fuck off mate. Let's go down the pub.'

But Noel didn't want to go down to the pub. He wanted to go to the gig. Noel loved gigs. You could get into places like the Boardwalk or the Hacienda cheaply, the drinks were very reasonable and you could see two or three bands in one night. Even if they were shit, you could still have a good laugh and maybe, just maybe, pull a woman.

'It was one of the great things about The Smiths' gigs,' Noel recalls. 'You'd go there and it would be full of blonde women. I'd say to my mates, "You should come down, the place is full of women." But, of course, they'd never come.'

On 29 May 1988 Noel was standing upstairs in the International Two waiting to see The Stone Roses. He had a spoonful of speed up his nose and a huge packet of it lying in his pocket. He knew full well that the next day he would have to be up early, working for Kennedy's, laying pipes for British Gas, and all with the hangover from hell. But you know what? He didn't give a fuck. Tonight he was out to party.

Anyway, Noel reasoned, someone like Tommy Coyle, the old geezer who worked with him, would help him through the downer with his biting humour alone.

Tommy acted like a dad to Noel. He would often take Noel aside and say in all seriousness, 'Now listen, son, take my advice. Don't marry a woman, marry a man. A man you can go to the pub with, you can go to football with, you can pull birds with, you can even go down to the bookies and spunk all your money away and still you won't have any arguments. I really wish I'd married a bloke.'

Just the other day one of the gang had announced they were now a born-again Christian. Quick as a flash Tommy looked up and said, 'How did you manage to climb back inside your mum's fanny then?'

But work was tomorrow. Tonight was now. Noel strolled over to the toilets, went inside and locked himself into a cubicle. He racked out a huge line of speed and, taking a crumpled £5 note, snorted it up his nose. Then he strolled back into the crowd and within two minutes he felt invincible.

The Stone Roses appeared on-stage. Fucking great band, Noel thought to himself. And, for a second, he tried to imagine what it would be like to stand up there in front of all these people, playing music. It must be incredible, he decided. And one day it'll be me there.

Then he noticed, to the left of him, a kid with a tape recorder, sneakily recording the gig. He didn't recognise the kid but they had in fact met before.

Graham Lambert was now a guitarist, but a year ago he had DJed at the Boardwalk at a Jack Rubies gig.

Noel had been in the crowd that night and he had cheekily gone up to the booth to ask Graham if he had a spare copy of The Pastels' single he had just played. Graham had taken the piss right out of him for that.

Noel looked at the kid again and then decided to approach him. The speed had kicked in nicely now. All of Noel's shyness had disappeared. Fuck it. Noel went over to Graham, asked him what he was doing.

Instantly Graham panicked, thinking that Noel worked for the band or the club, but Noel explained he didn't and would it be possible to get a copy of the tape when it was done?

Relieved that he hadn't been caught, the lads got talking about music. Noel told him he had just bought an Inspiral Carpets' record called 'Planecrash'.

Graham smiled at this news. 'I'm the guitarist,' he said.

By the end of the night they had swopped numbers and they stayed in touch. But, more importantly, this gig laid the seeds for what was to come. Liam was downstairs absolutely riveted by The Stone Roses and their singer, Ian Brown. Mark Coyle and Phil Smith were there working for the Roses. It would be as important a gig for Oasis as Spike Island, The Stone Roses' 1989 gig, would be for heralding the arrival of the 1990s British pop movement.

Noel, meanwhile, was getting very serious about his song-writing. Peggy remembers cleaning his room once and making the mistake of tidying up all the scraps of paper he had been writing lyrics on and then, when Noel saw what she had done he went mad, and she said, 'Well, if you kept your room tidy then I wouldn't have to go in there,' and Noel shouted back at her, and it was all such a palaver.

But Noel kept on writing lyrics, putting together chords. He even replied to an advert in the *Manchester Evening News*. It read 'Musician wanted for co-songwriting, must be into The Smiths.'

'That's me, Noel thought, and he got on the phone and, without telling a soul, went to meet this guy who was about the same age. Noel put down on tape what he thinks were about four of his songs. But this guy was a right student, as so many Smiths' fans were, so Noel never returned. But he had committed his first songs to tape. It was something.

Noel spent a lot of his time going to see local groups, such as The Happy Mondays or the Roses, and of course, he was always present at most Manchester City games. Then, one day, while talking to Graham, Noel discovered that the Inspirals had just sacked their lead singer, Stephen Holt. Noel saw his chance.

'I'll audition for you,' he offered. Graham thought it a great idea. If it worked out he would have a good mate in the band.

On 21 December 1988, with Christmas approaching, Noel told Peggy he was going to audition for a band.

'It's funny,' Peggy says, 'but as he was leaving the house I thought to myself, "This is really what Noel wants to do".'

Noel arrived at the Mill Studio in South Street, Ashton-under-Lyne. He was slightly nervous but, of course, like his brother, he never betrayed a fraction of what was inside of him.

He stood in front of a microphone and sang an Inspirals' song, 'Butterfly', and then a version of The Rolling Stones' 'Gimme Shelter'.

When he was finished he came home to find that a plane flying over Lockerbie in Scotland had exploded in mid-air. The news was shocking, but the verdict from the band on his vocal performance was disappointing.

'We felt his voice just wasn't strong enough,' Graham says. Noel agrees. 'I was shouting my bollocks off,' he recalls. 'I couldn't sing then, so I didn't get the job.'

If Noel was disappointed by the outcome he certainly never showed it. He had learnt not to express himself in front of others, feeling it was a sign of weakness to do so. He worked after all with a tough gang of pipe-layers for whom displays of emotion reflected badly on your masculinity. Girls cry, boys don't.

Around the April of 1989 Noel broke his foot. He was at work when a heavy pipe crashed down on him. He was taken to hospital and put in plaster. The worst part of the injury for Noel was being immobile. It meant he would have to stay at home day after day. Noel hated being bored. It really was the worst thing. All his life he would struggle to evade boredom. One day he phoned Graham and told him of his plight.

'I remember him calling us up on the mobile phone,' Graham says, 'and he said, "You know, I wouldn't mind roadying for you", because he now needed a job.'

Given his physical condition, Noel may well have been joking. He would after all be a 'one-legged' roadie. But Graham was keen to help his friend out who was so obviously bored out of his mind.

So in May 1989 Noel travelled with The Inspiral Carpets to their gig at the Duchess of York pub in Leeds, a venue that would later play host to a very famous incident in the Oasis story.

'Noel was on crutches,' Graham recalls, 'and I remember we had to help him up this fire escape.'

When the leg healed, Noel jacked in his job with Kennedy's (he had been moved to the storehouse where Liam would later work) and was taken on as a guitar roadie by the Inspirals. Not long after, the band employed another roadie called Jeff Scallon, and Noel was then made responsible for the band's guitars, keyboards and drums.

Soon after starting his roadie career Noel had learnt how all three instruments operated, quickly learning how to play drums and understand a keyboard. In footballing terms, he became an all-rounder.

There was also a sound-monitor man working for the band by the name of Mark Coyle. Mark and Noel shared many similarities. Like Noel, whatever Coyle chose to do, he did so with an all-or-nothing attitude. He too was Irish Catholic.

At the age of fourteen, Mark's ambition was to produce and engineer. He played guitar with a Manchester group called The Wild Strawberries in the early 1980s and later on worked as a sound engineer for The Stone Roses. Between their gigs he was employed by the Inspirals, where he and Noel quickly developed a major friendship that lasts to this day.

'Music and football is what brought us together,' Noel explains. 'He was really into The Beatles and he's also a full-on United fan, the dick. We had loads of arguments about City and United. Still do to this day. He's also a brilliant guitarist. He never plays in front of anyone now but let me tell you, he's top.'

Coyle could also play drums. Many times the two of them would arrive at venues, set up the equipment and then, either before or after the band soundchecked, Noel would get on guitar, Coyle on drums, and they would run through Noel's songs. Unbeknown to them, they were both preparing for what was to come.

If Coyley (as he is known) was Noel's closest male friend, then, apart from Peggy, the woman closest to him at this point was Louise Jones. Noel had seen her around in various clubs, mainly the Hacienda, and they had eventually got chatting.

Noel was still living at home, and Peggy, who got on well with Louise, remembers her coming round most nights to the house and sitting with Noel in his bedroom.

Soon, they decided to live together. Louise was manager at a Benetton shop in town and she had put her name down for a flat in India House, a large building situated in the city-centre.

Meanwhile, a friend of hers was moving out, so Louise and Noel took the apartment, effectively squatting. A year later, Louise's initial application came through and they moved upstairs to a larger flat.

But by now Manchester had found itself a new name: Madchester.

*

In late 1987, London DJs such as Paul Oakenfold, Nicky Holloway and Danny Rampling were about to change the course of club culture. It needed a shot in the arm. Dance music, at this time, was neatly divided. Rap over there, house over here. Many of London's clubs were élitist also. You had to dress a certain way to gain entry.

By travelling to Ibiza and witnessing an across-the-board musical policy that appealed to many, these DJs returned to London and started playing in a similar style. For instance, at Paul Oakenfold's late-night club in South London, he would play U2 and other rock sounds as well as house music. The introduction of Ecstasy pills into this scene then provoked the biggest youth movement since punk.

Ecstasy pills, first used in 1912 by German psychologists to help their emotionally-stunted patients express themselves, were at this time incredibly powerful.

Within twenty minutes of taking them users had lost all their inhibitions and felt an enormous well-being towards themselves and others. Suddenly white kids who rarely danced were leaping on to tables to gyrate the night away.

Clubs such as Schoom, the Trip and Spectrum were witnessing amazing scenes of public abandonment as a new culture quickly took shape. Nineteen eighty-eight was officially christened the Summer of Love.

The Hacienda in Manchester had been playing house music on a regular basis, well before London took note, although the clothes and the drugs were absent from the scene. It took, as Sarah Champion noted in her book *And God Created Manchester*, Shaun Ryder and Bez from The Happy Mondays travelling down to London, checking out the clubs and then returning home with the formula, for Manchester to emulate the whole scene.

Once it did, the town went crazy. It certainly had needed an injection of pure excitement. Economically, Manchester was still in serious decline. Manufacturing jobs had all but disappeared, unemployment was staggeringly high and a black-market economy based around stolen goods and drugs was about the only service industry showing any kind of growth.

Gangs, such as the Quality Street Gang, who had once ruled and operated Manchester in the same way as the Krays had in

London, had lost their power, taken over by a breed of new young drug dealers who mainly congregated in Manchester's Moss Side area.

This new breed of drug dealers were young (both Mark Coyle and Guigsy have witnessed or been threatened by eleven-year-olds holding small automatic pistols), unprincipled, fearless and determined.

They soon took over Manchester's house scene and made a killing·selling Ecstasy for enormous profits. Later on, they would flood Manchester with heroin and cocaine.

Noel initially resisted the house scene. His love was guitar music. He couldn't dance and he wasn't particularly conversant in any kind of black music. It was only when he moved down to London that he would be exposed to the likes of Lee Dorsey, Sly Stone, Marvin Gaye et al.

At his first visit to a Hacienda house night, Noel watched the crowd with a real detachment. He didn't understand the music, didn't understand why everyone was going mental on the dance floor. The next time he went, he took an Ecstasy pill and suddenly everything made sense.

This was easily the most powerful drug he had ever taken. As with his previous excursions with mushrooms or glue, the drug killed his guilt and shyness. But Ecstasy also attacked his anger. It made him far more open to people, less fearful or cynical about them.

Soon, he was dancing to the beat, albeit at the back of the club. By contrast, Liam hated the scene. All these kids dancing strangely with their bulging eyes and declarations of friendship ('you're my best mate, you are') sickened him.

But Noel was unstoppable. He went to raves such as Live The Dream and Joy. He would travel down to London to attend sessions at the Spectrum club and he would see people such as Alan McGee or Jeff Barrett, The Happy Mondays press officer there.

Noel even put aside his guitar for a while as he totally immersed himself in house's primal beat and its anthemic choruses which, when heard while on Ecstasy, made you feel as though you were really fulfilling heaven's promise of love eternal. (Another facet of this music was the large productions most of these records displayed. One of Noel's favourite tracks from this period was 'The 900 Number' by Mark The 45 King, a blistering mix of hip-hop beats and a wailing saxophone.)

For a few months, apart from isolated writing in the music press, this scene went unnoticed until the *Sun* ran a front-page exposé in August 1988 warning the nation of their children's exposure to chemicals. There were calls for the police to take action.

'We got arrested in Leeds,' Noel recalls. 'There were about four of us in this car and we bowled up to this rave in Leeds. But the police had put up this roadblock and because we were off our tits, we didn't care. So we bowl up in this car, pot smoke everywhere, Es and cocaine in the car, and this copper puts his head through the window and says, "You're all under arrest."

'So we were taken and put on this coach with all the rest of the people from Manchester. Everyone was emptying their pockets on the floor. There's Es all on the floor, Rizla papers, people eating dope. Then they took us up to this nick in Leeds. But that was full up, so they put us in the basement of the town hall, locked us in the corridor and handcuffed us to the radiators.

'Mike Pickering [founder of the group M People] was there, Graeme Park [a name DJ], some of the Mondays, and we all spent the night in this corridor, laughing, tripping, stoned.

'Next day we all appeared in front of the judge with the worst fucking hangovers going, and some people were actually put in jail for dealing and are still there now.'

Noel was given a fine and returned home. Undeterred, he kept going to the Hacienda, dropping Es and having a wild time. One night he and Louise returned home to India House, with Noel buzzing away.

'You had to use these zip cards to get in,' Noel explains. 'We opened the door and there's this big black guy standing there and loads of people in the corridor and on the stairs dancing away to this music. The guy goes to us, "Five quid to get in mate."

'It was mad. But for me the real Manchester scene was three years before when you used to go down to the Boardwalk and see The Happy Mondays, The Stone Roses and a couple of other bands for two quid, and it would be a pound a pint at the bar.

'But once that shit was in the papers, Mancunian phrases in the *Daily Mirror* like, "top one means well-done old bean", and the students moved in and all the clubs started to be run by gangs, that was it for me.'

Soon the music of The Beatles and The Jam and The Smiths would return to centre-stage in Noel's life but he was also enormously taken by records from The Happy Mondays, The Stone Roses and another new group, The La's.

Their single 'There She Goes', which was released three times before becoming a major hit, preceded an album that had taken years to record but which, on its release, made the band's leader, Lee Mavers, a force to be reckoned with by his contemporaries.

Even so, The La's remained something of an underground phenomenon. When their album, *The La's*, was finally released, Mavers, ever the maverick perfectionist, told every interviewer that the album was shit and that people shouldn't buy it. Most people complied with his request.

Mavers' reputation quickly spread. Stories of him insisting on 1960s dust being brought into the studio quickly circulated and only served to strengthen Noel's admiration for him. Noel was also pleased to learn that Mavers also rated a favoured LP of his, the Pink Floyd album *The Wall*.

While accepting that *The Wall* isn't a consistently good album, tracks such as 'Little Black Book' are classics in Noel's eyes.

But what Noel really admired about The La's album was how it was ahead of its time. First recorded in 1987, it signalled a return to classic pop songwriting and would exert a major influence on many up-and-coming groups such as Oasis, The Real People and Ocean Colour Scene.

When Noel finally did meet Lee Mavers, on 17 December 1994 at the Royal Court in Liverpool, Noel introduced himself saying, 'It's a real honour to meet you.'

'I bet it is,' Mavers replied. To this day, Oasis still hold him in the highest esteem.

As the house scene turned predictable and the Ecstasy pills lost their potency, Noel moved back towards guitar-based pop music, propelled there by the work of artists such as Mavers and John Squire.

But he never forgot how those glorious, transcendental house choruses, so reminiscent of Irish music and football-terrace songs, had made him feel. Soon he started incorporating them into his own music to devastating affect.

Noel had already made strides towards incorporating house

into his repertoire with the music he now started making with Mark Coyle. Mark often invited Noel over to use his recording equipment, and co-write some songs.

'What's the address again, Coyley?' Noel asked.

'It's 388 Mauldeth Road West,' Mark replied.

I know that place, Noel thought. Now where the fuck from?

Arriving there, Noel realised the house was opposite the fields he had played Gaelic football on. He told Coyle this and Mark replied that he too had played the game as a young kid.

The boys worked out that they had actually played against each other at one time. It seemed indicative of the nature of their deep friendship that they should have already crossed paths.

The boys set up their tape recorders, got out their guitars and started putting melodies and ideas over sampled drums. One song they recorded used a sample of Buffalo Springfield's 'For What It's Worth'. A few years later, the group Oui 3 employed the same idea and scored a major hit single.

There were other songs as well, but a lot of the time the boys got so out of it that they often forgot to press 'record', or put in the wrong tape.

'I'd go home to Louise, stoned out of my head after three days of being round Coyley's, and say, "You should hear this song we did, it was ace, only you can't hear it because we taped over it because we were so stoned".'

All those who did hear these tapes, Liam for one, would testify, that the ideas and songs 'were great'. But Noel or Mark never approached a record company with them.

As for Noel's relationship with Louise, someone like Bonehead found it hard to fathom out. By the time Noel had joined Oasis, a lot of the money that he earned as a roadie, and by all accounts he had received good wages, went on either enjoyment or equipment. It was left to Louise to cover the rent and bring in the shopping.

'You'd go round there,' Bonehead recalls, 'and Noel, who would be something like four grand behind with the rent, would have all his mates round to watch football. They'd be drinking beer, shouting, and meanwhile Louise would be in bed trying to get some kip to go to work the next day so that she could pay the rent. But you'd never hear her complain or anything.'

Naturally, Noel was away a lot of the time with the Inspirals.

He soon found out that he loved travelling. Touring has often been likened to living in a bubble and Noel enjoyed life there. He and Coyle, who shared rooms, would get up, roll the first spliff of the day, maybe take a line, amble into soundcheck, unload as little of the gear as possible, play their songs and then wait for the gig.

'We knew nothing about amps,' Noel recalls. 'We'd put them up and if they didn't work, we'd kick them like you do your TV when it's not working. If that didn't work, we'd turn them off, put them back on and if they still didn't work tell the band to get some new gear in.'

During gigs the boys, who rated the Inspirals as so-so, would smoke copious amounts of spliff and check out the girls in the audience.

'Once, me and Coyley were behind the amps when the band were playing,' Noel remembers, 'and we were so fucking stoned that the band came off, came back on and we didn't even know about it.'

Marijuana may have calmed Noel down, but travelling definitely appealed to his nomadic instincts. Like all serious artists, he hated being tied down and although everyone considered him a lager lad, he was sensitive enough to appreciate many of the different cultures that he was exposed to.

He fulfilled an ambition, first ignited as a kid by all those US cop shows such as *Kojak*, *Starsky and Hutch* and *Police Woman*, by going to America. Later on there would be trips to Japan, Estonia and South America.

But it was while he was in America that Noel found out through Peggy that Liam's group, Oasis, were playing a gig at the Boardwalk on 18 August 1991. There was no way in the world that he would not be there.

In the meantime, he had made perhaps the most important discovery of his life. One day at home, Noel had been playing *Exile On Main Street*, one of his favourite Rolling Stones' albums, 'for about the 300th time'.

It was while listening to the track 'Shine On Me' that Noel thought he heard Mick Jagger sing the word 'Maybe'. God knows why but the word stuck in Noel's head; he picked up his guitar and strummed some chords repeating the word time after time.

Then he found that if he left a gap between two chords and inserted the word 'maybe' into the space between, he was on to something.

Which is how Noel Gallagher wrote his first classic song, 'Live Forever', and how he discovered that not only was he a songwriter of undisputed talent but that he could now truly take himself seriously. In all his early songwriting attempts, he was smart enough to know that he hadn't arrived at the kind of standard that he expected and looked for in all things. With 'Live Forever' under his belt, he now knew for certain that he had a future. It was a strange feeling. Noel Gallagher had never felt anything like it before in his life.

Six

Everyone was asked to be in Kings Cross by twelve that day for the journey to Whitley Bay and Oasis's 232nd gig. By ten past, only one person was missing. Liam. Of course. Tour manager Maggie got on her mobile and tracked him down.

'He's just got up,' she announced, 'he'll be here in an hour.'

'Right,' Noel said, 'Scran it is.' Across the street was a café that the local cabbies used. Guigsy, Alan White, Noel, the new security guys, Kevin and Terry, Maggie and her assistant Melissa, ventured to. Here they ordered breakfast, talked about football and the press.

'Did you see the *Daily Mail*?' Noel asked Alan as they tore into sausages, eggs, beans and bread, washed down by pale cups of tea. 'They had this report about those pre-Brit Awards that I went to. They said I got out of the car looking like a window-cleaner with a hangover.' Noel grinned. 'Fucking top.'

Because the band had been in America, they had missed the TV programme on The Beatles, *Anthology*, that had recently been shown. Videos of the programme were now available on the coach. They all settled down as Liam finally got on. He looked totally wasted.

'What you watching?' he asked, the tiredness apparent in his voice – huge sunglasses covered his eyes.

'That Beatles thing,' Noel replied.

'Oh.'

Then Liam turned around, got into one of the bunks and slept the whole of the journey.

Noel, Guigsy and Alan White watched *Anthology*. They made no comment until footage of the band playing to thousands of screaming girls came on-screen. Noel screwed up his face in total disgust.

'Fucking screamers. Shut the fuck up. They get right on my tits, all that screaming.'

'Too right,' Guigsy replied.

At about five that afternoon, the coach pulled up outside the Windsor Hotel and everyone made for their rooms. Three hours later, after freshening up, Noel came down and was advised to go to the Bikini Bar, just around the corner. Liam stayed sleeping in his room.

The bar was aptly named. The barmaids all wore bikinis, while raised on a rostrum in the corner a DJ worked in the old-fashioned way, constantly addressing the crowd over his records.

'Right, it's Michelle's birthday today. Come on Michelle, get on the bar and give us a twirl. Come on everyone give her a round of applause.'

Michelle was helped on to the bar and started drunkenly gyrating to the music.

'Come on, Michelle,' the DJ cried, 'you can do better than that. Let's be seeing you. Do a strip.'

The crowd cheered her but not in a leering, nasty way. This was Friday-night funtime. Whitley Bay was on the piss but all they wanted was to laugh, to party.

Similarly, the majority of the crowd recognised Noel. But there was no tension, just a stream of people coming up with best wishes. The boys said, 'Top fucking band,' and the girls said, 'Oh you're lovely, you are. I love that song of yours, that "Wonderwall".'

Noel stood there smiling. He was among his own. And they bought him drinks and they cuddled him and then they gave him his space. Afterwards, the manager kept the bar open for an extra hour, and Noel went back to the hotel, drunk but appreciative.

'If that's what 200 people are like,' he said, 'imagine what the gig will be like tomorrow. And, best of all, Liam is going to be gutted that we all went out and he wasn't involved.'

The call-up time was for three-thirty the next afternoon. At three o'clock, the band were in the bar. Liam, refreshed, was standing by the bar and flirting with the pretty bargirl.

'Here Tracey, Tracey, I'm not getting on your nerves, am I? Tracey? I'm not, am I? 'Cos I'll stop talking to you. I will, Tracey. I promise. Scout's honour. I'm not getting on your nerves, am I?'

Tracey smiled and tried to serve other customers. Liam kept going. 'You're very pretty, Tracey. That's lovely hair you've got. But if I'm getting on your nerves, I'll stop, I will.'

Guigsy came over to buy a drink.

'How are you?' he asked Liam.

'How am I?' Liam replied. 'How am I? I'll tell you how I am. You want to know how I am? Well, I'll tell you how I am. Do you want me to?'

Guigsy, in a flat tone, said, 'Yes Liam, I would like to know how you are.'

'Okay. This is how I am. You want to know how I am, I will tell you how I am. You know the phrase, over the moon?'

Guigsy nodded.

'You know that phrase, right? And you know that other phrase, out of the cuckoo's nest?'

'Which is what you are,' Noel shouted from his seat.

'Well, right between those two phrases is how I am,' Liam said, ignoring his brother's jibe.

Then he turned to Bonehead who was sitting by Noel. 'Here, Bonehead, did you bring those CDs?'

Bonehead shook his head. 'I forgot.'

'You forgot,' Liam said.

'I forgot.'

Liam moved towards him. 'I ask you to do me a favour which is to walk into HMV, buy some CDs and come back, which, when you think about it, is dead fucking simple, and you forgot.'

'Well, why didn't you get them?' Bonehead challenged.

''Cos I'm the singer and every time I walk into HMV it's . . .' Liam mimed a photographer using a camera.

Immediately, Noel stood up and pretended to play the violin. 'Ahhh,' he said, 'you poor little thing.' Then Guigsy and Bonehead joined in.

'All together now,' Noel said and the three of them chanted, 'Ahhh.' Liam stood there half-smiling. 'Fucking wankers,' he muttered. Then he looked at Noel's jacket, a smart three-button number with leather collars and cuffs.

'At least I don't look like a geography teacher with that fucking jacket on.'

'Nor do I,' Noel quickly replied, 'seeing as my geography teacher was black and from Nigeria.'

Outside the window a cluster of fans peered through the bar window. Maggie came in. 'Right, bus is ready.'

The band quickly finished up their drinks and made their way outside. Liam and Noel signed autographs for the kids. Then they got on and went to the back of the bus and sat down with the rest of the band.

There was a momentary silence. Noel looked over at Liam and laughed. 'Come on,' he urged his brother, 'say something controversial.'

'Nah,' Liam replied, half-smiling. 'Nah, I've got nothing to say.'

Noel raised his eyebrows. '*You've* got nothing to say.'

'Look, at the end of the day . . .'

'Comes night,' Noel shot back.

'Depends where you live,' Liam retorted just as quickly.

'You know what he said to me the other day,' Noel said, now addressing Bonehead. 'He said, "The next single has got to be proper top".' Noel raised his arms as if in disbelief. 'Like, all the other ones haven't been.'

'Hang on, hang on,' Liam interjected. 'Get it right. What I said is that right now everyone thinks this band is the dog's bollocks, which is right and everything but what I'm saying is that the next single should be proper top. It's got to be even better. It's right, isn't it?' he asked, turning to Bonehead for some back-up. But the guitarist was too busy grinning.

'Anyway,' Liam said, turning back to his brother, 'what kind of audience do you want with a jacket like that? A fucking bunch of antique-car collectors?'

This was a thinly disguised jibe at Noel's chocolate-brown Rolls-Royce, his Christmas present from Creation. Noel pulled a stupid face and said, 'Might do.'

'Ah, sack it,' Liam said, and sauntered off to sit elsewhere.

Five minutes later the coach pulled up outside the Whitley Bay Ice Rink. Two minutes after that, Noel was on-stage playing his guitar. Guigsy, Bonehead and Whitey soon joined him. They played a new song, now entitled 'Me and My Big Mouth', then went into 'Don't Look Back In Anger', a raw version of The Beatles' 'Daytripper', then another run through 'Don't Look Back In Anger'.

Then Liam appeared and the band went into 'Round Are Way'. But the pacing of the song was too hectic. A minute into it and Liam was shouting, 'Slow down, slow down, it sounds like fucking Blur.'

The band ignored him. They all followed Noel who was now slashing at his guitar.

'It's too fucking fast, I can't . . .' Exasperated, Liam pulled back from his microphone and the song finally collapsed.

'I'm here to do my vocal,' Liam lectured them, 'so slow it down.' Noel started strumming the opening chords but did so deliberately slowly, like a single being played at half-speed.

'Faster,' Liam said. Noel upped the pace a little bit.

'Fucking faster,' Liam said. By the time they were playing the song correctly, Liam was in a temper. Halfway through the song he sat down on-stage and stared glumly ahead. At the song's conclusion, he stalked off-stage.

Noel didn't seem to care. He went over and picked up his acoustic guitar, settled down on his stool. Everyone expected him to play a recognisable song. Instead, he started playing another new tune. The chords sounded like a distant cousin to 'Wonderwall', and the chorus was riveting.

'Every sound I hear is made by me-eee,' he sang. Everyone present stopped what they were doing to listen. When he finished, Noel put down his guitar and said, 'That'll do.'

Behind the stage, Ocean Colour Scene, that night's support act, were preparing to soundcheck. 'Did you hear that new song?' Steve Cradock the guitarist asked. 'Amazing.'

As the Ocean Colour Scene boys soundchecked, Noel sat down for an interview with Richard Johnson from the *Sunday Times*. Then he joined Guigsy, Bonehead and Whitey in catering. Liam was absent, but as soon as he did walk in it was obvious that his temper had worsened.

He sat down and sullenly ordered some food from Mouse, who was doing the catering. When she delivered it in her normal ebullient manner, Liam said nothing. Instead, he stared at his plate, not bothering to pick up his knife and fork.

Behind him, Johnny Hopkins, Oasis's press officer and Richard Johnson sat at another table. The journalist wanted to talk to Liam at some point. But Liam had already refused. One of the road crew at Liam's table asked if anyone wanted any bread. Liam mumbled, 'No.' Everyone else said, 'Yes.'

When the roadie came back he handed Liam a roll.

'I said I didn't fucking want any,' Liam snapped and then returned to staring at his food. It was then that Melissa, Maggie's assistant, walked in. Liam had asked her to iron his shirt for that night's show. But she had been unable to locate the suitcase it was in.

'Liam, where's your suitcase?' she blithely asked.

Liam looked up in disbelief. 'What, you haven't ironed my shirt yet?'

The venom in his voice and eyes caught Melissa unawares.

'No, I . . .' she stammered.

'It's in my suitcase which is downstairs where I fucking told you it was. You know what a fucking suitcase looks like d'ya? It's the blue thing with handles and a fucking top and a bit of rope at the end of it, all right?'

Melissa's face turned red. Shamed, she walked out.

'Fucking twat,' Liam snarled.

Bonehead turned to him. 'You don't have to talk to her like that, y'know.'

'What's it to you?' Liam demanded.

'I'm saying, you don't have to.'

'Five fucking times I've asked her to iron my shirt, five fucking times. So don't tell me anything.'

'I'm not,' Bonehead shouted back at him. Their faces were now inches apart. 'I'm saying, don't . . .'

Liam violently pushed his chair back and stood up. Now he was towering over Bonehead. 'No,' he screamed, 'no,' his finger wagging in Bonehead's face. 'You don't put your fucking nose in my fucking business, ain't your business, all right? It's none of your fucking business.'

'Hey,' Noel shouted at his raging brother.

But Liam ignored him. He kicked the chair back and walked out of the room, shouting back at Bonehead, 'I'll see you any fucking time.'

Bonehead turned to Noel. 'He's off his tits,' he said.

'He's a dickhead,' Noel calmly replied.

Hopkins now came over to Noel and crouched down next to him. 'Is your brother all right?' he asked.

'He's getting too big for his boots,' Noel said, still eating.

Bonehead stared at the doors that Liam had just walked through. There wasn't anger in his face at being challenged or put down in public. It looked more like genuine worry. Everyone was used to Liam's tantrums but this felt a bit more serious.

By contrast, Noel was currently in a consistently good mood. The new songs he had in his head were well up to scratch. His band was the biggest in the land and getting even bigger. He was publicly respected for his craft and the gigs were a pleasure to play.

Certainly, that night's was no exception. The minute they walked on the crowd were on their side. The band always responded to such full-on encouragement. They never broke a smile but they put everything they had into it.

Liam waited by the side of the stage to make his entrance. He was too vibed up now to be scowling. He motioned to one of the roadies and jerked his head at Noel as he hammered out the screeching notes to 'Swamp Song'.

'He's good, isn't he?' Liam said.

'Fucking great,' came the reply.

'Yeah, but not as good as this,' Liam boasted and then he swaggered on-stage to thunderous applause. When the band reached, 'Cigarettes And Alcohol', Liam approached Noel from behind and then placed his back against him as Noel played. He knew it would get to his brother. He knew he would be gritting his teeth. But, as ever, Noel showed no emotion. Liam walked away from him laughing.

In 'Live Forever' someone threw a coin on-stage. Liam noticed it first. He stared at the coin lying on the stage and then he fixed his stare into the part of the audience it seemed to have come from.

'Do we look like we need money?' he asked with a perfect sneer.

The best moment occurred in Noel's acoustic set when he hit the familiar opening chords to 'Wonderwall'. As he went to sing the opening line, the crowd beat him to it. But they didn't stop there. They sang the whole song back to him. Noel didn't sing a word. He just leant back away from the microphone and played his guitar as over 10,000 people sang his song, absolutely word perfect. Their voices filled the huge arena. It was the first time that it had ever happened. But it wouldn't be the last.

Back in the dressing-room it was as if the gig had never happened. The mood was downbeat, constrained. Somewhere between Ocean Colour Scene's set, which Noel had watched with great enthusiasm from the side of the stage, and his own gig, he had been struck by a vicious stomach upset.

He lay on the sofa now waiting for the pain to subside. He could hardly bare to move. Meg was with him now. She had travelled up early that morning with Emma Greengrass, Oasis's marketing manager, to join him for the weekend and the huge show on Sunday in Edinburgh's Ingliston Hall.

Guigsy, Bonehead and Whitey sat exhausted on chairs and Liam sat scowling but motionless on a sofa. It was disconcerting to see Liam so subdued. Normally, he would be the one pacing the room, waiting for the party to start. Now he sat there, his long legs stretched out, his head tilted back and his eyes staring at the ceiling.

Johnny Hopkins and Emma sat talking softly away to the left-hand corner and Terry the security guard stood by the door. There was a soft knock and Terry let Marcus Russell in.

The Oasis manager looked happy. It had been a great show. Well above average. He looked over at Liam and nodded. The singer tilted his head slightly towards his manager.

'Do not,' the singer warned, 'ask me how I am. Just do not ask.'

'Okay,' Marcus cheerfully said. 'How are you?'

'Shit,' Liam said.

Marcus looked genuinely puzzled. It had been an outstanding show. What was the fucking problem? Noel groaned from the other side of the room. Marcus looked over.

'Noel,' he said with concern, 'can I get you anything? We can send out for something?' It was the hundredth time Noel had been asked that question in ten minutes.

'Nooo-o, all I need is a night off the booze and a good night's sleep,' he said irritably. Then he closed his eyes. Marcus looked back at Liam.

'People say,' Liam cryptically announced, raising a beer can to his lips, 'you've made your bed, now lie in it.'

'You haven't made your bed,' Marcus replied. 'You can do what you like.'

'No, I can't,' Liam retorted. 'My bed is already made.'

'You can make it how you want it,' Marcus pointed out. He reached over and grabbed the chair so he could face his unhappy singer.

'No,' Liam said, shaking his head sadly. 'I have to change the sheets.'

'You did what you had to do tonight,' Marcus said, 'you came on and entertained a lot of people.'

'Look,' Liam snapped back at him, raising himself forward, 'this Oasis shit, I don't fucking care about it. All I know is that when I walk on-stage I'm happy and when I walk off I'm not. So what's the point?'

Marcus shook his head. 'I can't help you there.'

'I know you can't,' Liam wearily answered.

He now looked over at Noel who had turned on to one side of his body and was facing them but with his eyes closed. He looked pale, weak.

'Hey Noel,' Liam shouted, 'Noel, how are you feeling?'

'I feel sick,' Noel replied. There was no energy in his voice.

'I bet you don't feel as bad as me,' Liam said.

The door opened and Kevin the security guy walked in.

'The good news,' he announced, 'is that the after-show party is over there.' He pointed through the crack in the curtains where you could see a bar situated on the other side of the hall. It was quickly filling up with people. 'The bad news is that it's a pay bar.'

Bonehead now looked up. 'A fucking pay bar?'

'Let's have a fucking carry-out,' Liam shouted in a mock cockney accent.

'Stuff your pockets,' Bonehead shouted. 'Bring a crate, two bottles in each pocket.'

'Fuck it, I'm going over there,' Whitey said. 'Anyone else?'

Liam stood up but then quickly sat down again. He was still troubled.

'Nah, fuck it,' he said.

'Come on then Bonehead,' Whitey said, 'let's get a faa-king lager dahn our necks.'

'I'll be over soon,' Bonehead replied, drying his neck with a towel.

Whitey left and Kevin motioned to Terry to accompany him. Liam looked back at Marcus, shaking his head.

'I'm not happy,' he said.

'Why not?' Marcus softly asked.

'Ah, loads of things,' Liam dismissively said.

'Well, if you don't tell me what,' Marcus reasoned, 'I can't help you.'

'Okay,' Liam said, leaning forward. 'Here's one for you. The coach we had in Europe was shit. Why couldn't we have a double like the one we have now, with two floors and everything.'

'Because ferries won't take them to Europe.'

'So why did the road crew have one?'

Marcus was stumped. He couldn't answer that one. The crew coach had been hired in Europe, the band's in the UK.

'Did you complain at the time?' he asked.

'There shouldn't be a complaint to begin with,' Liam pointed out.

'Fair enough,' Marcus conceded. 'I'll give you that one.'

'And tonight,' Liam continued, 'I couldn't get my shirt ironed.' His long arms stretched outwards. 'Now you might think I'm being some big fucking pop star about it . . .'

'What happened?'

'I couldn't get my shirt ironed, a simple thing like that. And I'm sick,' he added for no reason, 'of staying in hotel rooms. All I've fucking got, as the lead singer in this group, is my room with my ma. That's it. I can't stay there. Everybody else has a fucking place to go to. They've got a room where they can go and close a door, chill, play a record, do what the fuck they like. I ain't got that. All I've got is a poxy fucking hotel room.'

'I know what you're saying,' interjected Bonehead, 'but when I was driving the van to gigs, no one spoke like that, did they? It was just get off our tits and fucking have it.'

'But that ain't now, is it?' Liam pointed out. 'It's a lot different now. You can go home and that's it. Sorted. Close the door, chill out. I can't. Everyone knows where I fucking live and it does my fucking head in. Now if you think I'm being a big pop star or acting like a big pop star because I can't get my shirt ironed then say it and I'll leave the group. 'Cos I've got a life and when I've got enough for a house, that's it. You'll never see me again.'

Liam looked straight at Marcus, and Marcus decided to play his bluff.

'Personally, I think you're acting like a pop star,' he coolly said.

'Right.' Liam stood up and reached inside his pockets. 'This is what the big pop star has got on him. This is how much the big pop star is worth.'

Liam pulled out a handful of coins and a crumpled £5 note and threw the money down on the floor. 'That,' he calmly announced, 'is what I'm worth and you won't ever fucking see me again.'

Then he picked up his jacket, kicked a chair over and left the room. As he did so, Marcus shouted after him, 'See you tomorrow.'

'You fucking won't,' came the reply.

Kevin the security guard came over, knelt down and picked up Liam's money.

'I don't know what's got into him,' Marcus said.

'Look,' Bonehead said, 'the man needs his own gaff. He's Liam Gallagher and he needs somewhere. I've got a house, it's my house and it's got an attic and I'm going to give it to him. Here you are mate, here's a key, here's your place. 'Cos he's right. We've all got places where we can get away from the madness. He hasn't. He's permanently on tour.'

'Yeah, you're right,' Marcus agreed.

'I'm going to get him sorted,' Bonehead vowed. 'We'll get in the car and I'll take him round. You want this gaff? Here, have it. He's unhappy and that's not right. He's my mate and he's not acting like the person I know. He's unhappy. We'll sort it out.'

Bonehead drained the last of his lager and then left for the after-show party.

Noel who had been half-asleep throughout the whole incident now motioned to Meg that he wanted to get on the coach. He stood up shakily and he and Meg left, accompanied by Kevin. That left Emma and Johnny in the room.

Emma shook her head. 'I knew it was wrong to give them those Christmas presents,' she said, 'they should have all got the same thing. Noel shouldn't have been singled out.'

Liam meanwhile had walked out of the venue and got on the coach. He went up the stairs and then in a fit of fury he started smashing the back room up, kicking this, punching that. When he had finished, when the demon inside had subsided, he broke open a can of beer, sat down and glared out of the window.

His brother meanwhile lay on a cot bed downstairs, exhausted and sick.

Finally, everyone was on board and the coach began the all-night drive to Edinburgh. As it passed the Windsor Hotel, Tracey was stood at the bar telling some girlfriends about the day Liam

Gallagher had chatted her up.

'He's so tall, and those eyes of his,' she said.

'I like Noel,' said her friend, 'he's cute.'

A boy standing by the bar heard them talking.

'Bollocks,' he sneered. 'Those Gallagher boys have got it fucking lucky.'

The Downside of Smoking Pot

On 22 February 1995, the week that (What's The Story) Morning Glory? *stood at five in the US charts, Noel Gallagher took over Gary Crowley's show on Greater London Radio for one night.*

NOEL: 'Good evening, it's Thursday night, it's ten o'clock, you're listening to Noel Gallagher on 94.9FM. For the next two hours we're going to be talking to somebody who isn't very important and you're going to be listening to someone who *is* very important play his favourite music.'

Noel then plays 'Anarchy In The UK' by The Sex Pistols, 'Helter Skelter' by The Beatles, 'Tramazi Parti' by Black Grape and 'Jimmy James' by The Beastie Boys.

NOEL: '. . . And we're going to be talking to a mate of mine in a bit. His name is Digsy, he's been titled in the press as the Great White No Hoper, he's in the most unimportant band in Britain, he's going to be playing a few tunes later and hopefully we'll get him out of the studio without him pinching everything. That might be quite hard.'

Noel then plays 'Fight The Power' by Public Enemy, 'Get Your Rocks Off' by Primal Scream and 'Alright' by Cast.

NOEL: 'If you were reading the press a few weeks ago, John Powers, who's the singer out of Cast, was apparently visited by an alien who came into his bedroom and started mumbling, "Human, human, human." [*pauses*] That's the downside of smoking pot, kids. Just say no! We're going to move on with a band that is on my record label, which I actually own now; it's Creation Records and a band called Heavy Stereo. And when you listen to those DJs on the radio-stations who seem to know a lot about these bands what you have to remember is that they have these stickers on the back of CDs which say things like

129

[*adopts a DJ style voice*] "'Chinese Burns' is Heavy Stereo's third single and the follow-up to 'Sleep Freak', and 'Smiler', and was recorded along with the rest of their as yet untitled début album at Ray Davies's Konk Studios." Like anyone cares where it was recorded. Anyway, this is "Chinese Burns" by Heavy Stereo.'
Afterwards,
NOEL: 'I've just been told by my mate Arthur who's actually quite famous because he's on the cover of a video which is about football hooliganism, if there's any police officers listening out there, the geezer with the old 1980s England top and with a golfball stuck to the top of his cheek, shouting, "Enger-land, Enger-land, we'll take them on the beaches," well, he's a geezer called Arthur and he's just told me that if you ever want to get your kids to go to school, the best thing to give them is a Chinese Burn. That's not a cocktail, it's when you pull up the sleeves to your elbow, and you grab a wrist with both hands and you twist your hands really hard in an anti-clockwise and clockwise motion – to all you students out there, that's one back and one forward – and apparently they go off to school without a word out of them and they become proper car thieves. That's what I've heard. Anyway, next up we've got Northern Uproar, but if you come from down here it's Northern OOP-Roar.'
  Noel plays 'From A Window' by Northern Uproar.
NOEL: 'Next up we're going to play three tracks, and these are by yer Mod bands, you see, these are your Mod groups.'
  Noel plays 'The Riverboat Song' by Ocean Colour Scene, 'Out Of The Sinking' by Paul Weller and 'The Comfort Of Grace' by Dr. Robert.
NOEL: 'That was yer Mod squad and this is music.'
  Noel plays 'This Is Music' by The Verve.
NOEL: 'And I've got with me – I wouldn't say he's my best mate but he's one of them – Digsy from Smaller. Would you like to tell the listeners out in radio-land about your group and what you haven't been up to?'
DIGSY: 'Okay then, I didn't batter my kids yesterday, I didn't take them to school. But I've written some great songs.'
NOEL: 'Have you? So you've got a new single coming out on Better Records – it's getting better all the time, kids – but when's your album coming out?'
DIGSY: 'I don't know, mate.'
NOEL: 'Don't you think you better find out?'

DIGSY: 'Well, probably end of summer.'

NOEL: 'Now there's a rumour being spread around here – it's not the one about you wearing false breasts – but you were in a group called Cook The Books. Is that right?'

Digsy remains silent.

NOEL: 'All you sad students will probably know who Cook The Books are, and Digsy was actually on *Top Of The Pops* before I was, if you can believe it or not.'

DIGSY: [*now animated*] 'Why are you telling them that for? C'mon. Jesus wept.'

NOEL: [*laughing*] 'I have to. It's going to get exposed in the *News Of The World* sooner or later. So it's better coming from me, isn't it? I tell you now, kids, if you've got any Cook The Books records, keep hold of them. They're going to be worth at least . . . four or five pence in six years time. You're embarrassed now.'

DIGSY: 'I'm not embarrassed. I'm stunned.'

NOEL: 'Now the other rumour is that when they have open-day at his school, he has to borrow the kids next door.'

DIGSY: 'I do, I do. It's not my fault they're ugly.'

NOEL: 'It's not my fault, either.'

DIGSY: 'It better not be.'

NOEL: 'Live radio kids!'

Noel plays 'God I Hate This Town' by Smaller and 'I Wanna Be Your Dog' by The Stooges. Digsy then plays an acoustic version of his song 'He Loves You'.

NOEL: 'I've got in here a young chap, and this is the first time he's been on the radio since the last time he was on the radio, and the last time he was on the radio he was big, and I mean big. Huge! Robbie Williams, how are you?'

ROBBIE: 'I'm a bit tired actually because I spent the weekend with your brother.'

NOEL: 'You weren't going in any toilets, were ya? Because he's apt to go into toilets when the *News Of The World* are kicking about . . . So what have you been up to? Since you got sacked!'

ROBBIE: 'I've been blaming you and your brother 'cos it all happened after Glastonbury.'

NOEL: 'I know it did. But it wasn't our fault.'

ROBBIE: 'It was your fault.'

NOEL: 'No, no, no.'

ROBBIE: 'It was your fault. I went in and said, "Lads, I've had a great time. I met Oasis." And they went, "You're sacked!"'

NOEL: [*serious tone*] 'I'd just like to say to all the Take That fans listening . . . We planned it! We split them up! Seriously now, are you going to put some records out or are you just going to ponce about?'

ROBBIE: 'No, I've done the ligging for eight months now so I've got to come out with a record now. It'll be out in about a month's time. I hope.'

NOEL: 'Now, I keep reading in the papers that I'm actually writing it for you. Is it any good?'

ROBBIE: 'It's top. You've come out with a banging tune.'

NOEL: 'A banging tune? Is it the one with the saucepan lids?'

ROBBIE: 'That's the one.'

NOEL: 'It's a smash then.'

Noel then plays 'Aquarius' by Fifth Dimension, 'Imagine' by John Lennon ('What do you mean it sounds like "Don't Look Back In Anger"? That's out of order. He had us over. I'm telling ya.'), 'Jet' by Wings, 'Come Together' by Desmond Dekker And The Israelites ('except none of them came from Israel'), 'I Wanna Be Adored' by The Stone Roses, and 'Staying Out For The Summer' by Dodgy.

Digsy then plays an acoustic version of his song 'Just As Bad', and Noel continues with 'Eton Rifles' by The Jam, 'Anyway, Anyhow, Anywhere' by The Who, before Paul Weller arrives to play an acoustic version of The Style Council's 'Down In The Seine'.

NOEL: [*clearly bluffing*] 'You don't need me to tell you what that song was. Here's one of the other great British songwriters ever.'

Noel plays 'Waterloo Sunset' by The Kinks.

NOEL: 'I'd like to thank everyone who's been on the show tonight. That's Diddly Digsy Dairy from Smaller, Robbie Williams from the dole office, and Paul Weller from the top of the tree. This is Noel Gallagher saying thanks for listening and if I didn't play your record that's because it's crap! This is "Tomorrow Never Knows" by The Beatles.'

PART TWO

Seven

A cow. A fucking cow. The geezer wants to steal a cow. Can you believe it? Paul McGuigan and Noel Gallagher sit in a Manchester flat above a butcher's shop and exchange amused glances.

Tonight, no one in this room has any money. Not a penny. They have no spliff, no cocaine, no mushrooms, not even enough to buy a stick of glue to rub under their noses. One of the elder boys has already questioned everybody.

'You sure you haven't got any spliff, Guigsy. You're fucking mad for it, you pothead. Come on, you must have some.'

'I haven't, I swear.'

'Don't fucking lie.'

'Look, search me if you want.'

The TV is silently flickering in the corner, the curtains are pulled and there is music playing in the background.

The mood is depressing, claustrophobic and is only broken when this guy, the one with the disturbed eyes, suddenly comes out with this hare-brained scheme to procure some much needed cash.

'Here are, here are, how about this? We go up to the abattoirs, break in and nick a cow. We take it away, kill the fucker and then tomorrow morning take it down to the butchers and sell it. How top is that idea? Plus,' he excitedly adds, 'later on we can sell its skin as leather.' A couple of the guys look up eagerly. 'Yeah, up for that one. Right, who can steal a car?'

Noel wearily raises his hands. Ten minutes later, when it's all gone silent again, Guigsy and Noel make their excuses and leave.

'They're fucking nutcases,' Noel says as they tramp home.

'I know,' agrees Guigsy. Then he reaches into his pocket.

'Here, Noel.'

'What?'

'Got a bit of spliff, here.'

'Top fucking man.'

Paul McGuigan was born in Manchester on 9 May 1971. His father, Gerard McGuigan, was from Belfast, and had arrived in England on the same ferry as the young footballer George Best, who was nervously returning to Manchester United.

A few weeks previously, Best had walked out of United suffering from homesickness. After a brief spell in Belfast, Matt Busby, the United manager who signed him, had persuaded him to return.

Guigsy's father knew the brilliant winger but, as a fully paid-up Manchester City supporter, he wasn't overawed by Best's mercurial talents. But the men were friends. Indeed, some Sunday afternoons when Guigsy was a small child, Best would occasionally visit the McGuigan household where he would try to give Guigsy his United shirt, but Gerard would have none of it. He saw Best's 'kindness' for what it was, a wind-up.

'Best was always trying to get my dad at it,' Guigsy recalls. 'But,' he regretfully adds, 'I could have had his shirt.'

One time, Best gave Gerard a leather football signed by all the Manchester United players. Guigsy was told to take it outside and kick it against a brick wall until the leather became so scuffed, the autographs were illegible. Only then was the ball allowed to stay in the house.

On his arrival in Manchester, Gerard had met a young girl called Teresa.

They married and settled down in the Levenshulme area. Guigsy was their first child; a sister, Mary, following two and a half years later.

When Guigsy was but three and a half years old, Gerard took his son to see Manchester City play. 'There you are, son,' Gerard said, 'that's your team.'

Gerard's ambition for his son was simple. He wanted him to play professional football.

To that end, he would take his naturally right-footed son to the park and tie his right leg in three different places to a young sapling tree. Then he would pass a ball to his son. The point of this exercise was two-fold; to shape Guigsy into a complete footballer by becoming two-footed, and thereby emulate the playing style of Rivelino, the great Brazilian player that Gerard idolised.

When Guigsy started playing in football matches, he played left midfield. And he was good. Very good. He had balance, skill with both feet and instinctively knew how to read the game.

He also excelled at other sports, all of them ball games, such as squash, badminton, tennis and basketball. He represented his primary school, Chapel Street, at badminton and went on to play for Manchester.

At nine years of age he started boxing. Being short and stocky, he found it hard to box taller opponents who could keep him at bay with their longer reach. But the sport taught him how to land effective punches. It was a skill that would prove to be very useful in his later years with Oasis.

His secondary school was Burnage High School. This was an all-boys school, one of the biggest in the Northwest. There were about 1,500 pupils and the school was divided into two sites.

But a family tragedy interrupted Guigsy's schooling. When he was eight years old his father was diagnosed as having cancer of the stomach. The doctor gave him six months to live. Gerard died four years later.

'He had it for a long time,' Guigsy says, 'and in the end you want it to end. He went down to six stone and he was in hospital for a long time. When he came home I didn't really want to see him in that way.'

With the passing of his father, family life changed dramatically. If there was one lesson his parents gave their children it was that in life you can do anything you want to do. All you have to do is put your mind to it because nothing in life is impossible.

Now, following her own advice, Guigsy's mother, Teresa found work as a dinner lady and also enrolled at Fielding Park college. She took a year's refresher course designed to ease people back into studying, and later studied sociology, ending up three years later with a degree. She then found employment with British Telecom.

Mary McGuigan was also academically inclined. She left school with ten O-levels and four A-levels. She went on to university where she gained an English Literature degree.

Guigsy would pass five O-levels. But not before he found

himself suspected of murder. In 1985 a young Asian kid was stabbed to death at his school. As Burnage High was made up of predominantly Asian children, the murder was seen as racially motivated.

While the police investigated, Guigsy and six of his friends were suspended from school. They were made to sit their exams in a special building. The mothers of all the suspected children mounted a campaign, later successful, to have their children reinstated. Six months later a report, the Macmillan report, exonerated Guigsy and his friends of all wrong-doing.

Guigsy had always been a bit of an outsider at school. Through excelling at sports, he had come into contact with a lot of older boys and preferred their company. This trend carried on in his teenage years. One year, he bought a scooter, a white Vespa 50 but with a 125cc engine.

On a ride back home, it broke down. Guigsy was fixing it by the side of the road when a member of the Manchester Aces, a local scooter club, pulled up to assist him.

It was through this connection that Guigsy was exposed to Northern Soul music, Motown and Stax. The rawness of much of this music directly appealed to him.

At school most of his friends were into The Smiths or Bronski Beat. Their clothes were correspondingly quite drab. In contrast, the neatly attired Guigsy would drive into school on his scooter and enthuse about Marvin Gaye or early Who albums. Through his parents, he was also conversant with The Beatles and a lot of 1960s pop music.

They regularly received, through a mail-order scheme, a series of LPs that featured 1960s chart hits. Each year would be represented on either side of the record. There was also a copy of The Beatles' compilation *Love Songs* in the house, which Guigsy's mum played every Sunday morning while doing the housework.

But, as with Noel, music wasn't an overriding obsession at this point in his life; football took precedence.

Guigsy followed City religiously. He attended all their matches, home and away and at night, he dreamt of fulfilling his dad's ambitions.

That Guigsy was an exceptional player isn't in doubt. As a teenager, he had trials at Oldham, Stockport and Crewe. Oldham never rang back, Stockport told him that as a player he was 'too tricky', and Crewe were impressed with the three goals he scored in three games under their watchful eye.

But it wasn't to be. Playing for his local team in a cup quarter-final game, Guigsy jumped to head a ball and when he landed his legs gave way.

'When I came down, I couldn't stand,' he remembers, 'the pain was outrageous. The doctor told me that my knee was badly sprained. I didn't play in the semi-final but I played in the final.'

During that game, Guigsy's team went 1–0 down. Then they won a corner. The ball found its way to Guigsy standing on the corner of the penalty box. He coolly volleyed it back into the goal. Later on, one of his team-mates scored the winner.

The next day Guigsy couldn't walk. Following several visits to the doctor, Guigsy was diagnosed as having a torn knee ligament, and he didn't kick a ball again for the next two and a half years. Instead, he got further into music and resumed smoking marijuana.

He had taken his first spliff at age thirteen and kept smoking until he was seventeen. He could often be found over at Erwood Park with about fifty of the other lads from Levenshulme and Burnage. It was there that they would put their fifty pences in and try to make up enough to buy an eighth of hash.

Erwood Park is where he first met Noel, although there was no formal introduction as such. As Guigsy explains, Noel was just a face you saw in the park. After a while, it was just natural that they started talking.

He remembers Noel then as a chilled-out guy who smoked a lot of weed. In fact, it was Noel who first put Guigsy on to the more rockier and experimental side of The Beatles. Through the *Love Songs* album Guigsy intimately knew songs such as 'Norwegian Wood' and 'Yesterday'. But he was unaware of tracks such as 'I Am The Walrus', or 'Helter Skelter'. Noel pointed him in that direction.

There were other musical favourites as well: Jimi Hendrix, Bob Marley, The Faces, The Kinks, as well as blues acts such as Brownie McGee and B.B. King who Guigsy had discovered through his scooter club connections. This was a tenuous link at best. Guigsy only went on one scooter run. Strangely, he travelled in a van.

'I didn't get it until we were halfway there, then I realised what the van was for. Store any stolen scooters that might come our way.'

There was also another guy that Guigsy would see around. His nickname was Bonehead. He supported Manchester United but Guigsy soon realised that he was not as fanatical about his team or the game as people like him and Noel.

One night, at the Severe wine bar, where everyone went after the pubs shut, Bonehead and Guigsy got talking. They discovered a shared passion for music, Bonehead revealing he could play guitar.

'Couldn't do that, me,' Guigsy said.

'Yeah, you could,' Bonehead breezily replied, putting down his pint glass. 'It's a piece of piss. I'll come round and show you one night.'

And that's precisely what he did.

His story has been framed and hung in the main school corridor. It makes him so proud. Fifteen pages of his imaginative writing that tells of an old barge on a canal and a little boy who discovers a ghost living on it. Every day, he walks past and slyly glances up at it with a real sense of achievement.

'Oi! Bonehead!'

'What?'

'Is that your stupid fucking story on the wall?'

'Yeah. What about it?'

'You fucking teacher's pet!'

Paul Arthurs is eight years old. Even then, he's known as Bonehead. All his mates have quite longish hair but Bonehead has his cropped every week. It didn't take long for his schoolmates at St. Roberts in Longsite, Manchester, to bestow him with the name that he carries to this day.

He was born on 23 June 1965. His parents were Irish, his mother Delia being raised just ten miles away from Peggy Gallagher. Yet the two women never met. It was only when Bonehead met Noel and Liam that they discovered the close proximity of their families.

And, like Noel and Liam, Bonehead too spent his summers as a child in Ireland. Three weeks in the South with his mother's side of the family, three weeks in the North with his father's.

His parents had met and married in Manchester, both having

left Ireland in their teens. They would raise another four children (Martin, Maria, Celine and Frances), Bonehead's father Ben supporting the family through his work in the demolition business. They were also staunch Catholics.

'Church every Sunday,' Bonehead recalls. 'Didn't miss it. I was an altar boy as well. You got a choice. It's either the Boy Scouts or be an altar boy. So I was like, fuck wearing a dress, gotta join the Boy Scouts. But then this woman was gassing to my mum one day and she was saying, "Don't let him join the Boy Scouts, my son was in them and he got beaten up every day."

'It was like, right, altar boy for you. I must have done it for about three years, met the Bishop and all that shit. But then I got kicked out for laughing and drinking the wine. They have a good rider [the part of the contract that obliges promoters to supply drinks for bands] them priests. More than we get in Oasis.'

His parents were also musically minded and at an early age they paid for their son to take accordion lessons. Bonehead took to the instrument and his playing quickly progressed. He even joined an Irish group that played traditional music.

From there, he went on to piano lessons and then, in his teens, he picked up a guitar.

Academically, Bonehead also displayed early promise. He passed his eleven-plus, winning a place at St. Peter's Grammar school in Prestwich, North Manchester. It was a prestigious establishment but Bonehead grew to hate the place. Not only was it a lengthy bus ride from his home, but it was also, to quote the man himself, 'full of spotty middle-class bastards'. As his dislike of school grew so his studies slipped.

By the time he was thirteen, he and his friends would often stay on the bus and, using their free passes, travel on to Bolton or Liverpool to spend the hours wandering around town. Other days, he sat bored rigid in class, looking out of the window.

No doubt on such occasions his mind turned to music. Bonehead had an abiding interest in his elder brother Martin's extensive record collection. Along with all the classics that Martin possessed – The Beatles, The Kinks, The Who – Bonehead also listened to contemporary bands such as The Smiths.

He developed a real taste for quality music and it was with like-minded pupils that he hung out at school. They were dressed in the Casual style; Perry Boys they were called in

Manchester, with their designer label tops and wedge haircuts.

When Bonehead left school at sixteen, he did so with just one O-level to his name. That was in English. The rest of the subjects he took were marked 'U', denoting unclassifiable.

When his mum saw the results she asked, 'Paul, what are all these Us?' And her son replied, 'Unbeatable, Mum. It stands for unbeatable.'

'Ah, you're a clever lad,' she replied. 'I always said it.'

Not long after, Bonehead signed on to a Youth Training Scheme and was placed on a building construction course which, much to his surprise, he found himself really enjoying. He had finally found something worth working for. He stayed at the college for two enjoyable years, and this time he passed all his exams.

His first job was as a plasterer for a building firm in Stockport. He enjoyed the work, but the boss was a mean man and the rigid times he had to keep, clock on at eight, lunch at one, finish at six, didn't appeal to Bonehead's temperament.

To divert himself, he and his brother Martin formed a band with two other friends. They called themselves Pleasure In Pain. Bonehead played the synthesizer.

'We were sad as fuck,' he says now. The band stayed together for about a year. Their first gig was the Trap pub in Glossop ('I was proper shitting it,' he recalls), and they also appeared at an all-day festival in Manchester which featured only Manchester bands.

'There were about forty groups playing,' Bonehead recalls, 'so we all got about ten minutes each. It was mad.'

Pleasure In Pain faded away, although Bonehead now possessed an amp, an electric guitar, a bass and a drum machine.

One day at work his friend Jeff, who worked as a joiner, came to him with an idea. Fuck this job, he said, let's save up all our money for the next six months and then piss off to Europe.

'I was nineteen, I'd seen fuck all and I told him that's a splendid idea.'

They bought themselves mountain bikes, practised on them daily and stored away their cash. During these six months Bonehead also briefly met Guigsy who lived in the same area.

On a day he recalls with great delight, Bonehead walked into work and told his boss he was jacking it all in.

'You can't do that,' the boss snorted.

'Why not?'

'Well what are you going to do?' he asked.

'Travel round Europe,' Bonehead replied.

'Travel round fucking Europe?'

'That's right. Well done.'

'But what happens when you get back? What are you going to do for work?'

'Give a shit, dickhead,' Bonehead replied.

The day of his departure was bright and sunny. Bonehead picked up his bags, said farewell to his parents and set off for Europe. Just as he was approaching the railway bridge in Albert Road, Levenshulme, he saw a young guy, wearing shades and sporting a Mick Jagger haircut. Bonehead recognised him from round his way so he pulled up.

'You all right, mate? What you up to?'

'I'm just on me way home,' Noel Gallagher replied. 'The Inspirals played last night and I got right off me box. What you up to with all them bags?'

'Going to Europe. Going to travel round until me money runs out.'

'Europe? You're going to cycle round Europe? You're fucking mad.'

'I know. Top, isn't it? See ya when I get back.'

Bonehead and Jeff caught the ferry to Ostend and, over the next six months visited Vienna, Venice, Rimini and Paris, before coming home. Then it was back to the real world.

Not long after signing on, Bonehead's brother-in-law visited and mentioned that he was getting rid of a van of his, an old Mazda 1800 pick-up. It was a bit rundown, but Bonehead could have it if he liked; it would at least allow him to start up his own plastering business.

Bonehead went to look at the vehicle. To say it was rundown was to compliment it. You could only enter the vehicle if you knew the special way of using the handle. It was also necessary to start the engine with a screwdriver. Apart from that, it was fine.

Bonehead took ownership of the van and turned self-employed. He was now hanging out a lot with Guigsy, and the following Wednesday night he told him about his new job. This was the night they always met up on to go to the pub, drink themselves stupid, throw up in someone's garden and then stagger home.

Guigsy decorated Bonehead's van in garish psychedelic patterns and, along with other friends such as Tony French and Chris Hutton, they all piled into it in the summer of 1990, and took off to see The Stone Roses play in Spike Island.

The following week a picture of the van was printed in a local Manchester paper as part of their special on the event. The photographer was Michael Spencer Jones.

By now, Bonehead had started teaching Guigsy the bass, and the boys eventually formed a band called Rain, with Chris Hutton on vocals and, later on, Tony McCarroll on drums.

For Rain's first gig they put all their instruments through Bonehead's amp and used a drum machine to back them.

Not long after that they sacked Hutton, and then Liam Gallagher swaggered into their lives. He visited them at the house Bonehead now shared with his girlfriend and future wife, Kate.

Bonehead had met Kate at the Severe wine bar in Fallowfield. 'It was this mad cellar,' he remembers, 'with a top jukebox, and it was full of students and a few madheads.'

The night he and Kate met, Bonehead went back to her flat and they have been together ever since. They started living together at Kate's place and later on, having sold that flat, they took a place in West Didsbury which Bonehead then spent a year renovating. It was here that Oasis would be photographed for their début album cover. By Michael Spencer Jones.

In the first Oasis line-up, Liam would write the words and Bonehead the music. They first rehearsed at a hotel that had not yet opened for business. It was called The Raffles. Guigsy had got friendly one night with a girl who worked at the hotel and she had invited him back. With loads of space at their disposal, not to mention the hotel's amenities, the band rehearsed here until the hotel opened.

Paul Gallagher then found them rehearsal space at the Plymouth Grove Club but barely two weeks later they were ejected because of their constant spliff smoking. They then moved to the Greenhouse in Stockport which for twenty-five pounds a day allowed them access to a backline.

They came up with four songs: 'Reminisce', 'Life In Vain',

'Take Me', and 'She Always Came Up Smiling', which Bonehead automatically assumed was about the act of fellatio.

The band used Bonehead's van to transport their equipment. After Liam changed the band's name to Oasis and Noel subsequently joined, they started rehearsing at a studio called the Red House before moving to the Boardwalk.

Bonehead's van was a valuable possession for the band. It meant they could transport equipment and use it for their own personal gain.

Many was the time when rehearsing was finished for the night that Guigsy would ask for a lift down to Moss Side, to score some weed. Bonehead hated going down to Moss Side. So did the others. It was Manchester's notorious drug-dealing area and anything could happen.

On Bonfire night, for example, a lot of old scores are settled by the gun. The noise of fireworks exploding in the sky provided the perfect cover.

'Ah fuck off, Guigs,' Bonehead would say when the bassist said he had to score some weed. But he would always take him. These two provided the perfect counterbalance to Noel and Liam's increasingly tempestuous relationship.

Within the band, Bonehead was looked upon as a madhead, a man they would all nominate 'as the funniest man in Manchester'. Whether it was smashing up hotel rooms or diving into pools naked and drunk beyond belief, Bonehead was the band's humour.

As the band progressed, so their commitment deepened. To miss rehearsals was a major issue. One Saturday, a good friend of Bonehead's invited him and Kate to his wedding. Bonehead couldn't go. The wedding took place on a rehearsal day, he explained. His friends couldn't believe it, but Bonehead held firm. The band first, other things second.

'The way it worked at rehearsals,' Bonehead states, 'was that Noel would always come in with something new and then we would jam on it. But you didn't miss rehearsals for anything.'

On the day before Bonehead and Kate moved to their home in West Didsbury, the rhythm guitarist called up the Gallagher household and told Liam, 'I can't make rehearsals. Got to move house tomorrow and I've got to pack everything up.'

Liam just slammed the phone down.

Bonehead put the phone down and was just about to redial the number when the phone rang. This time Noel was on the line.

'Right you dickhead,' he ordered, 'get your amps and guitar and get your arse down to the Boardwalk, or you're out.'

Then for the second time in two minutes, a Gallagher slammed the phone down on him. Bonehead was amazed.

'I thought, I'm not having this, got to sort this one right out.'

Bonehead jumped into his van and drove to the Boardwalk. He pulled up just as Noel was arriving.

Within two minutes of trying to explain to Noel why he couldn't rehearse, the two of them were shouting, arguing and threatening each other with severe violence. Then Liam and Guigsy arrived.

'Look,' Bonehead shouted at Liam, 'I've got to move house. I can't do anything about it. I'll be here tomorrow.'

'See you tomorrow night then,' Liam casually remarked, and the three of them then disappeared into the Boardwalk, leaving a speechless Bonehead out on the street. It's the only major ruck he has ever had with Noel.

'You have to understand that we totally believed in the band,' he states, 'and the only way it was going to work was by grafting at it. You weren't going to rehearse two hours a week every Sunday afternoon and do something. In a band you either do it full-on or you treat it as a hobby. We decided to do it full-on.'

Eight

She came in through the bathroom window. Or at least that's what she and her friend look like doing as they wait outside Patsy Kensit's London home.

They have sat there now for hours on the wall opposite the actress's house and have not moved an inch. They simply stare.

It's Sunday 14 July 1996, and the object of their obsession, Liam Gallagher, sits in the kitchen staring back at them.

'They're off their tits,' he mutters to himself. Never in a million years would he have indulged in such behaviour, not even for his all-time hero, the man he sincerely believes lives inside him, John Lennon.

Since moving in with Patsy, Liam has got used to people waiting outside the house. The majority of them are photographers who know that one good picture of Liam and Patsy is front-page news. Oasis sells papers, so they go to every extreme. The other day Liam came out of the house to find a photographer hiding under a car.

'You daft cunt, what the fuck are you doing?' Liam said to him, shaking his head in benevolent disbelief. It was almost as if a champion boxer was taking some kind of pity on his beaten opponent.

Liam, much to his chagrin, can do nothing about it. He can't sue the photographers for taking pictures, nor can he stop the reporters writing their stories. So he plays up to them.

'They think I'm this,' he says, 'so that's what I give them. They don't understand it, so fuck them.'

For the media, it's a classic story; the beautiful well-heeled actress taming the man they have imaginatively dubbed 'the wild man of rock'. In reality, what bugs him the most is that everyone forgets that he is first and foremost a singer, one of the best in the land. He is also totally dedicated to his band and his craft.

'When it comes to Oasis, Liam is a musical purist,' Marcus Russell, band manager, says of him. Creation boss Alan McGee's comment is just as succinct, 'Liam Gallagher is one of the great soul singers of our time.'

Tonight, Liam is dressed in sandals, light green trousers and a pale striped T-shirt. On the shelf behind him is a picture of him that Patsy took on their recent holiday in Antigua. It shows Liam gazing out to sea. On the kitchen table to his right is an estate agent's catalogue describing in pictures and words the house he plans to buy. It is totally isolated, a huge building set amidst beautiful English countryside.

For many people, it is hard to imagine the man living in such sedate palatial surroundings. They are used to seeing him in clubs, dishevelled, eyes rolling. They know him for throwing punches or outrageous comments at the media. But over the last three months, Liam passionately insists, he has undergone huge personal changes. The reason he says is his relationship with Patsy.

'I'm growing older,' he states firmly, 'I'm surrounded by kids, a beautiful woman that I love, I'm getting money and I want to do my stuff. See, I've changed so much since we've been off.

'I'm not a monkey any more. I'm not into being in a scene where I don't respect anyone. I want to sharpen myself up. I don't want a heart attack. I don't want to get off my tits all the time.

'I want to get a nice gaff and come home to a beautiful woman, and that is Patsy. I want to be with her forever. She's got a kid [James, from her marriage to the Simple Minds vocalist Jim Kerr] and I love the kid and I love her. That's it.'

For many people who have known Liam down the years, those words are unrecognisable, because, frankly, from a very early age, Liam Gallagher has been kicking up an almighty fuss.

He was born on 21 September 1972 in St. Mary's hospital, Manchester. Surprisingly, his father Thomas doted on him. Unlike Noel or Paul, Liam can only remember his dad hitting him once.

'He liked me,' Liam states, 'because I was the youngest. But I didn't like him. He shouldn't have got married and had kids if he wasn't ready for it.'

Their father's obvious preference for Liam hurt Noel, and is a major reason as to why their relationship is one of the most complex ever to have been placed under the white heat of public scrutiny.

Noel, and Paul to a lesser extent, took the bruises, the punches, the cuts. Liam was left physically unscathed, but emotionally scarred.

Growing up, Liam was also, by Peggy's own admission, 'spoilt'. Therefore, his natural human confidence and spirit was never dented as badly as his brothers'.

At the age of six, and he looked so innocent then, he was hugely disruptive in his primary school, St. Roberts. His teacher one day confessed to Peggy that her youngest son's daily antics drove her to a nightly intake of Valium. That was Liam at six.

In secondary school, it was no better. He started fights, ran with bad boys, took drugs and alcohol, caused chaos in class and bunked off as much as he could.

It placed Peggy, as one of the school's dinner ladies, in an impossible situation. After every incident, a teacher would come to remonstrate with her: please control your son. But for Liam, attack is the best form of defence.

'He was a swine at school,' Peggy recalls with a smile, 'and he shamed me, oh, he shamed me. I'd say to him, "You bloody shame me," and he'd say, "You're too nice to those teachers, stop sucking up to them." I'd say to him, "That Mr. Foley [Headmaster], he's a nice man." But Liam wouldn't have it. "You don't know him, Mum," he'd say.

'I think in the end they felt more sorry for me than anything else.'

Liam had undoubtedly inherited large doses of that wild-hearted spirit which sustains and propels all Irish rebels. He simply didn't give a fuck. Ironically, later on in life, the more exposed that attitude became to the public, the more successful he became.

'I was a cunt,' he says of his primary school days. 'I was a cunt,' he says of his secondary school. No subject interested him. He hated reading, hated studying. It all seemed so fake to him. What does it really matter if you can't spell mar-ike-uana? You smoke marijuana, you don't fucking write about it.

Plus, Liam was no fool. He instinctively knew that for him

there would be no interesting job to wake up for, no nice house to come home to. He would join the rest of Manchester on the dole queue and on the make. So that's what he prepared himself for, not some old nerd's idea about how best to live your life, but how best to live on your wits.

Liam quickly learnt the art of fronting it. That is, you never betray your inner feelings in front of anyone. Someone offers you a fight and they're ten stone heavier than you? Show no nerves. Accept the challenge. Because, believe, nine times out of ten the dickhead will back off.

Liam also absolutely refused to bow down to anyone. No one. Teachers, policemen, whoever, he didn't care. And that included his brother Noel.

Yet, as both brothers confirm, their relationship wasn't that frictional until Noel joined Oasis. That's when the locking of heads, like antelopes in a fury, started. Previous to that they shared a bedroom together and, to be honest, didn't really see that much of each other.

There is a five-year age gap between them, which for children is simply too enormous to breach. By the time Liam started secondary school, St. Marks, Noel was embroiled in glue sniffing and burglary.

The only things that really interested Liam at this point were music, clothes, girls, sport and singing. It was a teacher who took him first to Maine Road to see City play. He became a City fan, though never as committed as his brother or Guigsy.

As a young boy he sang in the school choir and he often pestered his mother to buy him instruments. So she did. Peggy bought him a violin. But Liam's temperament wasn't suited to self discipline. After a day of trying, he discarded it. Then it was a guitar. Again, the same result. He was always restless, always looking for some action.

Singing was a different matter. There were no books to learn from, no lessons to carefully absorb. You just opened your mouth and that was it.

'I often sang around the house,' Liam says. Yet his first musical passion was hip-hop. He regularly played, much to Noel's annoyance, Mantronix records such as 'Bass Line', and he later learnt how to breakdance and body-pop.

He bought many of Streetsounds Electro records, compilations of beat-box music, and he also fell in with a girl graffiti writer called Gina. The pair of them would go round town, spraying various walls. Liam's tag-name, the signature you leave on your murals, was Galli.

He also knew how attractive he was to girls. It's hard to believe but he had once gone through a period of carrying a lot of puppy fat. But the weight came off and Liam shot up in height. With his magnetic brooding eyes, tall body and seeming lack of inhibition, he had no problem in persuading girls to do his bidding.

Indeed, in the flush of Oasis's initial success, Liam was easily the most sexually active of the band. Much to his early delight, his rock-star fantasies all came true. The girls would come to his room and there they would disrobe and he would eagerly take his pleasure.

But once he was physically spent, he instantly felt nothing but emptiness inside. So he would send them away, despite all the promises he had previously made to them about holidays, even marriage on a few occasions. He felt they were shagging Liam Gallagher, the pop star. They would never have gone to bed with him so easily if he hadn't been famous. They weren't there for William John Paul Gallagher.

But his mum always was, and that's why she was the only person he could reveal his dreams to.

'I remember Liam getting into music when he left school,' she recalls, 'and he sat out there in the kitchen and he said, "I know I'm not much of a singer but I'm as good as anything out there and that's what I'm going to do."'

Liam had a point: Manchester has a history of throwing up 'individual' vocalists. Morrissey, Mark E. Smith of The Fall and Shaun Ryder are three prime examples.

'I said, "If that's what you want to do, Liam, and you're happy doing it, then you do it." Then he'd be upstairs, shouting and bawling and he'd have the music on full-blast. I used to go up there and say, "Turn that bloody music down, Liam." He'd be singing at the top of his voice.'

Liam was expelled from St. Marks at the age of fifteen. His big problem was that of being born in September. Under the law, he would have to attend school for a few more months. Meanwhile, all his mates, people such as Syd, Daryl and Stef, were now out in the big world. So he refused to attend classes.

Peggy was worried sick. She knew that sooner or later the education board would come round and demand he join a school, any school. If he didn't, a court appearance would be the next step.

'I kept saying to Liam, you have to go to school because they will take me to court and I haven't got the money to pay them. Eventually, I went back to the headmaster and I begged him to take Liam back. He said, "Well only because I know you, Mrs. Gallagher, but if he puts one foot out of step until he's allowed to leave, he's off the premises."'

Liam saw the distress he was causing Peggy and that he simply couldn't handle. Suddenly, he changed, calmed down. He became, by his standards, a model pupil. No trouble, no cheekiness, no fighting. In fact, just before he left, the school even went so far as to find him his first job. He was employed making fences.

He started at eight in the morning and finished at four in the afternoon. He travelled to work by bike and was paid £60 a week.

'Everything was going nice,' Peggy recalls, 'until they told him to clean the toilets. See, everybody had to take their turn cleaning the toilets but Liam said, "I don't care what they do, I'm not cleaning no toilet for anybody." So he got on his bike, came home and that was that job done.'

His next job was as a sign-writer, but the company he joined hit bad times and were forced to lay off staff. The unwritten law in such cases is that the last person employed is the first person asked to leave. Liam was made redundant.

He then worked as a car valet before taking over Noel's old job at Kennedy's, an Irish building firm who did a lot of work for British Gas.

'He was in the office answering phones,' Peggy says, 'taking orders for different things. I think Liam and Paul worked there at the same time, but Paul was in a different gang. And then they finished with Paul because the building was finished, and Liam decided that no way was he going to go and dig holes for anyone.'

So Liam quit and then signed on. As Les, Noel's driver, once pointed out, it is the Department of Social Security that is the real Arts Council in Great Britain. They are the ones who support musicians financially.

To supplement his meagre benefit money, Liam and his friends would steal mountain bikes and sell them off. But he never involved himself in bona fide criminal activity. He had the temperament but the thought of distressing Peggy stopped him.

Another facet to Liam's character was that many of his friends tended to be a couple of years older than him. One example is Guigsy, who Liam met when he was about thirteen through playing football over at the Bluebell pub.

They saw each other regularly for about a year and then, as all teenagers do, they drifted apart. Later on, when Liam was about sixteen, they met up again. Guigsy was now hanging with this guy people called Bonehead. He sported a pencil-thin moustache and was a real character. He too didn't seem to give a fuck about anything and his individual sense of humour soon won Liam over.

Bonehead had been in the band Pleasure In Pain, playing keyboards. Now he, Guigsy and a singer named Hutton and a drummer called Tony McCarroll had formed a group, named Rain.

They invited Liam down to see them play at a pub called Times Square. Unknown to them, Liam was now desperate to join a band.

His desire had been ignited on the night of Noel's twenty-first birthday when both brothers, separately, had gone to see James, supported by The Stone Roses at the International Two, play an anti-clause-28 benefit gig.

This was the latest bit of vicious Tory law which directly attacked the gay community through censorship. The Gallaghers were arsed about the cause. Live and let live was their motto. But The Roses were playing and that was enough for both of them.

The Stone Roses had been around Manchester for years. They tended to play obscure little gigs but their melodic sound, combined with Ian Brown's semi-druggy vocals had won them a sizeable local following. At the time of this gig the band were just months from breaking big time.

While Noel stayed upstairs, speeding off his head, jabbering to Graham Lambert of The Inspiral Carpets, Liam was downstairs and in a trance. For one of the very few times in his life, Liam was speechless. Ian Brown of The Stone Roses was on-stage and he was, to quote Liam, 'doing my head in'.

Brown's performance that night taught Liam two things. You

didn't have to be a conventional singer to succeed and you didn't have to make a prat of yourself by trying to work at pleasing the audience. Just be yourself. Look at Ian Brown. He would amble on-stage, sing his words and then just aimlessly patrol the stage, or, if he felt like it, sit down and stare at the audience. It was this performance, allied with The Stone Roses's individual and melodic sound, which decided two things for Liam. First, he started exploring more guitar-based music, but, of far more importance, he now knew his future: he was going to sing and become famous. All his energies would go to achieving that goal. That was that. Liam came home and told Peggy of his ambitions. Then he did absolutely nothing about it. Actually, that's not quite correct.

He asked Noel three times to form a duo with him. The Gallagher Brothers. Liam knew enough to see that his brother was now deadly serious about music. Up in their bedroom, there were scraps of paper everywhere with Noel's doodlings on them.

But each time, Noel refused Liam. So Liam sat at home dreaming. Peggy recalls, 'He'd sit there in the kitchen for days saying, "I'm going to be famous, Mum." I'd say, "Are you, Liam? I hope you will be because I'm sick and tired of listening to you."

'"Oh yeah," he'd say, "but you just wait and see, I'm going to be famous and you're going to be the proudest mum in the world." I'd say, "Would you ever get off your bloody arse, Liam, and get out and get yourself a proper job, 'cos I can't keep you."

'My friend used to be out there in the kitchen and she'd say, "Well, really, he is determined and you've got to be positive."

'I'd say, "He's talking a load of old shite." She's always said since, "Do you remember when you used to say that?"'

When Liam went to see Rain, he had two major thoughts. The first one concerned their musical prowess: 'They were shite,' he sneers. The second was that he would have loved to have been up there himself.

'The singer was a dick and I knew they were shite,' he recalls, 'but I just thought it was top that they were in a band as I wanted to be in one myself.'

Unknown to Liam, the day after this gig, Guigsy had gone to see Bonehead at the house the guitarist was working on as a plasterer. Guigsy demanded that Hutton be thrown out.

'We were supposed to be doing "Wild Thing" by The Troggs,'

Guigsy explains, 'and the fucking dick who was the singer started making up his own words, singing "Wild Thing, you smoke a draw". I mean the geezer didn't even smoke,' Guigsy points out with real affront in his voice.

'So I told Bonehead, I never wanted to see this guy again. He said he was thinking the same thing. So after we got rid of him, we didn't do anything for a while.'

It was during this period of inactivity that Liam and a mutual friend called Baz popped round to the house Bonehead shared with Kate.

As they spoke, Bonehead played a tape of some of the songs they had written. Liam sat in a chair and started singing along. As he did so it quickly became apparent that he had something.

'Kate was in the bath,' Bonehead says. 'I went in and said, "Did you hear Liam singing?" She said, "Like a nightingale."'

Liam didn't just have the voice. He had the personality as well, an urgent need to be the centre of attention. Everywhere he went, he would take over. He made sure he was noticed. His qualifications to become a rock 'n' roll singer were impeachable.

The first major contribution Liam Gallagher made to the band was to change the name. The boys had named the band Rain after The Beatles' song (a Lennon composition) which had appeared as the B-side to 'Paperback Writer'.

Liam had a better idea. Studying the huge Inspiral Carpets poster that Noel had hung in their bedroom, Liam noted the tour dates that were run under the band's picture. The group were scheduled to play the Swindon Oasis Leisure Centre. For some reason, the name kicked a spark off in his head.

'Here are,' he told them, 'Oasis, it's a better name than fucking Rain.'

And he was right.

It was May of 1991, summer was approaching and Liam was constantly short of money. As soon as he'd get his benefit cheque, he would go straight to his dope dealer, order more gear and part pay off what he already owned. That was most of the money gone. What little was left would go to his mum.

Liam signed on every two weeks. Every now and then, he would be called in for an interview and asked what kind of job he intended taking.

Before, when they enquired, he never had an answer for them. This time he did.

'A singer,' he told them, 'I'm going to be a singer.'

'Mr. Gallagher,' the interviewer would say, 'I'm talking about a proper job.'

'That is a proper job,' Liam replied. 'In fact, it's a right proper job. See, I'm in a band now.'

. The interviewer's eyes widened, like a shark smelling blood. 'So are you being paid for any performances?'

'Well,' Liam had to admit, 'we haven't done any yet. But we will.'

'Okay then, but until you do I think you should seriously apply for what we call a proper job. I have to tell you, failure to do so will mean your benefit is cut off. Do you understand, Mr. Gallagher?'

Do I understand? Do I fucking understand. Who is this cheeky bastard? Liam felt his temper rising. He badly wanted to smack this guy right in the mouth. But he held himself in check. Instead, he coldly asked, 'What job you got in mind?'

'Well, there's a vacancy at a factory in Stockport. It's good work, good wages. I think you should go for it.'

That was it. He'd tried to be civil to this wanker but it hadn't worked. It never did with their kind. They understood absolutely nish. Where did these people come from?

Liam leant over the man's desk and said, 'Here are, I've got a better idea. You think that job is good, yeah?'

'Yes, I do, Mr. Gallagher.'

'Okay, then why don't you go and do it? Uh? I'll tell you what, you give me your job and if you think this other job is so great, you go and do that and I'll do yours. How about that?'

Then Liam Gallagher got up and walked out.

Liam spent most evenings with Bonehead, Guigsy and Tony McCarroll. He wasn't enamoured with McCarroll, but he was the best musician out of the lot of them and drummers were always the hardest to find.

Oasis rehearsed for four months and in that time they wrote four songs. Liam, after hours and hours of painful struggle, would come up with the words and Bonehead put music to them.

The other three members of the band were all working, Bonehead as a self-employed plasterer and Guigsy for British Telecom. It was through these jobs that Oasis managed to buy equipment, usually from a local music shop called Johnny Roadhouse.

Eventually the band got a booking, a gig at the Boardwalk in Manchester. It was scheduled for 18 August 1991, and they were due to support another local band called Sweet Jesus.

Noel found out about the gig through his mum. When he was away with the Inspirals he always called home on a regular basis. Peggy told him that Liam was due to appear on stage soon.

Noel checked his diary. He would be home from America by then. He would go and see them. If nothing else, it should be a right laugh.

Nine

It is getting near dawn when Noel Gallagher reaches over and picks up a battered acoustic guitar in Creation head Alan McGee's living-room. He strums a few chords to ensure it's in tune.

'Here are, Alan,' he says. 'Tell us what you think of this song.'

His left hand forms a C-major chord and his right hand starts strumming the strings. After a few bars of this, Noel starts singing.

'I'm older than I wish to be/ This town holds no place for me/ All my life/ I've been trying to find a way back home . . .'

The song finished, Noel rests his arms on the guitar's body and says, 'It's called "Rockin' Chair". What do you think?'

Alan McGee tries to focus on Noel's expectant face but it's useless. Everything in front of him has been transformed into a blur, as if his eyelashes are slowly wiping his eyes. McGee is drunk, pilled-up and wired. Actually, that's wrong. He has shovelled so much up his nose and down his neck he isn't sure what the fuck to call his high.

'Noel,' he finally replies, in a slurred Scottish brogue, 'I can hardly see you, let alone hear you.' Then he slumps back on to the sofa.

There have been many nights like this for McGee over the last seven years. They usually begin in a bar or at a gig with sizeable amounts of alcohol and cocaine being consumed, and, if there are any around, Ecstasy pills.

The bar or club finally closed, McGee likes to invite people back to his flat in the Docklands area of London. There, he will get out his records and try to convince people such as Noel of the greatness of the groups he adores.

'You got to hear this song, Noel,' he'll passionately say. 'After this, you cannae tell me you dinnae like Big Star.'

Noel will smile to himself, as if to say, come on, I'm listening and then McGee will put on '13' or 'Jesus Christ' or 'September Gurls'. After about a minute, McGee will exclaim, 'How great's this record? Listen to that drum sound, fucking amazing.'

Suddenly, another tune will spring to mind and he'll pull out another record and put it on before the first record is even half finished. 'Noel, just listen to this man's guitar.'

Noel could never make up his mind about McGee's taste in music. He never heard enough of it to form an opinion.

And McGee loved music. It was something that never let him down, there was always another new album to buy, another group to discover. For McGee, as it was for Oasis and so many people around them, music was a bottomless ocean that you could spend a lifetime exploring. This McGee intended to do.

He had been smitten at an early age. Noel had asked him once, 'What was the first record you bought?' and McGee replied, '"Get It On" by T. Rex.'

He had bought it in Glasgow when he was eleven years old and it had transformed him. Glasgow was McGee's home town. He had been born there in 1960. He attended primary school and then went on to King's Park secondary.

McGee didn't have too much of a bad time at school. He was an average student, not very good at sports, yet he was popular. He had plenty of friends and an abiding passion for music. He would often be seen around school with albums under his arms. One boy who noted him was a skinny kid in the year below. His name was Bobby Gillespie.

McGee spent hours in his bedroom playing records, dreaming of being in a band, becoming a star.

'I got into music because I had nothing else,' he says. 'It made me feel part of something at last.'

But there was one problem. To be in a band you had to play your instrument well. In fact, very well. In the mid 1970s, musicians were judged on the length of their solos, not the quality of their songs. Musicianship was in, and pop music, along with black music, was for the frivolous and the stupid.

McGee was sharp enough to know his own limitations. He was not a natural musician. He put aside his rock star dreams. But he never left music.

First he adored T. Rex. Then it was Slade. But, like all the young dudes who hit their teenage years in the early 1970s, there was no escaping David Bowie.

McGee remembers first seeing Bowie in glitter-type clothes on *Top Of The Pops* performing 'Starman'. He was dumbfounded.

'I hadn't seen anything like it before,' he recalls. 'I remember it being my holidays and Bowie had a blue guitar. I became a Bowie fanatic.

'See, by the time I was about fifteen,' he explains, 'I realised that I was never ever gonna be very successful with women. You get to that point when you're about thirteen, fourteen, fifteen, when you're kind of invisible, and that's how I got into music.

'It's ironic because once I got into music and started doing music I became visible to women. But up to that point I was this kind of invisible, freckly, red-headed creature. So music was my escape into some kind of other world.'

Sometime in 1976, McGee received a phone call. When he answered, Bobby Gillespie came on the line. McGee had never previously spoken to the young skinny boy whose father would one day run as MP for his local constituency.

'See,' Gillespie explains, 'I was more into football than music. But then "The Boys Are Back In Town" by Thin Lizzy came out, and that was the first record which really made me want to go and see a group. Thin Lizzy were playing in Glasgow and I didnae want to go on my own. I remembered Alan from school because he wasnae punching people out but walking round with records. I looked him up in the directory and then I phoned him, said, "Do you want to come along?"'

Aye, McGee said, aye I do. It was the start of a close friendship that has lasted to this day.

The next year punk happened and the boys grew even closer together. In April 1977 McGee heard 'Anarchy In The UK' by The Sex Pistols; it took the ground from under him.

As the encouraging message that anyone could and should be in a band started to infiltrate young minds, McGee reactivated his rock-star aspirations. The Sex Pistols had made that possible and McGee loved them for it. So did Bobby. To them, Johnny Rotten was a true hero. He had encouraged them to do something interesting with their lives. For that alone, their hearts would always be with punk.

Significantly, McGee also dug the group's manager, Malcolm

McLaren. As they both had red hair, soon McGee was aping McLaren's clothes and spouting his philosophies. Already, McGee was casting himself as the power-broker behind the scenes.

The boys never got to see the Pistols but in that event-filled year of 1977, they saw The Clash and The Jam. They were concerts neither would forget. But then, there were so many memorable concerts around that time. It was a truly exciting time for both music and Britain's teenagers. McGee and Gillespie had a lifestyle now, one that gave them musical principles, fashion and the chance of some top nights out. Plus, the barriers that McGee had previously faced about being a musician were now broken down. Anyone, said the punk manifesto, can be in a group; everyone should be in a group.

So McGee and Gillespie joined groups. McGee's first group was The Drains, where he played bass. The guitarist, who they secured through a radio advert on a sympathetic Radio Clyde show, was Andrew Innes. The group soon folded. McGee and Innes then invited Bobby to form a group with them.

This was at McGee's suggestion. He was far closer to Bobby than he was to Innes.

'Bob is much more my soulmate,' he reveals, 'whereas Innes was more like the guy I was in bands with. It's only recently that me and Innes have got on, to be honest.'

Their band was named Captain Scarlet And The Mysterons, after the TV series.

'We never used to do anything,' McGee reveals. 'We'd just go round to Innes's every Friday night and drink beer, and Bobby would roll around the floor and do Sham 69 songs, because Bobby used to love Jimmy Pursey. He loved the working-class thing. He still loves all that.'

The group never went anywhere. But after its demise, Innes and McGee were asked to join a group called H2O.

'This is before they had a hit or anything and the idea was that we were gonna become like The New York Dolls. Me and Innes were wearing make-up and glam-rock trousers.'

Again, the band didn't work out. But their soldiered on with their dreams.

Their next outfit was called Newspeak. This was at the end of 1979, and McGee was now seeing the girl he would soon marry.

Her name was Yvonne. McGee was in love and basically content with life. But Innes was constantly bugging him to get out of Glasgow and move down to London. If they were going to be serious about making it as musicians, that was the place where it would happen.

'If Innes hadn't made me come to London, I probably wouldn't have made it,' McGee points out. 'I'd probably be fourteen and a half stone with three kids and living in Glasgow right now. So we came to London and formed a group called The Laughing Apple.'

Once there, Innes caught a bad case of hepatitis and McGee joined British Rail as a clerk. Soon after, he realised that he wasn't cut out to be a major songwriter, or a minor one, come to that. Yet this final realisation in no way diminished his passion for music.

This is why one day McGee is to be found reading a fanzine called *Jamming*. In it, the editor, Tony Fletcher has written an impassioned article about punk's failure, the betrayal of certain bands of the punk ethos and the subsequent stagnation of the music scene. The article truly fired McGee's imagination. 'It was saying, you've got to get off your arse and how nobody had any morals or beliefs anymore. Everything he said was right.'

McGee decided to join Fletcher's crusade. He found premises at the London's Musician Collective in Gloucester Avenue and started the Communication Club. The first band he promoted was Fletcher's own band, The Apocalypse. For the first eight weeks, McGee would lose about £70 a night. His weekly wages from BR amount to £72 a week. His wife Yvonne wasn't too happy.

A year later, his luck changed. Using a sizeable amount of an unexpected tax rebate, he found a room above a pub in London's West End called the Living Room and booked a band named The Nightingales. The following week it was The TV Personalities.

Much to his amazement, people started to show up in large numbers.

'By this point, music had turned round and people wanted to go and see bands,' McGee points out. 'Suddenly, I was getting like 200 people and I started earning £700 'cos I was doing the club about three times a week. In the first few weeks I got completely plastered every night because I thought it would all stop. But it didn't.

'I realised it was there for keeps. I thought, fucking hell, I can make a living going out and spotting bands for the club. So I chucked my job in at British Rail.'

As the club grew, it was inevitable that McGee's feverish mind would one day hit upon the following thought; if he could spot bands that people in his club genuinely liked, then the next step, surely, was to record them. Start a label.

That's what he would do. A label. It would release records that mirrored his two main musical loves; psychedelia and punk. In honour of one of his favourite groups, he would later name it Creation Records.

Alan McGee bends down with a $50 note in his nose and places it above the gleaming white particles of cocaine. He sniffs hard and the powder shoots up his nose and into his eyeballs. He sits down on his bed in this plush Los Angeles hotel room and takes a sip of Jack Daniels and coke. Then he absent-mindedly rubs his stomach.

It fascinates and repulses him how misshapen his stomach has become through boozing. He remembers how skinny he once was. Especially in the late 1980s when the Ecstasy pills were unbelievable and you didn't need alcohol because, according to rumour, it killed your high. Those days were gone now and McGee had turned to alcohol as one of his main ways of getting high. He now weighed fourteen stone.

Alan feels the coke starting to take effect. An urgent need springs to his brain. Music. He must have music. He looks over at the tapes he has brought with him.

He selects the one that has written on it 'Rocks, Primal Scream demo', and he inserts it into the machine. A thumping Sly Stone drumbeat comes stomping out of the speakers, followed by some raucous Stonesy guitar licks.

Then Bobby Gillespie starts singing. 'Dealers keep dealing/ Whores keep a whoring . . .'

Proper. He loves this song. It's an anthem for the times. Decadent, rocky. This is the first single of 1994 from Primal Scream. It comes from their third album *Give Out But Don't Give Up*, the crucial follow-up to their critically acclaimed *Screamadelica* album.

That LP made the band. It scaled the charts, found wide critical acclaim and even gained the band an extra £20,000 when it won the 1992 Mercury prize for Best Album Of The Year.

McGee laughs out loud. Now he is remembering how the day after the band's win, no one could find the cheque.

'I thought you had it, Bobby.' 'Nah, man. I didnae.' 'Well, where the fuck is it?' 'Dinnae ask me man, I was fucking oout of it.'

The song finishes. McGee rubs his stomach again and forces his mind to focus. He has been willing himself to stay one step ahead in America because to be honest, he is currently walking something of a tightrope. In September of 1992, Sony, the huge multi-national, bought 49% shares in his label. It was an inevitable deal.

Running an independent label in a market which is dominated by the multi-nationals is a huge financial and personal risk. You can sign the best band in the world ever, but if you don't have good distribution and marketing resources at your disposal, your records don't get in the shops. You're stuck with them. Piles of the fuckers.

The personal strain is tremendous. One minute you're dealing with bands screaming for more money, the next minute you're desperately trying to collect on money owed you. It also doesn't help when you're, as Alan McGee is, firmly attracted to musicians who you happily view as 'dysfunctional'.

'I thought all musicians were like that. You're fucked up, you must be really special. Then I found it's not exactly true,' McGee ruefully relates.

When McGee started Creation, the first single he released was by The Legend. It was called '73 In 83'. Then came Innes's band, Revolving Paint Dream, followed by groups such as Biff Bang Pow!, Jasmine Minks and The Pastels. McGee found many allies in the music press, but the music was of varying quality. His first major success would come with his discovery of a group dominated by two warring brothers, The Jesus And Mary Chain.

They had played McGee's club in July 1984. Straight after the gig, McGee went backstage and said to the brothers who had formed the group, 'I'll manage you.'

The brothers were Jim and William Reid, and their relation-ship was, to say the least, tempestuous. 'They were either gonna kill each other or smash the club up,' McGee recalls. 'They were a complete mess but they looked amazing. Plus, they played "Vegetable Man" by Syd Barrett and I love Syd Barrett.'

In November of that year McGee put out 'Upside Down' by the band. This single sold 50,000 copies in a month. McGee quit the club to concentrate on his label.

Creation was soon established as a hip, favoured label by the music press. They were independent, signed non-mainstream groups and were seen to keep the punk ethic alive, a notion that remains vitally important to music writers even to this day. Later signing would include My Bloody Valentine, House of Love, Ride and Primal Scream.

Yet it seemed to escape everyone's attention that many of the groups McGee had spotted, he then signed on to major American labels; it was the only way he could keep his label afloat.

'How Creation survived the first ten years,' McGee reveals, 'is because basically I'm a barrow boy. Up until I did the deal with Sony, I used to take my tapes to America and they would be of groups such as Slowdive, Swervedriver, Teenage Fanclub, and I used to go round the record companies and say, "Give me £250,000 for the Fanclub or give me £120,000 for Slowdive." And that's how I used to pay the bills, by being a market-trader.

'But then it got to 1992,' he continues, 'and I owed something like £1.2 million. I'd even sold the name Creation to Charles Koppelam who runs EMI Records. I sold him the name for $500,000 and I didn't have anything else I could fucking sell. So I had to sell 49% of my company to Sony.

'They signed the label for two reasons. Number one, because I had a history of finding bands. Number two, because they thought Primal Scream were going to become superstars.'

In March 1994 Primal Scream released their third album, *Give Out But Don't Give Up*, and thanks to Sony's huge distribution network the album, despite receiving poor reviews, outsold *Screamadelica* by some 400,000 copies, selling in total 600,000 copies. But it wasn't enough. The album had cost £425,000 to make.

'So basically at that point we were right in the shit with Sony,' McGee explains. It would take something truly special to rescue both McGee and his label. How ironic then that Creation's initial success which had started with two brothers who wanted to smack the fuck out of each other, would now be saved, by two brothers who often acted like they wanted to smack the fuck out of each other.

One of them, Noel Gallagher, is now sitting in his chair laughing at McGee who is sliding further and further down the sofa. All McGee can think to himself, as Noel reaches for another drink, is how the fuck does he keep going and how the fuck does he keep coming up with these amazing songs? And when can I get some sleep?

Ten

Noel Gallagher stands with about twenty other people in the Boardwalk, Manchester, watching his brother on-stage for the first time in his life. Because they cannot yet afford a microphone stand, Liam holds the mike in his hand.

Bonehead, Guigsy and McCarroll look nervous, but Liam doesn't. He is, of course, fronting, even now asserting that 'he was mad for doing it'.

As is so often the case with any important event, time rushes by. One minute they're nervously plugging in, hands slightly shaking, and the next they're playing the last song.

In the Oasis mythology, Noel now comes backstage, tells the band that they're shit, offers to join and write all the songs and they start rehearsing the next day.

Not so.

He did heavily criticise them, and Liam would have then challenged Noel, pointing out that if they were shit what about him? Why not join and make us better?

Undoubtedly the offer would have appealed to Noel. He was now twenty-four and had never been in a band, despite having furiously written songs these past few years. And, Oasis was the perfect band for him to join. It contained his brother and people he knew, apart from McCarroll.

Him aside, they all spoke the same language, came from the same class. They all liked football, scooters, clothes and cars. They were all obsessed with music. Perfect then, but Noel had a problem.

He couldn't ditch his job with the Inspirals. He earned good wages. No way did he want to go back on the dole. So Noel prevaricated. What he did was to invite the boys round to his flat in India House to play them a few of his songs.

The band gathered round at Noel's and, guitar in hand, he played them a few of his songs. One was called 'Live Forever'. The others had titles such as 'Colour My Life', 'See The Sun', 'Better Let You Know', 'Must Be The Music', 'Snakebite', 'Life In Vain' [the title adapted from The Stones song 'Love In Vain'] and 'I Will Show You'.

The only song of theirs that Noel would even consider playing live was 'Take Me'. He liked the lyrics.

Listening to Noel's songs, Guigsy, Bonehead and Liam felt a growing sense of real excitement. It was obvious that they were now in the presence of someone who was obviously very talented. He not only had an ear for melody but his arrangements had class as well. They determined to get Noel in as soon as possible.

'I remember ringing Liam constantly,' Bonehead recalls, 'asking if his kid had made his mind up yet.' Indeed, one Sunday afternoon, as Noel watched the football, Liam turned up on his doorstep, demanding an answer.

Typically, Noel took the cool approach. A month after the Boardwalk show, Noel Gallagher finally committed himself to Oasis, but only under some strict provisos. The first was that they would give their everything to the band. No one would be allowed to miss rehearsals. Everybody had to make a 100% effort. Failure to do so would mean dismissal.

They would have to watch their drug and alcohol intake too.

'The rule,' Guigsy explains, 'was that you could do what you want but only if you can handle it. Like I don't drink before I go on-stage because I can't handle it, but I can smoke loads of spliff. Whereas Liam can drink a hundred beers before he goes on and he can do it.'

Noel would carry on with the Inspirals and while he was away the others would have to keep on working. Any money they had would be put towards the cause.

They all eagerly agreed. By laying down these conditions, Noel Gallagher confirmed himself as the band's leader. As time moved on, only his brother would ever challenge his right to that title.

Noel also pulled in his friend Mark Coyle to engineer their sound and help set up the equipment.

At first, the band were unsure of Coyley. He seemed quiet and contained. But they soon learnt that once he had had a few drinks, he livened up considerably. Plus, he was totally on their wavelength.

Noel and Guigsy would gang up on him and kick off a football debate on the merits of City or United. Mark would argue his case and then Bonehead would come in on Coyley's side. He too supported United. But he was never as committed as Mark.

'Well, you can shut up as well,' Coyley would say to his United ally. 'What the fuck do you know about it?'

Bonehead could only say, 'Yeah, you're right.'

Noel's first concert, Oasis's second, took place at the Board-walk on 15 January 1992. They played a set lasting no longer than half an hour. They didn't move an inch on stage and then they abruptly left. Some kids in the crowd heckled them.

The next morning at five-thirty, Noel made it to Manchester airport, having been up all night and then flew to Japan with the Inspirals and Coyley.

'It was our two-week round the world tour,' the Inspirals' Graham Lambert explains with a laugh.

The remaining members of Oasis eagerly carried on rehearsing. But it was only when Noel was in town that they would feel the excitement of it all.

Meanwhile, Noel and Coyley were having a real good time. The Inspirals played Japan, and then moved on to Argentina and Uruguay, where they played at the River Plate's famous football stadium.

In Estonia, they played a festival. Two stages had been erected and the crowd would move from one to the other. Directly before the Inspirals played, Bob Geldof performed. He ran overtime.

So, over on his stage, Noel got on the mike and started saying things like, 'All right Bob, you've done your bit. Come on, off you come. I mean you don't need the money after all that Live Aid business, do you?'

Afterwards, Geldof came to their dressing-room. All the Manchester boys ignored him. As he left, Geldof slipped over, and the band and crew fell about laughing.

Graham Lambert recalls that in this period Noel was totally besotted by U2's *Achtung Baby* album and that he finally learnt how to play that guitar standard, beloved of pickers everywhere, 'Stairway To Heaven' by Led Zeppelin.

*

The next Oasis gig was at Dartford Polytechnic on 19 April, which Noel had secured thanks to the connections he was making through working with the Inspirals.

To travel there the band hired out a van and Guigsy took his car. The band arrived, followed by about five of their mates. They went to the local pub where someone lit up a spliff. The band were chucked out and made their way to the college.

They had with them a plentiful supply of cocaine, speed and Ecstasy. By the time they got on-stage, they were seriously gone. Bonehead played with three cigarettes in his mouth, Noel was E'd up, Guigsy fell off the stage and McCarroll forgot to tighten the nuts on his cymbals so when he first hit them, his drum kit half-collapsed.

So much for the band handling their drink and drugs.

Meanwhile, in the audience, the Manchester friends kicked off a fight with some students. Later on, some of the offices were raised and money that the students had collected for their traditional rag week was stolen. The band and their friends had to fight their way out of the college and into their cars.

Guigsy was in no condition to drive so by the time they reached a service station on the motorway, he pulled over and he, Liam and McCarroll went to sleep. They were awoken in the morning by a copper banging on their window.

They explained that they had got drunk and wanted to sleep off their hangovers. The policeman accepted their story and walked off, failing to notice the rather huge spliff that was in Guigsy's ashtray. Top night out, then.

Noel had now informed the Carpets that he was in a band. In fact to everyone he met he told the same thing.

'I'm in a band, we're called Oasis and we're playing at such and such place. Come down if you want to check it out.' Then he left it at that.

At the Hippodrome in Oldham, Graham Lambert witnessed his first Oasis gig when the band supported The Revenge. He later saw them again.

'When Noel asked me what I thought I told him that I thought the music was still a bit unfocused,' he recalls.

But the interesting thing, according to Graham, was Noel's obvious prolific nature. Then, just as now, Noel wrote most days of the week. Once he got on a roll there was no stopping him. He would show up at rehearsals with a whole new batch of songs which would then take precedence over the 'older' material.

During this period, Noel astonished the band with the quality and maturity of his songs. He had now come up with songs such as 'Whatever' and a real band favourite, 'All Around The World'. There was also 'She's Electric', (Noel recalling his primary school days and blatantly lifting part of the melody from the kids TV show *Me And You*) and 'Hello', which were demoed at Mark Coyle's house at 388 Mauldeth Road West, although they wouldn't see the light of day until October 1985 when Oasis's second album was released.

'They never played the same set twice,' Graham recalls. 'Within six weeks they had a new set-list which I told Noel wasn't goo for getting record companies interested. But he never seemed that bothered. I also remember Bonehead playing acoustic guitar at a few of the gigs.'

By now, the band had moved into a new rehearsal space. This was at the Boardwalk in Manchester. They were given a room downstairs where they rehearsed maybe two or three nights a week, depending on their finances. Then they came to an arrangement with another group, Sister Lovers, to share the cost. Once that was done, Oasis were in there every night of the week, starting at five in the evening and finishing by ten o'clock at night.

The rehearsals would start off with any new songs Noel might have. These would have included 'Blue', a song that Liam says was Noel's first-ever epic.

Then the band would rehearse the songs they knew, maybe breaking off round about seven-thirty for a beer or a spliff. Then it would be back to playing until ten.

The room was small and sometimes there were pools of water on the floor. To liven the place up, Bonehead brought in some paint and they would sporadically paint the back wall in the colours of the Union Jack.

Noel had even written a song called 'The Red, White and Blue', and their fascination with the British flag caused a little consternation among some onlookers. One of these was the group they shared the room with, Sister Lovers.

In November 1992 one of the group's members, Debbie Turner saw Creation boss Alan McGee at a Bob Mould gig at the

Boardwalk. Afterwards, she invited him down to their rehearsal room for a spliff.

McGee entered the room where the most important band he would ever sign rehearsed and noted the flag. He was told that it was the work of this lads' band, Oasis, and there were various mutterings about the band's politics. McGee made a mental note to steer clear of them.

For the group, their interest in the flag had been prompted by bands such as The Who, who early in their career had used the flag in an ironic pop-art fashion.

'But because we were lads who liked drinking beer and going to football,' Noel explains, 'no one thought we would be into art or anything. It was like this song I had, "The Red, White and Blue". That song came about because one day I had gone down to Johnny Roadhouse to get some equipment. As I came out, there was some march going on. I'm standing there and this guy comes over and starts ranting at me for not taking any interest in his cause.

'I'm like, I'm arsed about your cause. All I want to do, mate, is be in a band. If this is your thing, then fine, I haven't got a problem with it, live and let live. But leave me out of it.

'He just went on and on, so I wrote this song about how if you look a certain way you instantly get labelled and I called it "Red, White and Blue", which was also about how things like the Union Jack get hijacked and if you use it people automatically think you're part of something you're not.'

The song was based around a riff not that dissimilar to Isaac Hayes's song 'Shaft', with Noel utilising his wah-wah pedal to maximum effect. But he soon shelved the song.

'All the band really liked it but I knew if we played it, it would cause more trouble than it was worth, which is why it got sacked.'

Because they were regular users of the rehearsal space, the Boardwalk would occasionally put the group on upstairs. This was probably done in some vain attempt to get the rent paid.

The band often missed payments. Buying equipment proved to be expensive and although everyone but Liam worked, the cost of maintaining themselves and Oasis consistently left them short of cash.

At the end of each rehearsal, the band would down their instruments and bolt for the door. The last one out had to hand the keys back which always meant making up some kind of excuse to the owners about paying tomorrow. Sometimes Noel would pay by a cheque that he knew would bounce higher than a kangaroo. Other times they would offer ten quid and solemnly promise to pay the rest the next night.

What bugged everyone was that they thought the place was a right dump. First off it was cold and leaked water, which was highly dangerous with all the electrical gear. It was also small and dark.

'Well before U2's Zooropa tour,' Guigsy says, 'Noel came up with this idea of turning off all the lights, getting a load of broken down TVs in and then just switching them on to light the room up.'

If you were to have seen the band practise at this time, you would have opened the door and, looking clockwise, found to your left-hand side, Noel playing his guitar. Guigsy would be in the far corner to Noel's left and Bonehead was placed in the right-hand corner, playing next to McCarroll's drums which had been set up against the wall. Liam stood in the middle of the room.

When the band jammed on an instrumental bit, Liam would sit cross-legged on the floor, spliff in hand, close his eyes and check the music.

If Coyley was taping a session there would be a mike placed over one of the pipes that ran above their heads. It was his job to set up the equipment and again the boys were initially impressed with his knowledge as he ran around checking amps and levels. It was only when equipment failed to work and Coyley's eloquent response was to try to kick it into life, that they realised they had a fellow chancer on board.

There was some graffiti on the door and further down the corridor, Liam had drawn a plane and written a remark under it about being careful when you land on runways, a biting comment aimed at all United supporters. But still it was here that the unique Oasis sound first started to surface. It happened through volume. The band always played loudly. Noel would put his switch right up to ten and then hammer the shit out of his guitar, venting all his frustrations. Bonehead did the same.

It was at some point here that Noel realised that if Bonehead kept playing barré chords, his fingers covering all the strings, all of the time, that then allowed Noel the freedom to pick out melodies, riffs and guitar lines. Align that with a very basic, almost punk-like rhythm section provided by McCarroll and Guigsy and the sheer volume they played at, and the Oasis sound starts to take shape.

The only missing element at this point is Liam's voice which was yet to take on the strength and character it now has. But that, with time, would come.

In their idle moments, the group would go and play tricks on other bands rehearsing. They would carefully open the doors to other rehearsal rooms and switch off all the lights as someone rehearsed. At other times, they would play knock-down ginger, banging on a band's door and then running back to their room.

If anyone complained, well, there's five of us here and you want to talk about it outside, mate? None of them ever did. But if anyone knew what the outside felt like, it was Liam. Every Friday night, after rehearsing, he would go upstairs to the Boardwalk's Friday club night.

He would stroll in, skin up and stand there blatantly puffing on his spliff. The bouncers would then come over and ask him to put it out. He'd tell them to fuck off. They would then grab him, push him through the backdoors, down the stairs and out of the club on to the street. He would curse like mad, and then do precisely the same thing the next Friday night.

'I went down those stairs so many times,' he recalls, 'it was ridiculous.'

His shenanigans were so regular that the Boardwalk management even wrote to the band saying that if Liam didn't stop then the whole group would be banned from the premises. The next Friday, there was Liam, spliff in hand.

He didn't care because he knew something that only four other people knew in Manchester. Oasis were going to be huge. It was just a fact. The songs that were rushing out of Noel were simply head and shoulders above everything else. And that fascinated Liam.

Here was his brother, this seemingly normal, restrained character, who loved nothing more than getting out of it or standing in the Kippax Stand urging on his beloved Manchester City team, suddenly unveiling these songs which contained in their words and sound, a torrent of emotions.

Their melodies were so simple yet so right, and the arrangements were just naturally crafted. There was no hint of the songs being calculated. It was just amazing. Oasis, with Noel Gallagher on their side, just could not fail.

Guigsy remembers how most nights after rehearsing, he and Liam would go back to his house and up to his room. There they would play Hendrix, Kinks and Who records and just tell each other how successful they were going to become.

'It's going to be fucking top,' Liam would say, settling back with a spliff in his hand and a contented smile on his face. Yet not even Liam, or anyone connected with Oasis for that matter, had any idea just how top it would turn out to be.

It is obvious then that this self belief, coupled with an innate suspicion of outsiders and a thriving arrogance, turned Oasis, with the exception of Tony McCarroll, into a tight-knit gang. The drummer was different. He never displayed a passion for anything.

Take music, Bonehead says. 'I wouldn't have minded if he had five records that he said were the best ever and that was it. But he didn't even have that. I don't think he owned any records or even a stereo.'

But Noel, Liam, Guigsy and Bonehead held tight. They would arrive at gigs and totally ignore everyone there. If anybody said anything, they were more than happy to kick off a fight, whether it be with the other bands or promoters. It didn't matter to them. 'Proper angry young men,' is Guigsy's curt description.

On-stage, they said nothing. They came on, played a short set, never moved, never communicated and then walked off. That was it.

Their attitude was, this music is great and to be honest we really don't think you deserve it. But here we are, here it is, and if you like it then that's how it should be. And if you don't, that just proves our point. Dickheads.

It was Oasis against the world, a feeling that all the best bands or solo artists are full of in their early days, and that year, 1992, the feeling was paraded at the Club 57 in Oldham where they supported The Ya's Ya's (whose bass player was one Scott Mcleod), three more times at the Boardwalk, and once at the Playback Roadshow on 22 June 1992.

This was an event that formed part of a nationwide drive to raise money for various charities. Martin, Bonehead's brother, knew the organiser and persuaded him to let Oasis play the day-long festival, which also featured acts such as Opus 3 and The Utah Saints.

After performing, Oasis handed over a tape to be auctioned of 'Take Me', featuring two mixes. They also autographed the cassette cover.

Their next prestigious gig would be in two months time on 13 September, an appearance at the Venue as part of Manchester's In The City season.

This was a scheme partly organised by Tony Wilson to rival the Music Seminar in New York which takes place every summer. It was also an attempt to drag the music scene away from its London centre, provide a chance for labels to display their bands and to allow A&R men to check out new talent. No one, it seemed, bothered with Oasis.

Yet for Liam Gallagher, such gigs aside, this was the time when Oasis should have been recorded.

'That's when we were really rocking,' he firmly states. 'I wish we could have made an album then.'

Eleven

Marcus Russell lay in his sickbed and hard as he tried, he couldn't shake off the thought of impending doom that seemed to permeate his whole being. He was twenty-nine years old and he felt as if his life was going nowhere.

His marriage was in trouble. Not because of his wife, Jane, she was a good sweet person. No, it was because the conformity that marriage demands wasn't to his liking.

At the time of his wedding, Marcus had told himself that the time was right now to settle down and build for the future. And for a while he abided by this new way of thinking. Yet he couldn't shake the nagging feeling of dissatisfaction that lived in the back of his mind. It just wouldn't leave him alone. It made him feel like a fake, someone acting out what he thought he was supposed to be, not what he really was.

And his job. What a weight on his shoulders that was. Marcus worked as an economics teacher in a Harlow secondary school. At first, it had been a challenge to stimulate the rows of disinterested kids that he faced every day. Already, some of them were muttering aloud, saying what was the point of taking exams when there were no fucking jobs to go to.

Inside, Marcus could only agree with them, but he took it upon himself to show them differently, to agitate their minds, at least get them thinking in a more positive vein. That attitude lasted about a year. If that.

Now he hated his job with a passion. His yearly budget didn't even begin to cover the cost of the materials his students needed, and the routine of it all numbed him.

He knew that in September he would be teaching the laws of supply and demand. In February it would be inflation. Year in, year out, the same books, the same lesson, the same bored expressions staring up at him. It was all a sham, his whole fucking life.

And now this illness, this viral arthritis that he had somehow picked up in Portugal, had come along to frighten the fuck out of him. For the past six months he had been confined to his bed. He was in reality, a cripple, unable to walk. Marcus Russell couldn't put one leg in front of the other.

The doctor had assured him that it would pass, but the illness had lasted so long that paranoia had now set in. He secretly wondered if his friends and family were keeping a terrible secret from him, namely that he would never walk again.

'Oh, don't be so stupid,' his wife Jane would say. 'You heard what the doctor said.' But who was to say that his diagnosis was right? There were plenty of examples of doctors getting it wrong.

'You men, when you're ill,' his wife would tut, 'you're like little babies.'

That was probably true, but you try and stay in bed in this tiny council flat bedroom here in Godforsaken Harlow and dream a better dream. And on top of all that, his thirtieth birthday was now approaching. Thirty! For fuck's sake. Another ten years and he would be forty, and then . . . he shuddered to think.

Five months later, things had slightly improved. Marcus was back at work, he was walking, and his wife had walked too. He and Jane were now separated. Marcus knew his days at work were also numbered.

He just needed time to figure out his next move. And it was as he was pondering that a phone call was placed to his flat. It was unexpected, but then as Lennon had once said, 'Life is something that happens to you when you're busy making other plans.'

The call was from Marcus's friend, Mike, a really close ally from his past, and it brought back a flood of memories. Mike was now living in Liverpool, but it was he and Marcus who had started the Drifter's Escape club (named after a Bob Dylan song) in their hometown of Ebbw Vale, South Wales, when they were just boys and so much younger than they were today.

They were sixteen at the time and Ebbw Vale was a vibrant, economically prosperous town. By day everyone had work and by night the pubs would be filled with singing men and women. It was a time when the future was secure and people could feel their lives moving forward.

The town was also a Labour stronghold ('put up a monkey with a red rosette and it would get 40,000 votes,' Marcus half jokes), built around a huge steel works that had guaranteed money for life. You could get a job there one day, leave the next month, travel around a bit and return home, safe in the knowledge that your old job would be waiting for you.

Marcus had worked in the steel works there after leaving grammar school with six O-levels, three A-levels and absolutely no idea what he wanted to be, except for a vague idea that it should somehow include music. In fact, he had actually worked as an unpaid roadie for a local group called Rock Cottage Barn when he was fifteen, but the work hadn't suited him.

His first proper job was working the blast furnaces. It was potentially dangerous work; he was, after all, working with scalding molten iron. But it gave him money and, more importantly, some much-needed breathing space to figure out his next move.

And, anyway, he was a teenager and there was plenty of living to be done. The future could wait.

It was 1969 and Marcus's main passion in life was music. In his youth, Paul, his elder brother, had put him on to The Rolling Stones, The Beatles and Phil Spector. Now he was into groups such as Family, The Doors, Captain Beefheart, progressive rock music.

To hear such music in Ebbw Vale, Marcus would go to the local pub. This was a big building with four different rooms. The soul types would be in one room playing their Small Faces, Northern Soul and Wilson Pickett tunes. The rockers would be in another room, and the hippies, where Marcus hung out, in another. Nobody ever mixed but there was very little trouble.

It was a good scene but it was disrupted the day the order came to pull the pub down.

'This bar opened up,' Marcus recalls, 'called the Bottom Bar. It was a big basement bar and that took on the whole youth clientele of the old pub. All of a sudden everyone was in it together and the common denominator was the spliff or a pint.

'After about three months all the stereotypes were gone. They had this jukebox and you could bring in your own records and put them on. That's how it all crossed over 'cos anyone could bring in a record. So you would hear everything.'

One night Marcus, his best mate Mike and a couple of other friends were sat around the Bottom Bar, drinking beer, shooting the breeze and eyeing up the local girls, when one of them suggested that they should expand the town's nightlife beyond just this bar. Why not find a spot, like that disused building, and put on groups? That's what the town lacked. All the bands they liked played everywhere but Wales. Why not bring them in?

'Then we thought, well, instead of talking about it, let's do it. We went to the council and said, "Look, you've got a bit space sitting there doing nothing. Why don't you do something with it? We'll run it and you can take all the money." Lo and behold they backed us.'

The first night the boys booked a local blues band and everyone turned out. The place as rammed. The council, once they saw the first week's profit, granted the boys a licence.

They named the club the Drifter's Escape, and for the next nine months it became the centre for alternative music in Wales. Mott The Hoople, Caravan and the original Genesis all played there.

'It ran for about nine months. Then it closed down, and then it ran for another three months. It was a good time. I didn't feel that I missed out because I didn't live in London or something. Never felt like we missed out. We were in touch with people like John Peel, and we used to write off to export or import record shops in London or San Francisco and get all the music we wanted.

'We'd read *Zig Zag* or the *International Times*, *Oz* was the other mag. I mean that whole culture was permeating our area, which was great because it really switched me on to music.'

The club didn't last. Kids there were openly taking drugs and it was only a matter of time before the authorities moved in and busted them. One day the council called the organisers in for a meeting. One councillor in particular was furious, condemning 'the wild scenes of fornication' he had witnessed, much to Marcus's open amusement.

Afterwards, Marcus and his mate went for a drink.

'What about that old codger who kept on about fornication,' Marcus said to his mate. 'I mean, I wouldn't have minded if any had gone on.'

His mate put down his pint, sheepishly grinned and said, 'Well, there was this one girl . . .'

So the Drifter's Escape folded, and Marcus packed his bags and moved to London for a while, working as a labourer. Despite his qualifications, he still had no clue as to his future employment.

But a girlfriend kept calling him, entreating him to go home. So he decided to rejoin the steel works. But Ebbw Vale was changing. So was Britain. Money and jobs were drying up. Soon, the Prime Minister, Edward Heath, would order a three-day working week.

'You could smell the death of the steel works,' Marcus notes. 'I got made redundant in 1973 and I knew that was it. I thought, hang on, I'd better get out of this town because if this place goes, everything's going to go with it, everything's going to die. I thought, I'm not gonna go labouring, I'll go to college.

'And that's when I moved back to London in 1974 to do an education degree, a BA in economics and history at Middlesex Poly. I was lucky. I had the A-levels to get out with.'

He also had entrepreneurial skills which, aligned with his musical passion, made it natural for him to apply for the job, at the end of his degree, as the college's social secretary. He had no other ambition than to make his life interesting by filling it with music.

'I've always been involved in music for the love of it,' Marcus states. 'For me, music was serious all the time. So when I was in college I was involved and through that I also got involved in promoting gigs outside of the college. The agents would go, "You ran that show at college really well, do you want to promote a gig for me at Alexandra Palace?" The college had one of the rooms down there.'

By this time, 1977, the musical landscape had massively altered. Punk rock, through groups such as The Sex Pistols, The Clash and The Jam, had brought in a much younger audience with new values and ideas. Marcus was in his mid twenties when the scene kicked into life and he felt too old for it. He just couldn't bring himself to go po-going with the fifteen-year-olds in the front row.

But he was enough of a musical fan to take the mood on board.

'At the time, I thought the only good music was old music. Punk just totally regenerated my interest in new music. I used to go to The Clash gigs – I didn't think they were as good as The Pistols, but their gigs were great. The Jam; the gigs weren't packed but they were a quality band, very, very important.

'I used to like odd tracks by bands such as Penetration or X-Ray Spex but I used to think The Pistols were the bees' knees. Well, the album was.'

Marcus bases that assertion on the one Pistols gig he saw. This was at Middlesex Poly and he was the promoter.

Despite the rising excitement caused by the band's imminent appearance, the gig turned out to be a shambles. The Pistols came on and in ten minutes the gig was over. The fans had rushed the stage and the band retreated to their waiting vehicles. The night ended in chaos and disruption.

Undeterred, invigorated even by the show, Marcus went on to promote gigs by Siouxsie And The Banshees, Generation X and The Stranglers. His natural left-wing political leanings were activated by punk. Marcus fought the neo-Fascist National Front in Lewisham in 1977 and attended many benefit concerts around that time.

Given his leaning towards 'classic' rock music, he was also taken by New Wave acts, such as Elvis Costello or the new American bands such as Television.

It was around this time he met Jane, his future wife and began a serious relationship. She too was a teacher and was waiting for the day when Marcus would eventually find a good teaching job and settle down.

'She was waiting for me to start on the S & N,' he says, 'the straight and narrow. Settle down, get a flat, get a job, wave goodbye to all your college friends. I thought I should do that then, put it all behind me. Little did I know.'

By his last year of teaching, Marcus had hooked up with a fellow school colleague called Sean. He too was disillusioned by his work and the British education system.

'He was mad as a hatter and bang into music,' Marcus recalls. 'He used to manage a punk band as well, The Sods from Harlow, who actually had a couple of good tunes. One of them was called "There's No Pictures Of Us". So I started hanging around with him and it was him who really got me thinking of doing something else other than teaching. Like he wanted to start a tape duplicating business or he'd come up with these other ideas. And it was around this time that Mike called.'

It turned out that Mike had started writing songs. And good ones at that. But he was also wise enough to know he couldn't sing them properly. But he did have another mate who was ace on vocals. What he wanted from Marcus was for him to use his previous connections in the music business to secure a publishing deal.

Marcus disagreed. What Mike needed, he told him, was to get a band together. Then they could go hunting for a deal. And, Marcus added, as the songs had undoubted potential, he would like to get involved. Which is how Latin Quarter became the first band that Marcus Russell ever managed.

Naturally, Marcus couldn't just quit his job. He had bills to pay, records to buy. So he started leading, in his own words 'a complete double-life'.

'We got a band together and I started trying to get them a deal. But it was while I was still teaching. So I was rushing home from work at four o'clock in the afternoon and then getting on the phone to London Records or rushing into town for a six o'clock meeting with A&M.

'And I didn't have a clue how to get a record deal, didn't have a clue about record companies. I was just selling the band, organising gigs and hoping that no one would find out what I was up to. I mean I couldn't tell the companies I was a teacher and I couldn't tell the school I was trying to be a rock manager.

'Then it got to the stage where I really believed they had a chance and I just jacked the teaching in, just jacked everything in to be a full-time manager. I thought, well if it means I've got to live on twenty quid a week then I'll do it. Give a shit. And that's how it all started.'

Marcus formed a company, called it Ignition, and then he signed on. Naturally, his first priority, was to find a deal for Latin Quarter. Eventually, he signed the band to a small independent label called Rocking Horse Records.

The label only had one other group. They were called Blue Zone and were led by a sixteen-year-old vocalist called Lisa Stansfield.

Once Latin Quarter were signed, Marcus's first ambition was to break them big in England.

'They were writing politically correct, melodic pop tunes with a reggae tinge, and a couple of the songs were gems,' Marcus recalls. 'So I was trying to get them away in England, get them in the *NME* and all the weeklies. There were some people who championed them in the press but the general vibe was, Nah, this is old hat, we're into Haircut 100, or something.'

Again, the unexpected occurred. The band's début album hit the charts in Germany. It would eventually rack up a quarter of a million sales and teach Marcus an invaluable lesson in pop management; there was more to life than just Britain. There was a whole world you could conquer. The experience literally opened his eyes.

'I very quickly learnt, you don't have to be big in England to sustain a career,' he explains, 'and then I looked at Latin Quarter's success in Germany. Over there, they were licenced to RCA, and RCA developed the band with a very long-term point of view. They weren't expecting a big reward straight away.

'They were prepared to wait. And then Sweden cracked and we thought, right, we'll start developing foreign markets and sod the *NME* and Radio One. And in the end they had success in England with "Radio Africa". So my first experience was really positive.'

In 1986, Marcus felt confident to take on another group, The Bible, who scored three or four minor hits. 'But in both cases,' he says, 'the bands self-destructed. It sounds a bit dramatic but I think everyone gets bugged by the level of success they have or haven't got. And I was unable to give them that confidence within that time.'

As Marcus struggled to keep both bands afloat, a dynamic news story broke in the *NME*. The Smiths, the Manchester band who had taken over from The Jam as the critics' and people's choice, were to split up. Unable to work with each other through now very apparent differences, Johnny Marr the guitarist, who had been revered for his exceptional songwriting ability, was now a free agent. And he badly needed a manager.

Both he and Morrissey had not only led The Smiths but had also assumed managerial roles. The contractual maze that The Smiths' demise now brought to light was mind-boggling. Plus, Marr was exhausted. He could no longer take on everything. He needed some cover.

To that end, he had visited his lawyer James Wylie to see if he could recommend anyone. Wilson brought up Marcus's name.

Sure, Marcus was a friend but Wylie also admired his thorough approach and the way in which he had handled his groups thus far.

'I'll ring him and see what he has to say,' Wylie told Marr. When the call came through, Marcus was flabbergasted and not a little scared.

'Johnny's profile is still very high now,' Marcus points out, 'but at that time he was like Lord God Johnny Marr.

'He could have picked any top manager from either side of the Atlantic and, in fact, he did have this American guy managing his affairs in America. I was a fan of Johnny's, but I've got to be honest and say that I fall into that category of people who love The Smiths music but could only take Morrissey in small doses.

'I respect him as a lyricist and as a singer but he's not my cup of tea. But I thought Johnny was fucking amazing, and double so when I actually met him and got to know him. He is such an open-minded guy, totally open-minded musically, and he's a great guy to while away the early hours of the morning just talking and boring everyone to death about the last twenty-five years in music.'

Marr and Marcus hit it off straightaway. Marr relieved his American manager of all duties and then appointed Marcus his sole manager, a position he still holds today.

'Johnny gave me shitloads of confidence basically,' Marcus states. 'He's a very giving guy, to be honest, very understanding, very encouraging, and it was a hell of a break for me. And it was through Johnny that I ended up managing The The.'

After leaving The Smiths, Marr had decided to spend his time playing with various musicians. Whoever caught his fancy, really. To that end, he had hooked up with The Pretenders. But then an offer came through from Matt Johnson, the man behind The The, to work on his new album. Marr phoned Marcus for advice.

'I said, Well, if that's the choice it's got to be The The. Because Matt was like the young-gun in town and with Chrissy [Hynde] it could take ten years to make the album. Matt was ready to go.

'And then, totally unbeknown to me, Matt was in wrangles with his manager and he ended up managerless and during that course of time, he said, "Do you want to manage The The?"

'I was like, Yeah, mad for it. And that's when I really got into worldwide touring because for me it was just the greatest band going. Johnny Marr, David Palmer on drums – what a drummer he is – James Eller on bass and Dave Collard on keyboards. You rarely get to see a band like that.

'So we did a world tour that lasted exactly a year and at the end of it my experience and knowledge had gone up like 3,000%.'

But the smile was soon wiped off his face. Within months of the tour's end, Matt Johnson fired him.

'Matt does albums in cycles,' Marcus explains. 'He'll write the album, promote it and then he retreats into the world of Matt Johnson, and during his retreat after *Mind Bomb* I think a lot of people were pissing in his ear saying, "You need heavy management. Marcus is all right, he's a nice guy, but you need someone who's going to kick arse with the chief executive of Polygram or whatever."

'He had what I think is an old-fashioned perception of what an effective manager is. And it really wasn't personal.

'If he walked in right now we'd have a fucking great night together. But he was just going through that cycle and for about five minutes I was really worried but Johnny was just amazing. He very quickly reassured me. He was saying, "I can't believe Matt's done this, it's the biggest fuck-up he's ever made," and he made me feel good about myself. And I'll never forget Johnny for that.'

The next musician to catch Marcus's eye was Andy Frank who was then in a band called S.K.A.W. (an acronym for the classic song 'Some Kinda Wonderful') and who had signed to Warner Brothers. Marcus had bought one of his singles and had been knocked out by the B-side, 'which was like West Coast blues-laced acid stuff'. The song strongly reminded Marcus of his teenage roots.

S.K.A.W. broke up and Frank then set up another band called Pusherman, who now record for Marcus's own label, Ignition Records. As all that was going on, Marcus found himself in May of 1993 talking to a very excited Johnny Marr.

The object of Marr's enthusiasm was an unknown Manchester band. Oasis.

'Oasis,' Marcus replied, thinking to himself that it was a bit of a strange name. 'What kind of music is it?'

Marr said guitar-driven pop. 'They're good,' Marr continued, 'fucking good.'

But Marcus was too busy with too many other things on his plate.

'If you're a successful manager,' he points out, 'you're

inundated all the time, not only with tapes but with people saying, "We should take on this or that", "Look at these", "Listen to that", and physically you haven't got the time to do everything.

'So, I gotta be honest, I never got round to doing anything. And then Johnny phoned me again and said, "Look, this guy out of Oasis has been offered a deal, can you recommend anybody?" So I got a lawyer for them, which was John Statham.

'And then John rang me and started saying, "These guys haven't got a manager and they want to know why you haven't been to see them." I was like, "John, chill out. I'm busy, I'm doing this, I'm doing that, you know what it's like."

'He said, "Fair enough, I'm only trying to find them a manager." Anyway, a week or two later I was up in Manchester visiting Johnny, and Andrew Berry, the hairdresser, was there. He said, "Oasis are playing, why don't you come and see them?"

'I was like, "Yeah", but actually thinking I wasn't going to go because I hadn't heard anything except the manager of another group who was saying, "Oasis, nah, if it was gonna happen, it would have happened by now." That was the vibe, believe it or not.

'Then Johnny said, "I'm going up there, fuck it, let's go into town and see them." And it was like, well, if Johnny's going to go, there must be something in it because he had never seen them either.'

So Marcus Russell, with Johnny Marr in tow, got into his car and drove to a student union bar called the Hop and Grape in Manchester. He got out of the car, walked into the gig and, again, the unexpected; his life changed forever.

Twelve

On 12 June 1992 Oasis woke up to find themselves splashed all over page twelve of that day's *Manchester Evening News*. The writer was Penny Anderson, one of the very first journalists to interview the band.

On a full-page spread (indicative of the press to come), she wrote, 'It is not very often that an unsigned band appear on these pages as the main feature, but Oasis deserve it.'

Noel had passed her a tape that Coyley had recorded at rehearsals. It contained songs such as 'Take Me' and 'Colour My Life'.

Although Penny felt the lyrics needed more work (a criticism that would echo down the years), and the songs were too lengthy, Oasis were 'the best demo band I have heard in years'. In the article, Noel, in an impish mood, and obviously pleased by the attention, describes their music as, 'Not pop, not rock but somewhere in between. Maybe pock?'

He then refutes any suggestion that Oasis are cashing in on the vogue for heavy guitar-based music heralded by the success of Nirvana's *Nevermind* album.

'I've always been into guitars,' Noel points out. 'We want to put keyboards on but keyboard players don't look cool on-stage, they just keep their heads down. There has never been a cool keyboard player apart from Elton John.'

It was, of course, a joke. But after the article appeared, Noel was pulled up several times in Manchester by people saying, 'So you really think Elton John is cool, d'ya?'

Later on in the article, using the Gallagher foresight, he prophesied, 'If we'd been around in 1989, we would have been signed by now but we would have been under serious pressure to deliver an album. But in eighteen months we're going to be five times as good.'

It was true. In that time Oasis would have two top-forty hits under their belts and one of the début albums of the decade nearly ready for release.

Another person to hear this demo tape was Phil Sachs at Factory Records.

Liam remembers the band going to meet him to get his verdict. 'He said that we sounded too Manchester,' he says with bafflement in his voice. 'We said, "Well that's what we are. We're not Turkish or Israeli, we're from Manchester." So we fucked him off, took the tape.'

It was fortuitous for Oasis to be turned down by Factory. Despite their success with groups such as New Order and Happy Mondays, Factory were heading towards financial ruin. By the end of the year, receivers had been called in and the record company's debts were estimated to be in the area of £2.5 million. Tony Wilson's empire may have turned Oasis down, but a meeting which would produce far more benefit for the band was about to take place.

The Real People, a Liverpool group, had been going since 1988. They had been formed by two brothers, Chris and Tony Griffiths. In December 1989 they signed to Sony Records and a year later, their début album was released.

In 1992 they toured America. While there, they also recorded a few tracks for their second album with the late Jimmy Miller, the famed 1960s producer who worked with The Rolling Stones and Traffic among many others.

On their return, the good news for The Real People was that they were offered a support slot with The Inspiral Carpets on their UK tour. The bad news was that they were about to lose their manager, Anthony Bodgiano, and that personnel changes at Sony had now removed all their supporters at the company.

Despite all this, their new single, 'Believer', had entered the charts at thirty-eight. But the group found themselves in limbo as Sony refused to back the band with any kind of serious promotion. It was in this context that the band set out on the road with the Inspirals.

'The Inspiral Carpets were all right,' Tony Griffiths of The Real People confirms, 'but Noel and Mark Coyle were dead sound and that's because they always gave us bevvies out of their riders.

'We got talking and all that and after a few gigs, I found out that Noel was actually into our band. He had bought our records and our album and seen us a few times.'

On one of the dates, Liam came down to visit Noel and see the band. After the gig, Tony met Noel's cocky young brother and immediately thought the same as everyone else when they meet Liam for the first time.

'I met Noel first,' Griffiths says, 'but meeting Liam was weird because the first time I set eyes on him, I just went, you're a star. I'd never heard him sing or nothing, it was just instant. He just had that look and attitude.'

It hadn't been the first time that someone had expressed such sentiments and it's probable that this was something that bugged Noel. He was the songwriter, the musician, the one who slaved for hours over his songs, constantly fine'tuning them and having to deal with bouts of real self doubt. Yet, because of his essentially shy nature, people never instantly singled him out. Noel could be just as destructive as Liam but never as impulsive. In contrast, Liam, with his boisterous presence and natural charisma, got all the attention and was the natural magnet.

At the end of the tour, Noel and Mark invited The Real People down to see Oasis play at the Boardwalk on 5 January 1993. They would be supporting Puressence, another band tipped for big things.

It would be great to be playing live, but Noel and Coyley's excitement was somewhat tempered by some very unwelcome news. The Inspirals had decided they no longer required their services. Maybe there had been too many complaints about their behaviour or maybe the band, as they explained to Noel and Mark, no longer had the finances to pay them.

Whatever the reason, Noel was seriously pissed off. He now had to sign on and there is nothing worse than having to adjust your living standards to a much lower level. Now he was no longer financially solvent, Oasis would also be affected in terms of maintaining themselves financially.

Guigsy and Bonehead still worked, Guigsy as a personnel officer for British Telecom and Bonehead as a self-employed plasterer. But both Gallaghers were now on the dole, while, according to the band, it was always hard to squeeze cash from Tony McCarroll. It would only be through the DSS that Oasis could expect any kind of regular income.

When the Griffiths brothers arrived at the Boardwalk, Tony spotted John Bryce, who used to work for Sony Records but had now moved to Warner Chappell Publishing. He went over, said hello, and together the pair of them watched the gig.

Liam came on wearing a pair of shades, and sections of the audience started heckling him, shouting 'Showaddywaddy', in reference to the dire 1970s glam rock 'n' roll group whose singer also sported shades. Liam told them all to fuck off.

Oasis then played their customary short set to an audience of about fifty people. Now they had two new songs in the set list. They were 'Rock 'n' Roll Star' and 'Bring It On Down'.

'They were the ones,' enthuses Tony Griffiths. 'I was standing there with this John Bryce and it was obvious to anyone standing there what was going on on'stage. It was just fucking boss. And I said to John, sort them out some studio time and Chris my brother will produce it, and he said, "Yeah, fucking sound."'

But Bryce found it impossible to convince his people in London of the wisdom of recording a band they had never seen or heard. So Tony and Chris decided to do it themselves.

'We'd been setting up our own studio in a place called Porter Street in Dock Road,' he explains, 'a big warehouse which had like three floors.

'We'd set up an eight-track studio in this boss large room and at the same time we were about to produce our album. But then all this shit happened with the record company so we didn't know what was going on. We didn't have any gigs to do so we basically ended up working for Oasis for three months. We recorded about twelve tracks and it was really, really good.'

Eight of these songs would appear on the demo tape that Noel would later hand over to Alan McGee, head of Creation Records.

The sessions, produced by Mark Coyle and Chris Griffiths, took place at nights, starting at about eight in the evening and going through until about seven in the morning. They set the studio up to capture the band totally live, with very little added to the finished results.

By all accounts the atmosphere in the studio was easy-going with both bands showing each other a lot of mutual respect.

Oasis even made a rough recording of a Real People song entitled 'Heaven Knows', and a lot of the sessions would veer into a party mode.

'I still had a publishing deal at the time,' Tony recalls, 'so we had money to get the beers in, gin and tonics, all that stuff, plus there was a lot of good coke around at that time as well.'

When the band weren't recording, they would retire upstairs where there was a pool table and a stereo. Captain Beefheart and Beatles' music was the order of the day.

'Slade as well,' Tony recalls, "cos our drummer, at the time, Tony Hodgson, he's got the best musical taste in the world, and he was going through his Slade period where he was digging out all these Slade records, and that's basically what we were listening to at the time.'

The boys would engage in endless argumentative banter about music and football. It amused Oasis no end how talkative their Liverpool allies were, especially when Tony and Chris introduced them to their older cousin Digsy, 'the funniest man in the world'. Digsy also played in a group called, and this is indicative of his humour, Smaller.

As for Noel and Liam, Tony saw little of their argumentative side, except that which is common to all brothers.

'It's complete shite,' he stresses, 'it's what the media want it to be. It makes it more interesting. I'm in a band with me own brother and we talk to each other like dogs, but that's the way you are, because you're brothers. I don't talk to anyone else like that.'

The songs Oasis recorded over these three months included 'Alive', 'Cloudburst', 'Do Yer Wanna Be A Spaceman', 'Strange Thing', 'Bring It On Down', 'Whatever', 'Married With Children', 'Fade Away', 'Rock 'n' Roll Star' and 'Columbia'.

All of the songs bar 'Strange Thing', are now available and very little has been changed on the finished recorded versions. The original recording of 'Rock 'n' Roll Star' boasts a slightly different intro and is played at a slower pace than that on the *Definitely Maybe* album. Liam has yet to come up with his unique phrasing. He sings 'sunshine' in a completely straightforward manner, although it's clear that his voice is starting to find its now unique sound.

On 'Bring It On Down' Guigsy's bass is to the forefront on the intro, sounding like John Entwhistle's playing on The Who's

'Pinball Wizard'. Liam's vocal is also treated in a much heavier fashion, filtered through for a megaphone effect.

'Columbia' has a different intro altogether and ends with a disembodied voice, sampled from the radio and deliberately slowed down, intoning things like, 'Take away the melody from your song . . . like an ever-flowing stream.' It's then replaced by what sounds like a Hare Krishna chant.

It was this song that would later cause some controversy. According to Griffiths, Noel had the chord structure for 'Columbia', an early example of his ability to bridge the gap between rock guitars and a dance music element. But he had no melody or lyrics. One night, Chris Griffiths sang a melody over it which began with the words, 'There we were / Now here we are / All this confusion / Nothing's the same to me.'

'That was the thing that started it off,' Griffiths recalls. 'And it was Liam who wrote the chorus, "I can't tell you the way I feel / Because the way I feel is oh so new to me," and it's like, Liam wrote that.

'Then I came up with some shite words for the third verse and Noel went fuck off and wrote something well better.'

A collaboration then, yet when the song was released, Noel Gallagher was the only name credited. Similarly, the fact that the eight-track demo of 'Alive' ended up on the B-side of the band's second single, 'Shakermaker', was also a contentious point.

'That kind of pissed us off a little bit, the fact that three months of our work was getting put out and Creation Records are making loads of money out of it. But see, we're not arsed. If we had wanted to sue Oasis we would have already done it. We don't want to come across as the dickheads of the music business jumping on the Oasis bandwagon, because as far as I'm concerned I'm in a boss group myself.

'I'm just amazed I was a part of it because the thing is we were always talking about us both being successful and, you know, let's all buy a studio on an island and go there. It's the shite you talk when you're all off your heads.'

It was during this period, late March 1993 to June 1993, that Oasis played twice in Liverpool. Once at Le Bateau and once at the Krazy House. At the first gig Smaller, Digsy's band, played support and about twenty people showed up.

'But nearly everyone there,' Griffiths recalls, 'was in bands from Liverpool, and me and our kid are going, "They're boss, aren't they?" And they're all laughing, going, "They're fucking Mancs." We've never ever been into that Liverpool versus Manchester thing. It's all shite, that.'

When Oasis had finished, Liam was spotted by some bouncers smoking a spliff. The bouncers went to throw him out. Liam, as ever, kicked off and Tony had to intervene to keep him in the club.

'Luckily enough, I knew the manager but I nearly ended up getting a fucking hiding.'

In April, the band played their Krazy House gig and then in May they appeared at the Boardwalk again, their sixth appearance there. Later on that month, Sister Lovers told them they had a gig booked at a place in Glasgow, King Tut's, supporting a Creation band called 18 Wheeler.

'We'll have that one,' Oasis said.

It was a girl that sent Alan McGee scurrying over to King Tut's club in Glasgow on the night of 31 May 1993. A girl. He wasn't acting on a tip-off about an explosive new group and he certainly didn't have business on his mind. Alan McGee went to King Tut's hoping to get laid.

McGee was in the middle of one of his regular break-ups with his then girlfriend Linda. The night before he had told his sister, Susan, about the bust-up and she had responded by saying, 'Come down to King Tut's, I'll be with a couple of mates, one of them is dead nice and she hasnae got a boyfriend.'

McGee had been unsure about going to King Tut's that night. He was hungover from the previous night's excesses, but he felt obliged to pop in as one of his bands, 18 Wheeler, were playing. When the chance of meeting a girl suddenly occurred, his mind was made up for him.

'I was such a cantankerous git in those days,' McGee says with a laugh, 'so I bowled in pissed, hoping basically to pull one of my sister's mates. Sure enough, the girl didn't show up.'

McGee actually arrived two hours earlier than he should have done. He naturally thought that all the bands on the bill would be playing during pub hours. He didn't realise that King Tut's had been granted a late licence. If he had known that, he would have arrived two hours later and missed the first act.

When McGee walked in his attention was instantly grabbed by a tall, young Mancunian wearing an Adidas top and sporting an eye-catching haircut.

'And I remember turning round in this pub and the minute I saw him I thought, he looks like Paul Weller, the kid looks like a fucking star. And that was Liam.'

At first, McGee thought Liam was part of the Manchester gang who were present. They had travelled up with Oasis and were making a lot of noise and acting in a threatening manner.

They had been put in this aggressive mood by the harassed owner of the club. He thought he was putting on three bands that night. Instead he had got four.

'Who are you?' he asked the gang of about fourteen Mancunians who had tumbled out of two hire vans bearing guitars and equipment.

'We're Oasis, mate,' Liam told him, 'and we're playing here tonight.'

'But I haven't booked you.'

'Tough shit, we're here, that's it.'

And then it was pointed out that although the promoter had bouncers on the door, this firm outnumbered them four to one and as they had just travelled for hours in a van they had paid for, they would be very, very annoyed if the band didn't play. *Capiche*?

The promoter took one look at the band and their mates and acquiesced. Oasis set up their equipment.

Meanwhile, McGee climbed the stairs of the pub to get a better view of the first band on. He was amazed when he saw Liam walk on-stage. He assumed he was part of the Manchester fan contingent. Probably one of their drug dealers.

Oasis went into 'Rock 'n' Roll Star', 'Bring It On Down', 'Up In The Sky', and finished with 'I Am The Walrus'. Fifteen minutes worth of work, if that.

Liam, who McGee described that night as 'absolutely charismatic and confrontational', held the mike in his hand as there was no mike stand. And because the stage was so small, Guigsy for the first and last time, played just behind and to the left-hand side of Noel who always stands centre right.

McGee watched the gig with an excitement he hadn't experienced in years. He absolutely swears 'that I knew I was going to sign them within two songs.'

But he didn't go backstage waving his cheque book in the air. He waited patiently for them to appear in the bar. When they emerged, he went up to Noel and introduced himself. Noel did a little double-take. He remembered McGee from his days of raving at Spectrum in London's Charing Cross. And, of course, he knew all about Creation Records. But this character standing in front of him looked nothing like the McGee from four years ago.

'Noel said to me, "The last time I saw you, you had tons of hair and sunglasses on", which was right because I thought I was Malcolm McLaren up until 1989. And then I said, "I want to sign you", and he goes "Do you want to hear a tape?" And I went, "No, you're real. I'll sign you."'

Even so, Noel still gave McGee a demo tape. The cover of the cassette was a picture of a swirling Union Jack going down a plug. It had been designed, from an idea by Noel Gallagher by Tony French, a friend.

'But he forgot to put the plug-hole in the middle of the flag,' Noel recalls, 'so we had to explain it to everyone.'

On the back of the tape was a number to call and a note to ask for Paul, Noel's older brother.

McGee promised to get in touch. Noel said goodbye, went back and told the rest of the band about the offer. He said that McGee seemed quite out of it so the news was taken by all with a pinch of salt, and then they travelled back to Manchester.

The next day, Noel was still unsure about McGee's offer. He couldn't work out if the guy was taking the piss or was for real.

The only person he could think to get advice from was the Inspirals' old manager, Anthony Bodgiano, whom everyone in town had nicknamed Scamiano.

'What's McGee like?' Noel asked him. 'I mean, if he makes an offer is he serious or is he just off his head?'

Bodgiano replied, 'If he says he wants to do it, he's probably serious.' Then he started enquiring about the vacant managerial slot within the Oasis team. Noel told him he'd get back to him on that matter.

Noel then phoned Creation and made an appointment to see McGee the following Thursday. The fact that McGee had agreed to see him was positive, even if Noel was still in the dark about the Creation boss's real feelings.

What he didn't know was that as Oasis had travelled home that night, McGee had staggered back to his Glasgow hotel, the Lorne on Sauciehall Street, and immediately got on the phone to every significant Creation employee to tell them he had just discovered the band of the decade.

One person he called was Johnny Hopkins, the Creation press officer. 'We were used to McGee's mad phonecalls,' he explains, 'but this time was different. You could tell he had seen something really special.'

Another call was placed to Tim Abbot, the marketing manager.

Abbot had come from a marketing background. He had set up his own marketing consultancy in the 1980s and worked on accounts with the likes of Levi's and Pernod. In 1988 he necked his first Ecstasy pill. In 1989 his business went down the drain. So he and a friend went travelling round Thailand and the Philippines.

On his return to Britain, Abbot started a club in the Midlands called the Better Way, which put on bands. One night McGee came up to see the Manic Street Preachers, Saint Etienne and East Village play there.

He brought with him his friend Bobby Gillespie and introduced himself to Abbot. They chatted during the soundcheck. The upshot was that at the end of the night they were all to be found at Abbot's house, E'd up and playing records until dawn.

Abbot's collection reflected his youth. There was plenty of Northern Soul, masses of other related black music with classic rock albums mixed in. McGee was impressed. He liked a man with a big record collection.

When he met Abbot again, six months later in Birmingham, McGee offered him some part-time work. Within a year, Tim Abbot was managing director of Creation Records, and his brother Chris was employed by the label as well.

'I got this phonecall from Alan absolutely arseholed in Glasgow,' Abbot fondly recalls. 'It was in the middle of the night and he was going, "I've just seen this fucking amazing band, it will turn the company round. This is the band I've always been looking for. It's The Sex Pistols crossed with The Small Faces. They're like mad Mancs, and trust Creation to sign a band from Manchester", which at the time was the most unfashionable city, A&R wise.'

On 3 June 1993, Noel, Liam and Bonehead travelled down to

London and made their way by taxi to 8 Westgate Street, Hackney, home of Creation Records. Press officer Johnny Hopkins remembers looking up and seeing three-fifths of Oasis for the first time.

'You were just drawn to them,' he recalls, 'they just had this massive presence which you couldn't ignore. Most other people who come in just blend in, but they were magnetic.'

While waiting to see McGee, Noel quickly studied all the pictures that the Creation boss had pinned to the office walls.

He saw artists that he liked, The Faces, Paul Weller. But there were others, such as Big Star, even Lynyrd Skynyrd whom he didn't have a clue about. Not that Noel would ever let a fact like that stand in his way.

Noel went down to McGee's office and the two started talking about musical likes. Noel kicked off by telling him that he was a huge fan of Big Star.

'And he told me all about the bands that I liked and because he was so into music, I was saying to him, "You're the first person since Bobby Gillespie that's totally tuned into my musical taste."' McGee now gives the laugh of someone who knows he's been totally had.

'Up until about six months ago I thought I'd found the ultimate musical soul brother.'

Noel and Liam then went and met the other employees. Downstairs, in what Abbot refers to as the 'bunker', there was a room whose walls had been plastered with pictures of various celebrities.

'It was like an A-to-Z of our minds,' Abbot explains. 'Everybody from Tommy Cooper next to George Best, Rod Stewart next to Kate Moss, Wilson Pickett next to Brian Wilson, all blue-tac'd to the walls. The carpet was sodden with booze, stank of fucking booze and it was a fucking shithole, grade A.'

It was here that the Abbots and the Gallaghers hit it off. Chris spoke mainly to Liam (indeed, they would holiday together later on in Portugal), while Tim, Alan and Noel chatted and chatted, Bonehead occasionally joining in.

For their part, Alan and Tim didn't try to sell Creation to Oasis. Instead they spoke about clubs, music, football (Abbot is a United supporter), all the things that motivated them.

At some point, it was pointed out to Noel that he should think hard about getting a manager. Bodgiano was an option but so too was Johnny Marr's manager, Marcus Russell. Noel had passed on an Oasis tape to Marr's brother, Ian.

'You have to understand,' Marr says, 'that I get loads of tapes so when my brother gave me that Oasis tape, I didn't play it for at least two weeks. My brother kept badgering me about it. Finally, I played it and it was great. I just thought it was brilliant. Anyway, not long after I was driving through town with my brother and he went, "Look, there's that guy from Oasis", and it was Noel walking down the street.

'So we pulled over and went and had a drink with him. Then I went to see them in Manchester University with Marcus.'

Marcus Russell had been astonished by Oasis's performance that night.

'Well, I thought they were fucking wonderful,' he enthuses, 'I mean, I thought they were a breath of fresh air. Honestly. But I didn't think there and then, I'm going to manage these, because I didn't know them.

'I got introduced by Andrew Berry to Noel's girlfriend during the gig and she said, "Oh, you're Marcus", and told me that the band didn't know that I was coming to see them. I told her, "It's no big deal, I'm just in town but I thought the music was a breath of fresh air because it reminded me of all the things that I've loved in the last twenty years."'

Oasis's set that night included 'Digsy's Dinner', 'Fade Away', 'Up In The Sky', 'I Am The Walrus', and the public premiere of 'Live Forever'.

On the way back from the gig, which took place in a small student union bar called the Hop and Grape (Marr and Marcus didn't stay to see Dodgy because of the attention Marr was starting to get from the crowd), Marr asked Marcus what he thought of the band.

'I thought they were really good,' Marcus replied, playing it safe. There was a silence. Then Marr turned to his manager again.

'You're going to manage them, aren't you?'

Marcus asked, 'Why do you say that?'

Marr replied, 'Because normally you immediately dismiss everything.'

'And that,' Marcus says, 'is when I first started thinking seriously about it.'

Meanwhile, as their future manager drove back to London,

Oasis had a problem on their hands concerning their equipment. Guigsy's car wasn't starting, and that meant they had to load his gear on to Bonehead's van. A huge speaker cabinet was left standing out on the street.

Someone would have to wheel it back to the Boardwalk, Noel pointed out. It's far too big to get into a cab and by the way, boys, it certainly ain't going to be me.

They groaned. When it came to packing all the gear away, Noel always played foreman.

Guigsy recalls, 'We'd be breaking all the gear down and he'd be there winding up leads or something going, "You want to do it like this", but he'd never get on it. Then he'd go, "Guigsy, can you give us the keys to the van, I'll go and open it up."

'And he'd be dead industrious 'cos he would grab something light and you'd think, well, he's a professional with the Inspirals, isn't he?

'Then he'd get in the van with all these leads and say, "I'll stay here and you pass everything up to me." And you'd be going up and down the stairs with all the amps and instruments. It took us months to cotton on.'

Who then to deal with this huge cabinet standing idly outside the Hop and Grape? Ten minutes later, passers by were intrigued to see Liam and Guigsy in the middle of the road, pushing a huge cabinet.

'You couldn't put it on the pavement,' Guigsy recalls, "'cos the wheels were those little round plastic ones and all the little paving stones would make it jump too much and you'd fuck up all the connections. So we had to push it on the road, like a pair of fucking dustbin men and we nearly got run over by two buses.'

'And there were all these cars,' Liam recalls, 'going, beep, beep, beep and we're going, "Fuck off," and all these people are watching us. But it had to be done.'

Of more importance to Noel was what Marr's manager, Marcus, had thought of the gig. Louise had told Noel that Marcus was present but he had quickly disappeared. What did that mean? Noel thought. That he wasn't impressed? Is that why he didn't come backstage?

The next day, Noel called him up at Ignition to find out. Yes, Marcus reassured him, I was impressed, very impressed. 'Do you want to have a chat about things?' Noel wanted to know. 'Sure,' Marcus replied.

'Well what are you doing now?' Noel asked.

Marcus gave out a small laugh. 'But you're in Manchester, aren't you?'

'Yes,' came the reply, 'but we do have trains up here, you know.'

Five hours later, Noel Gallagher and Marcus Russell sat talking in a café near the Ignition offices in London's West End.

Marcus told him what he thought about Oasis, how he loved them playing 'Walrus', and that the other songs were ace. Plus, he added, your singer looks fucking cool, a real star in fact.

Noel replied by telling him how he was sick to the back teeth by all these crappy bands like Suede and REM making it big, and here they were, a great band, with nothing to show for it.

'He was just explaining his vision,' Marcus says, 'and I bought it hook line and sinker. He was just totally and utterly faultless. I don't know what it was but I was totally convinced. At the end of the conversation, I was like, I'm there.

'He said, "Well do we get a contract?" I said, "No, I don't do contracts, but I want to be your manager and if that's fine by you, we'll shake hands."'

Noel put out his right hand and Marcus Russell shook it. He was now manager of the best new band in the country.

'What about the rest of the guys?' Marcus asked.

'They'll be fine,' Noel replied. 'Don't worry, I'll go back and tell them.'

Marcus said, 'I should come up and meet them.'

'I'll fix it up,' Noel promised. 'I'll call you tomorrow.'

Then musician and manager went their separate ways.

'And then it struck me when I got home,' Marcus recalls with wry amazement. 'I had just taken on a band and I haven't even got a tape of them. I've seen five songs live, met this geezer, and that was it. I was their manager.'

The Oasis magic, in the area.

Noel went back and told the band about Marcus. Then he sent one of the demo tapes of the Liverpool sessions down to him. The day after he phoned up and arranged for Marcus to meet the band in the City Inn pub, near to the Hacienda.

By the time Marcus got to that meeting he was utterly convinced that he had something truly special on his hands.

'I just fell in love with that tape,' he enthuses. 'After about a week of playing the tape, I started thinking, this looks like being the band I've been dreaming of ever since I started in the business.

'A rock 'n' roll band in the good old British tradition with great songs, who are up for it and for whom hard work is a piece of piss. They just had all those ingredients.'

All of Oasis, bar Tony McCarroll, were present at this meeting. There was a very good reason for the drummer's absence. The band wanted him out. According to them, the drummer hadn't progressed musically. When he first joined, he was easily the most proficient. Now he had been overtaken.

That was bad enough, but worse still was that none of the band got on with him. They just couldn't fathom it out. He seemed to have no interests, no overriding passions to dominate his life. To the Oasis way of thinking, he just wasn't right.

It showed, Liam says, in his general behaviour. 'I never,' the singer asserts, 'saw him clean his kit once, change the skins or talk about this drummer's cool or this drummer's great. He was coming along with these pieces of paper and I was like, "You don't need them. Just practise every day, that's how you get good. That's what I do."

'I sing every day. I'm always singing, Noel's always playing his guitar, Guigsy's always fiddling with the bass, Bonehead's the same. There's no point getting a piece of paper out 'cos the thing that makes a good drummer is trying things out, and the reason you can't do it is because you haven't got any records. Sit down and play The Who, The Stones, The Beatles, listen to them because that's where it comes from, not a piece of paper.'

Guigsy, who is the first to admit that his bass playing skills are not above the norm, says, 'For the first six months of rehearsals I always thought it was me fucking up. Then I realised that it was him. He just didn't progress.'

So, the band told Marcus, we want him out. Not a good idea, their manager told them. You've got a string of gigs coming up, you're about to sign a deal and go in the studio; if you sack him now you're going to lose three months while you find someone more compatible.

The thought of having to put everything on hold at a time when the band was so eager to get going, deterred them from their plan. Unlike Pete Best, the Beatles' drummer who was sacked just after the group signed to EMI, McCarroll was allowed to remain. For the time being.

Marcus then outlined his vision of the band's future.

First off, they were going to hit the road and play every flea-pit available. Live work would be the order of the day. There was no better way for building up a fan base that would remain totally committed to the band.

They would deliberately avoid London for the time being and there would be no hype surrounding the band. It would all be word of mouth, the best form of publicity there is.

The band eagerly agreed. They loved playing live and to be able to go on the road and spread the word to every boy and girl truly excited them. Especially Noel and Liam. For them, standing on a stage playing music to an appreciative crowd gave you the best feeling in the world. Nothing can touch it. Nothing, not even drugs. On-stage is where the Gallagher brothers express themselves emotionally and in doing so find a very real kind of happiness.

'The best thing,' Liam explains, 'is the crowd relating to it. That is the best thing. When I'm on-stage, that is me. You could shoot me thirty-five times and I won't feel it 'cos up there no one can touch me.'

'But let's not,' Marcus insisted, 'get obsessed with cracking Britain. As far as I'm concerned, with these songs and your attitude, there's no reason why Oasis shouldn't be successful worldwide. No reason whatsoever. Again, we'll go and play everywhere. Yes, success in Britain does tend to give you a leg up, especially in Europe, but it's not the be all and end all. Never forget that.' Then he told them about his experience with Latin Quarter.

'As for the Creation deal, I'll go and see Alan McGee as soon as possible and sound him out.'

Noel then butted in. 'What's important,' he told Marcus, 'is that we retain complete artistic control. I'm not having anyone, and that's anyone, telling Oasis what to do. That's down to me and the band. If it means we take less money, then arsed. If we do things our way we're going to make shitloads anyway.'

'Fine,' Marcus said, 'I totally agree with you.'

The band had listened carefully to Marcus and they liked him. He was straight'forward, down to earth, he had good ideas and he obviously believed in them. But what really swung it was when he outlined his deal with the group. No contract, I take 20%, here's my hand, if you shake it we have a deal.

'Which is what I wanted,' Liam recalls. 'None of that negotiation shit. I want to be straight with everyone. We're a top band, we make great music. You get your bit, we'll get our bit. But I tell ya, if anyone ever ripped us off, I'd do them, and I'd do it personally.'

Marcus may have only known the group a couple of hours but just by the obvious gang mentality they displayed, he knew enough to know that any kind of back'handed behaviour would undoubtedly place his general well-being in extreme danger.

No, what Marcus had in mind, was something different. Oasis had dedicated themselves to becoming a group that would be remembered years down the line for their musical excellence and ability.

Similarly, Marcus Russell's main ambition was to emulate his all-time managerial role model, Peter Grant, who had steered Led Zeppelin to world-wide domination in the 1970s. So when Marcus walked away from that first meeting with Oasis, he pinched himself hard.

He had just found the band with which to realise his ambitions.

On Tuesday 8 June 1993 Alan McGee met Noel Gallagher at Euston station and they went for an Indian meal. The first thing McGee did was to order a triple Jack Daniels and coke.

'I think that impressed Noel,' he says.

On the Thursday, McGee flew out to Memphis to oversee the Primal Scream recording sessions and then, three weeks later, on Friday 2 July, at eleven in the morning, he met Marcus Russell for the very first time.

The meeting took place in McGee's main office at Creation. Naturally, he was extremely keen to get negotiations underway. He knew that word of this phenomenal new group was starting to spread around the record companies. Marcus had already received firm offers from EMI, Polydor, MCA and Island Records.

But the keenest competitors by far were Andy Macdonald at Go Discs, and Malcolm Dunbar at U2's record company, Mother Records. Dunbar had told Marcus that whatever money McGee offered, he would double it straightaway.

Marcus resisted all offers. He and Oasis had already decided on Creation as the best home for them. Marcus's job now was to see if they were capable of breaking a band worldwide. If not, then and only then, would he consider talking to other companies.

When the meeting finished, McGee saw Marcus out of the building and then returned to his office. The phone rang. It was Noel, calling from Manchester.

'What's my manager like?' he wanted to know.

'Easily the best manager I've ever dealt with,' McGee replied.

It was true. McGee had been totally impressed by Marcus's thoroughness and determination. The main example of this was when McGee told Marcus that he wanted to sign Oasis for the world, not just the UK. But Marcus had done his homework.

'I'm not happy with Creation's performance world-wide,' he told McGee. 'I'm perfectly happy for the band to be on Creation Records in the United Kingdom but not elsewhere.'

McGee agreed that the companies who licenced his records outside of the UK had yet to deliver. He asked Marcus for a month or so to try and change the deals he had struck. 'I'll see if I can come up with something acceptable for you.'

'Look,' Marcus stressed. 'we want to sign with you and I give you my word that we won't talk to anyone. But you have to sort your end out.'

The two met again on Friday 17 July, this time with Garry Blackburn of Anglo Plugging present. He handled TV and radio exposure for all Creation acts.

McGee played Blackburn the demo tape. After it had finished, McGee said to the plugger, 'Garry, imagine you are playing at Wembley in a cup final. It is the eighty-ninth minute and it's nil-nil. You have got the ball and you have gone through, dribbled round the keeper and now all that is between you and victory is an empty goal. Garry, all you have to do is kick that ball into the net, and that ball right now is Oasis.'

It was melodramatic, highly theatrical but totally unnecessary. Blackburn had been totally convinced by the music.

For his part, Marcus liked McGee. He found McGee's knowledge and passion for music a real tonic.

'Here's a guy,' Marcus recalls, 'who actually loves Rod Stewart and The Faces, and I hadn't found anyone who'd had the guts to say so at that particular time.'

In July Oasis played just two gigs. One at the Boardwalk and then one at Le Bateau in Liverpool. This left most of August free, which is when Noel and Marcus travelled to New York to inspect various record companies.

At a meeting with a major A&R man, who shall remain nameless, they played him 'Digsy's Dinner', 'Sad Song', and 'Live Forever'.

'You guys are from Manchester?' he enquired. 'Well, it sure don't sound anything like Jesus Jones to me.'

This was a Manchester band that had just gained some popularity in the States. It wasn't the kind of analysis or show of support that either Noel or Marcus wanted to hear.

During their stay they also visited Epic Records, who had signed Pearl Jam. The band were now one of the biggest attractions in America. Marcus was impressed by the label's attitude and strategy. 'Long-term planning,' he explains, 'that's how they did it.'

On Marcus and Noel's return to the UK Oasis prepared for a showcase gig at Manchester's Canal Bar as part of the In The City season. Noel also gave McGee a tape of 'Live Forever'. The Creation boss took it on holiday with him to Honolulu.

On 9 August 1993 McGee called up Noel from the beach he was sunbathing on. 'Noel,' he enthused, 'this track, "Live Forever", it's absolutely amazing. It's a classic.'

Noel stood in his Manchester flat with two quid in his pocket on a miserable rainy afternoon listening to a man in sun-drenched Honolulu telling him that his song was great.

There is something very, very wrong here, Noel thought to himself.

Actually, there was something awry in Noel's life but it was nothing to do with music. It concerned Louise. The relationship was breaking down and Noel wanted out.

'It was funny,' Bonehead said, 'you'd go round to pick Noel up to go rehearsing, and Louise would turn up just as we were leaving with the shopping. They'd just kind of nod to each other and then go their separate ways.'

One night they had had an argument and Louise told Noel that the band he was in was crap and the music he wrote was shite. Noel picked that line up straightaway.

In any case, Noel wouldn't have been totally focused on his relationship. His band was obviously on the way. If Creation didn't get them then someone else would, that was for certain. Soon, he would be making his first album.

Better than that, one of his all-time heroes, Johnny Marr, was now making some very encouraging noises about Oasis, and that was sweet sweet music to Noel's ears. To get recognition from one of your peers, let alone someone you truly respect, can only serve to boost your self-confidence sky high.

When he and Marr had first met in May 1993 they talked about The Smiths, music, Manchester. Then the talk, as it had to, moved on to guitars. Noel told Johnny about a shop he knew about in Doncaster where they sold rare guitars. Marr had never heard of the shop.

'Fuck it, why don't we go there tomorrow?' Marr suggested, an invitation that Noel was never likely to turn down.

At the time, Marr was working with an engineer called Owen Morris and it was these three who got into a car and drove over to Doncaster. On the way, Marr offered Noel a spliff but Noel refused. He explained that his doctor had told him that his low blood pressure made marijuana bad for him.

'I have to stick to chemicals,' Noel explained with a laugh.

Marr asked him if he was now experiencing more vivid dreams.

'There's a medical term for it,' Marr explained, 'it's called something like daytura dream deferred. When you come off the spliff, you get your dreams back.'

Instantly, Noel's radar switched on. 'That's a top song title,' he exclaimed. 'Mind if I have it?'

The next day, Noel wrote a song called 'Daytura Dream Deferred'. At the shop, Marr, in front of Noel, who was still signing on, spent some £9,000 on guitars that according to Owen, 'He really didn't need, he was just showing off.'

But what's interesting here is Noel's reaction to Marr's extravagance. It wasn't one of jealousy or distaste. He simply thought to himself, one day that's going to be me. And he was right.

Marr now recalls meeting Liam for the first time.

'I went round to Noel's flat in India House,' he says, 'and he and Louise had this big fish tank with all these different kinds of fish in it. I didn't realise Liam was there until I shouted over to Noel in the sitting room, "What are these ones called?" Then I heard a voice behind me say, "Fish." That was Liam. Of course, as soon as I saw him, I just went . . .'

You would have thought then that around this period, Noel would have been totally fixated on his début album, planning every second of the music, thinking about the cover, what image to use, etc. Not so. That job was already completed.

Noel already had *Definitely Maybe* worked out in his mind. He was now planning the second album.

The proof of this is when he moved out of India House, stayed with Bonehead for a while and then moved down to Chiswick, London, to live in a flat that Ignition had found for him, opposite Eden Recording Studios.

Noel's main friends in London were the Abbots, and both Tim and Chris distinctly remember going round to see the song-writer, and Noel picking up an exercise book, showing them pages of lyrics and casually saying, 'That's the second album. I've got the music and everything.'

Prior to Noel's move to London, Oasis still didn't have a record contract. McGee had been unable to change his foreign licensees. He phoned Marcus and they met again. There had to be a solution to the problem and through their many discussions it finally arrived.

Marcus told McGee that out of all the companies he had visited in the States, Epic had caught his eye. Then it occurred to the pair of them that as Creation were licensed to Sony in the UK, why not let Oasis sign direct to Sony and let Creation licence the records. That way Creation would basically be their UK label but Epic could handle them worldwide.

It was the answer both McGee and Marcus had been looking for. A contract was drawn up and on Friday 22 October 1993 Oasis went to McGee's office and signed to Creation Records.

They were given a £40,000 advance, for which the band were obliged to supply Creation Records, via Sony, with six studio albums. Live albums or compilations didn't count.

The band all put their signatures on the contract. Oasis now had a record deal. To celebrate, they went to the Break For The

Border restaurant next to the London Palladium. Much alcohol was imbibed, and some of the group tried to play the bar band's instruments that were left on the stage.

A bouncer intervened and a very drunk Johnny Hopkins, who weighs about eight stone and measures about five foot eight in height, offered the bouncer outside for a fight.

Finally, Noel went off to 'see some girl', and the rest of the band headed down to the Falcon pub in Camden to see the band Whiteout, who they already knew.

McGee resisted that option and went to the Sabresonic club in Farringdon where Andrew Weatherall was DJing. Later on in the club, he bumped into Noel. Surprisingly, the guitarist was in a furious mood.

'What's the matter?' McGee asked. Noel replied that at The Falcon, Liam, Bonehead and McCarroll had got on-stage with Whiteout.

'This is my band,' Noel raged, 'and they shouldn't do shit like that. You wait until I see them.'

It really pissed Noel off, Oasis on stage with a second-rate band. Didn't his band members have any fucking pride in themselves?

'Come on,' McGee said. 'Let's go back to my place and play some records.'

At McGee's house there was an old battered acoustic guitar in the corner. At seven in the morning, Noel reached over, picked it up and played Alan McGee a song he had written years ago. It was called 'Rockin' Chair'.

A week later Marcus and McGee met up again with Garry Blackburn of Anglo Plugging to hammer out a strategy for the band's entry into the music world.

Blackburn already had good news. Steve Lamacq, a Radio One DJ, had booked the band for a session to be recorded on Wednesday 22 December and broadcast on 4 January. Oasis would be heard by millions.

What McGee and Marcus now wanted to do was to issue a white label of one of Oasis's strongest tracks, 'Columbia', to all radio stations round about the same time as the recording of the Radio One session.

The song wouldn't be available in the shops. It would only be heard on radio. It was a good choice of song to introduce the world to Oasis. 'Columbia' boasted a pile-driving rhythm, stinging guitar riffs from Noel, a contained vocal from Liam, catchy backing vocals, druggy lyrics, and managed to combine an obvious rock feel with a solid dance-orientated backbeat. Plus the title paid deliberate homage to the country that is notoriously known for its heavy cocaine production.

On 23 November 1993, three weeks after this decision was taken (and obviously with Noel's blessing as nothing could ever get down without his say-so), McGee went to see Blair McDonnell, the head of Sony Publishing, who wasn't convinced by McGee's new signing.

McGee had played McDonnell the Oasis tape in August. His response? Not interested. Manchester was three years ago. Forget it.

Now McGee was going in to threaten him. Get Oasis's publishing rights or let me out of our Sony distribution deal. McGee was anxious to secure the publishing deal as it would work in the same way as the recording deal, and he and Sony would become their publishers.

McDonnell was now a bit more interested but it would take another five months of McGee's persistence and haggling before Noel Gallagher, in April 1994, signed to Sony publishing for £125,000. It touched McGee that Noel chose Sony.

'He had better offers on the table,' McGee recalls, 'but Noel went with Sony I think because he knew that I and my partner, Dick Green, got a percentage.'

But such business details sometimes eluded Noel, especially after a session with a bottle of Jack Daniels. McGee remembers leaving Noel's flat in Camden early one morning and the songwriter taking him aside. 'Look Alan, I trust you, so for fuck's sake don't tell my publishers. But here's a load of new songs I've been working on.'

McGee took the tape and then looked Noel straight in the eye and shook his head sadly.

'Noel,' he said, 'for fuck's sake, I am your publisher.'

On 11 September 1993 Oasis played one of their most memorable gigs. It took place at the Duchess of York pub in Leeds. They will never forget it. There was no one present. Well, there was a couple sat in one of the corners. But then they got into a terrible argument and left. So Oasis played to the owner and the barmaid.

'We couldn't decide whether to do an encore or not,' Noel said. 'I mean I thought the crowd didn't deserve it to be honest with you.'

Still, it was a good warm-up for their In The City appearance three days later. But this time the buzz was about a group called Whiteout, and despite Garry Blackburn telling everyone he knew to check Oasis, the band went unnoticed despite receiving their first mention in the music press, a very encouraging *NME* review by Emma Morgan of their gig in late July at the Boardwalk.

'Shout to the rooftops and dance in the streets,' her copy began. 'Creation have not gone mad . . . Oasis are a genuinely fine guitar-propelled pop band.'

Later in the review she makes a reference to the undoubted Stone Roses' influence, and mistakes 'Digsy's Dinner' for something called 'Stray Dogs'. But there is no doubting her enthusiasm.

'Oasis,' she concluded, 'really are the shoots of vitality in a barren pop band.' Not bad for your first-ever mention in the UK music press.

Their Canal Bar show was also reviewed by Paul Mathur at *Melody Maker*. He writes that there were less than one hundred people present, but, 'Oasis are magnificent'. He refers to their obvious influences – The Stone Roses, The Faces, The Happy Mondays, The Beatles, The Sex Pistols – draws attention to 'Live Forever' ('an anthemic reiteration of the beautifully arrogant power of youth'), and concludes with the sentence, 'Oasis have got me. You're next and you'll love it.'

Along with this press coverage, Oasis also made their national radio début at this time, and appeared in front of TV cameras, all on the same day. Radio 5 had a weekly show called *Hit The North* which was presented by Mark Radcliffe and Marc Riley, formerly of The Fall.

During the In The City week they had elected to showcase the most promising bands that were playing in Manchester. Riley was a friend of Caroline Ellery, who managed the group Intastella. It was she who urged him to put Oasis on.

At first, Marcus Russell was reluctant for the band to be previewed at such an early stage, but they soon persuaded him otherwise.

That day they came in and played 'Bring It On Down', 'Digsy Dinner' and 'Cigarettes and Alcohol'. Peter Hook, the New Order bassist was co-hosting the show with Riley.

The band were downstairs in the basement and after they had finished 'Bring It On Down', Riley commented to Noel on the similarity between his guitar sound and the late Mick Ronson's, who was best known through his work with David Bowie.

Noel replied that they had actually dug up Mick Ronson from his grave but the smell was awful. Nearly as bad as that coming from Peter Hook's leather trousers.

'They were so lippy and arrogant,' Riley recalls, 'but it was great to have them on.'

Directly after the show the band then travelled over to Leeds to perform two songs for a local TV show called, *Something For The Weekend*. In this respect, the band had been helped no end by the help of two people who Noel had met and who also lived in India House. Liam Walsh and Alison Martin worked for a plugging company called Red Alert. Their aim was to help young bands get radio and TV exposure and in the band's early days they did as much as they could, such as securing them their first appearance in front of the cameras.

The press was also starting to pick up now.

In the 2 October edition of *Melody Maker* Oasis received another mention. In an article entitled 'State of the Nation' John Robb tipped Oasis as the band of the future.

On 7 October they supported Liz Phair at Manchester University and the *NME* reported (9 October) that she was heard to be complaining that Oasis spoke like 'New York drug addicts'.

A week later Oasis supported The Milltown Brothers at the same venue, before going off on tour with another Creation signing, The BMX Bandits.

They played Keele University on 27 October, and Sheffield University the following night. Then it was on to the Wherehouse in Derby on 1 November and the Wulfrun Hall in Wolverhampton two days later.

Still rabidly suspicious of any outsiders, the band didn't mix at all with the headlining group. On 4 November they played their first gig in London at the Powerhaus.

This was basically a showcase gig for the media, put on by Creation, and their next bit of press coverage wouldn't come until early December.

Meanwhile, Noel travelled up to Manchester to sign off. Much to his delight, he spotted Phil Saxe of the now-defunct Factory label in the same building, signing on. Revenge is so sweet, he thought to himself.

Noel also went to Louise's and gave her a cheque to cover the rent arrears. Then he returned to London and his new home.

Noel had experienced mixed thoughts about leaving Manchester. It was his hometown and he was fiercely proud of it. After all, it had, in his own words, 'given me my life view', but he also knew it was filled with people who would rather hold him back than see him succeed.

Guigsy felt the same way and he soon left town as well, taking up residence in West Hampstead, and then London's West End before moving to his current residence in North London.

But Liam and Bonehead refused to join the others. Liam found London 'too impersonal, I couldn't get my head round it', and Bonehead agreed. He had Kate to consider, too.

On 28 November Oasis supported the band CNN at Sheffield University, before regrouping in Birmingham to play support to Saint Etienne. One of their members, Bob Stanley, remembers Oasis well.

'Liam made a beeline for Sarah Cracknell, our singer, and was trying to give her lines of speed. At one time he actually locked us out of our dressing-room so he could talk to her. But Noel was friendly enough.'

No doubt Noel, although not a fan, would have admired Saint Etienne's pop, although their studied approach would have told against them. Noel is drawn primarily to passionate music.

This tour was the first time that Jeff Barrett had seen Oasis live. He was looking forward to the event. He had heard of Oasis through McGee and from his days as The Happy Mondays press officer knew Noel. Noel had also dated a Manchester friend of Jeff's, a pretty blonde named Hannah.

Jeff had now set up his own Heavenly Records label with his partner, Martin Kelly, who also managed Saint Etienne. It was Kelly who had specifically asked for Oasis to support them.

Jeff and Martin placed themselves at the front of the stage as the band came on. Within two songs they were vociferously cheering the band on. By the end of the set, they were left speechless by the band's sheer musical class, their charisma and their arrogance.

Afterwards, Martin Kelly quarrelled with Marcus over the band's payment while an elated Jeff Barrett went backstage and met Liam for the first time.

'I told him,' he recalls, 'that he reminded me of Nathan Gough who managed The Happy Mondays. Liam said, "Well, you can fuck right off," and I told him, "Well you'd better get used to my face, it's going to be right in front of you at all your gigs."'

Oasis were starting to get this now, people coming backstage and telling them how great they were. Their attitude, as ever, was, so you fucking should. You'd be a dickhead to think otherwise.

But it couldn't have escaped Noel's attention that the one song people kept on about was 'Live Forever', a point again made in Paul Mathur's follow-up piece on the band that appeared in the 4 December issue of *Melody Maker*.

Mathur had been taken by Johnny Hopkins to the band's rehearsal room in the Boardwalk. There they ran through a selection of their songs and Mathur returned to London to write lines such as, 'Songs like "Digsy's Dinner", "Whatever I", [sic] and in particular, the magnificent "Live Forever", are delivered with an assurance that belies their relative inexperience. And they seem to be averaging about a dozen new songs each week, most of which are gobsmackingly tremendous.'

Mathur also quoted Liam as saying, 'There's a lot of people who seem to be making records just to fill up the time. We want to write classics.'

(You can just imagine Noel reading that line and then turning to his brother and saying, 'Oh, *we* want to write classics, do we?')

When Jeff Barrett returned to London, he made a phone call to Stuart Bailie at the *NME*, who was then editor of the Live pages. Although Barrett had no financial or otherwise interest in the band, his love for music was so contagious, he had to spread the news.

'Stuart,' he said, 'this band Oasis? Well, everything you've heard about them is true. They're phenomenal.'

'Really?' Stuart replied. 'That's not what Johnny Cigarettes says in his review.'

Attending the same Birmingham concert, Cigarettes's opening line read, 'If Oasis didn't exist, no one would want to invent them,' and his final line said, 'But most annoying is the fact that they're too cool to have a personality or be more surprising than the dullest retro indie fops, too well versed in old records to do anything new, and evidently have few too brains to realise that any of the above is true. Sad.'

Noel insists that he was nonplussed by the review, and that is probably true. But to receive two differing reviews in the same week, one ecstatic and one totally and utterly dismissive, would have served to prepare him for the vagaries of the music press.

Such hiccups aside, there was undoubtedly a momentum starting to gather pace. *Melody Maker* writer Calvin Bush reviewed Oasis supporting Saint Etienne at the Plaza in Glasgow. After dismissing 'Shakermaker' he wrote, 'And then, Oh God, they play eight songs, seven of which are more marvellous than Lena Olin [Hollywood actress in *The Unbearable Lightness of Being*] in slinky black lingerie and a bowler hat. They are, frankly, incredible.'

The band next headlined at the Warwick University on 4 December before moving on to another tour four days later supporting The Verve, a group they actually had time for.

The Verve were led by Richard Ashcroft; Noel would later write a song, 'Cast No Shadow', with him and Paul Weller in mind. He would also make a dedication to Ashcroft on the *Morning Glory* album.

The tour lasted eight days and visited Wolverhampton, Manchester, Glasgow, Preston, Newcastle and Bradford.

The bands got on well with each other and there were several all-night sessions, playing each other CDs and tapes, taking each other's drugs and talking to the early hours.

The last Oasis date of 1993 was at the Krazy House in Liverpool, where they supported The Real People. Oasis were also back in the studio with The Real People, with a view to recording their début single. But Noel felt uneasy. He knew that bands have to make a major impact when they launch themselves upon the world.

'So I sat down,' Noel casually notes, 'and wrote "Supersonic" and "Take Me Away".'

In the studio was a large dog named Elsa. Someone had inadvertently spilled cocaine on the floor and Elsa had licked it all up. She then spent the next few days gazing at a wall. So when

215

Noel was busy scribbling out the lyrics, the image came to mind and thus, 'I know a girl called Elsa/ She's into alka seltzer.'

After the recording was finished, they then travelled down to London for the Radio One session at the Maida Vale studios. This is where their radio plugger, Dylan White, first met them.

'They were completely knackered. Noel was lying on a sofa and I asked them who the songwriter was. He said, "I am," and I said to all the band, "I'm going to shake your hands now because in the future there won't be any time."'

The songs included in their set that night were 'Bring It On Down', 'Shakermaker', 'Cigarettes and Alcohol', 'Up In The Sky' and the newly recorded 'Supersonic'.

Alan McGee was in attendance at the Maida Vale show and he remembers hearing 'Supersonic' for the first time.

'I kept thinking to myself, What's wrong with this song? It's too perfect.'

It was here that another piece of Oasis mythology was made. McGee holding a glass of Jack Daniels and coke sat down on a chair which subsequently collapsed. The drink spilt all over his white Levi's jeans.

In Noel's hands that incident became, 'Alan McGee was so excited by our performance that he poured a bottle of Jack Daniels all over himself.'

Face it, it does read a lot better than what really went down.

Thirteen

Liam Gallagher entered Mark Coyle's bedroom in the Monnow Valley Studios in South Wales and told him to get the fuck up.

'We've been waiting half an hour, you dickhead.'

Coyley made no response, just lay there sleeping. Liam went over and shook the engineer. 'Oi, Coyley, get up.'

Coyley hated being woken up. It did his head in. He was one of these people who had to get their required amount of sleep. Woe betide anyone who prevented him from doing so. He came to with a start.

'You fucking wanker,' he shouted, 'fuck off.'

'Piss off dickhead and get up.'

Coyley raised himself up, grabbed some shoes by the side of the bed and threw them at Liam. Then he grabbed the lampshade and threw that too.

'Fuck off, you madhead,' Liam shouted, ducking the objects, but a huge smile breaking out on the singer's face.

Then Coyley leapt out of bed and started running after the giggling singer. Outside, Oasis were sitting in their van waiting to travel to the Water Rats in Kings Cross, London. It would be their first proper concert in the capital, a prestigious concert people kept telling them. But they were unimpressed. To them, all gigs were important.

They already knew there was a buzz about this show. First off, 'Columbia' had brilliantly served its purpose by causing a real stir. It had received its premiere on Monday 6 December 1993 on Radio One's increasingly important and popular *Evening Session*, hosted by Steve Lamacq and Jo Whiley, and had been regularly played thereafter. It was the first time a demo had been put on Radio One's playlist.

In his report to Creation, plugger Garry Blackburn wrote, 'Reaction to this track has been fantastic, discussed at playlist meeting on Thursday 16th, now on C-list [lists devised by Radio One, A-list being those records that are most played] as of Monday 20th, and has been kept on C-list as of Monday 27th December. We will not go heavy on this . . .'

He goes on to say that Mark Cooper at BBC2's *Later* show, Gary Crowley at Carlton TV's *The Beat*, *The Word* and *The Big E* had been serviced, and that 'everyone very interested'.

Add to this, Marcus Russell's strategy of slowly building up a fan-base while deliberately avoiding a high-profile show in the capital, and it was no surprise that the gig had sold out in minutes, leaving a substantial amount of people waiting outside the Water Rats trying to get in.

No doubt the band would have had sympathy for those unable to buy tickets but, as Marcus would have pointed out, it was better at this point to play a small place and have people clamouring to get in, than to satisfy everyone straight away. Marcus would repeat this game-plan until even he, two years later, had to finally cave and book the band into the biggest gig ever seen in Britain: two nights in Knebworth Park playing to a quarter of a million people. And even then, that would still leave one and three quarters of a million people disappointed.

That night, 27 January 1994 Oasis played for forty minutes. They performed 'Columbia', 'Bring It On Down', 'Shakermaker', 'Supersonic', 'Digsy's Dinner', 'Up In The Sky', 'Live Forever', and 'I Am The Walrus'. There was no encore.

'I remember us being in this poxy dressing-room,' Bonehead says, 'and opening the door to look out and this club which had seemed so small when it was empty was now absolutely packed. It was top.'

'Nah, it was full of fucking journalists and media people,' Noel says dismissively, although the audience did also include musicians from The Verve, Saint Etienne and The Charlatans.

Two days after the show, when he should have been back in Wales, Noel was taken by McGee down to the MTV studios in London to witness Primal Scream's first live TV appearance for two years in support of their new single, 'Get Your Rocks Off'.

'It was the first time we had played live in ages,' Bobby

Gillespie points out, 'so we just kept playing because it felt so good. Then our drummer went out for something and I saw Noel there and just shouted at him, "Noel, the drums!"'

Unfortunately, as Noel strode towards the drum kit, the MTV producers decided enough was enough and turned the cameras off. Footage of the Primals and Noel performing 'Rocks' and The Rolling Stones' 'Jumping Jack Flash' was never recorded.

Noel had already met Bobby at a Paddington hotel about a month before. He was a big fan of the Primals' *Screamadelica* album and an admirer of their outspoken views. Bobby recalls Tim Abbot bringing Noel to their room, and he and Throb, the Scream's guitarist, performing various Sam Cooke and old soul tunes. Noel then asked if he could play a song.

'And he did a really beautiful version of "This Guy's In Love With You",' Gillespie recalls with obvious admiration. Eleven months later, Noel would support the Primals on their Christmas show at London's Shepherd's Bush Empire. Paul Weller would also appear with the Primals.

The reviews for the Water Rats show were unanimous in their praise, but at this point in their career, despite the gig's success, Oasis really weren't in the mood to celebrate. The reason was that the recording of their début album was now completed and not only had the sessions been agonisingly slow, but the finished tapes were nowhere near the sonic assault Noel and everybody else wanted.

In part, Noel had to blame himself, for he had made some unexpected decisions concerning the album. First off he had totally baffled the band by refusing to record 'All Around The World' or 'Whatever'.

'Nah,' he had firmly stated, '"All Around the World" isn't going on the first album and certainly not on the second one. It might go on the third album but probably the fourth. As for "Whatever", that's going to be our sixth or seventh single.'

That was fair enough, showing Gallagher foresight, but the second surprise proved to be costly: Noel's choice of producer David Batchelor.

Noel knew Batchelor from his Inspirals' days, when he had mixed them live. Batchelor had produced the cult 1970s band The Sensational Alex Harvey Band, a group renowned for their care-free attitude that had acted as a real precursor to the punk movement. He had then gone on to work with acts such as The Kinks in the late 1970s, and his musical CV strongly appealed to Noel. They had similar musical tastes.

'He [Batchelor] talked a great record,' McGee explains.

The other main contender at this point was obviously Coyley, but his inexperience in the studio went against him, a fact he was the first to point out. He would be more than happy to engineer and let someone more knowledgeable man the controls.

That man was Batchelor, but as the sessions progressed he was finding himself increasingly at loggerheads with the band owing to his production technique. Instead of recording the band live and then adding various parts, known as overdubbing, Batchelor insisted on recording each member of the band separately.

This method not only prolonged the sessions but the mixes that were being achieved didn't match up to the raucous sound the band wanted.

Noel's ambition was to make Oasis records as loud as The Who's *Live At Leeds* album, but these early mixes were far too tame for both his and the band's tastes.

'It didn't sound like us,' Guigsy explains. 'It was too nice. He tried to make us sound nice instead of just taping us.'

Ironically another Manchester band, The Stone Roses, whose audience Oasis would so dramatically swipe, were recording their new album, the long-awaited follow-up to *The Stone Roses*, down the road at Rockfield Studios.

In nearby Monmouth, Noel had bumped into their singer Ian Brown, who reportedly had said, 'Oasis, yeah, about time.'

(Later on, as everybody waited for Oasis to self destruct, it was the Roses, who took something like fourteen months to put this album, *The Second Coming*, together, who fell apart and not the hell-raisers from Burnage.)

The sessions dragged on. Liam vociferously complained about Batchelor, and McCarroll was routinely abused by every band member. Somehow, the hapless drummer was able to convince himself that the band's vicious insults were actually demonstrations of their regard for him which, of course, further aggravated his tormentors.

Things only really livened up when the band partied. This either meant massive drinking sessions in nearby pubs, or riotous affairs in the studio. But on one occasion Bonehead was at it so hard that he nearly got a hiding from Noel, and the band produced one of their most scintillating performances.

'It's about four or five in the morning,' Guigsy remembers, 'and everyone is drifting off to bed. But Bonehead's still going and he wants to speak to people. Everyone's in their rooms and it's pure country quiet where you can hear everything and you can hear him walking downstairs going, "What do I do? What do I do? I know, phone people up." So after he's tried a few people, he's decided, "I know, ring the Roses." So John Squire comes on the phone and Bonehead puts on a Rasta accent, "Hey man, is that the man Squire from the Squire family, we meet you at the corner, man, get you some toot." Then he puts the phone down and rings up again only this time he's an Indian curry shop owner with their takeaway orders.

'Bonehead's like laughing and crumbling to bits. Eventually he goes to bed. Then he opens up the window and starts shouting at the rabbits outside, "Ya fucking Mr. Bunny, go to bed, come on Mr. Bunny, beddy times."

'And that wakes the whole gaff up. Next morning, I'm eating breakfast and he comes down the stairs. He's like, "All right, Guigs?" and then he sits there just farting and laughing his head off. Then Noel comes down and he is double grumpy. Noel's like, "You better go to fucking bed, dickhead, because I don't want to see you," so Bonehead goes off and Noel sits down going, "I'm going to kill the cunt when he wakes up. Wait until he sobers up."

'So to calm Noel down I take him into town, buy him the papers and some Pot Noodles, crisps, cream cakes, all the stuff he likes, and then we pop into the pub at about half-ten and order a cab for eleven. Half-five in the evening me and Noel are still sitting and we are proper off our faces. Then we go back to the studio.

'Bonehead is now avoiding us, he's like, "Noel is going to kill me," and Noel walks into the studio and goes, "Right you bastards, we'll do 'Slide Away'." After each take we got more and more off our heads, but Noel's going to Bonehead, "You're staying straight, you're not getting off it *ever* again." Liam had fucked off somewhere but it was one of these takes that we used on the album.'

As this was the band's first real experience of a proper recording studio, they had reluctantly bowed down to Batchelor's experience. But as they struggled to find a way through, the unexpected news broke that they wouldn't be able to call on their record company boss for advice and support.

In early 1994 Alan McGee suffered a complete physical breakdown, caused by his massive drink and drug intake, and frenetic lifestyle. He would be the first of many to temporarily fall by the wayside as the Oasis juggernaut gathered pace.

'Basically,' McGee admits, 'I became a professional drug addict. There was this image of me as Alan McGee, the party animal and I was playing up to it. Cocaine, amphetamines, Ecstasy, speed pills, diet pills, Jack Daniels, and then taking Night Nurse to go to sleep.

'And it wasn't just the drugs, it was everything connected to it. The whole company was based right round me. It was the cult of personality, and there was no respite. I'd get back home in the morning and there'd be like twenty'three messages on my answer machine. I was just too available. There was no cut-off point.'

McGee entered the Florence Nightingale clinic in London's West End. On his first day, the fire alarm bell went off. Everyone was evacuated. Some patients tried to escape, others, like McGee, stayed outside on the street. As he was waiting to go back in a patient pushed past him, bent down and picked up an empty crisp bag.

'I've found my handbag,' she announced.

'That was the point,' he now says. 'I just went, all right, Christ, this is real. But I also realised I might be fucked up and I need a lot of therapy to sort my head out, but the bottom line is, that is a crisp packet and I know it's a crisp packet.'

It would take nine months, four in re-hab and five spent slowly readjusting his life, for McGee to take hold fully of the reins again. Dick Green, his partner, and all the other key Creation employees would now have to fill the space McGee had vacated. And they did so brilliantly, according to the Creation boss.

Despite his absence, McGee insisted on being involved in Oasis, even if it was at a distance. Therefore, he was totally supportive of the band's decision to scrap the Mono Valley sessions, replace Dave Batchelor with Mark Coyle and go to the Sawmills Studio in Cornwall to re-record the album.

The decision was taken back in London. After Mono Valley, the band had gone to the Olympic Studios in Barnes, London, to mix the album. This was the studio where The Rolling Stones and The

Small Faces had produced some of their best work. But it quickly became apparent that it was a fruitless exercise. The only track to survive these sessions was 'Slide Away', one of Noel's finest compositions, bolstered by one of Liam's most stirring vocal performances, apparently recorded in just one take. They also spent wasted time in Eden Studios, Chiswick, opposite Noel's flat.

With Coyley now producing and with a new engineer, Anjali Dutt, on board, the band decamped to the Sawmills studios in Cornwall. This time, Oasis were recorded live and the sessions went quickly and smoothly.

But when it came to mixing the album in Chiswick, again they ran into problems: the tapes still didn't sound right. The sound Oasis were after still eluded them. As they now had a string of dates coming up, it was left to Marcus to sort out.

'What came out of the Sawmills in recording terms was good,' he states, 'but when it came to the mixing stage, it wasn't happening.'

'I think Mark and Anjali were too close to the tapes to mix them, which is quite often the case. The person that records it can't mix it, they're too involved with what went on the tape in the first place. And that's where Owen Morris came in.

'I knew Owen wasn't just an engineer,' Marcus continues, 'although he wasn't a producer at the time. I knew him well enough to know that he isn't someone who just pushes the buttons but that he's got ideas and the guts to suggest them. Plus he's very good at dealing with musicians.'

It was an astute choice. One of Owen's all-time heroes is the producer Phil Spector, the man who created the Wall Of Sound. Spector's emphasis on volume and his penchant for having as many instruments as possible playing, was to play a massive influence on Owen's work. And now here come Oasis desperate to achieve a huge sound. The chemistry could not have been bettered.

Owen was also a huge admirer of the producer, Tony Visconti, who had worked with David Bowie in the early 1970s, the start of Bowie's golden years as the most influential musician in Britain. Noel wasn't really *au fait* with Spector but he loved Bowie's work from 1972, starting with the *Hunky Dory* album through to 1975 and the *Young Americans* LP.

In this period, Bowie also wrote one of Noel's favourite songs,

'All The Young Dudes', which he then gave to Mott The Hoople. Owen loved that record as well. He remembered it well from his youth.

Owen Morris was born in Caernafon, North Wales, but had spent his childhood near the town of Port Talbot in South Wales. He dropped out of school during his A-levels and found a job working in a Cambridge studio called Spaceward. It was there that he had met Marcus when he was managing The Bible.

Owen stayed there for nearly three years and then went to work on a Stranglers album that never saw the light of day. After that discouraging experience he asked Marcus to manage him. He was tired of engineering and he very much wanted to move into producing.

Through Marcus, he engineered the first Electronic album, the project started by Johnny Marr and Bernard Sumner from New Order. But after two years of working with Marr, Owen, frustrated at not being able to move into the producer's chair, ditched Marcus as a manager. A year later he had a huge falling out with Marr.

Owen had seen Oasis play at the Boardwalk in November 1992, and so when he heard they were signed to Creation and about to enter the studio he applied and was turned down for the producer's job.

Now Marcus, who he had retained friendly relations with, was on the line asking him to come in and mix Oasis. Naturally, he accepted. Marcus then sent him the Sawmills tapes and Owen realised he had a job on his hands.

'I just thought, fucking hell, they've made a real fuck-up here and I guessed at that stage that Noel was completely fucked off. Marcus was like, you can do what you want with it, literally, whatever you want.'

Owen's first move was to book two days in the Loco studio in Wales to pre-record Liam's vocals on 'Rock 'n' Roll Star' and 'Columbia'.

It was here that he first met Liam. 'Liam's version of events,' Owen states, 'is that he came in and said to me, "You're Phil Spector," and I said to him, "You're John Lennon." I don't know if that's true, but I do remember Noel shouting at Liam, "You are not fucking John Lennon and he is not Phil fucking Spector, now just shut the fuck up and get on with it."

'Those two mixes,' Morris admits, 'are total Spector and Visconti rip-offs. I just got out the Phil Spector tape-delays and used Tony Visconti harmonising tricks, and they're like total hats-off to those two.'

According to Morris, one of the problems was Noel's prolific nature. He had been allowed to put too much into the songs, filling up his compositions with numerous different guitar parts.

'But there was no cohesive thought to it,' Owen says, 'So I remember when I mixed "Rock 'n' Roll Star" I dumped about half the guitars, arranged them differently and then put a Phil-Spector-style tambourine on the snare drums.

'Then I thought, Noel is going to freak out now because I've just wiped about half of his guitars off.'

He called Noel into the studio and nervously played him the mix. After intently listening, Noel turned to the sweating producer and said, 'I like that tambourine.'

A relieved Morris then repeated this method with 'Columbia', stripping it down and again eliciting a casual but positive response from Noel.

'Very, very strange having so little feedback apart from, "Yeah, it's good,"' notes Morris.

Noel's nonchalant attitude disguised his shyness, but also he knew that to go overboard with congratulations leads to complacency. The best compliment he could give Owen was to ask him to finish the album. In reality, everyone was, in Marcus's words, 'ecstatic' about his mixes. At last, the sound that Noel had heard raging in his head all these years was coming to fruition.

Over the May bank holiday weekend, Owen entered Matrix Studios in Fulham, London, and mixed *Definitely Maybe*. He worked incredibly fast, mixing a song a day, which is an impressive pace to maintain in anyone's books. He was helped no end by Marcus, who would come to the studio every day laden with bottles of the producer's favourite red wines and various constructive comments.

The only mix that was met with any disapproval was Owen's first mix of 'Live Forever', where Owen had wiped off Noel's guitar solo.

'You're fucking joking,' the songwriter cried when he heard it, 'I spent months working that fucker out.'

*

As *Definitely Maybe* came together Oasis travelled up to Scotland to play a Sony Records convention at the Gleneagles Golf club.

On arriving, Noel went to the bar and asked for some drinks. After being told to put his money away as everything was free, he said to the barmaid, 'Well, if that's the case what's the most expensive drink you've got?'

The barmaid turned around and said, 'Those bottles of brandy which are a grand apiece.'

'Right,' Noel said, 'I'll have half a pint of that and one of these big cigars, please.'

Meanwhile, Liam was upstairs complaining that his room was too big. It was a foretaste of what was to come.

The next day the band got up early, but the conference was running behind schedule, so they put Noel, Liam and Marcus into a hospitality suite.

Mistake. The trio sat in a room with a waitress and ordered drink after drink. Then Noel had an idea. He phoned up press officer Johnny Hopkins and told him that Bonehead had broken into the lodge of the legendary racing driver, Jackie Stewart, stolen an air rifle and was now out on the golf course shooting at trees.

'It's true,' the songwriter insisted, 'I'm watching him right now.'

Hopkins duly reported this information to the press, and *Melody Maker* ran with it the next week, under the headline 'Oasis Gun Drama', thus further adding to the growing Oasis mythology.

Eventually the band were called for a soundcheck. But by now, they were smashed out of their heads. In fact, Noel had to lean against his amps just to keep his balance.

Even so, that didn't prevent them from producing a magnificent version of 'I Am The Walrus', which they later placed, after it had appeared on a limited white-label edition, on the B-side of 'Cigarettes and Alcohol'. The applause at the end is sampled from another artist's live album. The night ended at eight in the morning with Marcus roaming down the corridors singing Welsh songs and eventually having to be helped on to the plane home by Noel.

In February, Oasis were given their first foreign date, the Paradiso Club in Amsterdam. They never made it. The band, with Coyley and Jason in tow, boarded a coach in Manchester at midday and quickly consumed two bottles of Jack Daniels. Then they stopped off to get another bottle before finally boarding the ferry.

Once on board, they headed straight for the bar. They also located the duty'free shop where they started stealing bottles of champagne which they then openly consumed back in the bar.

The upshot of all this drunken mayhem was that the security guards were called and the band decided it was best to split for their bedrooms.

As Guigsy and Liam drunkenly walked down a corridor, trying to locate their room, Guigsy heard a noise, turned and saw a guard coming out of a side door about to use his truncheon on the unsuspecting Liam. Without any hesitation, Guigsy punched the guy. From nowhere, eight guards suddenly appeared and piled into him. Liam, then made a bolt for the stairs.

Guigsy was hauled downstairs, roughed up and thrown into the brig. About five minutes later he heard loud noises coming from the corridor and sure enough, here's Liam shouting that the guards have thrown him down three flights of stairs and if he's going into a cell they better not have any sexual desires for him.

The boys were incarcerated for the next twenty-four hours, left, locked up, without food or drink, dehydrating like crazy. One of the guards, a big mean'looking man, even drew a chalk line in Liam's cell and told the singer to lie down with his nose resting on it. If he moved over the line, he promised to attack Liam with his truncheon. Liam lay on the ground for three hours before the guard finally gave up watching him.

Meanwhile, a guard entered Bonehead and McCarroll's room and confiscated their passports. They would not be let into the country.

As the bassist and singer languished in the cells, the boat docked in Holland and Noel and the rest of the Oasis crew disembarked only to find out hours later that all four band members were now heading back to England.

The gig was cancelled and Marcus was informed of the incident. He then called a band meeting at which Liam defended himself by saying that it was proper rock 'n' roll behaviour.

'No,' Marcus vehemently said, 'playing to 300 people in Amsterdam is proper rock 'n' roll behaviour, not getting arrested so no one can hear you're music.'

Noel was furious too, and had been the first to give Guigsy and Liam an angry lecture. Even Bonehead was upset by their behaviour. For two weeks they were blanked by the rest of the band, and the guard that Guigsy had hit was paid £1,000 not to press charges.

In March, Oasis made their first national TV appearance. Karen Williams at Anglo Plugging had secured them a booking on Channel Four's *The Word* to promote their first single 'Supersonic', a full month before it's release.

McGee had actually argued for 'Bring It On Down' to be Oasis's first shot at the single chart, but Noel had firmly resisted the idea. As his contract gave him artistic freedom, McGee backed down.

For their TV début, late on a Friday night, Noel wore a red shirt and no shades. Liam sported a flight jacket, Bonehead a green cord jacket and Guigsy a burgundy jumper. Presenter Mark Lamarr introduced the band and Oasis ditched the song's intro and went straight into the first verse.

They didn't smile or really acknowledge the cameras, although during the third verse Liam whipped out his own Hi 8 camcorder and started filming the audience. At the end of the song, he said, 'Cheers, goodnight,' and sauntered off the stage as Noel bent down by his amps to extract a few seconds of feedback.

'Woops, bit of feedback there,' said a smiling Terry Christian who, two years later, would co-author a book about the Gallagher family with Noel's and Liam's older brother Paul.

This TV appearance went some way towards capturing the band's prowess as a live act, and served to whet everyone's appetite. It was patiently clear that Oasis had something that placed them well above their contemporaries. The sound, the look, the attitude, it intrigued and excited onlookers.

With that in mind, Oasis again took to the road, this time with Whiteout, who had just signed to Silvertone Records, The Stone Roses' old record label. The idea was that both bands would headline every other night. They started in Bedford on 23 March. Oasis played first, and the next day they all travelled up to London to play the 100 Club where Oasis now headlined the gig.

Ted Kessler wrote in the *NME* of their performance: 'At times tonight Oasis assumed the mantle of Best Live Band in the country with joyous arrogant Mancunian confidence. They may never be this good again . . .'

The tour moved on to the Forum in Tunbridge Wells, Kent, this was 26 March, and then the Oxford Polytechnic where Oasis stole a television out of their hotel so that they could watch Manchester United play Aston Villa while at the gig. Villa won and Coyley kicked the television to pieces in disgust.

The following night, in a move reminiscent of The Beatles in May of 1963 when they supported Roy Orbison, it was mutually agreed that Oasis should headline every night. Like it or not, after Oasis had finished playing, the majority of the crowd walked out leaving Whiteout to play to near-empty halls.

'It was funny,' Noel recalls. 'We had this old van to travel around in and Whiteout had this big coach that the record company had given them, but after each show all the kids were round our dodgy old van.'

It was on this tour that Marcus decided to relieve Bonehead of his tour manager duties and employ Margaret Mouzakitis, better known as Maggie, to take over. It is a position she still holds. Marcus also took on Phil Smith, a close friend and Stone Roses' roadie, who was now free due to their recording commitments. Halfway through Oasis's first US tour, Smith was recalled to the Roses' camp.

'When Maggie joined,' Guigsy remembers, 'we thought, brilliant, she'll get us loads of drugs and girls. But she wasn't having any of it, and that's exactly what we needed at that point.'

Guigsy is totally correct in his assessment. Set free on the road and finally receiving the acclaim they knew would one day be theirs, Oasis were starting to get a real taste of the stardom they had dreamt about.

What more could you ask for? Everything they had read, envied and fantasised about rock 'n' roll bands now applied to them. Girls wanted to bed them and geezers wanted to be them. Gone were the days of playing to twenty disinterested people in some shabby flea-pit. Gone were the days of signing on and not having enough money for records, clothes or drugs.

The word was out now, and accordingly Oasis ran wild as they saw all their boasts being totally vindicated. They would book into hotels, drink their mini-bars dry, go and play songs that would drive an audience into a frenzy, and then party into the early hours.

Rooms would be smashed, girls would be bedded and then, in the early hours, with copious amounts of alcohol and chemicals coursing through their veins, they would do a runner from the hotel leaving their bills unpaid. Top, they would say to themselves as they discussed the previous night's gig and events, fucking top.'

On 28 March Oasis played the Jug Of Ale in Birmingham, which is where Noel met up again with Ocean Colour Scene (having first met them at a Paul Weller gig in Oxford). He had heard a demo tape of theirs in the Creation office because Johnny Hopkins had been keen for Creation to sign them. But McGee wasn't convinced.

Noel was, and he actively helped their cause by booking them as support on numerous dates as they looked for a deal. Two years later, when Ocean Colour Scene's second album, *Moseley Shoals*, was selling over half a million copies, Noel was heard to say to their MCA A&R man at Knebworth, 'You better take good care of my boys.'

The tour finished two dates later, the bands having played the Fleece And Firkin in Bristol and Moles in Bath. After four days' rest, Oasis started their own tour in support of their forthcoming début single, 'Supersonic'. On the vinyl version, two new songs would be available, 'Take Me Away' and a live version of 'I Will Believe'.

CD buyers would be treated to an extra track too, in this case the white-label version of 'Columbia'. This bias towards CD single buyers continues to this day, seemingly a strange anomaly for a band brought up on vinyl, until you realise that bands earn far more from CDs than they do from records.

The band's tour started with three consecutive gigs, Lucifer's Mill in Dundee on 5 April, La Belle Angel in Edinburgh the next night, and then down to the Tramway in Glasgow.

It was after this gig, at Glasgow's Forte Crest Hotel, four days before the release of 'Supersonic', that Liam and Noel sat down with John Harris, then of the *NME*, to deliver an interview that would set the tone for all their future press.

At this point, the *NME* were overtly keen to make Oasis, through repeated coverage, 'their band'. They had already run a page interview in their 2 April issue, written by Emma Morgan. In it, Noel again foresees their future.

Are you worried about living up to expectations? Emma asks.

Noel shakes his head. 'It'll all be apparent when "Supersonic" (the first single) comes out,' he replies. 'Then it'll all be WAY-HEY! from there.'

Now Harris was here to write a much larger piece. To put it in context, it's obvious that the ferry incident is still rankling Noel. Liam, sensing his brother's annoyance, is determined to defend himself publicly.

The article begins with Noel and Liam squaring up to each other, Liam shouting, 'Let's fucking go then, you DICK! Let's have a fucking fight.'

Harris then goes on to recount the colourful Oasis history to date, before moving on to Noel laying into the group Smash and then Miles Hunt, formerly of The Wonderstuff, who, unknown to Noel, is booked to interview the brothers for his MTV show.

Harris then throws in a question relating to the band's image as rock 'n' roll pigs, and Liam responds by saying that he is into it and is dying to get 2,000 people into a gig to see *him*.

Noel then interjects. 'That's not what he's on about.'

'He is.'

'No, he's fucking not. He's on about getting thrown off ferries.'

Which is the point when an almighty row, captured and later released as the single 'Wibbling Rivalry', now erupts, perfectly illuminating the tension between the brothers.

For Noel, there is music and that is the most important thing; without it no one would be attracted to Oasis or any other band. The rest all comes second.

But for Liam music is nothing without the attitude. That is the key. Otherwise you end up like Andrew Lloyd Webber.

'Who's Andrew Lloyd Webber?' Noel asks, laying a trap for his brother.

'I haven't got a clue,' Liam responds. 'He's a golfer or something.'

Whether they were bluffing or not, the fact remains that in their first major interview, which thousands upon thousands of people would read, Noel and Liam Gallagher had no qualms about exposing their tempestuous relationship.

They fight and scream and argue. They end up threatening

each other and they also enter into surreal dialogues concerning conkers and, naturally, John Lennon.

What gave this article true impact was its totally unguarded nature. It was not, as it could well have been given Noel and Liam's streetwise cunning, a staged conversation designed to generate headlines, because the next morning, a worried Noel sat with Marcus at breakfast and confessed that he thought they might have blown it with the interview. In fact, the reverse was true.

'For me,' Johnny Hopkins states, 'it was one of the great rock 'n' roll interviews.' Hopkins had sat in the room as the interview took place. It was he who had attempted to separate the brothers when they nearly came to blows and it was he who knew that every writer in town would now make a beeline for the band. Oasis were now indisputably and undoubtedly great copy.

The next night Oasis played the Arena in Middlesborough, having just learnt the shocking news that Kurt Cobain of the group Nirvana had put a shotgun to his head and blown his mind out.

The group, who weren't Nirvana fans but would later admire his work with the release of Nirvana's *Unplugged In New York* album, dedicated 'Live Forever' to him.

It was a symbolic gesture. The grunge rock movement Cobain had inspired, saw America finally succumbing to punk rock music. But grunge's nihilistic viewpoint, which found its main appeal with bored, white middle-class kids, ran directly against Noel's way of thinking, and as a counterpoint, he wrote 'Live Forever'.

On 11 April 1994 'Supersonic' was released. The band were in Stoke playing the Wheatsheaf. The next day they made their way over to the Duchess of York in Leeds. This time the place was rammed. Again, a lot of people were left outside.

The next night in Liverpool at the Lomax streetwise kids were discovered outside the gig selling useless ticket stubs to gullible fans. The band admired that kind of behaviour. It's exactly what they would have done if they were in their shoes.

On 17 April, during a break from touring, the band were boosted by the news that 'Supersonic' had entered the charts at thirty-one. It was a good if not spectacular opening on their chart account.

A video had been shot of the band on the roof of a taxi company in London's King's Cross. Directed by Mark Szaszy, it was a straightforward film of the and playing live interspersed with various shots (filmed at Heathrow on the day the IRA launched a mortar attack on the airport) of, surprise, surprise, aeroplanes flying supersonically overhead.

The single itself set the pattern for most of their future single releases. The A-side, a full-on Oasis rocker, the B-side, 'Take Me Away', a beautiful demonstration of Noel's skills as a ballad writer, and then a live song coupled with a rarity such as 'Columbia'.

Lyrically, both 'Supersonic' and 'Take Me Away' would bring to light major themes Noel would constantly return to.

His use of rhyme in 'Supersonic' works on the most basic level, totally in keeping with his pop throwaway sensibility which had been weaned on all those glam-rock singles from the 1970s.

Noel's sensibility is such that he can admire three-minute pop stompers (and extract from them their basic appeal), and he can swoon to Burt Bacharach and other deeper works. On Oasis singles, he would display both sides of these art forms.

Thus 'supersonic' goes with 'gin and tonic'; 'doctor' with 'helicopter'; 'home' with 'alone'; 'tissue'; with 'Big Issue'. For some this was the proof they needed to ridicule Noel's intelligence.

But compare this deliberate pop throwaway style with the far more personalised approach to 'Take Me Away', in which Noel expresses his fierce need to escape from the world, and returns to a recurring Gallagher theme (first heard in the opening lines of 'Supersonic': 'I need to be myself/ I can't be no one else') of how people try to be everything but themselves, something he too experiences.

No doubt about it, Noel found lyric writing the hardest part of his job but he was by no means a poor lyricist, although he was sometimes a lazy one.

Certainly the press were divided over 'Supersonic's merits. *NME*'s Keith Cameron (another writer to pick up on 'Live Forever', in his review of the Tramway show) made 'Supersonic' Single Of The Week, and poured praise all over the band. He called the song 'a paragon of pop virtue', and wondered how on earth Oasis were so self-accomplished; he totally understood

Noel's deliberate nonsensical but funny images in the lyrics, and concluded by calling Oasis, 'Simply a great rock 'n' roll band.' .

Peter Paphides in the *Melody Maker* totally disagreed. He told his readers that the single sounded like Blur four years ago, a comment which would have seriously angered Liam.

Blur, at this point, were about to regain some of the ground they had lost after being initially touted as the band most likely to break big. Their album *Modern Life Is Rubbish* was set to lay the ground for the following year's *Parklife*, an album which would sell in huge quantities. Oasis dismissed most of their contemporaries as casually as you would flick dust from your coat, but Blur, with their mix of mock cockney songs and student backgrounds, badly riled Oasis, especially Liam. He smelt fakery, and that always upset him.

In mid May, on a night out on the booze, he would get his chance to express his disgust at them when he and Noel met Blur's guitarist, Graham Cox, at the Good Mixer pub in Camden. It was well known that Blur often frequented these premises so Liam had insisted on visiting the pub. Much to his delight, he spotted Graham straightaway and the brothers Gallagher went straight over to him. After roughly introducing themselves, they then started insulting his clothes and then his band.

Then they started singing, to the tune of 'Lazy Sunday' by The Small Faces, 'Blu-uur are cocknee, cocknee cunts.' At which point the fuming guitarist complained to the landlord. The brothers were swiftly ejected and informed they were banned for life from the pub.

Undeterred, they then walked over to the Underworld pub, near Camden tube station, where they fell into a fight with some of the locals and were again ejected and banned. Another top night out.

In the same *Melody Maker* issue that carried Paphides's dismissal of 'Supersonic', Calvin Bush, very much a fan, wrote a page-long interview on the group, finding Noel in a very bullish mood.

'Listen, right,' Noel forthrightly states, 'if anybody doesn't buy my music, I'm gonna be the most upset man in the world. We write music for the guy who walks down the street to get his copy of the fucking *Daily Mirror* and his twenty Bensons every day, and he's got fuck-all going for him, he's got no money.

'Even if somebody can't afford to buy our record, if they put on the radio while they're cleaning the house, and whistle along and go, "Fucking hell, did you hear that tune?" *That's* what it's all about.'

Such virulent sentiments hadn't been expressed in the music press for years, and no doubt slightly alienated the middle-class students who make up the core of the readership.

But then Noel, as he increasingly tended to in interviews, went on to twist facts so as to glamorise even further the Oasis story. He told Bush that at the King Tut's gig, McGee jumped on-stage during their second song and offered to sign them on the spot. Right. Noel also revealed that he only listened to old music, but that three records of late had impressed him: Paul Weller's *Wildwood* album, Grant Lee Buffalo's *Fuzzy*, and Beck's single 'Loser', 'which blew my fucking head off'.

Undoubtedly, Noel had been captivated by Beck's unusual use of a bluesy acoustic guitar set to a heavy hip-hop drum sound, and carefully filed this musical combination away for further use. Certainly 'Wonderwall' utilises the same ingredients, but in a very different fashion.

It is also in this article that 'All Around The World' is first mentioned, Noel insisting that Oasis will enter the Eurovision Song Contest with it and win by 'at least, oooh thirty points'.

In truth, when he first wrote the song in the early 1990s, 'I knew that people wouldn't be ready for it, they wouldn't get it. I had to put it aside and wait, which is why it didn't go on the first album. Then I briefly thought about putting it on the second album but then I went and wrote "Champagne Supernova", and you can't have two seven-minute epics on one album, can you?'

At time of writing, this song, one of Noel's most stirring and beautiful efforts, is down for the third Oasis album, provisionally entitled 'Be Here Now'. To give you an idea of its potency, it is as if McCartney had written 'Hey Jude', and then kept it hidden for years.

On 29 April Oasis resumed touring. They played the Adelphi in Hull, then it was on to the Coventry University where 200 kids were left outside. The next night, 2 May, it was the Wedgewood Rooms in Portsmouth where *NME* writer Simon Williams met up with them to write the band's first *NME* cover-story. They were, again, a journalist's dream.

After the gig, back at the hotel, the barman unwisely vacated the bar. Swiftly, two of the Oasis crew snatched numerous bottles of beer and stowed them away. Bonehead then decided to go for a swim in the pool next to the bar area.

The party moved over to the pool where all of a sudden, and obviously off their heads, Noel and Liam started viciously tearing into each other. When Guigsy tried to separate them, he too was punched.

As they wrestled on the floor, someone started throwing poolside chairs at Bonehead in the pool. Then a few tables were aimed at him. The commotion brought sleeping residents to see what the fuck was going on, and a girl, standing behind her boyfriend on the balcony, kept unwrapping the towel she was wearing and flashing her naked body at the band.

Finally, at six in the morning, the Oasis party were informed by the night watchman that he couldn't serve them any more drinks as he was off to bed, and by the way, the police were now on the way over.

The next day at lunchtime Noel and Liam laughed off their fight and mutually agreed that they should never have been booked into such an establishment.

'It's true,' Noel says, looking over at the swimming pool, 'Those plate-glass windows are just saying, throw a chair through me.'

The gig that day was at TJs in Newport and the band stayed in the King's Head Hotel. Coincidentally, the hotel bar was named the Oasis, and Liam duly posed in front of the sign for photographer Kevin Cumming's camera. This was used as the *NME*'s cover-shot.

Cummings also suggested a photo session with Noel and Liam wearing Manchester City tops. Cummings is a Mancunian and a fervent City supporter, attending every game he can.

No surprise then that the boys readily agreed to his suggestion. With Brother, City's aptly-named sponsors, emblazoned across their chests, they posed by a corrugated iron fence that had BLUES graffitied on it. The *NME* used two pics. One was of Liam with his arm slung nicely over Noel, the other of them mock fighting.

The point these pictures made was that Oasis were a major

band coming directly from the football terraces and the first in the 1990s to place football on an equal level with music.

Ask Noel Gallagher what the best day of his life was and he – the man who will play the biggest gig ever in Britain, write songs that will remain with people forever, and become a multi-millionaire – will unhesitatingly point to the day in 1989 when he and his fellow City fans stood in the Kippax Stand, E'd off their heads, and watched Manchester City beat Manchester United 5-1.

This kind of attitude not only preceded football's massive current popularity but mirrored a cultural shift that was best exemplified by the success of *Loaded* magazine, launched in 1994 and which reflected Oasis's appeal. Indeed, every time Noel met a *Loaded* writer he would tell them, 'Get a *Loaded* TV show together. I'll present it from my sitting-room. It'll be top.'

Loaded's appeal lay in its unabashed celebration of young masculinity. It had no qualms in running pictures of scantily-clad girls, devised its own language to compliment laddish behaviour – 'Good work, fella' – and, just like Oasis, celebrated and advocated total hedonism.

Such was its appeal, that within a few months *Loaded* had overtaken every other men's magazine on the market, and forced competitors such as *FHM*, *Arena*, *Maxim* and others to incorporate some of *Loaded*'s philosophy.

In parallel with Oasis's rapid ascent *Loaded* became the publishing phenomenon of the 1990s, and it was no surprise that when they first featured Oasis, the band were photographed playing football.

Similarly, women in the 1990s also adopted a far more aggressive approach. They too had no qualms about expressing their sexuality and they demanded not only equality but, as countless articles would testify, far more from their men, both in and out of bed. Many of these 1990s girls were to be found at Oasis concerts. The Oasis appeal wasn't limited just to a male audience.

Liam, naturally, was the complete *Loaded* man, but his public image, like the rest of the band's, wasn't a calculated act. He was the real thing, straight from the I-really-don't-give-a-shit school of thought. Therefore, Oasis could blow up at any time.

Noel had already foreshadowed this feeling in his song 'Hello'. Written way before Oasis entered the public consciousness, he states, 'We live in the shadows/ And we had the chance but threw it away.'

Over the next two years that's precisely what Oasis looked like doing. But those who predicted it forgot one crucial fact: music. At this point, no one else bar the band members, had any real grasp on the true nature of Noel's songwriting ability. How could they? They hadn't been privy to hear songs such as 'All Around The World' or 'Stand By Me' or 'Daytura Dream Deferred'. But the band had.

They knew that Noel, despite his unstoppable appetite for anything that would drastically alter his mindset, wasn't only hugely talented but also utterly disciplined.

He tries to write every day of his life and even when he isn't working his musical radar refuses to turn off. All you had to do back then was study him carefully and there he would be, fingers tapping away, his eyes darting around, his mind on twenty-four-hour alert for anything that might inspire him. Of course, not all that flowed from his muse was great, but the majority of it was excellent.

The rest of the band knew that Oasis had it in them to create records that would resonate down the years, just like all their idols had. How many times had they sat there, listening to The Beatles, The Kinks, Marley, Bacharach, Hendrix et al., and thought how great it would be to make music that successive generations would get off on every time?

Now, with Oasis, they could achieve that very goal. That is why throughout every major bust up, music was the glue that served to keep them together. That came first and they knew that to throw away something so precious would haunt them for the rest of their lives. But Liam, above all, would and always will, test that strength. Which is why a million and one men wanted to be just like him.

The tour continued and the momentum increased, visiting the Wherehouse in Derby on 4 May, followed by a night off and then on to the Charlotte in Leicester, the Old Trout in Windsor and the Roadmenders in Northampton.

At all these gigs fans were left outside as the band's reputation for brilliant music and outrageous behaviour spiralled into public knowledge.

Oasis were now constantly being mentioned in music press

gossip columns. 'Jokey' articles, such as *NME*'s 'At Home With Oasis', based around Noel and Liam's tempestuous relationship, now became regular columns.

There hadn't been a band as open as this about their behaviour since Primal Scream. But the cost of such coverage, as Gillespie and co. were to find out, was that writers zeroed in on their personal lives and forgot about the music.

Johnny Hopkins was aware of this potential trap. His policy was to encourage writers to discover the band for themselves and then make their own minds up.

'And that worked,' Marcus points out, 'because they came to the gigs and saw with their very own eyes a brilliant rock 'n' roll band with all these wonderful tunes.'

They would also have noted the crowd's fanatical reaction to the band as they played the Army And Navy in Chelmsford, the Boat Race in Cambridge and then back to London for a gig at the Venue in New Cross.

After soundchecking at this gig, Noel had gone out to the pub for a drink and then returned to the venue. A tall bouncer at the door refused him entry, not believing he was in Oasis. Noel finally convinced him of his credentials. The bouncer's name was Terry and two years later he, alongside Kevin of Top Guard, would be employed by the band as personal security guards.

At this gig the band ran into a little fracas with Sheffield band Shed Seven over the banners they had erected on-stage, and *NME* duly reported that back at the Columbia Hotel, Liam and a girl he had just taken to bed, had been disturbed by Alan from Shed Seven banging on his window.

On 14 May Oasis played the Leadmill in Sheffield and then prepared for the release of their second single, 'Shakermaker', a song that had already gained notoriety by its obvious use of the vocal melody from The New Seekers' song 'I'd Like To Teach The World To Sing', which was also immortalised in a 1970s TV advert for Coca-Cola.

Noel, in a new Mancunian mood, hadn't only lifted the melody wholesale but seized upon the obvious drug connotations by inserting the line, 'I'd like to buy the world some coke.'

In the 21 May issue of *NME* it was reported that the band had refused, despite the threat of legal action from Coca-Cola, to remove the line.

'We might have to write-off half the royalties,' Noel fumed, 'but fuck it. For someone in a suit to come along and say we've got to change a song we've been playing for two years isn't on. If we ever get to pay back our advance, which most bands don't, then it's just going to be another five grand on top.'

A week later *Melody Maker* ran with a Creation press release which stated that the line hadn't even been recorded. The only way it could surface would be as a live version of the song and that had never been considered a possibility.

Knowing this, Noel's fiery quote to the *NME* was obviously designed to whip up a controversy that never existed in the first place and so keep the band in headlines. Oasis did not need the press but they were now in a position to start playing games. And they liked that power.

The band had now been booked to appear at the Glastonbury festival and judging by the attention they were receiving 'Shakermaker' looked likely to outsell 'Supersonic'. Again, Mark Szaszy was employed to direct the video, this time shooting the band performing in the backyard of Bonehead's house and playing football in a nearby field. There were also shots of Liam and Bonehead being driven around in a car by Brian Cannon, their friend and sleeve designer.

On 1 June Oasis began their third UK tour, kicking off at Edward 8 in Birmingham and then on to Cardiff University. After this show, Noel was interviewed in his room at the Moathouse Hotel by Lisa Verrico of *Vox* magazine. Halfway through a speech attempting to play down the band's rock 'n' roll image, thereby switching the attention to music, his attention was caught by a table flying downwards past his window.

He went over, opened up his window, and looked up to see a grinning Bonehead gleefully surveying the damage he had just wrought. 'What was that about the stories of hotels being smashed up being untrue?' Lisa asked a sheepish Noel. The next night they played the Island in Ilford, and *NME*'s Stuart Bailie expressed the dominant feeling that was growing around Oasis. Brilliant, superb band but 'they might self-destruct tomorrow'.

The next night, at Creation's Undrugged show, ambitiously held at the Royal Albert Hall to celebrate the label's tenth year, Alan McGee, who was still recuperating, sent his uncle on-stage to introduce Oasis, who were minus Liam. He had a sore throat.

McGee's uncle told the audience, 'Since Alan can't be here tonight, he's asked me to convey his best respects to you all; and he wants me to introduce the next act, and he says, his quote is, "They are the best reason to believe in rock 'n' roll in 1994." Oasis!'

Noel and Bonehead, armed with acoustic guitars, then came on-stage to outshine every other act that night. They opened with a beautiful version of 'Live Forever', played a ragged 'Shakermaker' and then finished off, with the crowd now clapping along, with 'Sad Song'.

Later at the Embassy Hotel, they partied to the early hours with most of the other acts who had performed. As part of Creation's anniversary, the label had given *NME* a tape of all their acts to give away with one of their issues. Cleverly, the last track on the tape was Oasis's 'Cigarettes and Alcohol', further cementing their reputation as a great singles band with total attitude.

Two days later, 6 June, they were back on-stage at the Arts Centre in Norwich, and then it was back to London for an appearance on Channel Four's *Naked City* show.

Oasis performed two songs, 'Supersonic' and 'Shakermaker', and then Noel was interviewed for the first time on TV. The interviewer was Caitlin Moran, to whom Bonehead would later complain about the lack of free beer.

'We've put two million on your viewing figures,' Bonehead snorted, 'and we can't get free ale? You're fucking joking, aren't you?'

Noel wore his shades for the interview, a wise decision. That day he had downed some Ecstasy and his pupils were badly dilating. His fellow-interviewee was Peter Cunnah from the group D:Ream, but by the end of the chat he was probably wondering why he even bothered to show up. Noel dominated the conversation from start to finish.

'How has being famous affected your friends, Noel?' asked Moran.

'I haven't seen my mates in about six months. Apart from the ones that work for us.'

'Do you get your friends to work for you so you can tour round in a big group?'

'No. It's so we can exploit them. The thing is, if we didn't have them working for us they'd be burgling our houses, so it's best to have them with us. [Noel then looks over at his friend Chris Johnson standing in the audience.] Innit, Chris?'

The next day the band made their way to the Marquee in London, a gig they all had been looking forward to. The band soundchecked and then at about six that evening, Noel and Liam sat down in a music shop on nearby Denmark Street to be interviewed by *The Beat*'s Gary Crowley. Then they walked back to the Marquee.

This venue had witnessed performances from all of Oasis's favourite acts, from The Who to Jimi Hendrix, The Sex Pistols to The Jam, and from the outset, Noel had wanted Oasis to combine elements from all these groups; to be as debauched as the Stones, as destructive as the early Who, as reckless as the Pistols, as meaningful as The Jam, The Smiths and the Roses, and maybe, just maybe, as culturally significant as The Beatles.

Now at the Marquee, it was Oasis's chancc to prove they could do it, that *they* were now the Young Guvnors. Naturally, they succeeded. The place was packed with expectant fans and the band stormed through their set, egged on by the jubilant crowd.

'Absolutely electric,' Crowley called it.

The next night the band went home to Manchester and played the University, and then it was over to the Avenham Park in Preston to play a free festival Heineken beer had sponsored.

For some reason The Boo Radleys had been given top spot and the band's Martin Carr was later quoted in *Melody Maker* as saying, 'I feel a real twat with Oasis because they're the first other band I've really loved since joining a band myself . . . I can't talk to them properly because I keep on thinking, "You bunch are fucking ace".'

On-stage someone threw a glass of beer at the stage. Liam threatened to leave the stage, stating, 'We're not fucking Blur.'

They travelled to Glasgow for two shows at the Cathouse and then it was over to Paris to make their French début at the Erotika club.

'It was fucking ace,' roadie Jason Rhodes recalls, 'as we were packing up the gear, this stripper came on-stage and started her act.'

The band returned to Britain for a gig in the East Wing of the Brighton centre and two days later, 20 June, 'Shakermaker', c/w 'D'Yer Wanna Be A Spaceman', the demo version of 'Alive' and

'Bring It On Down' (live) was released.

Two days later, their *Naked City* appearance was screened, and both *NME* and *Melody Maker* made the song their respective Singles Of The Week.

Paul Mathur wrote that 'Shakermaker' was one of the hundred greatest songs ever written, and Mark Sutherland, after hearing the song, wrote 'you know you are dealing with greatness'.

Meanwhile, as 'Shakermaker' flew out of the shops, and picked up fifteen plays on Radio One that week, the band travelled down to the Glastonbury festival. On the Saturday night, after watching Paul Weller upstage Elvis Costello, that night's headlining act, in a backstage bar-tent Noel briefly met the ex-Jam frontman for the first time.

Weller told him that he liked 'Supersonic', and Noel stood there, shyly nodding, unable to talk, either through being awestruck or totally out of it. It was hard to tell which.

The next day, Oasis strolled on to the *NME* stage and by the end of the set had the girls sitting on their boyfriends' shoulders and most of the crowd wildly applauding as they tore into 'I Am The Walrus'.

Channel Four later screened three of their songs, 'Fade Away', 'Digsy's Dinner', and 'Live Forever'. That the *NME* tape had reached the public could be gauged when Noel hit the opening riff to 'Cigarettes and Alcohol', and the crowd screamed in delight. Then he stopped, looked at them as if to say 'Gotcha', and launched into 'Live Forever'.

They came off-stage to be greeted by a grinning, happy Marcus. 'Shakermaker' was in at number eleven in the charts.

'Way-hey' they cried and then proceeded to get even more blitzed, partying, in fact, with some of The Stone Roses.

Two days later, Oasis sat down to watch themselves on Carlton TV's now-defunct show, *The Beat*, hosted by Gary Crowley. This was the first time Liam and Noel had ever been interviewed together on TV and they proved to be a good double-act.

Crowley begins with a question about their signing to Creation. 'You didn't have to send out a demo tape, did you?'

'Nah,' Liam replies, 'we got signed by fate, y'know.'

'But they dropped us after the first single,' Noel jokes, 'and then Creation signed us.' The boys break up with laughter, Liam flicking his fingers in salute.

243

'Well, what was the story with Creation, 'cos Alan McGee saw you . . .'

'Well,' Noel starts, 'in the beginning, Gary, there was a big bang from the sun and from there came these gases and from there . . .'

The brothers then talk a little about Creation, 'the right label for us', and then Liam says, 'It's one of them things, innit? You walk down the road, you trip over, you break a leg and you're gutted. We go and play a gig and get signed. One of them things, innit?'

It's such quotes that endears so many people to Liam. Indeed, throughout the interview, much to Noel's amusement, Liam takes over, answering every question.

In one of his replies, Liam states, 'There's a lot of nice girls coming to our gigs and it's [he checks himself and adopts a posh accent] bloody nice to see it. But I suppose there is a lot of lads coming, thinking we're this mad hooligan band and we're not. I ain't no hooligan [at which point Noel starts laughing], I'm just me. They're probably coming to see all this way-hey, way'hey, but we're not.' Liam pauses. 'Did you understand me?'

'I like the bit,' Noel says, 'where you say you're not a hooligan 'cos I've read things where you've said, "I like fighting, me."'

Liam responds, 'Yeah, I'm up for it but I don't go out of my way. Someone comes up then I'm up for it. You have to be. It's a tough tough world out there.'

'What's it like being brothers in a band?' Crowley asks.

Both Noel and Liam fall silent. Then Noel exclaims, 'He's speechless, look at that,' and bursts out laughing.

'I think it's all right, me,' Liam says. 'I think it's very, very funny.'

They probably had smiles on their hangovers when 29 June arrived and Oasis woke up to grab the opportunity that every young British musician desires: to perform on *Top Of The Pops*.

Bruno Brookes introduced them under a TV caption that read, New UK Talent From Manchester, and Oasis swopped places. Tony McCarroll was placed right at the front of the stage. Guigsy and Bonehead stood behind him and then, on a higher level, the Gallagher brothers. It was reminiscent of The Jam's final appearance on the show when Weller put everyone forward and hid himself at the back.

As a backdrop, the sinking Union Jack image from the demo tape was used. Liam wore glasses, a brown cord jacket. Noel sported shades and the jacket he would wear on the cover of the début album, and the band, serious expressions one and all, mimed to the song. And that was it. All those years of watching and dreaming what it was like to be on the nation's biggest pop show, and you found out that you spend hours hanging around in a dressing-room and then you get just over three minutes to mime to your song.

And this sold records? Usually, but number eleven was as high as 'Shakermaker' would go.

Oasis now entered the Maison Rouge Studios in Fulham to record, much to the band's pleasure, 'Whatever'.

Owen Morris produced, and this was the first time he had really worked with the band as a unit, the first time he had met Bonehead and Guigsy. He looks back on the experience as 'one of the best weeks of my life'.

He recalls, 'Top nights with Bonehead, shaving his head and having wine-drinking competitions with him, all of us really pissed. Noel was the one I hung out with the most 'cos he was doing all the work, really. He was doing a lot of drugs then.

'Noel Gallagher, E'd off his tits, popping pills the whole time and the rest of the band just getting drunk. I had a week with them and it was just proper full-on chaos and "Whatever" was the soundtrack to it.'

The chaos Owen refers to wasn't confined to the studio, but spilled over to the Columbia Hotel where the band were staying. This is the hotel that most visiting bands use and is designed for that purpose. The staff's tolerance of misbehaviour is somewhat higher than most other hotels. Bollocks. Oasis took them to the limit and then pushed them right over.

They were handed a lifetime ban after a raucous night which began with fights, smashed chairs and tables, broken windows, and ended with somebody throwing a rock through the back window of the Managing Director's posh car.

Oasis packed their bags but give a shit, really. There was always somewhere else.

At Maison Rouge the band spent about four days perfecting

'Whatever', the time mainly being consumed by recording the song's live string arrangement.

They also recorded Marcus, the Abbots, Brian Cannon, Jason and others, applauding and whistling. This was packed at the song's conclusion, a mini football crowd having a major celebration.

In the remaining time, they put down complete versions of 'Listen Up', 'Fade Away', and Noel demoed a new song entitled 'Some Might Say'.

The band were doubly excited because now not only did they have an album ready to go and a new single to follow at Christmas, but they were, at last, about to fly to America at the same time as the yearly music seminar held in New York.

America. They had watched it unfurl on their TV screens all their lives. Cop shows like *T.J. Hooker* and *Police Woman* and *Kojak*, but not that one with the two women detectives, Cagney and whatever, nah, that was boring.

Anyway, now they would see it for themselves.

'I remember,' Marcus says, 'sitting them down and saying, America is going to be hard work, it's nothing like Britain. This is like fucking around compared to America.

'And they were going, "We're fucking mad for it, we're going to have it large."'

Before they departed, Noel, much to Liam's disgust, walked on-stage at a London college to deliver a version of 1960s garage group The Seeds' song 'Pushing Too Hard', with Ian McNabb, formerly of The Icicle Works but now being backed by Neil Young's band, Crazy Horse. That was the bait that lured Noel.

Now a committed Young fan, Noel said, 'It was insane. I was on the dole a year ago and now I'm playing with Crazy Horse.' After the show, Noel reportedly ran through 'Supersonic' for the Crazy Horse gang. How mad was this?

Liam, ever the purist, wondered why the fuck his brother would want to play with a bunch of tired old rockers.

'We couldn't really hear what Noel was up to when we were up there 'cos it as so loud,' McNabb told Cliff Jones in *Guitar* magazine, 'but I've just listened to the DATS of the gig and I was gobsmacked. Noel was playing like Peter fucking Green.'

Noel smiles at the comment. 'I didn't even know the fucking chords before I got up there.'

It is in this same article that Noel reveals that Johnny Marr has given him a guitar that Pete Townshend once owned, and that it drives him crazy when journalists ask Liam about Oasis's music 'because he hasn't got a clue where it comes from'.

With Liam in mind, Noel defines his and his brother's relationship as 'A classic case of hating the one you love. He wishes he was me 'cos I can write the songs, and I wish I was as brassy and cocky as him and I'm not. There you have it.'

Then, in a flippant quote that Liam won't forget for a long time, Noel says, 'I live in my own world and in that world the only thing that really matters is music. If the Devil popped up tomorrow and said it's a straight choice between music and relationship – be it mum, girlfriend or even Liam – I'd sign on the dotted line.'

When Liam read that, blood shot to his head. Dickhead, don't ever insult Mam like that again. It was a kind of blasphemy.

On their first night in New York, Sony took the band out for a meal. It was here that an executive told Liam that he was lucky to be signing to his label. Liam gave him the look. Lucky? Us? Listen, mate . . .

The next night, Liam had a similar to-do with an influential MTV executive who poured scorn on British bands who came over thinking that they could crack America, only to fall at the first hurdle. Liam could see his point, but Oasis were different. The MTV guy disagreed and, of course, Liam flipped at him.

'He said to the guy,' Marcus recalls, 'look, we've only been here for five minutes, give us a break. See, in that period America was very cynical about British guitar music. They'd seen one failure after another and I think the last poor fuckers to get it were Suede.

'I was very conscious of that, and had long meetings with the company about how to swerve the cynicism, break it down slowly. The whole strategy was quite painstaking. How to approach the media and the radio because we can't do it the same way as everyone else, blah, blah, blah.

'And then in the small hours of the morning at the Paramount Hotel this MTV guy is saying to Liam, "You've got no fucking chance," and this guy just kept on and on, about how they've got their own music, Pearl Jam, Nirvana and in the end Liam lost his rag. He said to him, "Me and you, outside."

'It was the talk of the industry the next day and the reason it was the talk of the industry was because some guy had enough guts to stand up to an MTV executive and say, "Fuck you, you're wrong and I'm not kissing your butt."

'The next day I was approached,' Marcus remembers with a smile, 'by a couple of sad-fuck promotion people who said, "I think you should have dinner with this guy to smooth it over."

'I said, "I'd rather have pins stuck in my fucking eyes." I said, "I'm proud of this guy and I'm not embarrassed by it." I said, "I would have been fucking cheering from the touchlines if I was there." That's where Liam's quote about Kurt Cobain being a sad cunt came from.'

Marcus pauses. 'And that's why the guy's wife burst into tears. She was a friend of Kurt Cobain's.'

Oasis played the Wetlands Hall in Brooklyn, New York. In this way, they circumvented Manhattan, the heart of the seminar. It was a paying gig, a fact Noel insisted on. No fat-cats getting in for free around here, mate. Sonya from Echobelly was in the audience, so were a few of the other British musicians.

Then it was a party and the next day, 21 July, it was on to Central Park to shoot a video for the next single, 'Live Forever'. This was directed by an American, Carlos Grossy, for British transmission. Later on, they would reshoot the video in London with a British director, Nick Egan, for American transmission.

Egan also reshot 'Shakermaker', when the band returned to the States. In both videos his ideas would be based on cult films by the director, Nicolas Roeg: *The Man Who Fell To Earth* for 'Shakermaker' and *Performance* for 'Live Forever'.

Grossy's video showed Liam sat on a chair suspended to a wall and then, in a symbolic foretaste of what was to come, the band buried an unsuspecting, uncomplaining Tony McCarroll.

Part of the shoot also entailed filming the band performing in Central Park. The band set up with their tiny amps and, in between takes, jammed on a few songs.

But Liam's mike was left off as there was nothing to put it through.

So what? Fuck the video. Let's do a free gig. It'll be boss.

No said Noel, and pointed out that they would have to hire equipment in and at ten-thirty at night, even if this is New York, it's out of the question.

Why?

Again, the temper, again the insults, again Liam stalking off, this time into a darkened and dangerous Central Park, calling Noel a sad pop star, telling people about, 'That fucking Elvis over there.'

The band returned to Britain and Marcus immediately called Liam and Noel into a meeting. Their relationship had now reached such levels of bad temper that it was affecting everyone. They would have to get it back on an even keel or the band would implode.

The brothers agreed to ease off each other and went back to homes in Manchester and London. It wouldn't be the first time that America would severely test Noel and Liam Gallagher.

Britain was a different matter.

In the ten days leading up to 31 July, the date of the band's next big show, the T In The Park Festival in Hamilton, near Glasgow, the band shot a video at the Borderline club for 'Cigarettes and Alcohol'.

Again, they used Mark Szaszy. They came early and set up their gear. Szaszy filmed them playing. In between takes, they fucked around with new ideas for other songs of theirs, 'Fade Away', for example. This was Noel's homage to punk, a 100-mile-an-hour, heads-down rocker. Noel now changed the tempo, slowed the song right down, and as he did so the song's potential shone through.

Then he started running through a new chord sequence he had written and the band jammed on it. It sounded very Neil Young but there was undoubtedly something there. A year later people would know it as 'Hey Now'.

Owen Morris walked in with his mix of 'Whatever'. They played it through the speakers and everyone agreed that it was top. The drinks came out, and so did the pills and the powders.

After filming close-ups of the band, a specially-invited audience was then let into the venue. Meanwhile, the band were backstage being filmed with a host of models.

'That must have been top,' someone said to Liam.

'Fuck off mate, one of the stupid bitches dropped beer all over my shirt.'

*

249

Oasis came back to the stage and played to the crowd who reacted in the manner the band was now becoming accustomed to: with total enthusiasm.

The shoot finished and the band, now off their heads, went their various ways, made their various plays.

On 31 July, British summertime, it rained. Oasis were in Glasgow ready to travel to the T In The Park Festival. But there was a hiccup. The band's coach driver had pulled up at a garage and mistakenly filled his tank with diesel, not petrol. The band had to wait hours for the AA to arrive.

The gig served to cement even further their live reputation. The Celtic bond between band and audience defied even the rain.

On 9 August, more chaos, more headlines. Would it ever be possible for them to play a show smoothly? It didn't look likely.

Oasis are on-stage at Newcastle's Riverside and Noel has just gone into his solo on 'Bring It On Down'. He's already aware of a guy down the front who keeps mouthing the words 'Dennis Tueart' at him, this being the Geordie footballer who was a local hero but then played Judas and crossed over to Manchester City's 1974 football squad. His transfer was still obviously bothering this man.

Oasis haven't yet employed security guards to watch out for them. Why should they? Band and audience are the same, aren't we?

The crowd are pressed against the stage, except for this guy. Suddenly, he's on-stage and he's burying his fist into one of Noel's famous eyebrows. Pain shoots through Noel's head, blood gushes out, splattering the stage.

Next thing Noel know he's pummelling this guy with his fists, and Liam, of course, is next to him and wading in as well. Panic in the hall of Riverside.

The guy escapes and the Gallagher brothers back off to the dressing room.

Liam returns to say they won't be back.

The band then quickly head for the van as the angry crowd start spilling out on to the streets, annoyed at being denied their gig. So are the band, who cram into the van with Maggie. The van slowly wends its way through the people; the band, wisely, are out of sight, their heads just beneath the windows.

At the Irish Centre in Leeds the next night they sit in the dressing-room and listen to the Radio One broadcast of that show.

Marcus meanwhile is on the phone. He wants bodyguards, and quick. The Leeds show is fine but the truth remains that while everyone had been gleefully building the bubble they had forgotten one thing: 'It's a tough, tough world out there.'

And a very real one. This is Oasis's first reality check.

In the Eye of the Hurricane

Noel Gallagher came to with a start and for a brief two seconds wondered where the fuck he was. The floor he lay on was freezing cold and for some reason there was a bath next to him. Then he remembered.

Round about four, with the ceiling spinning round, he had passed out drunk in his hotel bathroom. He was in Cardiff and, that's right, he had just played two gigs at the large International Arena across the road. On the Tuesday night, Heavy Stereo, a new Creation signing, had supported, while the following night the Manic Street Preachers played their first gig since losing, in mysterious circumstances, their guitarist, Richie James.

Oasis themselves had performed brilliantly over the two nights, but then they were so well drilled these days through constant playing, that they rarely played below a certain standard.

Noel shivered, pulled himself up and then checked his watch. They were flying to Dublin today and he was due in the lobby at one-thirty.

Battling, as usual, with his hangover, he showered and packed his bags. Then he realised that the ring he had left on the chest of drawers was gone. He searched the room carefully but still he couldn't locate it. Now he started to get angry. This was a personal item of his and someone had entered the room and stolen it. It was the only explanation he could think of.

No doubt, he bitterly thought to himself, it will sell in a Sotheby's auction twenty years down the line and sell for thousands. He had to admit that this fame game was really getting on his tits now. It had been fun at first but now it was turning into a real drag, a real fucking drag.

He came downstairs in a grumpy mood. Everyone was

waiting on him except Liam. Very early that morning he had appeared in the lobby of the hotel with Patsy Kensit at his side and announced that they had decided to travel back to London before rejoining the group in Dublin the next night.

On the way home they had phoned Chris Evans' Radio One breakfast show. There had been reports in the papers that the couple had recently been arguing and that a split-up was imminent.

They told Evans the stories were totally untrue; they were in love and happy as could be. The DJ would later broadcast the interview to millions of listeners all over the country.

When Noel heard this story on the way to the airport, he was incredulous. 'The dickhead, what's he fucking playing at?' he asked, shaking his head. 'He's in love.' Noel sneered, 'I'll give him in love, the twat. He's going to get some right proper stick for this.'

The flight over was uneventful and by seven that night the band were ensconced in Dublin's Westbury Hotel. 'I'll give you a shout if I decide to go out,' Noel told Kevin the security man, 'but I doubt it very much.'

Then Noel checked into his room, gave it about ten minutes or so, and then sneaked downstairs and out of the hotel. He needed to spend time alone, get his head in shape.

Noel moved quickly through the Dublin streets, the hood of his green jacket pulled up tight over his face. No one recognised him and the next day over morning coffee he was exultant.

'Fucking gave Kevin the right slip,' he told Alan White and Bonehead, raising his fist in triumph. 'Walked all over town, top time.'

It was 22 March 1996 and about eleven in the morning.

The band decided to go shopping and Kevin accompanied them. It was his firm, Top Guard, that had been given the Oasis security job. The majority of their clients were boxers, but as this was one of the biggest jobs they had ever landed, Kevin had personally taken charge.

Halfway down the crowded main street, they were recognised. Kids stopped in their tracks and then surrounded them. If they went into a shop, mobs of them would wait outside.

By the time they reached the end of the street, about fifty kids were walking with them. Noel was the main target and he manfully struggled to sign their scraps of paper, but it was getting ridiculous.

So they headed over to shops situated in a main student area where things might be cooler. On the way there, a guy in his mid-twenties stopped Noel.

'I went to see Bruce Springsteen last night at the Point,' he informed him. 'That's where you're playing isn't it?'

'It is indeed,' Noel replied.

'Well, I had the pleasure of meeting Bruce and I asked him what he thought of youse lot. He said, he was glad that there was a good rock 'n' roll band around.'

'Did he?' Noel said, with obvious disinterest.

At lunchtime, after visiting a few record and clothes shops, the boys stopped at a quiet café for lunch. They ordered the usual: eggs, sausages, beans, chips, bread, mugs of tea.

Alan White had just bought a Motown Records compilation and over lunch he pulled the inner-sleeve of the record out. On each side was printed the covers of other Motown albums.

'Let's have a look at that,' Noel said. He studied it for a minute and then said, 'We should do that. Put all the sleeves of our records on the next album.'

'Yeah, but it wouldn't fill the page like that,' Bonehead pointed out. 'That's all right,' Noel replied, 'we could use the rest of the page up with sleeves of all our favourite records. It would look ace.'

'Top idea, Noel,' Bonehead agreed.

Noel handed the sleeve back to Whitey. 'Another great idea from Brian Cannon, our sleeve designer,' Noel said, sarcastically.

After eating, the boys wandered back to the hotel. When they arrived there were something like a hundred shining young faces waiting for them.

'Noel,' they cried and rushed forward.

Kevin quickly placed himself in front of Noel and then guided him through the screaming mob. As he did so, the most beatific smile appeared on Noel's face as if he had been waiting all his life for this to happen.

Later on that evening Liam and Patsy arrived. They went up to their room and within minutes had got into an almighty row. There were tears and crashes, shouting and screaming.

Finally, Liam stalked off. To cool down, he sat in a chair by the lifts, glaring directly ahead of him. Anyone who approached him quickly backed off.

When he had finally shaken off his sullen mood, he went out for a drink and found himself in a bar with Michael Hutchence, the INXS singer. The two had a history. They had had a run-in at the MTV awards in Paris, earlier in the year, supposedly concerning Hutchence's girlfriend, Paula Yates, who had made no secret of her desire to bed Liam. This was their first meeting since that incident.

In the bar everyone conspired to keep them apart. But the wild-hearted singer wasn't having that, and soon there were words and insults thrown between both men. The next day's papers wrongly reported they had exchanged punches.

Meanwhile, the fans kept up their vigil outside the hotel. Some even spent the night outside and in the morning woke up knowing that as today was the first gig, at some point the band would have to make an appearance. There were fans at the front door and fans by the other exit.

It was a drizzly day but the fans couldn't care. They sang 'Wonderwall', 'Don't Look Back In Anger' and then 'Wonderwall' again, and then they screamed because they thought they saw a band member peeping out of a bedroom window but it was only Terry the security man. So they groaned, started singing again.

At one-thirty the band assembled in the lobby which was situated a floor above the street. Downstairs in the car park, three massive cars had their motors running. Kevin and Terry ushered the band into the staff lift and they shot down to the car park.

Then they hopped into the cars and were driven out into the street where a police escort was quietly waiting. A few quick-minded kids spotted the band and surrounded the car, banging on the roof as it sped off.

The incident left the group in hysterics. They had seen all this in Beatles' documentaries and now it was happening to them. Unreal.

On the way to the Point, the car passed two leather-clad bikers, standing by the pavement with their bikes. Noel immediately pushed open the car-roof, stood up and shouted 'Sweaties!' at them. 'That's what we used to call those bastards in Manchester,' he explained to Alan White, sitting back down.

At the Point, the band made straight for the stage. They ran through a few numbers, including 'Free As A Bird' by The Beatles, and then Noel soundchecked his acoustic guitar. The first song he played was 'Ticket To Ride'. But unlike The Beatles' recording, he played it as a ballad and it was achingly beautiful, Noel instantly locating the soul of Lennon's bitter-sweet lament.

Better was to come. Ireland have always held Oasis in great esteem. Every gig they had played there has been a staggering success, the crowds instantly relating to the Irish element of Noel's music.

'If you look at Gaelic bands, and I'm not likening us to any of them,' Noel said in the dressing-room, 'but if you look at the likes of U2, The Skids, Simple Minds, Stiff Little Fingers, The Undertones, they always had these rousing, fist-in-the-air choruses. And I suppose it's also because we have this rootsy, folk feel on some of the other songs which you get subconsciously from your childhood.'

Whatever it was, that night at the Point the Crowd was the wildest, the most committed, the most passionate the band had encountered in a long time. Given the reception Oasis receive at all their gigs, it was really saying something.

From the front row to the back, a distance of hundreds of feet, the response remained the same; absolutely phenomenal. The crowd stamped, cheered, threw themselves around, lit lighters during Noel's set and sang themselves hoarse.

Oasis played out of their skins, putting everything they had into their playing.

It was the kind of gig they had dreamed about when they were nobodies and scuffling around Manchester. Now it was theirs for the taking and they weren't going to let it pass.

Straight after this amazing concert, Noel and girlfriend Meg jumped into a car with a representative of Sony Ireland and were whisked away to *The Gay Byrne Show*, a live TV chatshow, the most popular programme in Ireland. Noel had agreed to make this appearance, mainly because it was one of Peggy's favourite shows and partly because it would sell him a shitload more albums.

On the way to the studio he was still visibly shaking from delight at the gig. 'That crowd,' he said, shaking his head, 'fucking unbelievable.'

By the time he walked on to the TV set to rapturous applause, he had somehow managed to compose himself, to make it look as if he had been out sightseeing all day and had now strolled in for a chat.

It was a gentle, innocuous interview. Noel, dressed in a green-patterned, button-down shirt and light brown army trousers, opened up with an acoustic version of 'Wonderwall'. Then he spoke with Gay Byrne, who asked him about songwriting and pressure.

Noel answered with grace and humility, aware that this was one interview Peggy and her friends were bound to watch. There was no way he would embarrass her by getting out of order.

He told Byrne that the gig he had just played was one of the best he had ever been involved in and that the band were too busy working to take much note of the massive hysteria surrounding them.

'In the eye of the hurricane is where it's calmest,' he said, unconsciously quoting George Harrison from The Beatles' *Anthology* on TV.

A member of the audience asked him how long it could last for and Noel told him he hated predicting the future.

'Look at The Beatles,' he pointed out, 'people used to ask them that and they'd say, ten months or whatever. But thirty years later they're still releasing records.'

With time running out, Noel picked up his guitar and then, just as he had done with 'Ticket To Ride', he transformed 'Live Forever', this time from a celebratory song into a reflective, at times mournful ballad.

The crowd listened in absolute silence and then burst into genuine applause. Noel shyly acknowledged them (it was after all a performance that any mum could be proud of), and then he was gone, back to the Point where the bar was still open and there might be a chance of getting some gear.

It seemed unlikely. Dublin was going through something of a drugs drought, and most people were settling on alcohol to do the trick. The band arrived back at the Westbury at about two in the morning.

The bar was next to the lobby but everyone sat out in the hotel's massive sitting-room. The atmosphere was calm, a kind of end-of-great-party vibe, until Noel happened to look over at a girl staring him out.

'You okay?' he asked her.

'I'm fine,' she said aggressively, 'how the fuck are you?'

'I'm great,' Noel warily said. Already, he had a sense of what was coming.

'I bet you are,' she bitterly said. Noel caught the inflection in her tone.

'What did you say?' he asked.

'Do you care?' she replied.

'Look,' Noel said, 'have a drink, whatever, but don't get cheeky, okay?'

'Oh,' she said, tossing her head back, 'and what are you going to do about that? Have me thrown out?'

'If I wanted to I could, so shut it.'

'Oh, you could, could you? Well, kiss your mother's arse.'

'Right.' Noel put down his drink and looked over for his security guards.

'Terry, Kevin,' he shouted, motioning for them to come over.

'You're joking, aren't you?' the girl said.

'No, I'm not.'

Kevin arrived.

'Throw this one out,' Noel said simply, not even bothering to look at her.

'Oh for fuck's sake,' she shouted. 'Who the fuck do you think you are?'

At which point, Liam's ears pricked up. Three nights before in Cardiff, a similar incident had occurred. Liam had been sitting with Terry, Kevin and a fan. But the fan kept giving Liam lip, eventually flicking a cigarette at him. Liam stood up and walked away to another table.

Kevin and Terry had grabbed the guy and threw him out of the hotel. As they did so, Liam looked over and shouted, 'Oi, don't fucking do that, he's only a kid.' He had been insulted but he was still on the guy's side.

Now he saw Noel throwing out what he thought was a fan and he came over to see what was happening.

'What are you doing?' he demanded.

'Throwing her out,' Noel lazily replied.

'What the fuck for? What's she done?'

'None of your business.'

'Yeah it fucking is. You can't throw her out.'

'Yes I can, I just have.'

'You fucking dickhead.'

At this, Noel leapt to his feet.

'Look you,' he shouted. 'If I want to throw her out, I will and it's nothing to do with you, all right?'

'No, it ain't fucking all right,' Liam shouted back. Instantly, the brothers quickly moved towards each other and now their faces were nearly touching. In that very moment, for Noel and Liam Gallagher, the world had just disappeared. All they knew, all they saw, all they heard was each other. It was of no use whatsoever to try and separate them because they wouldn't have even known that someone else was near them.

'She insulted our mother, all right,' Noel shouted. At that, Liam immediately backed off.

'Okay, okay,' he said, raising his arms in compliance. 'Got you.'

'You're the fucking best, Liam, okay,' Noel continued, real passion in his voice, 'the best there is, but you don't mess in my business.'

'Okay, okay,' said Liam, 'sack it, fine.'

And he walked away. Noel sat back down but the party was over now, destroyed in a few explosive minutes.

The next day at the soundcheck, Noel revealed a new song. He shouted to Hugh, 'Get this one down on tape otherwise I'll forget it and won't make any money, ha, ha, ha.'

Then he started slamming out a burning riff and some huge chords and after a minute or so, the rest of the band joined in. They jammed on it for over five minutes and Noel looked more than satisfied as he walked off-stage.

The band's mood was high. They knew what to expect from the crowd and couldn't wait to get back on-stage. It was all such a buzz. In the kitchen, Phil Smith, their old roadie and friend was waiting for them. He had travelled over from Manchester, where he shared a house with Mark Coyle, to see them.

The last time Noel had seen Phil was at their house. The three of them had sat in their sitting-room, playing easy-listening records while Phil and Noel made abusive comments to Mark about his support for Manchester United.

That day, Noel had been to a meeting with Francis Lee, the

City chairman, at City's training ground. City wanted to print the name Oasis on their shirts the following season.

'But tastefully,' Lee pointed out. 'Woven into the fabric like.'

Noel made no commitment either way, just quietly listened and then told Lee and his representatives to call Marcus. It was obvious that he wasn't 100% sure about the idea. But he had met Francis Lee.

'So you coming to the game against Coventry, lad?' Lee had asked him.

'No way,' Noel replied, 'every time I go to see City they lose. It's true. Once the players see me, they go, Oh shit, he's here, we've had it. Then they don't play well at all. I'll watch it on telly, me.'

Noel left the meeting and that night he went over to Phil and Mark's house. When he got there he told them that he had given their number to their all'time idol, Burt Bacharach, who was trying to get in touch with Noel about some future recording.

It was Mark and Phil who had put Noel on to Bacharach's music. They all adored him equally. Noel often said that his own music could never match the quality of Bacharach's. It pissed over most other people's, and when it came to the man who composed 'This Guy's In Love With You', probably Noel's all-time favourite song, then forget it.

That night, everytime the phone rang, the boys would momentarily freeze and then either Phil or Mark would calmly go and answer the phone. But it was never him.

Now, in Dublin, Phil was telling Noel, Burt had actually called a couple of days later. 'So we've framed the phone,' Phil told him excitedly, 'because that's the phone Burt Bacharach rang our house on.'

Jill Fumanovsky, Oasis's main photographer, was also present. She had brought over pictures from their recent American tour and the band pored over them for at least half an hour. Noel rarely chose one of them smiling.

Later on, most of the band watched the Manics set from the side of the stage and then, five minutes before they were due on, they sat listening to a tape of the new song they had played at soundcheck.

'That's fucking top,' Liam enthused.

'I've got a great melody to go over it,' Noel said to no one in particular.

'You should bring the drums in here,' Liam said.

'Fucking hell,' Noel said, exasperated. 'I haven't even written the song yet and he's telling me how to play it.'

Again, the gig was a huge celebration, a true meeting of band and audience in which everyone present lost themselves in the music and the occasion, only to come back to reality as 'I Am The Walrus' faded from the speakers.

Backstage, Bono, singer with U2, came to greet the band and invite them back to his huge house. The band declined the offer, and sat exhausted in the dressing-room as people swirled all around them.

Eventually, Guigsy went over to U2's club with Ruth, Mouse from catering and a few others. Much to his annoyance, Hutchence was there and Guigsy sat there staring him out.

'One move and I'll chin him,' he snarled. 'He doesn't talk to my mate like that,' Guigsy said, referring to the incident with Liam the night before.

Someone from the club came over and invited Guigsy and his party to the closed-off section, and thus trouble was averted. At two in the morning Guigsy, Ruth, Maggie and Melissa walked back to the hotel.

Most people had gone to bed but in the sitting-room area Liam sat on a chair saying, 'I'm going to have the cunt, I'm fucking going to have him. I don't care who he's with, I'll chin the cunt.' Terry and Bonehead sat by him, trying to calm him down.

'No, Liam, leave it,' Terry said in his thick London accent. 'Let him have his drink and just fucking ignore him.'

'He's right,' said Bonehead, 'ignore the cunt. That's what will get to him. He wants you to go over there and do something.'

'Well, I fucking will,' Liam asserted.

The two women closest to Liam weren't at the hotel. Peggy was staying in another hotel with her sisters and Patsy was now in London. She had flown back that morning.

Meanwhile, Thomas Gallagher, allegedly paid by the *News Of The World* to book into the same hotel, sat in the same bar as his youngest son and looked over and waited.

'What's he fucking doing here?' Liam demanded. And then he was up and away, making his way straight towards the father he hadn't seen in years.

Terry gave chase and just as Liam got to his dad's table, he swiftly blocked him off.

'You fucking cunt, I'll break your legs,' Liam shouted trying to get round Terry.

'You couldn't break Albert Tatlock's legs,' Thomas sneered.

'You cunt, I'll have you.'

Liam went to punch him but everytime he moved, Terry expertly moved with him. Liam threw his arms up in disgust and walked away, back to his seat. He looked hurt, devastated.

Suddenly, Noel entered the room, walked past his father, and went straight to Liam.

'Liam, come with me.'

'No, I won't.'

'Liam! You come with me right now.' Noel was in no mood to argue, his voice made that patently clear.

Liam stood up and Noel took him by the arm and guided him to the far side of the room. They disappeared behind some curtains.

Bonehead watched them disappear and said, 'It had to happen. We've been waiting years for this. We knew it had to come some time. And now it has.'

Kevin came over to where Bonehead was.

'I think we should clear the bar. He's gone now.'

'I think that's exactly what should happen,' Bonehead said in total agreement.

The bar swiftly emptied to leave Noel Gallagher and his brother alone, speaking words that no one could hear.

Finally, Noel went back to his room.

As he came in, Meg woke up and Noel told her what had just gone down.

'Oh my God,' she cried, 'are you all right?'

'Yeah, I'm fine,' Noel said. And then he couldn't resist it. 'Fucking hell Meg, you're meant to be my wonderwall, and you were fast asleep when it all went off. What kind of wonderwall are you?'

The next day a security guard was placed outside both Noel and Liam's rooms. Thomas had already left. Noel ordered up a bottle of Jack Daniels and a bottle of coke, and he and Meg partied all day and all night. Close your eyes, the monster has gone.

Liam surfaced mid-afternoon and went downstairs to the bar. He seemed happy and relaxed. The thing they had dreaded ever since fame came knocking on their door had taken place. The storm was over, spent. Now they could relax in the sunshine. Maybe.

A waitress came over and Liam ordered some sandwiches.

'What room have you got?' she sweetly asked.

'I haven't got a room,' he said.

The waitress laughed. 'Course you have,' she said.

'Nah,' he said, warming up. 'I haven't got a room.'

'But you're staying here.'

'I am,' he confirmed, 'but I haven't got a room because the TV is on the floor, the mattress is in the bath, the bed is upsidedown, and I don't call that a room.'

Both he and the waitress laughed.

Sitting with him were Tim and Chris Abbot plus their parents. They too ordered sandwiches and just as they arrived the fans outside started singing 'Wonderwall'.

'I think your fans want you,' Tim said.

Liam picked up his place, stood up and went and pulled back the curtains to gaze down at them. The fans looked up and screamed. Liam pretend to offer them a sandwich. They screamed even louder. He pulled back the curtains and returned to the table.

'Now that,' he announced, 'is fucking fame for you. Screams when you're having your sarnie.' He shook his head.

Behind him, on another table, lay copies of that day's tabloid newspapers who all carried pictures of Liam and Patsy. The main story alleged that Patsy was pregnant by Liam.

Liam took a bite of his sandwich and said, 'How mad is this?'

He said it to the Abbots. Really he was saying it to himself.

PART THREE

Fourteen

Well before he signed to Creation, Noel Gallagher was playing his career like the best poker-player in town. He knew that he held all the aces in his hand. He had no idea why he had been handed these cards. That would puzzle him for the rest of his life.

But facts were facts. He held them, and now it was a matter of timing, when to show, when to hide, when to bluff.

'Live Forever' was the first ace he laid on the table. If the first two Oasis singles had suggested that something special might be happening, 'Live Forever' was the irrefutable proof that something *was*. It's a classic record.

Noel knew that once he had placed it on the table, his reputation would rocket sky-high. It came coupled with an acoustic version of 'Up In The Sky' (the title adapted from Jimi Hendrix's 'Up From The Skies'), 'Cloudburst', and a live version of 'Supersonic', and was released the day before Noel's forehead was gashed open in Newcastle.

Unlike the preceding two singles, 'Live Forever' was lyrically direct and musically ecstatic. It began with a hip-hop-like drumbeat and ended in a squall of musical chaos and Liam insisting that we would all 'live forever'.

This life-affirming record worked on two levels. First, it reached out to people by using the classic Us Versus Them sentiment ('We see things they'll never see'), and secondly, the music was so uplifting that it gave you every reason to believe that even death could be beaten.

Liam said 'I wanted a band that could make music which would make you high without having to take a pill,' and this was it.

It was the song that made everyone who wasn't yet quite convinced by the band, hold up their hands and say, 'All yours, boys,' just as Noel knew it would. He knew also that it would be the first Oasis single to penetrate the club fraternity, those not bothered by indie music or pop sensations. They would hear it blasting out of radios and say, 'Who's that record by again?' This was because the song's sentiments mirrored the euphoric feeling that Ecstasy gives to its users.

In the perfect world it would have shot in at number one but it went in at number ten and reached no higher. It should also have been *NME*'s Single Of The Week (it was undoubtedly, most people's Single Of The Year), but instead, John Mulvey called it 'a terrific record', and added, 'It TOTALLY gives off the impression that the Gallaghers believe they can make the world dance around their little fingers just when they like, which they can nowadays, more or less.'

Noel Gallagher winked, having cashed in the first of many chips. On 11 August it was the Wulfron Hall, Wolverhampton again, and then on the 13th, Sweden for the Hultsfred Festival. One performance and the country was theirs.

'They came on,' Andres Lokko, founder of the influential *Pop* magazine, recalls, 'about six-thirty in the evening which is always a good time to play. They were on the second stage and you know that feeling when you discover a band and go, "Yes, this is my band." Well, that's what happened to 20,000 Swedes.'

In triumphant mood, Oasis returned to their hotel where they met up with The Verve, Primal Scream, and a very unfortunate barman who had the thankless job of informing them that there would be no more drinks that night. Wrong.

After various threats, the bands rethought the situation and put Plan B into action. Okay mate, off you go to bed, we'll just sit and talk here for a little while. We'll be fine. See ya later. Goodnight.

Then the screwdrivers came out, the bar was dismantled and then thoroughly ransacked.

Three hours later Bobby Gillespie was banging on an acoustic guitar, him and Liam screaming the Stones' 'Satisfaction' at each other, until Malloy, the Primal's head of security came over, picked Bobby up and carted him away.

'Liam!' Bobby shouted over Malloy's shoulders, 'We're gonna live forever.'

When the booze ran out the two groups then contemplated

their next move. One of them then came up with a suggestion. Wasn't that a church they saw on the way coming in? And what do churches use at masses? Wine. Lovely, red wine. C'mon!

The boys left the hotel, found the church and then broke in. They searched everywhere, the vestry, the altar. Reluctantly, they went back empty-handed to the hotel. As they walked back to the bar they had just vacated, a sizeable amount of policeman, alerted by a horrified guest in the hotel, were now heading their way. The police arrived at six, surrounded the hotel and the bands were led out to their coaches, like convicts on a chain gang.

Next day, Oasis were front-page news in Sweden. Do we need this filth? the paper asked.

Two days later, 15 August, Oasis played the Rock City in Nottingham and began three rollercoaster days that contained two triumphant shows in London. The Forum on the 16th (where Paul Weller came backstage and Noel finally managed to start chatting), a *Top Of The Pops* appearance on the 17th for 'Live Forever', and then the Astoria on the 18th, when Donna from the group Elastica sat in Liam's dressing-room after the gig and complained about the *NME* ignoring loads of great unsigned bands.

'The *NME*?,' Liam shot back, 'the fucking *NME*. Listen, we spent three years slogging our guts out and none of those fuckers wrote about us. But we did it. We made it and we did it without the *NME*. Don't worry about those wankers.'

'I suppose you're right,' she said.

'Damn, fucking right I am,' he said, pacing up and down the tiny room. Afterwards, there was a party at the Leisure Lounge in Holborn. There were queues round the block while inside envious young musicians stood at the bar dreaming of the day that this would all be theirs. Oasis were the hippest band in the world, and the drug dealers made a killing.

In a newsagents nearby, Oasis stared out from the cover of the *NME* (again), *Melody Maker* and the *Face*. The latter magazine asked if the brother's tempestuous relationship would split them apart, failing to note that at the photo shoot, Hopkins stepped in to wrap things up quickly as he could sense trouble rising between Liam and Noel.

The *Face* tagged Oasis as the The Sex Beatles, and Noel thought, 'Fuck, why didn't I think of that name.'

Later, when Richard Ashcroft left The Verve, Noel remembered the name and suggested that he use it for his new outfit.

'No, I've got a better name,' Ashcroft replied, 'The Heat.'

'Fuck,' Noel said, 'Why didn't I think of that?' mentally kicking himself again.

Even the newspapers were now smelling a story they could get their teeth into. London's *Evening Standard* gave over a page to the band on 11 August, with Noel adding more fuel to the fire.

'Liam's the star,' he told Sam Taylor. 'He's the singer, and singers have always been conceited tossers; look at Morrissey, Mick Jagger, Roger Daltrey . . . Liam's a genius frontman but he'd be nothing without me.'

The next day, the *Guardian* ran a piece and on Sunday it was the *Observer Review*, plus a patronising *Sunday Times* article that compared Oasis with Suede, concluding, 'If they don't want to go the way of Suede, they had better put that mirror aside.' As if.

On Tuesday it was the *Independent* with Noel vowing, 'People stop proving themselves, which is something I will never let happen to this band.'

On Monday 22 August they finally appeared in a paper they read. The *Daily Mirror* ran a piece about the Newcastle show. This is when you know for sure that any lingering doubts about your popularity are mistaken, when the tabloids move in.

Of course, Oasis were prime material. Sex and drugs. This one would run and run and run and run and . . .

The fans were starting to have their say now. 'Seeing Oasis from the front at the T In The Park was worth every bruise, and whoever writes their set-lists can't spell the word "Alcohol". Tiny bit ironic, that,' Liam's Next Groupie From Glasgow wrote in the *NME*. Other letters severely caned the guy who wrecked the Newcastle gig.

'I'd like to buy him tickets for Blur, Suede and Ride gigs,' wrote Tom Bradshaw from Solihull.

In the same issue, these letter-writers and thousands of other readers read a glowing review of the début Oasis album. 'Of course, as Liam Gallagher himself advises,' *NME*'s Keith Cameron concluded after pulling out all the superlatives, 'in the spiralling mantric conclusion to "Rock 'n' Roll Star", "It's just rock 'n' roll." Quite so, young man. That's all *Definitely Maybe* is. But when it's this brilliant, it's enough.'

Over at *Melody Maker*, Paul Lester was telling his readers, 'Just buy this record before tomorrow and if you don't agree it offers a dozen opportunities to believe 1994 is the best year ever for pop/rock music, then you're . . . wrong.'

Noel basked in such praise, but a part of him would also have taken issue with that last line. 1966 had a little bit more going for it than Suede, Blur, Gene, et al.

On 28 August the band made it to Holland without the usual fracas and played the Lowlands Festival. Even Dando from The Lemonheads was there that night. His group had had a hit in the UK with their version of Simon and Garfunkel's 'Mrs. Robinson', and they were receiving a lot of respectful press. Dando hooked himself up to the band that night, and in the early morning hours, he and Noel wrote a song together, entitled 'Purple Parallelogram'.

'I can't even remember writing it with him,' Noel later confessed. 'I have no idea what the song sounds like.' Two years later, Noel probably had a better idea of its content; his publishers swiftly blocked the song being placed on the new Lemonheads album, *Car Button Cloth*.

But Dando, like most people who came into contact with Oasis, had obviously been smitten by the band. He travelled back to Britain with them to see *Definitely Maybe* showcased in shop windows and record racks everywhere. Way-hey!

The band were on their way to an in-store signing at the Virgin Megastore in London's Oxford Street. At least 1,000 fans gathered outside the shop, but only 200 were allowed in to witness them playing a seven-song acoustic set with Dando on-stage in the background, clapping his hands and occasionally banging a tambourine behind a seated Liam, Noel and Bonehead.

It was here that the trio (Guigsy and McCarroll watched from the sidelines) ran through 'Sad Song', 'Slide Away', their first three singles, and then a live premiere of 'Whatever'.

Oasis then sat down and signed autographs for something like two and a half hours, the part of the job Liam especially hates. Pens, paper, writing, it reminds him too much of school.

'We wanted to do it for them,' Noel said about the hundreds of people left outside as they played, 'because without them we're nothing.'

Outside, the fans talked about how Oasis had taken music away from the rave scene and used words like 'best', 'fresh', 'unique', 'confident', and amazing'. The people know, they always do.

This was all said for the benefit of Granada's TV cameras who were shooting a twenty-five-minute documentary on the band that would be screened two months later. The TV crew, along with Dando, accompanied the band to the next show, Tivoli in Buckley, Wales. At the soundcheck, they interviewed Noel and Liam. But separately.

'The reason,' Liam stated, 'that we're in every paper is because there's something to write about. We're playing the game, we mean it, we're honest, we've got the best songs and that's why we're in everybody's face.'

He analysed their music as being poppy with a hard edge. Then Noel spoke. He said that if his band put people on to The Beatles or the Stones, then that was worth everything. Even losing Louise.

'I've lost a lot of friends,' he noted, 'split up with my girlfriend. I was going out with this girl for about six years, living with her and all that. Hopefully, I'll get over it.'

And songwriting?

'The music and the melodies I can write every day,' he casually said from behind his huge shades, 'but the lyrics I have to wait for. The music's a doddle.'

That night, as drained and excited fans streamed out of the gig, Evan Dando, armed with an acoustic guitar, stood on the roof of the hall and 'serenaded' the crowd with songs.

Next it was back to Sweden, where their record company had unintentionally let the album out a week earlier, prompting real fears that Oasis would lose UK sales by fans snatching up import copies. That didn't happen.

They booked into a hotel the night before the show and the band went out on the town.

Next morning, Marcus rose early for a breakfast meeting. He was sitting in the hotel lobby with a Sony employee when the hotel's manageress angrily approached him, waving a copy of the day's newspaper at him.

The Sony employee translated. Oasis were on the front page because the paper couldn't believe, after the Hultsfred bar incident, how such a bunch of louts had been let back in to the country.

The manageress agreed. She had just said as much to an employee. 'But they're staying here,' she had been told, 'that's the manager over there.'

Now she was demanding to enter all their rooms at nine in the morning (they had all crawled into bed two hours ago), and check for damage. If there was any, they would be thrown out.

Marcus tried to dissuade her but then he had to laugh. 'Okay, go and wake Oasis this early. Go on.' From every room there came insults, swearing and threats.

When they were on the road all the band shared rooms except Noel. He was now insisting on having his own room, the first member of Oasis to do so. After all, he smiled, I'm not called the Chief for nothing.

Liam and Guigsy shared rooms and that left an unhappy Bonehead forced to go in with Tony McCarroll. 'One fucking word out of you,' he'd say to him, 'and you'll get it.'

But that was nothing compared to the abuse Guigsy heaped upon McCarroll's shoulders. Sometimes it was so vehement, so cruel, that even Liam and Bonehead were moved to take the fuming bassist aside and say, 'Here are Guigs, leave him alone, chill out a bit.'

Guigsy couldn't help it. If only McCarroll would keep his gob shut. But he didn't and when he didn't he came out with lines like, how he loved that Beatles song 'Ringo In The Sky With Diamonds', or, check this one, Europe was an island

That killed Liam, that one. 'I'm fucking thick,' he shouted at the drummer, 'I ain't been educated but even I know that Europe isn't a fucking island, you great big fucking dickhead.'

After the Swedish show, the band flew over to Ireland. Fittingly they played their first Irish gig, the Tivoli in Dublin, on the day the IRA announced a ceasefire. 'Mental gig,' Marcus remembers.

The next night at the Limelight in Belfast, as the band were halfway through, ironically enough, 'Bring It On Down', a lone loyalist bomb was heard to go off outside. Marcus missed that gig, opting instead to return to London for business meetings.

The next day, Oasis flew high above the sea that Peggy and Bonehead's mum had crossed all those years ago, and landed in

Manchester. Marcus was there, a grin all over his face.

Definitely Maybe, he told them, had not only shot in to the charts at number one, it was the fastest-selling début album in history. Oasis were, believe it or not, in *The Guiness Book Of Records*. They'd outsmarted even Michael Jackson. And Pavarotti, Domingo and Carreras, the Three Tenors whose album had been hotly tipped for the top spot that week.

Creation put out a smug press release boasting that Oasis would outdo three fat blokes singing any day of the week.

Definitely Maybe would stay in the charts for years to come.

So, on this victorious night, where better to perform than the Hacienda, witness to their teenage years and run by the very company that first turned them down. Oasis tore the place apart. But they did so with some revenge in their hearts. You didn't fucking listen, did you? See what you missed?

Europe was starting to take notice as well. MTV's *120 Minutes* had screamed a lengthy interview with Noel and Liam in August, the last time they would sit down together for the cameras.

Miles Hunt of The Wander Stuff was the interviewer. He'd read Noel's scathing comments about him in the *Melody Maker* and he confessed to being a little nervous about meeting them. But the boys had no axes to grind. They were saving that for each other.

On set Noel hid behind his shades and stared impassively. Liam sat next to him with a Not Bothered look on his face.

The interview began okay but the friction soon built. It started with Miles asking about the guy who had whacked Noel in Newcastle. Noel replies, 'It was because he found out I was sleeping with his girlfriend.'

'Was it?' Liam asks, slightly perking up.

'Yeah,' Noel says, staring straight ahead.

'Nice one,' Liam notes but with no energy. Months before they would have been verbally bouncing off each other after Noel's comment. But today there is bad air between them.

Soon it comes to talking about the band's history, and the rift opens wide up for all to see.

'He's took over the songs,' Liam says, 'but he's not took over how the band is run or how I'm gonna run my life. He hasn't taken over me.'

'Yes I have,' Noel interjects, but Liam ignores him and continues, 'He's took over the structure of the songs and how they should sound and he's given us discipline, which is right. But he's not taken over the vocals or the guy who stands in front of that microphone, because that's *me* .' He spits it out.

Noel sits, quietly seething, as Miles then turns to him and asks, 'So you do all the songwriting?'

Coolly but very carefully, Noel says, 'I do all the music, all the lyrics and, oh, I co-produced the album.' Top that, bruv, who can't stop seeking all the attention.

Noel, having asserted himself as the Chief, is then asked to choose a video and he selects 'Hung Up' by Paul Weller, a song that he would later nominate as Weller's best solo song for a photographic book that was published the following year on Weller.

Their other MTV appearance that month, for *Most Wanted*, was thankfully more pleasurable. Noel, Liam and Bonehead, played live, all three sitting on stools, with Bonehead at the electric piano.

Although *Definitely Maybe* has just been released they totally ignore that and instead premiere 'Whatever' for the TV cameras. At the song's conclusion, to the melody of 'All The Young Dudes', the Gallagher brothers put in a Manchester City chant, singing, 'All the young Blues/ Carry the news . . .'

They then perform a gentle 'Live Forever'. Class.

Oasis were moving at breakneck speed now, acting as if they were somehow scared that they would wake up tomorrow and find everything had been a glorious dream, the curse that afflicts all working-class people when their ambitions are actually realised.

Abroad now, to Germany, and where better to début Oasis than in Hamburg where The Beatles honed themselves into the tightest band of their generation, before the screaming started and it all went to waste, gig-wise.

Oasis played the Logo where the promoter breezily said, 'No, we don't need any barriers in front of the stage.'

Marcus replied, 'If you don't put them up, we walk.' Reluctantly, the promoter ordered that barriers be put up. After the show, he came to Marcus and said, 'Thank God you did that. I never thought the crowd would go that wild.'

Over now to the Arena in Amsterdam and from there home for a brief stay and then on to concerts in Japan (Japan!), where they hadn't even released a record yet but the gigs were all sold out. How mad was that? (On the flight over Noel and Guigsy sat together struggling with their hangovers while the rest of the band were busy inviting two girls to one of their gigs. When they showed up Guigsy was introduced to one of them. Her name was Ruth and they've been together ever since.)

The Quattro booked them for a week-long tour, starting on 13 September and ending on the 19th. Four nights in Tokyo, one gig each in their Osaka and Nagoya premises. It was absolutely mental.

Pictures came back of Noel crushed against a wall by about thirty Japanese girls, another beatific smile spread across his mouth.

The girls waited outside the hotel. They screamed when they saw the band come out, they screamed at the gigs and they screamed in delight when they got to party with them all night.

One night the band were taken to see a Beatles' copyist band called The Parrots and they were so good, so on the nail, that Noel joined them on-stage for a couple of numbers. Then back to the hotel and more girls, more drinks.

In Danielle Soave's account of all this glorious madness for *GQ* magazine, she notes Liam squaring up to Tony McCarroll in the hotel, shouting, 'You better get your shit together or you're out of this band.'

Naturally McCarroll was also driving Guigsy to distraction. One night, the bassist finally snapped. He told McCarroll that, swear to God, if he didn't shut up and go away, he was going to get a knife and plunge it into his gut.

McCarroll, immune to insults after all this time and usually able to convince himself that all was cool, chillingly realised that the bassist wasn't joking. He was deadly serious.

Panicking, McCarroll went up to Noel's room and banged on the door. Noel opened up with a brusque, 'What?'

There was a girl lying on the bed behind him. McCarroll told Noel about Guigsy's real and frightening threat.

'Well, you tell Guigsy,' Noel barked, 'that I'm the first in the queue to fucking knife you, and if Guigsy does it before me I'll have him as well.'

McCarroll walked away, not knowing how seriously troubled Noel was by his presence in the band.

The album Noel could hear in his head would demand a higher level of proficiency from all the players. He was determined to show that on his next recording he could go deeper and startle people even more with his range. With *Definitely Maybe* Oasis had trounced the opposition. Now Noel wanted to stamp all over them. *Definitely Maybe* was a great album but it showed just a few aspects of Noel's talent. To really prove himself, he and the band would have to cast the net much wider, like all his idols had done. And Noel doubted very much that if McCarroll stayed that would be a possibility.

That said, Noel couldn't forget that McCarroll had been there from day one. Like him or not, he had slogged it out with the rest of them and even if he was a total misfit, his efforts couldn't be discounted.

But something, Noel knew, before he turned his attention back to the smiling girl in his room, would have to give.

And it did. But it wasn't McCarroll who walked. It was Noel Gallagher.

He had met Brian Cannon through The Verve; Brian had designed their record sleeves. Noel liked his style and when they first met, they got on well together. They shared similar tastes and Brian was from the North as well, Wigan, to be precise.

Brian was also younger than Noel so when it came to the presentation of Oasis, Noel insisted on using the designer. Part of Noel's vision was to give outsiders a chance. They would work together although Noel made it plain from the outset that his was the final word.

At an early meeting, Brian showed Noel various logos and they decided to parody and echo the Decca Records design by inserting the word Oasis into a small box. The background would be black but Oasis would be in white.

For 'Supersonic' Brian had called in Michael Spencer Jones to shoot the band in the Monnow Valley Studio. The photograph was then printed so as to bleach the band's faces white and emphasise the slightly garish colours around them.

For the 'Supersonic' sleeve, the colours were similarly treated but the band were absent. Instead, they depicted an Oasis tape playing and everything else in the room melting as the music played.

For 'Live Forever' they changed tack and decided on a blown-up black-and-white picture of the house in Menlove Avenue, Woolton, where John Lennon had stayed with his Aunt Mimi.

On the *Definitely Maybe* album cover they again used a domestic setting. But this time it was Bonehead's old house in West Didsbury. The beauty of this sleeve is that it gives no indication whatsoever of the fiery, antagonistic music contained inside.

In the photograph, the band are totally static. They all, apart from Liam lying on the floor and staring at the ceiling, are watching Sergio Leone's *The Good, The Bad And The Ugly* on a TV. The only moving object is a swirling lampshade.

Around them are various Oasis reference points, such as the pictures of Burt Bacharach, Rodney Marsh and George Best. George Best? But he's United. Ah yes, Noel replied, but he was first and foremost an Irishman.

As the band nonchalantly laze around this flat with its potted plants and wooden floor, the impression given is one of tasteful restraint. Now put on the record and feel the opening track, 'Rock 'n' Roll Star' leap right out of the speakers and throttle your ears.

Brian Cannon, not surprisingly, was a big fan of the group so when the chance to go to Los Angeles to shoot the picture for their next single and to see them play arose, he happily accepted. He had no idea that on that trip he would see them fall apart. Nor did the country he left behind.

Britain was now besotted with the group.

All the talk was of Oasis. They were everywhere. *Top Of The Pops* had let them play an album track, 'Rock 'n' Roll Star', on the show, the *Daily Star* had now run a page feature, where they called Oasis, 'The wildest and most outrageous rock band since The Who,' and in *Vox* magazine, Noel endeared himself to every serious music lover by saying, 'I realise that without them [the band] I'm nothing, in the same way that without me they're nothing. The money won't last for ever and we'll all end up broke one day, 'cos bands like us always do. But in ten years' time, when we've got a few albums in the shop, my name will be in brackets by the songs. That's something that will last forever and it's all I want from this.

'I'm not mithered [bothered] about being on the cover of this or that, or being a sex symbol or a voice of a generation, all I'm arsed about is going down alongside Ray Davies, Morrissey and Marr, Jagger and Richards, Lennon and McCartney, Pete Townshend, Paul Weller and Burt Bacharach.'

Over at Creation Records, the company's money problems now wiped out in a stroke by Oasis, McGee had turned his obsessional nature towards healthy living. He now worked out every day in the gym. He refused all alcohol, drugs and tobacco. His high came from activating the endorphins in his brain through regular exercise. He now weighed eleven stone and he'd never felt more positive in his life.

Similarly, but in totally different ways, Tim Abbot was seriously enjoying life. He was working and playing with the most sensational band of the decade. Which is why, when he was woken at five in the morning by a call from Noel in America, he was initially pleased to hear from him. But when Noel said, he'd come over and see him tomorrow, Abbot got confused. Oasis had just started their first proper US tour.

'He said,' Abbot recalls, 'that's it, the fucking band's over. They're all fucking pricks. They don't deserve it. Can you arrange to get me guitars and me baggage back, and can you phone Marcus and apologise, and tell him I'm sorry for all the trouble I've caused but I can't go on.'

Five hours later, Abbot was on a plane bound for America.

They didn't like it, this strange land with its neon lights and funny ways. America threw them. There was an underlying falseness everywhere. People flew American flags in their back garden and said things like 'Now have a nice day' as if they meant it.

Then there were the others, like the record company people, who would come up and say, 'Hi there, Loam, where's your brother, Nile?'

In their hotel rooms they would switch on the TV and just as they were getting into some dumb cop-show, it would suddenly switch to these really stupid, false adverts that treated the viewer like he was some retard.

It would annoy them so much, they'd change the channel only to find a religious nutter talking about God and asking for millions.

But the real killer was that they had landed in a country that didn't know them. For the past year, Oasis had been the kings. They'd known nothing but success and huge attention. Everywhere they went in Britain, people stopped and stared. In the US they were barely known. It was like going back to the fucking Boardwalk or something.

Marcus had warned them about this and Noel knew the score. But it got to the others.

They started in a small club called Moe's in Seattle, Nirvana's hometown, on 23 September, and the next night played the Satyricon in Portland. The next day they travelled to San Francisco, where they were booked to appear on a radio show called *Live 105*.

The DJ had secretly invited Blur to the session thinking that the bands would be overjoyed to see each other. Wrong. Blur walked in, Damon said, 'Hello,' and Liam called him a wanker. It was pretty much downhill from there.

On the 27th they played what Marcus refers to as their first hicksville gig, Melarky's in Sacramento. The crowd gave them a good reception, which was encouraging.

Then, on their day off, they arrived in Los Angeles where they discovered crystal meth, the most potent form of speed known to man. Use it and you don't sleep for days. Then the comedown kicks in, guaranteed to depress and tire you to the point of such exhaustion that you lose patience with everything and everyone around you.

The first mistake some of the band made was to sample the drug and then stay on it, all day and all night, searching as always for the high. The second was to attend a party that Epic had unwisely thrown on the roof of the band's hotel on the afternoon of their début gig at the Whiskey.

Epic splashed out $50,000 on the bash, and Noel was moved to ask Marcus, 'What the fuck is going on? We haven't even put a record out and they're treating us like fucking Bon Jovi or something.'

Noel was starting to feel the pressure. This was an important show for the band whose rule on drink and drugs is simple. If you can handle it and play a gig to the best of your ability, then fine. If you can't . . .

Of all the band, Noel not only knew his limits but would never test them when a gig was at stake. The best high in the world was playing your songs and watching an audience go ballistic.

He was also determined that Oasis would be the first British band in years to crack America. That's why he'd kept schtum that first night in New York when his brother had gone off at the Epic guy. He had seen how things worked in the States when he was with the Inspirals. Like it or not, you needed these people on your side, because that way you could achieve something far greater than simply telling a record company guy to fuck off.

Anyone could do that. But to succeed in the States meant you could actually help change the musical climate of the country. How top would that be. Your songs having such effect. Of course, in doing so you made enough money to last several lifetimes and that little fact wouldn't have escaped Noel's attention either.

Like it or not, the Whiskey was a prestigious show. All of the LA music scene would be there, including Epic who, despite their generosity, had yet to be convinced that Oasis weren't one of these two-bit Brit bands with loads of press and little talent or stamina. This gig was Oasis's first chance to prove they were a cut above the rest and, of course, they blew it horribly.

Liam came on wired-up to the eyes and spoiling for a fight. Behind the amps he had racked out lines of crystal meth and every now and then he would disappear for a hit.

Noel apart, the rest of the band's playing was sluggish.

And as it went on, Noel got angrier and angrier. Then he saw Liam go behind the amps and when he reappeared, he shouted at him and Liam turned and hit him with his tambourine.

Standing in the audience, watching the debacle, Marcus flew into a temper. When the gig finished he marched into the dressing-room where Liam and Noel were sitting, locked the door, and went berserk.

Noel, equally as angry, then went to hit Liam, and Marcus had to step in between them. Meanwhile, outside listening to the crazed and angry shouting, Guigsy, McCarroll and Bonehead waited to get in. They stood there with their Epic employers.

The door finally opened after an hour. Noel marched out and found tour manager Maggie. 'How much money have you got on you?' he demanded. She handed over about $800 and Noel returned to his hotel.

'If you are an instigator,' Marcus points out, 'and you don't feel people appreciate what you instigate, you get hurt. Noel was really hurt bad and he didn't know where to turn to or *who* to turn to in a country that you feel very alienated in very quickly, in a city, let's be fair, that isn't exactly fucking reality. And you add it all together and you very quickly come to the conclusion, as Noel obviously did, that there's better things to do in life.'

In his hotel room, Noel phoned a girl he knew in San Francisco and asked if he could come and stay with her for a while. Then he found out the time of the next flight, and off he went to the airport, without a word to anyone.

At the girl's flat he called two people in England. The first, of course, was Peggy.

'He was going on and on about Liam,' she recalls, 'and that he was on his way home. I said, "Noel, you'll probably work it out, why don't you talk it through with him?" He said, "No, Liam is this and that," and then he said, "After all you've sacrificed for us." I said, "Noel, I didn't sacrifice anything for you because you were mine, it was my duty to bring you up."

'He said, "I know, but you put everything aside and you had to do without things." I said, "That was my job, Noel." You see, Noel would be thinking, she sacrificed everything, but as I've always said to him, "Noel, while I'm here this is your home. It doesn't matter what you do or what you don't do, this is your home."'

His second call was to Tim Abbot who, after putting the phone down, organised his flight to Los Angeles ('cost three grand, the bastards') and then flew out to LA to meet up with a band that was now devastated by Noel's disappearance. None more so, in fact, than his younger brother.

'Liam,' Marcus says, 'was going out of his mind, absolutely. He was sitting and staring at the wall. He just could not contemplate Oasis not being together. It really showed me how together they are. Most bands would have gone crying back home, but I said, "Fuck it, stay here, there's a chance Noel is going to come back and we'll carry on with the tour."

'But the worst bit for everybody was the first two or three days when he was out of contact. We were really worried for him. We didn't know if he was in fucking Manchester, Ireland, Canada, Columbia. It was horrible.'

After two days of waiting and worrying, someone suggested getting hold of Noel's telephone bill for the room. When they looked at it, the only digits that seemed strange was a San Francisco number.

Abbot dialled it.

'This girl answered,' he says, 'and I said, "It's Timmy Abbot, a friend of Noel's, I believe you might know of his whereabouts." She said, "Call me back in a minute." I went up to my room and called again. She answered and then put me on to Noel. He went, "All right? how are you?" I said, "What the fuck is going on, man? Everybody's really fucking worried. Where are you?"'

Noel, believing Abbot was still in London, refused to reveal his whereabouts until Abbot told him he was with the band in LA and asked to come and see him. Noel agreed to that. But he still wouldn't give the address.

'Call me from the airport tomorrow,' he told Abbot.

'I thought, fucking hell, how can someone have a number-one album, have all this at their fucking feet and throw it all away. Everything had been achieved. The album was the biggest, fastest-ever-selling début album. Number one, Beatlemania in Japan, what else do you want?'

At that precise moment Noel Gallagher wanted out of Oasis. The next day Abbot flew to San Francisco, phoned Noel from the airport, who gave him the directions and an hour later he was being deposited in the Chinatown section of the city.

He rang a bell, and a pretty Asian girl answered and led him into her darkened flat, full of antiques.

'I was expecting to find this absolute, strung out, wasted, dishevelled fucking kid who I hadn't seen in weeks and who had lost it Brian-Wilson-style, and there he was in a beautiful ski jumper and we like hugged, and then he held up a big bag of coke and a bottle of Jim Beam and said, "Fancy one?" Fancy two, mate."

Assured now that Noel wasn't cracking up, far from it, they spent two days shopping, hanging out and generally relaxing. The bonus was that the girl whose flat they stayed in owned a great record collection, full of the music they dug.

'Then after about day three,' Abbot says, 'I thought, I've got to get him away to have a real chat with him because two's company, three's a crowd. I said, "Look, I've got a credit card, where shall we go? Have you ever been to Las Vegas? Let's get out, me and you, and have a crack."'

The idea appealed to Noel and the next day they departed.

Meanwhile, Abbot was making secret phonecalls back to the band. They, especially Liam, had demanded that he keep them informed as to Noel's state of mind, a request he couldn't refuse, but which totally divided his loyalties. He knew that if Noel caught him phoning the band the slight chance he had of getting Noel to rejoin would instantly vanish. Oasis really would split up for good, and Abbot wouldn't only lose a friend but gain a life-long enemy.

'I didn't want to break his trust,' Abbot points out, 'but I'd go out and phone the band and Liam would be saying, "I'm not bothered about anything as long as he's all right."

'I said, "I don't think he's going to talk to you to be honest but he's all right."'

Noel and Abbot booked into a Las Vegas Hotel and shared a room. In the morning, they began talking about America and Noel kicked off, stating how he found it all so false, so alien.

'So I told him, it's part of the plan, part of the masterplan. America was always the thing in my head with Creation. I'd just been through it with Primal Scream, and we nearly made it but we didn't deliver. Yeah, they ain't gonna understand you, so don't let it get to you.

'"This country is all make-believe and we're smarter than that. What you've got is communication and it will rise above all that." Anyway then we get in the cab and the driver starts on about UFOs.'

Now that Noel had started to talk about his feelings, Abbot felt free to start pointing out various factors. Like how America and its strange culture was all new to the other members.

'Me and you,' he said, 'we're old heads, but this is a band who've gone halfway around the world and they've never been out of the UK. Then they get to Los Angeles and it's Murder Mile because of the methedrine. I've seen it happen before with Primal Scream, I saw the methedrine madness around them. Look, America is bonkers but you can enjoy it.'

Later that night, they talked again, 'about life, families, parents, school, music, the whole lot'.

Then Noel went for a shower and Abbot reached for the phone

to call LA. Then he stopped himself. Enough was enough. He couldn't keep up the subterfuge.

'Because if there's one thing about Noel,' he points out, 'it's his absolute fucking honesty.'

When Noel re-appeared, Abbot told him he was going to call Marcus, tell him how things were. Noel said fine, and even spoke briefly with his manager to tell him he was all right. Then he handed the phone back to Abbot.

'I said to Marcus, get all the troops on the coach and drive to Austin, Texas, 'cos we've got a studio booked and Owen Morris is due to fly in.'

The studio had been booked for the band to record B-sides for the single after 'Whatever'.

'That was three days away,' Abbot continues, 'and I thought, we might be over the hump here.'

Abbot's hunch was proved correct the night he and Noel visited a casino, sat with their drinks waiting for a show to commence and then experienced the strangest thing.

'This American woman,' Abbot recalls, 'leant over and said to Noel, "Excuse me, but I must just say you are the spitting image of George Harrison, and my husband here, we've just got married, have a pact, it's written up, that I could be unfaithful with George Harrison, and you look just like him."

'I said to her, "Does that mean I've got your husband?" Anyway, they joined us, they were probably in their late forties, and she'd seen every Beatles' concert in her hometown of Philadelphia and she had every Beatles' record and knew every song, and she was besotted by Noel. Then she asked him, "What do you do?"

'He said,' Abbot states, ' "Funnily enough, I'm in a band," and then he caught himself, and said, "Well, I'm not sort of in it any more," and then he kind of pulled out and started com- plimenting the other side of America, the people who do appreciate, who do love music and how it affects them. Anyway, we got smashed with these people and swopped addresses, and she said, "When your band comes through Philadelphia why don't you come round, we'd love to come and see your show." Noel said, "Yeah, I'll do that."

'And that was the watershed,' says Abbot, 'because he'd really been touched by this complete stranger. I think he suddenly realised the power, how he could share his love for The Beatles and for music and that he had a thing he could do.

'So I said to him, "I'll tell you what John Lennon would do. He'd go out on top with a final single. What you've gotta do is polish off the B-sides. So why don't we go to Austin?" He said, "I'll think about it." Anyway, he slept on it and the next day, he went, "I've been thinking, shall we go to Austin?"'

Yes! Abbot quickly booked two flight tickets.

Funnily enough they arrived at Austin airport at exactly the same time as Owen Morris.

'And that was pretty weird,' the producer remarks, ''cos I turned up at the airport and Tim was there with Noel. Noel was like, "How are you?" I went, "All right, funny meeting you here, where's the rest of the band?" Noel said, "Dunno, I've left the band. I want to do this session and that's it."

'So we arrived at this hotel and Noel went straight to his room. I went down to the bar and all the band were there. They were like, "Is he all right?" and I said, "It's all cool," and started getting drunk with them. Then, about midnight, Noel came down and straight away it's all love and kisses, and Liam, more than anyone, is like, "Come here brother." Guigs and Bonehead were made up and it was all hunky dory.'

The next day, Oasis were back doing what they did best, playing music.

The first track they recorded was '(It's Good) To Be Free', a song that pitted, to great effect, Noel's insidious guitar riffs against Bonehead's electric piano. It was then wrapped in that powerful, unremitting and now-familiar Oasis sound.

They started about midday and by ten that night they had a rough mix of it. They put the music down first, so Liam stayed at the hotel. No way was he going to sit around waiting hours to do his vocal.

'And this session,' Owen recalls, 'is when it really started to kick in with Tony McCarroll. Noel was in this booth by himself and he had a microphone shouting instructions to the rest of the band. Tony didn't play it right the first time, second time, third time.

'He got it right in about six goes and Noel was really getting annoyed at him, saying things like, "If you don't get this right I'm gonna come out of here and kick your head in." Eventually, he got the rhythm down and the rest of the band played their parts with Noel playing some amazing lead guitar. He was on this demented coke trip from the week before.

'The next day, at about ten in the morning, we did "Talk Tonight". Noel was still writing it but we did it in about two hours. He just wrote it and sang it and that's one of the best recordings. Amazing feel on it, totally brilliant.

'Then the rest of the band turned up and Noel was like, "Ha ha, we've already recorded the track without you wankers."

'Then we did "Half The World Away", which has got that shuffling drumbeat on it and Noel said to Tony, "You aren't going near the drum kit on this one. Fuck off, right now." So Noel played the drums on that.

'Then I flew back to Britain the next day to start on The Verve album. The session was good, but very weird, very strange, that whole Tony vibe was very unpleasant.'

Both 'Half The World Away' and 'Talk Tonight' are major songs and beautifully realised statements. Noel started the latter in San Francisco and completed it in Austin before then writing 'Half The World Away'. For this song, Noel inverted the chords to Burt Bacharach's 'This Guy's In Love With You', added an electric piano which echoed that song's theme, and in doing so produced an effecting ballad that would act as a poignant diary to his then emotional state: 'And when I leave this planet/ You know I'd stay but I just can't stand it/ And I can feel the warning signs/ Running around my head.'

The themes of escape, panic and faraway loneliness are present also in the haunting 'Talk Tonight'. This time Noel is a thousand million miles from home, sitting on his own, although there is still the Burnage boy inside reminding him of his luck: 'Sleeping on a plane/ You know you can't complain.'

It's a fair bet, too, that when he wrote lines such as 'You take me walking/ To where you played when you were young,' and 'I landed, stranded/ I hardly even knew your name,' Noel had the woman from the Las Vegas casino in his mind, remembering her vivid teenage Beatle stories and, just as Abbot had noted, reminding himself of his initial impetus and the healing power of music. Now, he was thanking her as best he knew how, that is, in a song.

The American tour started up again on 14 October at the Uptown Bar in Minneapolis, the night Quentin Tarantino's film, *Pulp Fiction*, opened for business. Then it was Chicago on the 15th, Detroit on the 16th and Cleveland on the 18th.

At their Canadian début, on the 18th at Lee's Palace in Toronto, Patsy Kensit turned up to see Oasis for the first time. Her friend, Simon Halfon, a British sleeve designer who was living in the US at the time, had urged her to go and she duly attended, although it was some time before her and Liam got together.

Then it was down to the Local 186 in Allston the following night and forward then to Met's Café in Providence. The next show, the 9.30 club in Washington was, Marcus says, 'a really rough gig', and the band moved quickly out to finish the tour with two dates, one at Maxwell's in Hoboken, the birthplace of Frank Sinatra, the first American pop star to be screamed at, and then concluding at Wetlands in New York, where key Epic employees, who had been informed of the bust-up in Los Angeles, attended the concert with some trepidation.

'It was an amazing gig,' Marcus states, 'one of the very, very few times they've ever done an encore which is an indicator of how good they felt for that tour, because they had got through it.

'By the end of that tour, which was the longest they'd ever done, they really were playing with a packed punch and the record company knew it had gone off the rails, and three weeks later we turn up in New York, and what they got was a mega rock 'n' roll band. It just added to the whole thing of who Oasis are.'

In between the furore in Los Angeles and the restart in Minneapolis, the new single, 'Cigarettes and Alcohol', was released in the UK on 10 October. It came with the live version of 'I Am The Walrus' (attributed to the Cathouse in Glasgow), 'Listen Up', another real gem, plus the punk-style 'Fade Away'.

It scooted into the charts at number seven and the accompanying video was easily their best yet. With the band looking both menacing and wasted, and with a bevy of similarly emaciated and trance-like models waiting for them in the dressing-room, this film updated the sex, rock 'n' roll and drugs culture, and placed it right in the middle of the 1990s. It was an old story told in new hands, and it brilliantly served its purpose. Now a million young men wanted to be in Oasis and a million young girls dreamt about getting their hands on them.

But there was no breathing space for the band. On now to Europe and four dates in France, starting on 3 November in Lille, then shows in Paris, Lyon and Marseille.

After the Paris show, which took place with lesser British talents at the Les Inrockutibles Festival, Liam was accused by Simone Foerst, deputy manager of the Amiral Duperre hotel, of being discovered 'urinating in a corridor', a charge he denies to this day, saying that a Gallagher was caught but it wasn't him. Or his brother.

The next morning it was discovered that Noel had gone missing. He was tracked down by the band's security guard, Inm Robertson, who two years later would be sacked after an altercation with Liam, and who would then write a book about Oasis.

Between the 6th and the 16th of November, Oasis were in Britain. On the 9th, Noel attended the Q Awards at the Park Lane Hotel. Oasis had won the Best New Act category. His acceptance speech was brief and to the point. He told the audience, which also included the Labour Party leader, Tony Blair, 'To the readers – I'd just like to applaud your wisdom. Thanks.'

As he went back to his seat he was still trying to work out how *Definitely Maybe* had lost the Best LP award to the new Blur album *Parklife*, but he was photographed with Damon Albarn and spoke cordially to him.

At the same time, Noel had started a relationship with MTV presenter Rebecca de Ruvo, whom the *Daily Mirror* would describe as 'a leggy blonde', despite her small stature.

Noel had met her in New York through Evan Dando and he later discovered that Rebecca shared a ground-floor flat in Maida Vale with two other girls. There was Kadamba, an actress who would later have a fling with Liam, and footballer Matthew Le Tissier's cousin, Meg Matthews, then running Flavor, a DJ booking agency she had set up with her friend Karl Castillo.

Noel first met Meg that terrible day in November when Manchester United caned Manchester City 5–0, and Noel sat with Tim Abbot in the Landmark Hotel as miserable as sin. What made it even worse was that City hadn't scored a goal, not like United who had at least managed one against City on the happiest day of Noel's life.

Abbot gloated, and Noel regularly snapped, 'If you say one

more thing I'm going to kick you out of this room.'

The room, Meg recalls, was a tip, a rock 'n' roll bedroom. She had accompanied Rebecca and Kadamba to see Noel and remembered 'things being strewn everywhere, a complete mess with his Q Award on top of the TV. I think his bill came to something like five grand, and that was just his drinks tab.'

Her first impression of Noel was 'friendly and quiet, a nice guy. I didn't feel anything for him but they were doing a gig in Amsterdam about a week later and Tim was going to me, 'You've got to come to the gig with Rebecca." But Rebecca wanted to go to the MTV Awards so me and Kadamba went to Amsterdam.'

On the 16th, Oasis kicked back into life again with three dates in Sweden, followed by four German concerts before the band returned to Amsterdam.

It was on this tour that Liam was spotted in a Swedish service-station stealing a bag of plastic razors. Their total value was somewhere in the region of £1.50. He was caught by two policemen as he tried to board the coach and ceremoniously frog-marched back to the shop to hand them over. The incident made the front-page of the papers the next day.

Afterwards, on the coach, Liam firmly blamed Noel for the incident.

'How the fuck can it be my fault?' Noel demanded. 'How do you manage to shift the blame on to me? Tell us, I really want to know.'

Liam looked at his brother. 'It's your fucking fault because it was you who showed me where the razors were. You pointed them out to me.'

'But I didn't say steal them, did I?'

'Nah, but I didn't have any money.'

'So why didn't you ask to borrow some?'

'You should have known that I would have to borrow some. But because you didn't lend me any and you showed me where they were then it's your fault I tried to steal them.'

Noel thought about this for a few seconds. Then he said, 'Liam, I have no idea how your brain comes up with this complete and utter shit, and nor do I want to know, but I tell ya, I have to hand it to you.'

Back in Amsterdam, Noel met up with Meg, Kadamba and

Abbot. After the gig, they visited the red-light district, went for drinks and then returned to the American hotel where 'we just sort of sat up, talking and chatting', Meg recalls. 'We were like mates. I didn't feel anything. Well, you don't if your mate's seeing someone because then they just sort of become androgynous to you. We just hung out and had a brilliant weekend.'

Meg went back to London and Oasis moved back to Germany for a gig in Essen on the 27th and then on to the Botanieve in Brussels the next night. It was non-stop. Back to Britain now and another UK tour, kicking off at the Guildhall in Southampton and then up to the Octagon in Sheffield.

At that gig the promoter said to Marcus and the band, 'I want to show you the next place I want to put you on in Sheffield.' They then drove over to the Sheffield Arena and walked into the 12,000-seater.

Noel looked around at the huge hall and said to his manager, 'He's fucking joking, isn't he? We'll never sell this one.'

Three days later, 4 December, they played the Corn Exchange in Cambridge, and queues stretched right round the block. Then they drove back to London to shoot the video for 'Whatever' at a Wimbledon studio.

A day later, they assembled at the BBC studios in Maida Vale to record a session, to be transmitted near Christmas, for the increasingly prestigious *Later* show.

Noel brought in an eight-piece string section to back the band on 'Whatever' and 'I Am The Walrus', and he also delivered 'Sad Song' on acoustic guitar.

The next night came real proof of Liam's impulsive nature. On-stage at Glasgow's Barrowlands hall, a rowdier crowd than usual in front of them, Liam walked off-stage, complaining of a sore throat.

Noel, sensing a potential riot, came back on and played an hour-long acoustic set. It was then decided to cancel a proposed Australian tour with Primal Scream in January so as to give Liam's voice a rest. Plus, Bonehead's girlfriend Kate was expecting to give birth in January. It would be a good time to rest up.

They returned to Glasgow twenty days later to make up for the previous show, by which time they had played Wolverhampton, Cardiff and the Hammersmith Palais.

At that show, Oasis used the string section and at one point in the show a fan threw a letter on-stage.

'It says I've made some guy's girlfriend pregnant,' Noel said, reading out the letter to the crowd. It wasn't a great gig but the shows at the Royal Court in Liverpool (where Noel finally met The La's' Lee Mavers), and the Academy in Manchester were.

So was the Brighton Centre on the 29th where The La's made a rare if somewhat erratic live appearance and Ride replaced The Verve. It proved to be Ride's last-ever gig, the band splitting up the next year.

Oasis finished 1994's live schedule at the Town Hall in Middlesborough on 30 December. Discounting the aborted Newcastle show, this was their 105th show in 1994, over three times 1993's twenty-seven appearances. There were also twenty-three Noel Gallagher songs now in circulation. And many of them were appearing in a lot of people's top records of the year. *Select* magazine's lists were typical: 'Supersonic' and 'Live Forever' were the two best singles of the year and *Definitely Maybe* was placed second behind Blur's *Parklife*. Oasis were also second in the Band Of The Year category, Blur (that fucking name again!) in at one.

It was ironic then that for their *Top Of The Pops* appearance in support of 'Whatever', it would be Blur's Damon Albarn introducing the group with the words, 'They're wonderful.'

For some reason, giant model dandelions had been placed on-stage and Noel waved one behind Liam as he sang. The next morning, on Channel Four's *Big Breakfast Show*, Oasis were named 'Band Of The Year'.

The only hitch was the news that The New Seekers were seeking damages from Noel for his blatant steal of their song 'I'd Like To Teach The World To Sing'. Noel always denied getting the melody for 'Shakermaker' from there, pointing instead to the Beatles' instrumental 'Flying' as his source of inspiration. Eventually the matter was settled out of court.

But Noel remained non-plussed. Nothing could stop his band now. They had trampled all over the likes of Suede, The Stone Roses had fallen badly, and even though Blur's *Parklife* album refused to leave the top ten – give a shit. They'd get to them next year.

*

Noel and Meg were now a couple.

His relationship with Rebecca de Ruvo, such as it was, had slowly fizzled out, and because he was now living alone in a small rented flat near Primrose Hill, Meg told him that he could stay at her place over Christmas, until in fact he sorted out some better accommodation. Rebecca would hardly be there.

Subsequently, Noel and Meg went to Christmas parties together, stayed up all night drinking and talking, and became firm friends.

On the day he was filmed for the 'Whatever' video, Meg woke him on the sofa with a cup of tea, a can of Coca-Cola and a pile of vitamin pills.

'I was going to him,' she recalls, 'you have got to take these vitamins and he was saying, "What are you talking about? Vitamins? You're fucking joking, aren't you?" '

The video itself, directed again by Mark Szaszy, was a cheerful black-and-white film, Oasis larking around in a studio with the string section in tow. It was Christmas, there were smiles and lots of them. It had been a great year.

To cap it off, on 19 December, 'Whatever' c/w '(It's Good) To Be Free', 'Half The World Away', and a live version of 'Slideaway' was released. The next week, the song that Noel cheekily described as 'possibly one of the greatest songs ever', was at number three in the charts.

The week before its release, the song had already received a massive twenty-six plays on Radio One, and NME had called it 'the best single of 1994'.

But for the Oasis detractors, the ones who believed that Noel Gallagher was nothing more than a charlatan, 'Whatever', with its obvious Beatles' influence, was the proof they needed to issue a warrant.

Such charges would never have been made had Noel released the equally powerful '(It's Good) To Be Free' as the A-side, and recorded 'Whatever' as an acoustic B-side song. But where was the fun in that for the new Mancunian?

With 'Whatever' (whose string melody Noel had sung into a cassette and then given to a 'proper' arranger to score the song), Noel could insert all kinds of Beatles' references, like making Liam's voice sound just like Lennon's on the 'Here in my mind' lyric or recording the strings just as Beatles' producer George Martin would have done.

He didn't care about the accusations that would be made. This emphasis on The Beatles had a pleasant side-effect. It neatly diverted attention right away from other sources such as The Stooges, The MCs, The Stones, early Bee Gees, U2, The Jam, Pink Floyd, Stones Roses, et al. Noel was having far too much fun to let any of that worry him, and the single itself was perfect for the times. Loud, uplifting, he could already hear it blasting from a thousand Christmas radios.

As the single was being readied for release, Oasis played a live set for Radio One listeners from the Maida Vale studios. Commercial radio were still not playing Oasis and, as the band's radio plugger Dylan White pointed out, it was a recently revitalised Radio One who had supported Oasis from day one.

Oasis now had five days off for the festive holidays. Meg had invited Kadamba and another friend, Angie Parker, to spend Christmas with her and her parents in Liverpool.

As Noel was due in Manchester, the four of them travelled up together. In the car, with Noel sitting in the front seat and Angie driving, Meg mentioned that after the Primal Scream show at Shepherd's Bush, Abbot had returned to her house and somewhat the worse for wear had crashed out on her bed as she lay sleeping.

'He did what?' Noel snapped, turning round to face her and obviously very annoyed.

'And I thought,' Meg says, 'that's weird. Anyway, we got to Peggy's and went in for a cup of tea. Liam was sitting there and I think he was a little nervous of me because I remember him accidentally kicking a cup of tea over and trying to clean it up.

'Then we left and went back to Liverpool and I just crashed out at my mum and dad's because I felt absolutely wrecked. In the morning, my gran said that Noel had called to wish me a Merry Christmas and I just thought, I'm missing him. It was the first time I had felt like that.'

They spoke by phone that day and Noel invited Meg to a party in Liverpool. He also asked her to come to the re-arranged gig at Barrowlands. Ocean Colour Scene were supporting.

On the night of the party, Meg slept with Noel in his hotel bed but nothing happened, the pair of them too nervous to make that first move, falling in and out of sleep, and further in love.

The next day they travelled by coach to Glasgow. After the show, they went over to a club that played house music all night long. Noel soon got bored and left with two girls, telling Meg that he was going back to the coach.

On his way out, Lisa M., Meg's friend who would later start dating Liam, stopped him and asked him what he was doing. Hadn't he sussed that Meg liked him?

'Does she?' he replied, obviously quite pleased.

But when Meg got to the coach, Noel was nowhere to be seen.

The coach was leaving at two in the morning and five minutes before they were due to move off, Meg heard various people saying, 'Oh, don't worry about Noel, he's probably pulled, he can make his own way back.'

'So, I thought to myself, right, I'm going back to the club because I feel a right twat. I don't know any of them, I only know Noel and I'm not going to sit here for eight hours on my own on this bus. With two minutes to go, Noel walked on the coach with this big grin on his face and he says to me, "Oi, come over here." So we went and sat in the front seat and he told me what Lisa had said. And then we snogged all the way back to London. It was lovely.'

On the 29th, Oasis played Brighton. Before the gig, Noel went off to have a shower. Meg, who hadn't bought a clean set of clothes, grabbed an iron and started ironing her shirt. Noel came out of the shower and said, 'What the fuck are you ironing a dirty shirt for?'

'And I was so embarrassed,' Meg says, "cos you know what it's like when you don't really know someone. And then at the gig, he goes, "This is for the girl in the dirty shirt, she knows who she is," and he said it twice. Coyley's got it on tape and I was cringing.'

Later, when Noel heard the tape, another spark went off in his mind. The girl with the dirty shirt, good song title that.

On the 30th, they played Middlesborough Town Hall and the next night, New Year's Eve, Noel and Meg arrived at the Sunday Social party in the Albany pub in London. Standing at the bar, a young, good-looking kid came up to Noel and wished him a happy New Year.

'What's the best thing to have happened to you in 1994?' he asked. Without hesitation, Noel replied, 'Meeting Paul Weller.'

The couple only stayed for about ten minutes after that. But that wasn't surprising. Noel had booked a bedroom suite at the pricey Landmark Hotel. He and Meg would see in 1995 with a bottle of Jack Daniels and each other.

At that moment in time, they really couldn't have asked for any more.

·Everybody's talking about Britpop, trip-hop, Noel rock, Dad rock, but every smart band there ever was always avoided such categories.

The music press had thought up these titles. They needed a movement. History had taught them that movements are good for business. They sell papers. So do slogans and this latest batch was the work of writers trying to get a grip on the influx of bands whose music had been so strongly informed by the past.

To some, it looked like a conspiracy. As if everyone involved had secretly planned this coup and now here they all were, back-slapping mates, appearing at each other's concerts, appearing on each other's records, all of them enthusing about The Beatles and Bob Marley and Jimi Hendrix and The Rolling Stones, The Small Faces and early Who music.

Some writers were enthusiastic about this shift in music, but others hated it. They found the music too traditional and not progressive. They pointed to trip-hop or jungle as the way forward. Strange noises, different beats, other textures. It was reminiscent of the 1960s when the underground bands were the future and the craftsmen were the past.

What people failed to note was that the 1990s groups, now gaining favour, now selling gigs and records, had emerged separately. It was the forces that had brought them to this point that were of far more interest.

Most of these new musicians had grown up in the 1980s when music was judged by record sales and sounded fake, vapid. They had heard the empty sound of these people's souls and been told to wake up before they go-go. It meant nothing. So they went back to basics.

Throughout the 1980s The Beatles' music was considered *passé* which might explain the often dire nature of much of that decade's music. But in the 1990s, the musical tides threw them back on-shore and re-asserted the band as a major influence.

For many groups who formed in the 1990s the only contemporary music that moved them was hip-hop and later, house. Young music, in other words. From the street and off the street.

And the first UK group truly to inspire them were The Stone Roses. Lee Mavers and The La's might have had the songs but the Roses had the look and the attitude to go with their music. They came over as if they, like their audience, spent their nights in clubs, high on hope, and then saw out the early morning hours listening to The Beatles, The Byrds and Neil Young.

Not surprisingly, members of Oasis and Ocean Colour Scene were all present and correct at the Roses most famous concert, their gig on Spike Island.

Now, at the start of 1995, these new groups had assimilated their influences and tied them in with their own songwriting abilities. As if to add even more encouragement, news started breaking concerning The Beatles' re-emergence.

Later that year would see the release of three anthologies of out-takes and unreleased material, a TV special that would document their story, and, as if that wasn't enough, some brand-new Beatles' recording would take place.

There was a major new book on them as well, Ian MacDonald's *Revolution In The Head*, which Noel read voraciously. Noel avoided fiction and concentrated on quality literature about his favourite obsessions. John Lydon's biography *No Irish, No Blacks, No Dogs* was another favourite. In fact if anything summed up the differences between MacDonald and Oasis, it would be the critic's brutal dismissal of The Beatles' song 'All Together Now'. He said the song was 'trite enough to have been chanted for several seasons on English football terraces'.

That sentence jolted Noel. What the fuck was he on about? That's the ultimate accolade; 30,000 people singing your song on a cold Saturday afternoon. On the sacred terraces.

Noel had imagined such an event all his life and at the start of the 1995-96 season he saw this ambition, like all his others, turn to fact when the Manchester City fans rewrote and sang 'Wonderwall'.

One very influential Manchester City fan who would have been present when this singing first occurred was Tony Meehan. He was once in charge of promotions at Manchester City and understood better than most the increasing link between music and British football.

'The new rock 'n' roll' was what some magazines had dubbed 'the beautiful game', pointing out that the likes of footballers Ryan Giggs and Eric Cantona commanded a following comparable to any pop group.

It was Meehan who had organised for Noel, Liam and Guigsy to model the new Manchester City shirt in July for adverts. He also arranged for them, along with Johnny Marr and Phil Smith, to walk out on to the Maine Road pitch just before a league game against Blackburn. The crowd was delighted.

Later on, he persuaded City to give the band their own box at the ground and he also invited them to a dinner where ex-City players such as Mike Summerbee were present.

'That was funny,' Guigsy remembers. 'Summerbee was at the table and he said, "You know lads, I can't do it anymore." We thought he was saying that he was so fed up he was going to give up watching football. Somebody said, "Can't do what anymore, Mike?" and he said, "Drink five bottles of wine and shag all night." '

Meehan was also one of the men who had started a vigorous and successful campaign to have Francis Lee, an ex-City player and legend, installed as chairman of the club. The fans were very disillusioned with Peter Swales, the current chairman of the club. On the day he appointed Brian Horton as new manager there were demonstrations outside the ground. Noel, Guigsy and Liam took part along with other hundreds of fans in venting their disgust by smashing windows and front doors. Swales would eventually stand down and Lee would take charge. But the club's fortunes would further plummet under Lee's chairmanship. In 1996, a week after Oasis's Maine Road shows, the team were relegated to the First Division.

During this period, when Oasis were resting, as Bonehead and Kate awaited the imminent arrival of their daughter Lucy (Noel was made Godfather), Meehan suggested that Noel should write a song for the club. Noel agreed and sat down to pen a tune.

'But instead,' Meehan recalls, 'he wrote, "Acquiesce".' And that was far too good to give away.

In January, Oasis attended the *NME*'s Brat Awards, a ceremony organised in direct contrast to the record-company-sponsored Brit Awards. The Brats were specifically set up to honour the bands that the Brits always ignored, and to promote the *NME* as the paper of the new.

Oasis received the Best Live Band award. Liam said, 'I'd like to thank you very much and it's a good job Shed Seven didn't win it.'

Noel added, 'I think that's enough said.'

Oasis were then called up again and given Best Single award for 'Live Forever'. This was voted for by the readers. The writers went for Blur's 'Girls And Boys'.

Liam said, 'I'm glad Elastica didn't win it.'

Noel added, 'I'd like to accept this on behalf of "Hung Up" by Paul Weller, "Rocks" by Primal Scream. I'd like to finish by saying, indie schmindie, jungle schmungle, techno schmecno, new wave, no chance.'

They went back to their tables but soon returned to pick up the Best Album Of The Year award.

Liam said, 'I'm glad nobody else has won it.'

Noel put in, 'I'd like to thank Alan McGee, Marcus Russell, Brian Cannon, Chris Abbot, Johnny Hopkins, and I hope that Menswear win the best-dressed band award next year.'

Alan McGee was then given an award for his services over the years. 'Creation for the nation,' Noel shouted.

Afterwards Noel was interviewed for MTV by Donna from the group Elastica. He told her that any award they received because of kids voting for them would always be special. It would be a sentence that he would find himself repeating a lot.

After the ceremony, in which a dance troupe had strutted their stuff to 'Cigarettes and Alcohol', there was a fracas when Noel and Liam were asked to pose for photos with Blur. Noel agreed but Liam was having none of it. He threw insults at Blur by telling Damon his band were full of shit, and was then kissed on the cheek by Graham, Blur's guitarist. Noel had a go at Liam for his truculence, called him 'a pop star'.

'Yeah, yeah, yeah,' Liam muttered. The next week Noel and Damon graced the cover of the *NME*.

Noel also took time to travel down to the Manor Studios in Oxford where Paul Weller was recording his album *Stanley Road*, the follow-up to the successful *Wildwood*.

Weller asked Noel if he fancied playing acoustic rhythm guitar on a song they planned to cover, Dr. John's 'Walk On

Guilded Splinters'. Sure, Noel said, love to do it.

He put on a guitar, went into the studio and asked casually what key the song was in. Once told, he played along to the song which was blasting through his headphones.

After he was finished, he came back into the control-room, where a smiling Weller said to him, 'You don't know that song, do you?'

Noel had to agree. He'd never heard it before in his life.

But what really struck Noel that night were the songs Weller had thus far recorded. These included 'Porcelain Gods', 'Whirl-pool's End' and 'Wings Of Speed'.

'I'd just written "Roll With It', Noel reveals, 'you know, "You gotta roll with it/ You gotta take your time," and hearing those songs by Paul, I thought I've got to do better. I really do.'

Over the next three months he would write 'Don't Look Back In Anger', 'Cast No Shadow' and 'Wonderwall'.

For America, Marcus Russell had devised a separate strategy than that for other countries. America demanded a fresh approach. Marcus knew that the record companies there were unconvinced by British bands and to crack America took not only months of touring but also full support from the company.

Marcus's plan was to take Oasis not only into the major cities but into the backwaters as well. It was his way of showing the record company how serious they were about establishing themselves.

'Then you go back to them,' he explains, 'and say, "Right we told you we were going to do that. Now we have, can we have more support on the next tour?" That way you build it.'

In terms of records, singles were given to radio stations but weren't put into the shops. In fact, the first Oasis single to be released in America would be their eighth single, 'Wonderwall'.

Pop singles act as nothing more than adverts for albums in the US. Marcus's aim was to establish Oasis as a serious album band that had more than just one hit single in their possession.

Meanwhile, there were still many more towns to play.

On 28 January, the band's second US tour began in Seattle. After the gig, Pearl Jam, who shared a similar liking for Neil Young, came backstage.

'Their whole vibe,' Marcus recalls, 'was, "You guys are actually serious." They could see what we were trying to achieve.'

The next day on the flight to Canada, Bonehead's tooth left him writhing in such agony that he needed surgery as soon as he landed. The gig itself, at the Commodore Ballroom in Vancouver, was broadcast live on the radio.

The following night, in the Roseland Theatre, Portland, Liam's voice went again and in frustration he smashed up the dressing-room. But in San Francisco's legendary Fillmore theatre, they played a stormer and then, in contrast to the Whiskey debacle last time they were over, they fired up the Palace in Los Angeles.

Then it was back on the road to out-of-the-way towns such as Salt Lake City, Mesa in Arizona, Denver, Dallas, Austin, Houston, Memphis and Atlanta. The final show was on 18 February.

On the 19th they flew back to Britain to attend the Brit Awards at Alexandra Palace the following night. Oasis were given an award for Best British Newcomer, while Blur picked up four awards.

The band accepted the award from The Kink's leader, Ray Davies, and Noel said, 'There's quite a lot of people we'd like to thank but we've paid you too much money to show off your egos. I'd like to thank Ray Davies for influencing me. I'd like to thank George Martin for producing the best band there ever was, The Beatles, and I'd like to thank all our parents. Live forever!'

Then it was on to South Wales and the Loco Studios to record their new single, 'Some Might Say'. It would be Tony McCarroll's last recording session with Oasis. Discussions regarding his abilities had already taken place between Marcus and Owen Morris.

'Because Tony's big problem,' Owen explains, 'was that he only had two beats. He'd shuffle on some songs or stomp on others and it wound the band up chronically because they couldn't do anything other than that. So we were like, "Let's get him lessons." '

Which they did. They put him together with the ex-Bible drummer, Dave Larken, who gave him various exercises. His viewpoint was that Tony was potentially a great drummer but that he only used one of his arms properly. He told Tony to get a small practise kit and work on various routines devised to cure the problem.

'And I met up with Tony the day before we were doing "Some

Might Say",' Owen recalls, 'and I said, "How are the lessons coming on, Tone?" We were setting up the drum sound and stuff before the rest of the band turned up. He was like, "I haven't done any of them, I haven't had time." It was like, oh fuck, here we go.'

The new single had already been demoed at Maison Rouge and, according to Owen, differed enormously from the version they finally emerged with. It later surfaced on a Japanese-only CD.

'The demo has got a great groove on it, proper, slow Stonesy sort of groove, it's a lot slower,' Owen explains. 'But what happens when Oasis get in the studio is that Noel is all hyped up and he starts playing double fast. And at the end of it, when me and Noel were listening back to the tape, we were like, this is too fast compared to the demo.

'So we got the band back in and Noel was saying, "You fucking bastards, it's all your fault." But it was him who had started it quicker. We did three takes and picked the best one. But me and Noel were like, "We've proper cocked this up."

'The drums were all over the place, proper tragic bit of drumming on that track because it just loses it on the first chorus. So on the mix, we had to try and hide the drums which for a rocking track is very unfortunate, and we ended up with a mix that we were vaguely happy with.

'On the other hand 'Acquiesce' turned out really well, so the band were like, "Let's put that out as a single instead." But Noel was like, "No, the game plan is 'Some Might Say' comes out first, that's the single. I decided on that eight months ago."'

Some Oasis members weren't the only ones who were unsure about Noel's decision. In fact, Alan McGee, according to Noel, didn't like the A-side at all and argued strongly for, 'Acquiesce'. It wasn't hard to see why.

For many people, it is a superior song to 'Some Might Say', and gives the first-ever mention of the album that would catapult Oasis to worldwide stardom. As the jagged guitar chords announce themselves on the song's intro, you can hear Noel in the background, singing, 'What's the story, morning glory?'

He had picked up the title from a girl who had called him in America and announced herself with that very question. The phrase itself came from a musical entitled *Bye Bye Birdie*, which many American high schools stage every year. 'What's The Story, Morning Glory', is one of the show's centrepiece songs and accordingly it was swiftly adapted as saying by many school-children.

On hearing it, Noel's antennae had shot up. He jotted the phrase down and started writing the music for it while on tour. As ever, he had no lyrics bar the chorus.

Yet if he had counted on polishing it off at Loco, the edgy sessions for 'Some Might Say' had prevented him from doing so, building up as they did, into a major row with Liam.

The argument occurred when the finished tape of the single was played back in a studio packed with friends.

'On the demo,' Owen explains, 'we had this weird psychedelic bit, a backwards guitar bit that we thought was a bit naff. So me and Noel had finished doing all the overdubs and there was a lot of cocaine around, too much cocaine in fact, and we played it to the band and all these hanger-ons.

'Liam just totally exploded in front of everybody. He was going, "You fucking dickhead, you don't know what you're doing. Where's the guitar bit?"

'Noel's like, "Get him out of here or I'll fucking kill him. I know what I'm doing, you fuck off." Liam storms off and then everybody quickly leaves the control-room, leaving just me and Noel.

'I'm now thinking to myself, Liam's probably right, and Noel is sat there going, "He's a fucking dickhead, a wanker, what the fuck does he know?" And I said, "Well, maybe he's right." And Noel starts going, "Don't you come down on his side or you're sacked."

'Three hours later, Noel's calmed down and he comes into the control-room and says, "Maybe he's right, you know." So then he put the guitar part down but he played something different. He changed a couple of the notes so he then felt justified in saying to Liam, "I've got an even better one now." And so everybody was happy. But it was a real coke-fuelled session, everyone really on edge.' (A salient point in Liam's case is that when he was smoking spliff he was far less inclined to furious outbursts than when he was ingesting large doses of cocaine.)

The band then resumed their US tour, but in Noel's mind Tony McCarroll's die was cast. He would have to go, although there was no way they could sack him just yet.

From 3 March to 25th they had American dates to fulfil, followed in April by a video-shoot for the single, and three more shows that would culminate with a massive show at the Sheffield Arena; Noel had been proved wrong as the gig had quickly sold out. After that, it was back into the studio to start work on their second album which Noel would call *(What's The Story) Morning Glory*.

What's more, the tabloids were now regularly featuring the band. The *Sunday Mirror*, under the headline, Oasis Drug Scandal, published a story on 19 February that began, 'Top British pop group Oasis have caused a storm in their hometown by boasting about drug taking.' They later quoted Alf Morris, a Labour MP, as saying, 'What Oasis should be telling the Americans is how many people battle every year to win a university place.'

The US tour started up in New Jersey and went to Washington, Virginia Beach, Philadelphia, New York (where they met and got on with tennis player John McEnroe), Providence, Boston, up then to Canada for two shows, back down to Cleveland, and then Detroit and Indianapolis, where Liam was hit on-stage by a pair of spectacles and the band threatened to down instruments. The night before he and Bonehead had gone to see another UK band, Bush, and po-goed down at the front.

The tour moved on to Chicago and then the Orbit Room in Grand Rapids where Liam walked off-stage after three numbers and Noel had to finish the set. The next night they played Prince's club in Minneapolis and there met Nigel Dick, a British video director now living in the US. He would go on to shoot videos for 'Wonderwall' and 'Don't Look Back In Anger'.

The last gig in Milwaukee was perhaps one of the best of the tour, and then the exhausted band flew home. It had been a serious slog around America, but it had gone a long way to breaking them there.

On their return Oasis travelled to Chatley Heath, Surrey, to shoot a two-day video. The video had been budgeted at around £40,000 and filming was due to begin on 29 March.

They booked into a hotel but on the day of the shoot, Liam was nowhere to be seen. Finally, someone called him at the hotel. The idea is shit, he said, I'm not having it. Then he put the phone down. Liam, the purist.

Marcus then rang him and informed the singer that it would cost the band a day's worth of filming, some twenty grand, if he didn't show. Give a shit, Liam said, I'll pay it. The single doesn't need a video anyway.

The video was cancelled and in its place they cobbled together a film using different bits from their previous videos, including the American version of 'Supersonic'.

Now, they had three gigs left to play. Two warm-up dates, one in Southend and the other in Paris at the Bataclan, and then back to Sheffield for their biggest gig to date.

At the Southend show, Noel broke the set up and, for the very first time in the UK, sat on a stool and played an acoustic set.

In Paris, on 19 April, it was reported that Liam had an altercation with McCarroll. Not so, he says. 'I was standing in this bar and this mad bird that he was seeing walked in and started fighting him. He was down on the ground so I started eating these cherries and spitting the stones on him as he was rolling around.'

Meanwhile, Noel had other things on his mind, like polishing off a song floating around in his head, entitled, 'Don't Look Back In Anger'.

For the past few months, he had been listening to a private tape, given to him in America, of John Lennon starting his biography. On it, the former Beatle says, 'I love that thing they said about George Bernard Shaw, that his brains had gone to his head.' So did Noel. It was the impetus he needed to start work on what proved to be an exceptional song.

That he was excited by it can be gauged by the fact that he premiered it publicly on acoustic guitar at Sheffield Arena. Paul Weller and Johnny Marr were in attendance, and Ocean Colour Scene and Pulp played support. A sign of what was to come.

'That was funny that gig,' Noel recalls. 'I remember being on-stage in this huge hall and Liam saying, "Why are all those kids being held back by the barriers?" and, I'm shouting, "I don't know, I'm trying to play my guitar, you wanker." '

Which is when Liam and Noel told the crowd to fuck the barriers and the bouncers, and come further forward. Instantly, a mass of people vaulted themselves forward, an image that Noel would refer to after the show as 'like a revolution or something'.

Later that night, back at their hotel, Noel leant over to a friend and said, 'Do you realise that a year ago we were just about to put our first single out and today we played to 12,000 people?'

It had been an astonishing twelve months by anybody's standards. Two days later 'Some Might Say' c/w 'Talk Tonight', 'Acquiesce' and 'Headshrinker' was released.

Both *NME* and *Melody Maker* made it their Single Of The Week, and both reviews stated that it wasn't the best Oasis single to date but it had so much punch it literally swept all before it.

The next week it entered the charts at number one. In the same week, Paul Weller's new single, 'The Changingman', came in at seven. One of Noel's ambitions was to eclipse Weller's record with The Jam of having three singles enter the charts at one. And there he was, six places above him.

At a party in Soho, after Oasis had played *Top Of The Pops*, Noel sat in a chair, excitedly telling people, 'Weller's single has gone in at seven. That's the first top-ten entry he's had in years.'

'Yeah, but Noel, you're in at number one.'

'I know, but Weller's in at seven. It's fucking top, isn't it?'

Meanwhile, Tony McCarroll was back in Manchester trying to adjust to life without Oasis. After the Sheffield show, Marcus had called him in for a meeting and told McCarroll what he had heard all these years but refused to believe. If he didn't shape up, he would be out. Now, it was true. He had played his last-ever gig for the band.

Fifteen

'When I read "Oasis is Noel's band" it fucking sends me mad. It's no one's band. Take one away and there's nowt left.'

It lay at the core of everything, the way his brother ruled the band, dominated it with his songwriting and took all the major decisions. It badly angered Liam, made him feel that if he, Liam, sat down one day and wrote a song nearly as good as 'Hey Jude', it would be very, very doubtful that Noel would choose to record it. And that did his head in.

He also believed that the success they now all enjoyed was as much about him as it was Noel. Sure, we know who writes the songs. And fair play, each one's a cracker.

But would they be so potent sung by anybody else? Could they be so perfectly realised without his unique voice placed right in the centre? And who were all the boys modelling themselves on? And who were all the girls rolling over for in early-morning hotel rooms? Me, Liam. Li-Am the walrus, koo koo ka choo. That's who.

It bugged him the most when Noel pocketed all his publishing money. Did his head right in. Oasis wasn't about money. It hadn't been formed for that purpose. It had been created to further music, and therefore Noel should share his good fortune. It was a band. All or nothing. I'd do it. Give a shit, here's the dosh, lads. But Noel refused.

As for himself, Liam was determined to have it large. He had waited years for recognition and success and now he had it, there would be no letting up. Liam would play as hard as he worked. On days off, he would wake up with a hangover at about four in the afternoon. By six, there would be a drink in his hand. By nine, the night, a promise full of pleasure would be beckoning to him and he would not, could not resist. The only thing that bugged him out was the media attention.

On 28 February 1995, he had got into a drunken fight at the Dry Bar in Manchester. Not only was it reported in all the papers, but some scumbag had given *The Word* the camera tape of him being ejected. They'd screened it, the fuckers.

But Liam, in his rampages around town never forgot other principles.

'I remember going down to that club Brown's,' McGee recalls, 'and Liam was there. I hadn't seen him in quite a bit and he was surrounded by all these women, gorgeous women trying to get his attention. So I went over to say hello and he said, "Sit down, sit down." So we started chatting and I said, "Liam, look if you want to pull these women I'll go away, I don't mind, in fact I perfectly understand. I'd do the same thing in your shoes."'

Liam looked at McGee.

'They can wait,' he said. And then, 'So come on, how you been? Still signing shite bands on our money, are ya?'

Noel and Meg were in Camden now, living down Albert Street in a small flat. It was obviously a serious relationship but initially Meg found Noel hard to get used to.

To begin with, Meg's job wasn't working out. Flavor, the company she had set up, was failing. Too many phonecalls, not enough results. Noel told her that she should quit, find a less stressful job. It was taking too much out of her.

But Meg couldn't help it. That's how she was. Determined. But also a realist. She knew the job was driving her into the ground with worry and stress. Reluctantly, because she had failed, Meg quit.

'And then all of a sudden,' she states, 'I was penniless, I didn't have a job and I felt like he was thinking that I'd given up my job because of who he is and that I was just going to stop work. But that isn't like me. I desperately wanted a job, so that's when I started doing the doors on clubs, just to show him that I was a hard worker.

'Then he started work on *Morning Glory*, and I can understand when you're writing that you have to be cut off but at the same time I wasn't feeling strong.'

According to Meg, Noel, once seized by an image or something on the TV or in the pub, whatever it was that kicked off his antennae, would drop everything and disappear into their small kitchen and furiously write. It's how the lyrics for 'Champagne Supernova' came about.

'I bought this sugar jar which had a little man hanging on it nearly buried by sugar,' Meg says, 'and then he just went into the kitchen and wrote that song.' That jar is to be found on the inside sleeve of *Morning Glory* ('Someday you will find me / Caught beneath a landslide . . .').

But Meg was also finding it hard to get a reaction from Noel. He wasn't a tactile person nor was he one for sitting round discussing his feelings. He was brilliant at entertaining people and his humour was contagious. But go deeper and the barriers snapped up. And that threw her. In Meg's world, if the two of you sit down to watch the TV, you do so on the sofa, cuddling. That's what lovers do. Noel sat in his chair, alone. Self-protected.

'Sometimes I used to think he was like that with just me, but then I sort of got to know that he's like that with everyone, his friends, people close to him, everyone. I'd hear him on the phone or talking and he never gave anything, never expressed himself.'

But he did. It all went into the songs. And he knew it more than anybody. In 'Hey Now' he wrote, 'And time as it stands / Won't be held in my hands / Or living inside of my skin / And as it fell from the sky / I asked myself why / Can I never let anyone in?'

Which is why when his dickhead brother moaned at him about the money, how the band were all on wages but Noel was filthy rich, he could never see his point of view. Didn't Liam have an inkling of the work he put in? Did he not also hear the voices in Noel's head telling him that he was nothing more than a piece of dogshit? Did he not see that Liam was one of the very few people on the planet Noel could totally trust? And that if he wanted money all he had to do was ask. Damn right, Noel took the money. And as much of it as he could.

And it was in this frame of mind, that Oasis regrouped at the Rockfield Studios in Wales to make the album that would first break, and then make them.

Noel first heard him in the corridor of a rehearsal studio. His playing was so clear it made the songwriter stop in his tracks and ask, 'Who's that on the drums?'

The answer was Alan White and, like Noel, he had a brother named Paul. He also had a third brother whose name was Steve who was undoubtedly fast becoming the best drummer in the country.

The brothers White had grown up in Eltham, South London. Paul, the eldest, had little aptitude for a musical instrument. He went off to do a variety of jobs: bricklaying, plastering, cab driving.

But Steve was different. At ten years of age, he had persuaded his parents to buy him a drum kit that cost £30. Steve set it up in the front-room and then hammered away on it. That noisy arrangement couldn't continue, so their father turned the loft of their house into a practise room, hung a few curtains up to muffle the noise, and then said, all yours, son.

Alan, the youngest of the three, was too young to notice. He was born on 26 May 1972 and attended Deansfield Primary School. It was just as he was about to enter Crown Woods secondary school that he started to get the drumming urge.

At the dinner-table, Steve would always be tapping away. Next thing you knew, so was Alan. He was buying records now, 'Dancing In The Street' by Martha And The Vandellas was his first purchase. But he soon graduated to James Brown. It was the drum rolls you see, the ones that Clyde Stubblefield, Brown's funky drummer, would insert into each record, that truly caught Alan's attention.

Certainly those funky drums said more to Alan than school did. Alan didn't have time for most subjects, a bit of art, a bit of English, that was about all that interested him. But he was good at long-distance running, and played a bit of football as well.

He supported Charlton FC, the local team. His dad would take Alan and his brothers to see Charlton play and that was that. Like Guigsy and the Gallagher brothers, he had no choice in the matter, really.

Alan was about ten years old when his elder brother Steve hooked up with Paul Weller and started an enduring and fruitful musical partnership that has lasted to this day. When Steve was not with Weller, he was busy encouraging his brother.

Steve was the first to teach Alan about drumming and drummers. He would show him licks, play him various records. Steve's beloved jazz albums Alan couldn't get with, but the funk stuff – The Meters, Sly Stone, James Brown – now that really gripped him.

When Steve was away touring, Alan would steal up to the loft and practise. He was a soul-boy drummer. And he was getting good. Promising enough, in fact, for Steve to recommend that he take lessons from his old teacher, Bob Armstrong. He'll sort your hands out, Steve said.

Alan's parents were cool about their youngest son's interest. Their way had always been to encourage their children. Their philosophy was simple. Follow your instincts. You want to drum? Then drum.

Alan left school with no exam results worth talking about and secured a job in the clothes shop Next, situated by London Bridge. He started at ten in the morning and was finished by three in the afternoon. It was a tidy arrangement. Straight after work Alan was home to practise. Every two weeks, it was over to Bob's for drum tuition. Alan rarely missed a lesson or a day without drumming. Steve had taught him, by his own example, the real value of discipline. You want to make it, then practise. Don't fuck around.

Then one hot summer morning on the train to work, Alan ripped his trousers at the crotch. He had no boxer shorts on underneath. Alan got to the train station, praying that no one would notice. He made it to a phone and called up his boss. They had never liked each other.

'I said, "I'm calling from the station, I've ripped my trousers and I've got to go home and change them. I'm going to be late,"' Alan recalls. 'He said, "Oh no, you come here straight away. Get back on the train, hold your trousers together and walk over the bridge." I said, "I'm not walking over London Bridge with me hampton out" [hampton being cockney slang for the penis, as in Hampton Wick, dick], and he said, "If you don't come in now, you ain't got the job." So I put the phone down and that was the end of that one. I just dossed around for a bit.

'Then I got a job in Footes the drum shop which is in Golden Square, London's West End, and I worked there for about two and a half years.'

Meanwhile, Alan kept up his lessons with Bob Armstrong, who was a keen exponent of the Moella technique, a graceful style that allows you, through a certain use of the hands, to play two beats where others can only play one.

Alan put this technique to work both at home, and at work, where he was also making a lot of useful contacts.

He also bought his first drum kit from Steve, ('paid 500 quid, he ripped me off') and he was now using it to back a folky singer called Tamara. Alan White made his playing début at the King's Head in Fulham. He can still remember it.

'I was shitting me pants but I was well excited. I thought it would have been a bit more difficult but it wasn't as bad as I thought it would be.'

This association lasted about a year and a half but then Alan got bored, wanted to move on. That's when Steve, who had played on a session with a band called Star Club, recommended Alan to them. They called; Alan passed the audition.

Prior to his arrival, the band had signed a deal with Island Records and had recorded an album.

Two singles duly followed. The first, 'Let Your Hair Down', received positive reviews, good air-play and looked like it was going to put them on the map. But it never quite took off. Nor did the follow up, 'Hard To Get'.

That's when the band decided that America held the most promise for them. They embarked on a gruelling tour, came home and were told by their record company to record a second album. The band, Alan, Steve French, Owen Weiss, and Julian Taylor ('the best bass player I've heard in my life') started work.

Then their A&R man got it into his head that the reason for the band's lack of success was down to their guitarist, Steve. He started lobbying to have him removed. Realising that if he stayed the band would be dropped, Steve quit and travelled over to New York. He needn't have bothered. His departure was such a blow to the group, they never quite recovered their momentum. Alan thought, fuck it, the game's up, I'm outta here.

So on to the dole, you shall go. Alan signed on for about a year and spent some time pondering how the band had all been left broke but everyone who had been around them were now driving new cars.

The band did reform but under a new name, Paint. It was hardly inspiring. Alan found himself on the Camden pub circuit – Dublin Castle, the Monarch – and he felt himself going nowhere. Again, he quit.

Not long after, Dr. Robert, who was now launching a solo career after the demise of his group, The Blow Monkeys, invited Alan to record with him.

'I did some of his album,' Alan states, 'and I worked with him for about three months. I well enjoyed it, he's a top man, Robert, and he had some wicked songs. The one I'm really pleased I played on was a song of his called "Circular Quay". It's beautiful and I was really pleased with my playing on it. Then we went out to Japan and did a tour which was good. I was quite content working with him, but then Noel called.'

Alan was working in a rehearsal studio with a Creation artist named Idha when Noel walked by and heard him. He noted the name with interest, especially when he discovered he was Steve White's brother. When Tony McCarroll was sacked, Alan was the first drummer that Noel called. Alan wasn't there when the phone rang. But his mum was.

'Some bloke who sounded like he was off Coronation Street called you today,' she told her son when he walked in that evening. 'Noel Gullagugga, something like that.'

Alan stepped back. 'Do you mean Noel Gallagher?' he asked.

'Yeah, that's him. The number's over there. Do you want a cup of tea, love?'

The next day Alan phoned back.

'I said, "All right, Noel? It's Al, I believe you want a chat." And he said, "Yeah, I want you to be in my band." I said, "Don't you want me to audition?" He said, "No, don't worry about that. I've heard you play. As long as you're not eighteen stone and you've got a nice jacket and a nice pair of Levi's, you're in."'

They first met at the Café Delancey in Camden. Noel remembers, 'I didn't know what he looked like until this guy came up and said, "All right, Noel? How's it going? Fancy a Nelson?" [Nelson Mandela, Stella lager] I knew it would be cool then.'

Noel was staying temporarily in Fulham at the time, at Johnny Marr's flat, so after a drink they went back to the flat and Alan played him a tape of the records he'd appeared on. Noel said, brilliant, you're in.

The next day, they got together at John Henry's rehearsal space, studio six, in North London. They jammed for a couple of hours and then went down the pub to meet Guigsy.

Alan walked in and did a double-take when he saw the Oasis bassist.

He recalls, 'We met him in this pub down the road and I thought he was about thirty-five years old. He had mad hair and it was all grey. He had a drink and he was shaking. I thought, fucking hell, it's like someone out of the Stones who's done too much. Then I found out he was only my age, and I thought, this band is having it. Guigsy has got grey hair, Bonehead's going bald, Liam is always in the paper having a ruck, what the fuck have I let myself in for?'

They returned to the studio and now the three of them played together. Noel then said, 'We'll come back tomorrow and play some of the new album.'

Alan said, 'But I don't know any of the songs.'

Noel replied, 'Doesn't matter, no one else does either.'

The first thing they learnt was 'Roll With It', then 'Don't Look Back In Anger', then 'Hello'. A week later, Alan met Liam and Bonehead for the first time.

'Luckily,' Alan observes, 'We all got on really really well. I thought, reading all the press, it might be a bit of a bind because they're so Manchester, they might think I'm a complete lunatic from the South. But after a couple of weeks, I really settled in. I couldn't believe how easy it was.'

Liam, of course, had to test the new drummer. On the day they met, Liam swaggered into the studio and said, 'Allright, let's do that Beatles song "It's All Too Much."'

Alan said, 'Fine. 1-2-3-4,' and counted them all in. Liam was okay after that.

The following Wednesday the band travelled down to the *Top Of The Pops* studio to perform 'Some Might Say'. Now it was starting to hit home to Alan. Here he was drumming for a band that had just soared in at number one and he was about to make his TV début with millions of people watching.

As ever, there was a lot of hanging around. But it was a sunny day. The band got the lagers in, lolled around in the sunshine and got to know their new member. There was no friction, and how could there be? They were from the same class. Different worlds, different accents, but they all came from the same part of town.

'I was well over the moon,' Alan recalls, a victim of listening to too many Charlton footballers being interviewed.

God only knows what Tony McCarroll thought that night as he watched Oasis play their first number-one single on TV. The last time he had been on TV with them was for Channel Four's *The White Room* show where Noel had chosen to highlight the single's B-sides, 'Acquiesce' and, ironically for Tony, 'It's Good To Be Free'.

During their slot, Liam stared out at the crowd with such a mean impassive look on his face that some audience members actually averted their eyes when they looked at him. Backstage, the mood within the band hadn't been good.

Still, it had been a powerful performance, made even better for Noel when he crossed over to the other stage and performed 'Talk Tonight', with Paul Weller backing him on electric piano and vocals. It was a performance that may well have rankled the ever-protective, ever-jealous Liam.

Afterwards people came up to Paul and said things like 'that was brilliant, fantastic', and Paul snapped at them, 'Well, go and tell Noel, he wrote the fucking song.'

This was the last time Tony McCarroll had appeared on TV with the band. When he sat down to watch them again, it was their *Top Of The Pops* appearance for 'Some Might Say' which finished with Noel triumphantly holding his guitar aloft, like he'd just won the FA Cup.

That is, if McCarroll could bear to watch the band that would now take over the world.

It had all started so well. The band, coming off a number one single, were eager to record the new album. Not only would it be a buzz playing and learning a whole new batch of Noel Gallagher songs, perhaps one of the most pleasurable aspects of their job, but it also meant that when they returned to touring, they would have a new set-list to perform. They loved *Definitely Maybe*, but they'd played it over a hundred times by now.

They were booked in for six weeks at Rockfield Studios in South Wales and quickly their producer Owen Morris, picked up on the renewed energy they were displaying. Alan's presence, he believes, was a major factor.

'He chilled the vibe within the band because now that whole Tony tension had gone,' he explains. 'Also, Alan doesn't take any shit. I haven't seen them but I have heard stories about Liam having a go at him, and Alan going, "Come on then, hit me," and standing up to him.

'And he's got total respect off Noel because Alan's a phenomenal musician and they were all in love with him, going, listen to him do all these rolls, he's the new Keith Moon.'

The first track they recorded was 'Roll With It'. Noel had shown up about two in the afternoon, blind drunk. As he lolled around the studio, roadie Jason got his guitars together while the rest of the equipment was set up.

Five hours later they were ready to go. Their method of recording was to put the music down first and then let Liam sing over the finished result.

Noel had sobered up a bit by now but he was desperate to get something down. It was seven in the evening and the football was on TV in half an hour.

'He was drunk,' Owen explains, 'which is probably good because he started the song nice and slow; he couldn't play fast if he wanted to. All the band were playing at once and it was just noise, all out of control. We did about five takes and while they were watching football, I had a listen back to them and it was like, the first take is the one. So we went with that.'

Liam put down his vocals the next morning and then they went on to 'Hello'. The same thing. The band put down the music within a few takes and then Liam later added his vocals.

'And that night after we put down "Hello", Owen says, 'is when Noel played me "Wonderwall" '.

That night was also when more battle-lines started being drawn up and the tension between the brothers became truly palpable.

It began when Noel played Liam both 'Wonderwall' and 'Don't Look Back In Anger' and told him he had to make a choice as to which song he wanted to sing: 'Because, believe me, I'm taking lead vocal on one of these tunes.'

According to Owen, Noel wanted to sing 'Wonderwall', which makes perfect sense. He had written the song with Meg in mind. It was the only way he knew to properly express his love for her, with the song detailing her struggle to find work but celebrating her ability to bounce back against the odds.

'So we finished "Wonderwall",' Owen continues, 'and Liam's, "Right, I'm singing that one." And he did a blinding vocal, a brilliant vocal.'

Then it was on to 'Champagne Supernova', the intended centre-piece of the album. Again, the music was put down at an astonishing pace, Noel recording something like twenty different fuitar parts in one day. But the vocals weren't right. Liam's voice was now starting to strain for the notes.

'He had been singing for three days,' Owen notes, 'And he'd also started drinking quite heavily.'

They moved on, sweet irony, to 'Don't Look Back In Anger'.

It was Friday night now and sleeve designer Brian Cannon arrived to celebrate Owen's imminent birthday, 13 May, the next day.

The music for 'Don't Look Back in Anger' was recorded that night and then Noel, Owen and Brian got utterly wasted. They finished up about three the next afternoon, so Saturday was ruled out.

The others didn't care too much. Guigsy had brought along various items to while away the hours. These included air rifles and a cricket bat.

On Sunday, Noel went back to the studio to put down his vocal and Liam went off to the pub. He was now intensely annoyed and frustrated. At this juncture, he was surplus to Oasis's requirements, and that hurt.

At the pub, he was instantly recognised and started drinking heavily. Owen and Noel were back in the studio and Owen recalls getting aggressive drunken phonecalls from Liam, going, 'You old wankers, come on, I'll get you later on.' So there was aggro in the air.

Alan was at the pub with Liam. 'Then we came back and I went down to the studio to see Noel,' he remembers, ''cos I wanted to see how everything was going. And then we came back after about an hour and a half to the house and the place was mobbed with hundreds of kids. Liam had invited everyone back.'

Noel took one look at the scene and exploded with rage. he ordered everyone to leave, insulting a girl who Liam wanted to stay. That seriously upset the singer who now started upending tables, chairs, plants, anything he could get his hands on.

Absolute mayhem broke out. Guigsy was threatening to punch out a guy who had walked into his bedroom, Bonehead and Alan had grabbed the air rifles so that Liam couldn't get to them, and objects were flying everywhere as people departed.

One girl locked herself in Alan's room, frightened to death.

'When Liam loses it,' Owen points out, 'it's scary.'

That night Liam lost control and lashed out at everyone and everything around him. Among other things, he headed for the studio, determined to smash up Noel's guitars. He was frustrated by iron bars on the windows and heavy doors that were firmly locked.

According to Owen, he later traded punches with Bonehead.

At some point, he also started in on Noel, who promptly picked up the small cricket bat that Guigsy had bought and started viciously smashing his brother with it.

After he was finished, Noel went back to his room, but Liam wasn't finished. He then tried to kick down Noel's door, badly hurting his foot in the process. It was a ground-floor room so Noel climbed out of the window, came round the front, and asked if anyone could drive.

'I said, I can drive,' Alan recalls. 'And Noel said, "Right, take me home." So I got in the car with him, didn't even get anything, just the keys out of my pocket.'

Liam, now realising what was happening rushed out on to the drive as Alan's car started to move away and started chucking heavy black plastic rubbish bins at them, the dustbins bouncing off the bonnet.

In that one night, Liam had vented all his anger and pain, and had done so on the people closest to him. For Noel, it must have been like watching his father again.

In the car on the way back to London, sensing that Noel had calmed down a bit, Alan said, 'Fucking hell, I didn't realise I had joined The Troggs.' That put a smile on Noel's lips, but in reality he was deeply worried by his brother.

'Later, in the car,' Alan reveals, 'Noel was saying that he couldn't believe Liam could do such a thing. He [Noel] was freaking out, saying, "I don't want to do this any more, I just can't be arsed. I'm gonna fuck off and do my own thing." I thought great, I've only just joined and it's back to the dole.'

So Noel Gallagher quit the band for the second time in eighteen months. It was typical Oasis. In a week they had gone from an absolute high to a crashing low. It was as if they couldn't do anything without some kind of turbulence to validate their actions.

'It's the worst one I've seen,' Alan says, 'and I'm quite sure it's probably the worst any of them have seen because it was horrible. Some of it was funny, but at the end of the day it wasn't very nice at all.'

Noel retreated to his flat in London, and Brian took Liam over to Wigan to chill him out. The next day at the studio, Owen and the rest of the band received a call from Marcus Russell telling them to pack their bags. Noel had left the band.

Incredibly, the damage to the room wasn't too bad. After Guigsy had cleaned up, the result was a door off its hinges, a smashed television, the table was wrecked and so was the drinks machine. The studio had seen it all before. They billed the band for the damage.

Meanwhile, Noel spent some of the week alone in his Camden flat. Meg had gone off on holiday to Portugal and he was left pondering his future while feeling both guilty and worried by his brother's outburst and their subsequent fight. They had fought before but he had never ever seen Liam so violent. It worried the shit out of him.

Meg returned on the day that Go Discs held a party to celebrate the release of Paul Weller's *Stanley Road* album.

Paul had agreed to play a set prior to the party at the Nomis rehearsal studio where he keeps an office. Noel showed up with a tape of the songs they had recorded and played them to Weller and his band before the gig started. 'Don't Look Back In Anger' and 'Champagne Supernova' were instantly singled out for praise.

After the mini-gig everyone went over to the album launch where Meg, who was unaware of what had happened, had arranged to meet Noel.

'When I came over,' she recalls, 'He grabbed me and hugged me, and I was going, "Tell me you love me, I haven't seen you for ages." He was going, "Yeah, yeah, yeah," but I could see in his eyes that something was up.

'Then we went home and he was pacing the flat and I let him pace around for a bit and then he told me what he'd done to his brother and it was like a masive kick in the teeth to him that had affected him really badly.

'It really fucked him up. He was so gutted at what he'd done to Liam. The next day he got word that Liam was all right, but he was still thinking, I've kicked the shit out of my own flesh and blood.'

On the day that Everton beat Manchester United in the 1995 Cup Final, Noel took off to Guernsey to meet Meg who had invited him over to a family reunion. Two hours before he left the flat, Meg called and said, 'Don't bring anything with you. When I told customs you were coming over they searched everything.'

But Noel wasn't too interested in bringing cocaine anyay. He had more pressing things to think about. Like, should he really leave Oasis, and what was to become of Liam?

After staying in Guernsey, he and Meg then travelled to Jersey where he played her a tape of the songs, including 'Wonderwall'.

Meg suspected it might be about her but didn't like to ask. She only found out for sure when Noel revealed all in the interviews he undertook to support the album.

That was a good couple of months later.

While Noel was in Jersey, Marcus called Owen and asked him to go back into the studio and mix the songs already laid down. Owen complied and worked on 'Roll With It' and 'Hello'.

'They were shit mixes,' he states, 'I was properly not in the mood.'

At the start of the fourth week, Marcus rang him again. Good news. Noel was thinking of coming back. Soon after, Liam showed up at the studio. He and Owen spent their time going to the pub, the singer insisting that the band wasn't finished but doing so in a very low-key way.

Liam now says, 'I was a cunt, he was a cunt, and it had to be dealt with. That's all.'

One by one the rest of the band returned to the studio, and a chastened Liam apologised to them all. But there was still no sign of Noel. Then on the Sunday, casual as you like, as they were eating their roast dinner, Noel walked in.

'The same thing as in Austin, Texas,' Owen recalls. 'Liam's like, "Hi, brother, I fucked up, I'm sorry." Noel's like, "You dick-head". Then he gave him a Beatles' belt that he had bought him.'

Now, they had two weeks left to finish the album.

'I can't remember what order we did things in that week,' Owen says. 'But we did, "Morning Glory", "Hey Now", "She's

Electric", "Bonehead's Bank Holiday", "Step Out", which didn't go on the album, and "Cast No Shadow".'

Noel had started to write this last song on the train back to Rockfield. The train had drawn to a halt under a bridge, so Noel got out his guitar and started writing a song about the nature of songwriting. As ever, the music came quickly, but he was still working on the words when he and Liam went in to record it.

'It was the only time I've seen Noel and Liam stood together in the studio,' Owen recalls. 'Noel was still writing the words as Liam was singing it and they were both stood there really close to each other. Liam would sing and then Noel would say "Hang on", and then change the words and say, "Okay, sing this". It was beautiful and Liam's vocal on that song is amazing. Liam is fantastic vocally, he's got a real soul to him.'

As ever, music had healed and brought the brothers together.

Noel also cut a solo version of the song written by Lennon, 'You've Got To Hide Your Love Away', and late at night, alone with Owen in the studio, he would run through some of his unrecorded pieces, tunes he was saving for the right time, the right album.

'I've got endless DAT tapes of Noel's songs,' Owen says. 'I've got about twenty to thirty songs that have never been out, and they're all outrageous songs and he's progressing, the songs are getting deeper and deeper.'

The last album track recorded at Rockfield was 'Swamp Song', a tune that would be inserted at various point throughout the album, Noel probably getting the idea from Paul Weller's *Wildwood* album.

But they couldn't use the mix.

'Noel started too fast again,' sighs Owen glumly.

Sixteen

News of Tony McCarroll's sacking was swiftly reported by all the media. MTV news added that Oasis had also turned down proposed support slots for both Bon Jovi and David Bowie, but would support REM at their Huddersfield show on 25 July. Oasis later pulled out of that one as well.

'The Bon Jovi show,' Noel was quoted as saying, 'It's not worth the humiliation, and as far as David Bowie goes, twenty years ago maybe, but not now. He's an old git.'

Noel now spent his time mixing *Morning Glory* with Owen Morris in the Orinoco Studios in South London. During these sessions, which went smoothly, Weller arrived to play lead guitar and add backing vocals to 'Champagne Supernova'. he also contributed harmonica and guitar to 'Swamp Song'.

'I noticed a harmonica in his bag,' Noel reported, 'and said to him, "What key is it in?" He said, "D." I said, "Right into the studio, we've got a song here for you." '

Noel had originally entitled this track 'The Jam', but now with Weller playing on it, he thought the title too corny, and changed it to 'Swamp Song'. Later on, Paul told him he should have kept the original title. It was far funnier.

On 'Supernova', Weller's expressive guitar solo ends just as a deliberate Beatles'-style backing chant of 'Yeah, yeah, yeah' enters. Meanwhile, Noel sat at the mixing desk and weaved these elements into the fabric of his own song. It wouldn't be the last time that such connections would be made.

In early June that year, both Oasis and Weller were nominated for the Mercury Music Prize Best Album Of The Year award. Neither would win, the prize instead going to the Portishead album *Dummy*.

Meanwhile, in an astute piece of marketing, Creation offered all six Oasis singles on a three-for-£10 basis. It was also revealed that sales for both 'Whatever' and 'Some Might Say' had now reached a quarter of a million.

Pop music was big business again. In the early 1990s, the industry had hit a slump. Only the introduction of CDs into the market, allowing companies to re-sell their back catalogue, had managed to disguise the impending crisis. Most pundits pointed to the rapid growth of computer games as proof positive that pop no longer swayed the young.

Sega over songs, Gamebody over gigs. But it was a bad call. By 1995 the UK music industry wasn't only reporting their best domestic figures ever, but the success of Oasis, Bush and perennial artists such as The Rolling Stones and Eric Clapton, gave the business over £1.25 billion in overseas sales. If nothing else, it was desirable once more to be in a band. Music really mattered again.

'That's all I want from this,' Noel recently commented. 'If Oasis means that five years after we've finished there's 1,000 new bands out there, then we've done our job.'

On 17 June 1995 the *NME* ran an interview with Noel. In it, he foresaw a limited future for the band.

'I don't see this going on forever, I see it as three albums and that's it,' he told journalist Ted Kessler. 'I don't think I can do any more with Oasis after that. There's only so many anthems you can write. I don't know for sure, but I'd say the next album will be the last.'

Provocative stuff, although Noel was quick to play the quote down, saying he had been misunderstood. Oasis would continue, he insisted, but the music had to change. Had to. He couldn't keep writing in this vein for much longer. In many ways, he was preparing people for *Morning Glory*, which deviated strongly from their début album. No doubt he was nudging Liam, too.

'I think the sound of *Definitely Maybe* was a bit one-dimensional,' Noel continued. 'Everything was the same tone and whack it up to ten and off we go. There are a few songs on the new one that could've gone on *Definitely Maybe*, but overall I think there's a lot more variety in the songs and a lot more going on generally.'

The real test for Oasis at this point was their headlining appearance at the twenty-fifth anniversary of the Glastonbury

Festival. It was planned to be Alan White's live début with the group. As it turned out the band inserted a warm-up show at Bath Pavilion the night before. A relieved Alan White made his first appearance in front of hundreds of people rather than thousands. The last band to have played the venue was The Jam, some thirteen years previous.

After the show, which opened with 'Swamp Song', and included in the set about a quarter of the new album, the band returned to the Holiday Inn in Bristol where Liam and Brian Cannon partied longer than everybody else, staying up till nine to greet a bemused breakfast crowd.

At four the next afternoon they travelled to the site.

It wasn't a great show. The immense size of the crowd threw Oasis. They'd never played to an audience that big before. Then Liam invited Robbie Williams on-stage, and Noel hunched his shoulders up and pointedly turned away. Someone threw something at the stage and Liam offered everyone there a fight.

And so it went on, the kind of gig that would pick up pace and then inexplicably stall. The sound didn't help either, the wind scattering it to the skies. Only a rallying finale hinted at what could have been.

If Noel learnt anything from the gig, he later commented, it was that he would have to be much more careful with the set-list. They had played five new songs and that, he believed, had derailed the crowd's expectations of riotous behaviour to the songs they knew and cherished.

The only one to emerge with any real credit was Alan White. Back in the studio, Noel and Owen pieced together 'Swamp Song' by adding the drums from his Glastonbury performance to the final mix. They were beat perfect.

The band returned to the festival site the following day. Thanks to the Creation offer, all of their singles were now in the top forty. Liam arrived with the singer Lisa M., one of the very few girls to claim a serious relationship with him.

To play around with the tabloid's curiosity about his turbulent love life, Liam also had his photograph taken with Meg's friend Fran Cutler and told the reporter they were to be married. This story, much to everyone's amusement (with the exception of Fran's boyfriend), duly appeared the next day.

Noel spent a lot of his time at Glastonbury in a white mini-bus parked backstage and it was here that he first met Sean Rowley, who was swiftly dubbed Travis Bickle after Robert de Niro's psychopathic character in the film *Taxi Driver*.

Rowley fully endeared himself to Noel that afternoon when he agreed to be filmed for Channel Four's *My Glastonbury* spot. Asked how the festival was for him, Rowley answered by whipping out a small bottle of amyl nitrate and deeply inhaling before walking away.

'That,' Noel said, falling about with laughter, 'is the best bit of TV I have ever seen.'

When it was time to photograph the *Morning Glory* album cover, Noel insisted that Sean be used. In the resulting picture, shot at five in the morning in London's Berwick Street, Rowley walks towards the camera whilst Brian Cannon passes him by.

'I love people who don't give a fuck,' Noel said. Incidentally, Brian Cannon's Glastonbury had not gone too well. He was arrested by the police on the Sunday and spent the night in the cells.

Tim Abbot's Glastonbury was more productive. Having now left Creation Records to set up his own Better Records label (Digsy's group, Smaller one of his first signings), Abbot saw which way the wind was blowing for Take That's Robbie Williams. His public presence at Glastonbury and open cavorting with the 'bad boys of rock' was bound to dirty his carefully manufactured squeaky-clean image.

Soon after Glastonbury, Williams announced his departure from Take That. Not long after, Abbot started managing him.

A week after Glastonbury, Oasis began a series of appearances at European festivals that would also include two shows in a tent, the biggest ever to be erected in Britain, on Irvine Beach in Scotland. For Oasis now, everything had to be the biggest and the best.

The first show was at the Rosskilde Festival in Denmark, a performance that Noel rates as one of the best ever from the band.

Prior to the gig, Liam was asked by MTV about Noel's quote concerning Oasis splitting up after the next album. He said, 'I'm not up for splitting up. If he splits it up, he'll get loads of grief off the fans, so he can do it. All the fans can burn his house down, so let him do it.'

Liam went on to say that Noel had loads of albums inside of

him and that 'maybe a good slap around the jaw might change his mind'.

That night Liam took to the stage wrapped in a Union Jack flag, and the press reported that he had 'cavorted' with model Helena Christensen.

On 3 July Oasis played Milan, and on 5 July Lyon in France. On the 7th it was Switzerland, on the 8th back to France before travelling overnight to Germany, and then home to prepare for the Irvine Beach show.

They played two nights here, Friday 14 July and Saturday the 15th. At the latter, Cast, who had been formed by ex-La's member John Power, played one of their earliest gigs and Liam told their manager they wouldn't be using them again as they were far too good. Ocean Colour Scene also played the bill.

Oasis themselves delivered two blistering sets that had the next week's papers salivating. The most pertinent review was that of Taylor Parkes in *Melody Maker*. A self-confessed cynic of the band's merits, he admitted his intention to bury the band. Instead, he declared praise.

'On Saturday,' he wrote, 'they played what I'm close to accepting was the most exciting live rock 'n' roll show I have ever seen in my life.'

In the following week, Noel and Owen finished mixing the album, completing the work on 25 July. It was then announced to the press that the album would be preceded by a new single, 'Roll With It'.

The date of release was 14 August 1995. The next thing they knew, Blur announced that they too were releasing a new single, 'Country House', from their *Great Escape* album. The date? August 14 1995.

Oasis shrugged their shoulders and carried on touring. They played Madrid on the 18th and Zeebruger's Beach Festival in Belgium on the 21st. Then they flew over to Ireland to play an ecstatic show at Dublin's Slaine Castle.

'There were so many people going mad at the front,' Noel recalled, 'and they were all squashed up and everything. The gig had been getting better and better but by the time we got to "Live Forever" I thought, play this and people will die.'

And some kids did. During the festival, three people dived

into the moat that separated the band and audience, and drowned.

On their coach pulling out of the festival Noel and Liam fell into a serious fight and punches were exchanged. The next day another punch to the solar plexus, but this time from an unexpected source.

Mark Coyle quit his position as sound engineer.

Coyley was experiencing severe problems with his hearing and would need time off to recuperate. Though he never showed it, the news hurt Noel. Coyley had been there from the start and Noel considered him one of the very few close friends he had. With his departure, another familiar face had now disappeared.

As it turned out, Coyley's hearing recovered sufficiently for him to produce the Smaller album the following year. And Noel made a guest appearance on it.

Oasis took a bit of a breather as preparations for the release of their second album got underway. Noel took time out to stand on-stage with Paul Weller at his headlining slot at the T In The Park festival, hammering through a version of 'I Walk On Gilded Splinters' and a fiery 'Swamp Song'.

On 26 July Oasis regrouped at a King's Cross studio and, under the direction of John Klein, shot a video for 'Roll With It'. The audience was made up of fans who had successfully secured tickets from a phone-in competition, and the band later played a full gig for them.

Oasis then announced five gigs to take place in September, and the release of a live video, shot at their Southend show entitled *Live By The Sea*, the original working-title for 'It's Good To Be Free'.

Meanwhile, the media hype surrounding the release of both the Blur and Oasis singles was building to unmanageable proportions. It began in the music press, moved into the tabloids and ended up as a major news item on ITV's *News At Ten*, *The Channel Four News* and the BBC's *Nine O'Clock News*. Pointed references were made about The Beatles and The Rolling Stones in the 1960s, when each group would inform the other of upcoming releases.

This time, such an arrangement was impossible. Both bands stood stubborn, each side claiming that the other had started it.

A slanging match now erupted, most of the venom emanating from the Oasis camp.

One example. Press officer Johnny Hopkin's quote, 'Oasis versus Blur? More like Oasis versus Chas and Dave.'

Or Noel, on discovering that the Blur single contained the phrase 'Morning Glory'. 'Blur can steal our lines but it would be impossible for us to do it as I can't think what would go with "bag of shite".'

The hype introduced the word 'Britpop' to a nation, and as Noel shrewdly observed, 'The only ones who will really benefit in the end will be the record companies and the record shops.'

Much as Oasis didn't want this showdown the war of words continued. And it was just that. To put this public squabble into perspective, in America, where war had broken out between West and East coast in the rap community, Tha Dogg Pound, an LA group, shot a video in New York and were forced to run for cover when somebody opened fire on them.

Noel was quick to turn the charade into class-war, stating that Blur were middle-class twats who shouldn't mix it with working-class lads.

In the meantime Oasis had put out feelers to discover how they had become embroiled in a fight they never wanted to be in. It soon became apparent that it had been of Blur's making. Their single, as reported in the *NME* 8 July edition, had originally been slated for a 28 August release.

To add further insult, Oasis heard Damon Albarn being interviewed by Chris Evans on Radio One. Evans played the Oasis single to him and as it ran, Albarn started singing, 'And I like it, I like it,' to the tune of 'Rockin' All Over The World' by Status Quo.

That infuriated everyone in the Oasis camp. 'They're taking the piss now,' Noel stated, before ordering a series of T-shirts that had 'Quoasis' emblazoned across them. He then wore it on the day of a *Loaded* magazine photo-shoot and for the benefit of the MTV cameras.

'It should be about music but it's not,' he said. 'It's about who's the biggest. But everyone knows we've got the best songs.'

On 9 August, Noel and Meg left a Britain that was experiencing its hottest summer in years and took off for a week's holiday in Sorrento, Italy. Noel spent his time hiding from the sun and refusing all food except hot dogs or steak and chips.

While there, he wandered into a scooter shop called Auto Motors and bought five Velocifero scooters in different colours for himself and the band. It cost him £5,000.

'The guy who served me,' spins Noel, 'was saying, "*Mama mia*," thank you Lord, thank you.' He wasn't, of course. But it sounded good.

Noel arrived back in London on Wednesday the 16th, two days after the release of both Blur and Oasis singles. Straightaway he was given some bad news. Creation had let their marketing manager go due to a pay squabble. In the ensuing confusion, thousands of Oasis singles hadn't been given proper barcodes. It spelled disaster. And probable defeat.

When someone buys a record in a chart-return shop the assistant logs the sale by placing the barcode into a computer which then relates the sale to the chart compiler's headquarters.

If the barcode is failing to work then the assistant will sell the record without registering it. Potentially, thousands of Oasis singles would be bought and never registered.

'The biggest week in pop history,' Noel screamed, 'and my record company isn't up to it.'

In comparison, EMI were a model of marketing technique. They issued two formats of Blur's single. One contained three previously unavailable live tracks. The other contained a brand new song, plus a duet between Damon and French vocalist Francoise Hardy on the Blur song 'To The End'.

Their video, directed by the controversial artist Damien Hirst, also stuck out in comparison to Oasis's, who had plumped for a straight-ahead and not particularly interesting live performance.

In front of Noel on his kitchen table, as he assimilated all this bad news that Black Wednesday, were the music press reviews.

Melody Maker's David Stubbs reviewed both singles together. He pointed out that neither single was the band's best work, but asked readers to, 'Check the way Noel's guitar dips its shoulders and slips inside your defence mechanism after the first few bars, sending you tumbling towards the chorus – Oasis are never as "straight", as their detractors would have you believe.'

At the *NME*, Mark Sutherland was unequivocal in his judgement. Blur's was 'nothing short of a classic pop single', while Oasis's 'ludicrously intensive campaign suggests prolific workrate is finally taking its toll on Noel Gallagher's once seemingly bottomless well of cracking choons'.

Noel tossed away the paper in disgust. He was 60% sure now that Oasis would lose. Then Marcus called. Blur had again upped the odds. They had just announced their decision to play in Bournemouth on the same night as Oasis. This was going too far now. Any more of this and fuck the niceties. We'll have him, Burnage style. (Oasis subsequently grabbed the higher moral ground by moving their show to the following night, explaining that they didn't want their fans to be embroiled in any trouble.)

That night, Noel caught a cab over to the Kensington Hilton and met Paul Weller. They had a few drinks at the bar and then the two musicians returned to Noel's Camden flat and spent the night getting wasted. So wasted in fact that when Marcus arrived at midday to pick Noel up and take him to *Top Of The Pops*, Noel was, in Weller's memorable phrase, 'frothing at the mouth'.

At the TV studio, Noel and Liam decided to swap roles. Liam played the guitar while Noel swayed dangerously by the microphone singing the song. The BBC only realised, one tabloid reported, because, 'Noel stuck his tongue out when he should have been singing.' After the show, Noel went home and collapsed.

The following Saturday, Oasis flew out of the country to start a Japanese tour. On Sunday, at seven that night, Radio One announced the winners of the singles battle. Blur, straight in at number one.

'Roll With It' c/w 'It's Better People', Rockin' Chair', and a live version of 'Live Forever', taken from Glastonbury, number two.

In the week that some 1.8 million singles were sold, 'Country House' claimed 274,000 sales, 'Roll With It' 216,000. Now Oasis really knew what it was like to lose at Wembley in a Cup Final.

Noel moved quickly to shrug off the defeat. He pointed back to February 1967 when Englebert Humperdinck's 'Please Release Me' kept the best-ever Beatles' single, 'Strawberry Fields' c/w 'Penny Lane', off the top of the charts.

It was a hasty excuse that couldn't disguise the horrible taste that Oasis felt in their mouths. The next interview Noel undertook was with Miranda Sawyer for a major *Observer* profile of the band. In it, he told her about Blur, 'the bass player and the singer – I hope the pair of them catch AIDS and die because I fucking hate them two.'

Sawyer is herself from Manchester and wasn't surprised to hear Noel using such language.

'It's the kind of thing people around Manchester say,' she claims.

'People say, I hope so and so dies. When Noel said it, I thought he was a bit of a prick but I also thought it was quite funny. I certainly didn't expect it to be blown up like it did.'

Nor, would it seem, did her editors. In the published piece, the *Observer* didn't flag the comment in any way and left it buried somewhere on the second page.

Yet it was undoubtedly an intemperate remark whose insensitivity was highlighted a few weeks later when a woman whose boyfriend had just died from being an HIV carrier related that he had requested Oasis records to be played at his funeral.

Melody Maker were the first to highlight it. Two days, after the *Observer* appeared, they reported that Noel had brought the whole Blur/Oasis clash down to new levels of indecency. This was picked up by the rest of the media, and the story grew and grew.

Meanwhile, Sawyer, prior to flying to New York for a holiday, had been contacted by *Melody Maker*, who, she claimed, misquoted her. On her return, she spoke with Oasis's press officer Johnny Hopkins who said she should write a rebutal to them. This she did, which they then pulled apart.

'I couldn't do anything right at that point,' she says.

She also totally refutes Noel's later statement that he retracted the comment directly after saying it. 'If he had then I would either have not written it or pointed out the retraction.'

Miranda described Noel's mood throughout the interview as 'jovial'. 'Whether he was drunk or not I couldn't tell. It was a phone interview that took place at six in the morning over here and because of the phone lines it was hard to tell.'

Jovial or not, by the time he got back to England, Noel would have another public row to defuse.

Japan was a good place to be when the news came through. If anything, the audiences were even wilder now that they had Oasis records to play in their bedrooms. One fan stencilled a picture of

Peggy and her three sons that had appeared in the UK press across her shirt, and two others sported the new Manchester City shirt, even though the season had only just begun.

The band played five nights in Tokyo at three different venues. Two at the Club Citta, one at the Liquid Room, two in the Garden Hall. After one of the shows, two girls arrived backstage with pills and powders.

The band plus followers returned to the hotel and partied all night in the swimming-pool, managing by five o'clock in the morning to have an irate manager informing them that they were banned forever from his hotel. Liam had removed every emergency exit sign he came across; sixteen of them were discovered in his room.

Then it was on to Osaka and two triumphant nights in the Imperial Hall. They then boarded a plane for London, knowing full well that on their arrival home, Noel's AIDS comments would be whipping up a storm of bad publicity.

The Terrence Higgins Trust, an organisation dedicated to helping people who are HIV positive, said they were 'deeply shocked'.

At the London Lighthouse HIV hospital, spokesman Ben McKnight took a cooler approach, agreeing that the comment was insensitive, but adding, 'This is just them whipping up more publicity rather than thinking of how people might be affected.'

Damon and Alex from Blur refused to comment, and Oasis moved quickly to limit the damage. Noel released a press release apologising for his remarks, stating, 'As soon as I said it, I realised it was an insensitive thing to say and immediately retracted the comment. I was horrified to find the journalist concerned chose to run with it. Anyone who knows me will confirm that I am sympathetic towards the plight of HIV carriers as well as being supportive of the challenge to raise awareness about AIDS and HIV. Although not being a fan of their music, I wish both Damon and Alex a long life.' After that, things began to cool down.

When Noel returned home that Wednesday afternoon he was to find a message on his answer machine asking him if he would be available to be photographed with The Stone Roses for a potential *NME* cover. The story would be based around a unique venture that Oasis, prior to their departure, had agreed to participate in.

The project was the *Help* album, a record that would raise cash for the victims of the Bosnian War and attempt to enter the record books by being recorded, produced and distributed within a week. The idea came from Tony Crean at Go Discs Records.

Stunned by the phase of absolute brutality that the war in Bosnia had now entered into, Crean had been galvanised into action. His idea was to secure the services of young British bands who would all enter studios from midnight on Sunday 3 September and deliver a finished track by Monday the 4th. Midnight was the deadline.

The master tapes would be cut and flown to pressing plants on the Tuesday and manufactured as cassettes on the Wednesday. They would then be flown to Polygram's distribution centre in Chadwell Heath on Thursday and distributed to the shops on Friday, ready to be put on sale on that Saturday.

Such a mission had never been attempted before and its success lay totally with the full participation and professionalism of those involved.

On hearing the photo request, Noel jumped a cab to photographer Steve Double's studio in London's East End. He was in a good mood that day. Alan McGee had taken on Meg and given her a job as artist liaison. Now she had something to get up for in the mornings.

At the studio, Noel had his photo taken with Ian Brown, Robbie Maddix, who had recently joined the Roses, and Sice from The Boo Radleys.

The musicians were then interviewed by *NME*'s Mark Sutherland. Noel didn't mention Sutherland's recent poor review. Instead, they all spoke of their concern about the war but, unlike the Red Wedge movement of the 1980s which had inadvertently placed musicians in politician's clothes, they professed to having no solutions, just plain human compassion.

The following Sunday, Oasis entered the Maison Rouge Studios in Fulham just before midnight. Already, Liam and Noel had fought over the recording.

'What song are we doing?' the band has previously asked Noel.

'Remember how we played "Fade Away" at the Borderline? Like a ballad? That's the song. And I'm singing it.'

Liam, naturally, had to fight him on that one and after the squabble was over, Liam agreed to supply backing vocals, and the band, with Johnny Depp guesting on guitar, laid down a beautiful version of the song. Lisa M. sang backing vocals and Fran Cutler provided the 'And you know that' which ends the record. By five o'clock, they had left the studio, Noel with the tape in his hand.

Crean hadn't only got the likes of Portishead, The Levellers, Radiohead, Suede, Neneh Cherry, Manic Street Preachers, Blur, The Charlatans and The Chemical Brothers to contribute, he had also swung it for Paul Weller to enter Studio Two in Abbey Road and record the Beatles' song 'Come Together'.

In the preceding week, Weller had written a letter to Paul McCartney telling him about the project, offering an open invitation to attend the session.

It was precisely where Noel was heading that day. He told Liam about the arrangement but his brother said, 'Arsed'. 'If I meet Macca, I meet him. But I'm not going out of my way for him.'

Noel showed up at Abbey Road, the studio where his most favourite group ever had conspired to make some of the most riveting and far-reaching pop music of our times.

There was enormous doubt as to whether McCartney would show but at two in the afternoon, suddenly, he was standing there with wife Linda. Later, he played electric piano, bass and sang backing vocals. He also taught Weller's band a song he had written the day before but there was no time to record it.

About an hour after his arrival, Noel put down his guitar part in the small control-room that had recorded nearly every Beatles' song. McCartney to the right of him, Weller to the left, the subsequent film of this moment not only symbolised British pop in the 1990s, but also Noel Gallagher's musical journey. There would never be another day like it.

Soon after, Noel left the studio and hurried over to Radio One to preview 'Fade Away', and publicise the album. Then he returned to Abbey Road, finally heading for home at around midnight.

It was as if he, the good Catholic boy, was now publicly atoning for all his sins.

*

They put Plan B into action on Monday 28 August. The tabloids (not the music press) announced that Oasis would play the Earls Court Arena, London on 5 November 1995.

The seating would be removed to allow an audience of 20,000 people. Ticket prices would be held at £14 per head.

Blur's biggest show to date had taken place that summer at London's Mile End stadium with an audience of 17,000. Oasis tickets would go on sale the next day.

The following night Noel called Marcus for an update on sales. He was told that demand was so heavy, Oasis would now play two nights at the venue. Forty thousand people would see them. They would be Europe's largest-ever indoor shows. It put a smile back on the band's faces.

They then sat back to await the reviews for *Morning Glory*, each one of them expecting praise to shower upon them like golden pennies from heaven. But in that turbulent summer of 1995 nothing would go as planned.

To begin with there was a major problem with 'Step Out', the song that clearly lifted the verse from Stevie Wonder and Henry Cosby's song 'Uptight'. It had been sent over to America for clearance, and the songwriters had come back demanding a massively high royalty rate. The song, which had been chosen to open side two of the album, was swiftly removed. However, this was at such a late stage that Creation had already sent out CDs containing the song. (These CDs are now highly-valuable collector's items, as are the white labels of 'Columbia', 'I Am The Walrus', 'Acquiesce', and Brendan Lynch's mix of 'Champagne Supernova'.)

'It was a bit of a nothing track,' Noel told *Loaded* magazine. 'If I could go back now I'd definitely swap "Rockin' Chair" for it, but we had to make a snap decision and I was wrong.'

On 30 September *NME* and *Melody Maker* ran full-page reviews of the album. They weren't what was expected. John Robinson in the *NME* wrote that the album felt like 'the morning after the night before'. He railed against what he perceived to be a deliberate shift in Noel's songwriting, away from fast furious rock 'n' roll towards a rock classicism, and ended by saying that the album contains 'tales of a group that has peered over the edge and could lose their footing . . . Ultimately a nervous peek through the curtains, not a bold rise and shine'. He gave it seven out of ten.

David Stubbs at *Melody Maker* was much harder, more scathing. 'Now we realise that the reason they are inarticulate is that they are not very bright', was one of his opening salvos, before going on to call the album 'occasionally sublime but too often laboured and lazy', finishing with, 'Oasis are fallen, fallen short of the stars. They sound knackered'.

Worse was to come in *Vox* when Steve Sutherland complained that the album contained 'too much Paul Weller and too little John Lydon, too much Noel, not enough Liam', before concluding, 'Measured against *The Great Escape*, Blur are better'.

And so it continued.

'A wasted opportunity if you're being generous,' wrote David Cavanagh in *Q*. 'A shot in the foot if you want to be more melodramatic.'

The most favourable reviews were to be found in the quality newspapers such as the *Independent* and the *Guardian*. Marcus also pointed out to the band that the UK reviews were more than nullified by the rave notices that had started to pour in from Europe.

The band were surprised by the reaction. All five of them had been playing nothing but the album songs for weeks and they were sharp enough to know what was good and what didn't work. It would only be Liam, later on, who would point out that their fast recording pace sometimes left songs feeling too rushed or, worse, made them miss opportunities to play and sing them better.

It was generally agreed that for the next album they would take their time, but they still harboured few doubts about *Morning Glory*. They were immensely excited about it. Indeed, Bonehead had got himself barred from the Swiss Cottage Hotel when he climbed up on to the roof in the early hours and blasted it out for all the residents to hear.

He was staying in London because Oasis were back in the studio, continuing from where they had left off on the Sunday to record two new songs as B-sides. They were 'Round Are Way' and 'The Masterplan'.

After the basic recording had finished, Liam, Alan White and Guigsy then travelled to Paris to conduct interviews whilst Noel stayed with Owen in the studio mixing the songs.

Security guard Ian Robertson accompanied them. It was here

that he and Liam clashed really badly, when he entered the singer's room to drag him out to a press conference. As Liam had company, he didn't take too kindly to the intrusion. All day, he brooded over Robbo, as he was known.

'All I know,' Guigsy says, 'is that later on I was in this bar doing an interview. It was about ten at night and Liam started kicking up about something. So he got off and as he walked by, he was like, "You can fuck off as well, dickhead."

'Then about three hours later he comes back in going, "You fucking dicks," and he's got a coat on but no shirt. His coat was open and he was bare chested and he's going, "You fucking dicks, fucking nobs," so I just got off. I was like, "I'm going home, I'm not doing any press." So the next morning, I refused to do any more interviews and went home.'

About a week later, Liam called Guigsy and apologised. Ian Robertson, meanwhile, had been relieved of his duties.

'I spoke to Noel about it,' he said, 'and Noel said, "I agree with you but he's my brother." I have to go with him. And that was that.'

After completing their work at Maison Rouge, the band then started rehearsals at Brixton Academy for the upcoming UK tour. The call was for five that evening but by seven o'clock, Guigsy had failed to show. The band were used to late appearances but that was usually Liam's forte.

Guigsy was the solid one, the guy who swept up behind them, who remained in the background with his big spliffs but kept a careful eye on everything. He totally understood the band's psychology, knew their character traits. It was him who could calm a situation, cool down tempers. It was Guigsy who could sit there and faithfully predict how someone was going to react at least five minutes before they did. It was Guigsy, good old dependable Guigsy with his laid-back demeanour, and his encyclopaedic knowledge and passion for football, his wisecracks, and an ability to find flaws in people's arguments and gently pull them apart, who acted as a real antidote to the mayhem. But cross him or the band just once and then his temper would flare and he would defend his friends, his family to the last, just as he had done on the ferry to Amsterdam.

And while everyone had been waiting for either Noel or Liam to crumble under the stress of their complex, fiery relationship, it was Guigsy who woke up on the first day of rehearsal and literally couldn't drag himself out of bed. His body had given up on him. His nerves were shot right through. Every time he even thought about a bass guitar a feeling of abject sickness erupted in his stomach.

He stayed in bed, closed his eyes and slept for twenty hours straight. Then he went round to Marcus's house. It was Friday. Guigsy told him, 'Look, if I can't get out of bed I can't tour, therefore I can't be in the band so you'll have to get someone else.'

At first, Marcus thought he was severely hungover.

'No, no,' Guigsy insisted, 'You don't understand. I can't physically do it. It's not that I don't want to be in the band, I literally can't be in the band.'

Then he left to see a doctor and Oasis were forced to handle another major crisis.

Late that night, as they lay in their beds, they heard the words on the wind creeping through their windows and into their minds, telling each and every one of them, that they were finished now, the game was over. Now they would slowly descend to whence they came and they would do so with the eyes of the world upon them. As they listened, their collective fists clenched tighter and tighter.

By their own admission, they had completely taken their eyes off Guigsy. Maybe alarm bells should have gone off the day Alan White joined and he saw the bassist badly shaking as he lifted the glass to his mouth. Or maybe they should have taken more time out.

'There was hardly any daylight between the *Definitely Maybe* campaign and the *Morning Glory* campaign,' Marcus admits. 'I knew that, but that was part of the whole thing, to get across that this band was a phenomenon and not just some band putting albums out now and again. And Guigsy wasn't ready in his mind to go out full-on as you have to be to do it. And he had enough guts to come round and tell me.'

The focus will always be on Noel and Liam. Those are the two that people look out for, keep their eyes upon. They are also the ones that the media make a bee line for, rushing past the others to get to the source.

Guigsy, Bonehead and Alan White never had a problem with that. For them, just to be part of such an important band, their names now enshrined in musical history, was enough. They each knew their worth and what they brought to the table. They knew that they were working with an exceptional songwriter and a unique singer.

In tow with these two, they had travelled the world now, experienced life to the full, gained financial security and made homes with their loved ones.

Guigsy, by his own admission, will tell you, 'I am not a great bass player but somehow my playing fits into this band and that's how it is.'

But now his body had failed him. On the first day of rehearsals, it refused to move. On the second day, he went to the doctor's. It was important that he did so. Unless Oasis supplied a genuine doctor's certificate, they would be liable for thousands of pounds by cancelling the tour.

'I had this disease,' Guigsy reveals, 'where it means you've got no radiator in your system, there's no cooling system. It's something that you're born with. It means your blood pressure goes up and up and up, and it just stays there, it doesn't come back down.

'So doing things like cocaine, sends it further up until your body can't take it any more. Your body's working too fast inside and you just crumble. Which is basically what happened. But it took some time to find out.'

With Ruth and his family away in Manchester, after being examined Guigsy travelled North to spend time alone in the house he had grown up in. Since gaining success, he had been pleading with his mum to move to new accommodation, an area where nobody knew what her son did for a living.

The house had already been burgled once. But all they took was a selection of Guigsy's CDs. Weird. But it was a pointer, he would tell his mum, of what was to come. Teresa McGuigan stood firm. I'll move if I want to, she said.

Guigsy spent a couple of days in the house, totally alone. Then he returned to London.

'I basically chilled out,' he says, 'I didn't speak to hardly anyone, didn't go out, didn't leave the house except to have loads of blood tests, went to about four of five different doctors, urine tests, hair tests, I had everything until they finally diagnosed me. Then once they found out what was wrong, they prescribed me these tablets and it was proper way-hey the very next day. Everything was back to normal.'

But the cure wasn't really so immediate. As Guigsy slowly healed, Oasis moved the tour back a month and then sat down to work out a temporary replacement. Alan White suggested using Julian Taylor from his old band Star Club. But Liam wasn't having that.

'He's got to be from Manchester,' he stated, 'Can't have any more cock-nees in the group. No offence, Alan, but you know what I mean.'

Eventually, they decided to approach Scott Mcleod of The Ya Ya's. He agreed to join on a temporary basis and rehearsals finally got underway at John Henry's studio. During this period, Liam and Noel also attended a birthday party in King's Cross for James Brown, editor of *Loaded* magazine.

Everybody had a drink, everybody had a line, everybody had a good time. But as they were leaving, one of the guys on the door called Liam a dickhead. Before even he could react, Noel was upon him.

'Don't you ever call my brother that,' he roared. And then the two brothers laid into him before exiting and going their very separate ways.

Seventeen

On 12 September 1995 Oasis attended the Mercury Awards at London's Savoy Hotel. They didn't win but part of the ceremony involved every nominated artist receiving a plaque and making a speech.

Noel stood on-stage and said he'd like to thank . . . then he read the menu out. Liam said, 'I'd like to thank myself', and Noel added, 'all six of him'.

In Europe, MTV ran part of the interview they had conducted with Noel in July. This included his acoustic rendering of 'Don't Look Back In Anger'. Noel ended the song and said, 'Better than Blur anyday'.

It now felt like the world was dividing itself into two camps, Oasis or Blur. In football, there was Cantona (Oasis) or Shearer (Blur). In snooker, Ronnie O'Sullivan (Oasis) or Stephen Hendry (Blur).

But perhaps the best example of this was Irvine Welsh's *Trainspotting* novel which was now selling at a phenomenal pace, the first time in ages that an authentic British working-class writer had smashed his way into the smug literary world, making no secret of his roots or his pure 1990s lifestyle.

If Irvine's outlook was Oasis, then the other recent publishing success, Nick Hornby with his two books *Fever Pitch* and *High Fidelity* was Blur.

Noel would meet Irvine Welsh the following year at the Cannes Film Festival where *Trainspotting*, the film of the book was being shown. Noel and Meg hung out all night with the Scottish writer who, every twenty minutes or so, would grab the Oasis man and roar, 'I knew you'd be a good bloke, Noel, I knew it, you wee fucker.'

Irvine's huge success would slightly open the gates for other like-minded writers, such as John King and his *The Football*

Factory novel, in precisely the same way that Oasis now had A&R men scurrying around towns desperate to sign the 'new Oasis'.

Again, there were parallels with the 1960s. Just as many of the major groups socialised together then and made various guest appearances on each other's records, so many of the new 1990s groups forged a similarly healthy relationship. Most groups didn't see each other as rivals but as complementing each other.

Indeed, after their Irvine Beach show, Noel imagined people such as Primal Scream, Weller, Ocean Colour Scene and Cast all releasing albums on the same day and advertising the fact by being photographed together holding up each other's albums. He was also keen to host a huge open-air concert and call it Mods In The Park.

The success of Oasis had also introduced other elements into the culture. Now, instead of things being 'wicked', they were 'top'. People you didn't like were 'dickheads', and you were 'arsed' about things you didn't care about.

Hedonism, drugs, Mods, scooters, The Beatles, again and again, the echo of the 1960s provided the underlay for 1990s pop culture. The only difference was economic. Most teenagers had money in the 1960s; in the 1990s, British society was characterised by the huge and ever-increasing gulf between rich and poor. The latter had to withstand, among many things, attacks on free medicine, social security and council housing. This laid the conditions for what the Right-wing termed as the underclass, the poorest of the poor. In one of their earliest recordings 'Bring It On Down' Oasis firmly represented the latter.

To that end Noel publicly supported the Labour leader, Tony Blair, bringing to mind the relationship that existed between The Beatles and Harold Wilson, the then Prime Minister.

Noel met Blair at the Q Awards and was astonished when the Labour leader informed him that he listened to the first Oasis album on his way to work by car.

In football, the 1960s were also brought to mind when England hosted the Euro '96 competition. In June 1996 at Wembley, England would again outplay Germany, just as they had done thirty years previously, but this time they would sleep with defeat in their mouths.

But Oasis wouldn't. *(What's The Story) Morning Glory?* Despite the reviews, smashed its way straight in at number one, the week their UK tour finished. Oasis had played Blackpool, Stoke, Bournemouth and Gloucester. Vital Distribution reported that an extra 150,000 copies had been ordered by shops in the first week, topping up the 400,000 that were originally sent out.

On 10 October, Oasis left for yet another US tour. There were signs now that America was starting to move their way a little. In its first week of release *Morning Glory* had sold some 250,000 copies in the US, an encouraging sign.

Also, the industry publication *Music Week* had just held a US radio workshop in London's Hurlingham Club. Eight of the most prominent radio planners in the States were played one track each from new successful UK bands. The playlist included, Supergrass, Blur, Pulp, Black Grape and Oasis.

The panel voted 'Morning Glory' as the track most likely to succeed in their country, Brian Phillips of Atlanta Radio adding, 'This isn't even the best track on the album. If this doesn't work then I give up.'

Encouragingly, Black Grape's 'Kelly's Heroes' came second, and Ash's 'Girl From Mars' third. Blur's 'The Universal' and Pulp's 'Common People' were deemed 'too English'.

Compared to previous excursions, this was a short US tour. Earls Court was looming and nobody wanted an exhausted Oasis taking the stage.

The journey started in Baltimore, then on to gigs in New York, Danbury, Boston, Pittsburg, Buffalo, Toronto, Detroit and Chicago.

The band would also slot in a crucial TV appearance in New York on the massively popular *The David Letterman Show*. The show was televised from the Ed Sullivan Theater, the exact venue and stage on which The Beatles had conquered America in February 1964, with a performance containing just five songs.

After the Pittsburg show, tour manager Maggie was sitting by herself on the coach when Scott Mcleod, the temporary bassist, sat down beside her.

'I want to go home,' he stated.

'Yeah, don't we all?' she lightly agreed.

'No, I want to go home.'

Which is what he did. While the band slept, he demanded that Maggie get him a flight to Manchester. He flew out the next day, with four gigs to go. When they woke up, Oasis were stunned to find another member had flown the coop.

'What is it about bass players in this band?' Noel wondered. 'One minute, this guy is signing on, then suddenly he's in the biggest band in Britain, getting a decent wedge, and he pisses off.'

They had to laugh.

Liam then put forward a suggestion. 'Why don't we fly out that bass player Whitey was talking about. Get him in.'

Noel looked at him in amazement. This is what had first been suggested.

'Liam,' he said, 'You are either a genius or the biggest dickhead on the planet. I really can't work out which one.'

Which of course was a major part of Liam's appeal. He really was a one-off. Take for instance his comments on his brother's avid interest in UFOs. Noel firmly believes in their existence Liam is somewhat more pragmatic.

'If I saw an alien,' he said, 'I'd tell it to fuck right off because whatever planet he came from they wouldn't have The Beatles or any decent fucking music. So they can fuck right off, I ain't going nowhere with them.'

About God, he said, 'If a guy suddenly appears before me with a big beard and locks and all that caper and performed some fucking miracle, and then said to me, "Liam, I am God" I'd say, "Fair enough, it's a fair cop. I didn't believe in you but fair play, you've got me." But until that day comes he can fuck right off.'

Liam never had much time for God. Back in his childhood he and his brothers desperately tried to get their mother away from Thomas but her religion held her back.

That meant more violence against all of them, more pain. Liam expressed his through his aggression and Noel took on his father the best way he could. Through music. You play guitar, dad? Well, so do I. But better. People know you in town? People all over the world know me, mate.

The success of Oasis was Noel's private revenge on his father, and a major factor in his unceasing workrate.

Music was the Gallaghers' saviour, not religion. Music put them in a different world, a far far better world. That was their heaven on earth, their salvation. Nothing else.

Noel wasn't a believer in any sense. He was just waiting for the UFOs. But Liam had, without reading any books, become a natural Buddhist. His firm belief is that the soul never dies. The body does but your spirit survives. You really do live forever. Which is why he is adamant that Lennon's spirit is inside him.

He thinks that it happened when he was a teenager and he had a out-of-body experience. Suddenly, he was looking down upon himself and in that moment, he says, Lennon slipped inside him.

'I don't care if it sounds fucking mad,' he viciously states. And he doesn't, because he believes in the spirit and he believes in music. Those are the two most unshakeable beliefs Liam has. Again, he embodies two major elements of the 1990s. Laddishness and spiritualism.

Noel says, 'I believe in black and white. Liam's all over the shop.'

Bonehead says, 'You're all fucking mad. What are we going to do about Scott?'

Cancel the remaining gigs, go to New York and play the TV show was the answer.

Which is what they did. They arrived at the Ed Sullivan Theater to discover that the actor William Shatner would be one of Letterman's guests.

Noel said to Liam, 'Guess who's on?'

'Who?'

'Captain Kirk.'

'Whose that?'

'Captain Kirk. William Shatner.'

'Don't know him.'

Noel stopped for a second. Then he said, 'T.J. Hooker.'

'Oh him. Really? Fucking ace.'

Bonehead played bass and the band ripped through 'Morning Glory', the song that had been released to the radio. Then they flew home. They had no bass player and the biggest gigs of their career was just two weeks away.

Marcus phoned Guigsy to see how he was and inform him about Scott's unexpected disappearance. Guigsy said, 'Fuck it, if the doctor says it's all right and you can get us a couple of days' rehearsals, let's fucking do it.'

It was the first bit of good news since the album's release, made better when Guigsy's doctor said, 'Fine, just come back for a check-up every seven days.'

A relieved Marcus booked the band into John Henry's studio.

'I don't think we even played our old tunes,' Guigsy says. 'We just started jamming for a couple of hours and then we went to the pub for a bit because I didn't want to come back as a stretcher case, I couldn't do that. I had to go back as me again.'

On 30 October, Creation released the eagerly-awaited new Oasis single 'Wonderwall' c/w 'Round Are Way', 'The Swamp Song' and 'The Masterplan'.

In the three weeks preceding its release, Radio One had played 'Wonderwall' forty-three times, and commercial radio had now realised the error of their ways and now they too were busy giving the song plenty of air-space.

In terms of Oasis singles 'Wonderwall' was a complete departure for them. Every single so far had been up-tempo, and most of them were about optimism in the face of adversity. 'You gotta roll with it.' 'You got to make it happen.' 'We're going to live forever.' 'Get a grip on yourself, it don't cost much.' 'You need to be yourself.' 'Some might say we will find a better way.'

'Wonderwall' was far more personal. It was acoustic-based, although backed with a beat that verged on hip-hop, and it showcased a different side to Liam's vocals. Within a month of its release, it had become the most popular song of the year. It was sung everywhere. In pubs, on football terraces, everywhere that people congregated. It not only further increased their popularity in the UK but it broke America for them.

Better still, the single also contained two major songs. Earlier that year, Noel had attended the fifth anniversary of the 6Ts club, a monthly Northern Soul session held at London's 100 Club.

It wasn't so much the music that grabbed him. Rather it was the dedication of the crowd to the music, their fashions and unique dances. He also dug the fact that when you weren't non-stop dancing, you could take time out to browse through the record stalls that were placed in the club itself.

'Round Are Way' then was his tribute to the scene. The song (reminiscent in parts of The Jam's 'Eton Rifles') thrives, like so many Northern tracks, on a straight-ahead beat (the drums being phased in tribute to Kenny Jones's drums on 'Itchycoo Park', an effect that Noel wished he'd used on 'Wonderwall') a blaring horn melody and celebratory lyrics ('Round are way/ The birds are singing') that match the music's untainted joyfulness.

'The Swamp Song' is edgy and cocaine tight, and 'The Masterplan' is one of his finest musical achievements and can only be found on the B-side of the CD version of 'Wonderwall'. Overall the package is probably the best Oasis single to date. But it never made the number-one slot. Robson and Jerome, two actors from the hit UK TV series *Soldier, Soldier*, kept it off the top with their version of 'I Believe'.

Even though Oasis were the biggest band in the country, Noel would have to wait to secure his four number ones.

On the day of 'Wonderwall''s release, Oasis managed to sneak into Camden Town's the Underworld pub that had once banned them, to check out a new young Manchester group called Northern Uproar. Then it was on to a late-night drinking club in Farringdon.

They rose the next morning with hangovers and caught the train to the La Luna venue in Brussells where Guigsy fitted himself back into the side.

On the last song, Liam's voice went. He kicked the microphone stand into the crowd and walked off.

The next day they arrived back in Britain, on 1 November, and resumed rehearsals. That lasted two days.

On the Friday, Noel went down to Earls Court to see how the preparations were going. Their road crew had just one week to erect the necessary equipment, a task that normally takes three weeks.

The next day, the new Mancunians woke up determined to show London and the world just who was boss.

That morning, Meg was up by eight o'clock. She stood in her small kitchen talking on the phone so loudly that she eventually woke Noel up. She was in something of a frenzied mood.

Meg had been handed the task of organising the two after-gig parties and, of course, everybody but everybody was screaming for tickets. Apart from key friends, Oasis and Creation personnel, journalists, radio and TV people, there was also U2, George Michael, and maybe Madonna was coming. Oh, and don't forget Elton and Bowie, maybe the Stones, they all had to be accommodated.

Oasis were non-plussed by the big-name guests. U2 were fine, but the guest they were really excited about seeing was John Squire of The Stone Roses.

'If he comes,' Liam said, 'it will be the first night out he's had since 1987. How mad is that?' The only guest that Noel was disappointed to find couldn't make it was Paul Weller.

Meg left the house at about ten. Noel got up, watched BBC1's *Football Focus*. Soon after, Les arrived to take him to the show.

In the car, Les said, 'Noel, where do The Who live?'

'Don't know.'

'Live at Leeds.'

On Marylebone High Street, they were caught up in a traffic jam. 'Where's the fucking police escort when you need it?' Les asked.

'Put the radio on,' Noel requested.

Les flicked the dial. The unmistakable sound of Blur came through. Les quickly changed stations.

'Put that back on,' Noel said.

Les complied and Blur's new single 'The Universal' filled the car. When it finished Noel, who had listened intently through-out, said, 'I'm sorry but I can't hear a tune in that song.' He gazed out of the window.

'Can't fucking wait to see The Bootleg Beatles tonight,' he said. Oasis had offered the support slot first to Richard Ashcroft who now left his group, The Verve, and then to Smaller, but both acts turned them down. Now, Britain's best Beatles' copyist band would take their place. Later, when he met their guitarist, Noel asked, 'Do you play anything other than Beatles' songs.'

'No,' came the reply.

'Nor do I, mate,' Noel said with a smile.

The traffic finally eased up and soon Les was driving past Earls Court arena, where two massive pictures of Noel and Liam flanked the main entrance, before turning right and then into the backstage area. The first thing Noel saw when he got out of the car were the five Velocifero scooters.

Then he walked out into the arena and greeted all the road crew. They were all desperately scurrying around, determined to get everything in place for the soundcheck. Their expressions were grim, like runners in a marathon. High above this hive of activity, massive black drapes had been hung on the ceiling to improve the sound.

'Imagine having to put those fuckers up,' Noel said, craning his neck.

'Well,' Hugh the sound engineer noted, 'if The Inspiral Carpets had made it that would have been your job, Noel.'

'Like fuck,' he replied.

A few minutes later the rest of Oasis showed up and Noel gave them their scooters, handing them over like he would a cigarette. The band were delighted. They gleefully leapt upon them, revving them up and then careering round the backstage area, swerving cars and people like gleefully demented Mods on speed.

Finally, they parked up and Liam came out into the main hall and looked around in wonderment at the huge hall his vocals would resound around that night.

'I was fucked at that Brussells gig,' he reveals. 'Last number and my voice went. Just threw the mike away and hit about ten fans. But this,' he said, gazing around the hall, 'fucking, mad for it. I'm going to come on that stage and just say, "Come On!"'

A couple of minutes later Oasis ran a soundcheck. They played 'Hello' and then 'Acquiesce'. Then Noel stopped and pointed to his mike and Jason came on to fix it. As he did so, Noel strummed the chords to 'Hung Up'.

Liam then appeared on stage. He stood by the mike and as the band remained quiet, he sang an acappella version of 'Shaker-maker', dispelling any doubts that the Brussells gig might have instilled about his voice.

The band started up 'Champagne Supernova', but this time it was Liam's mike that failed. Frustrated, he threw his tambourine away and moved away to sit and sulk on the drum riser.

A roadie ran on-stage and fixed it as the band continued playing 'Supernova'.

Liam then went back to the mike. As Oasis finished the song, the string section started to gather on the riser high above them. To soundcheck them the band would have to stop playing. So they left the stage and hopped on their scooters. Then they drove out of the venue.

Already, there was a huge number of fans congregating outside and as the five scootermen of Oasis roared towards them, the surprised crowd started cheering them.

'Sausages for sale,' Liam unexplicably shouted at as he passed by.

'Afternoon,' Noel said.

'These are fucking top,' Liam said as he pulled up by the band's dressing-rooms, two big caravans stacked with beer, bottles of Jack Daniels and the usual assortment of crisps, sandwiches and soft drinks.

'We should take them on tour,' he continued, 'get a trailer thing to follow us around. Take two of them with us.'

'Take only two,' his brother ruefully pointed out, 'and we'll be fighting like fuck over them.'

With the string section now ready, the band returned to the stage to play 'Whatever'. When they finished, Noel shouted to Hugh, 'How did that sound? Could you hear the strings?'

'Just about,' he replied doubtfully.

'That's all right then,' Noel said. Then he caught himself and turned to the players. 'Sorry about that. Didn't mean it like that.' The five players smiled, trying not to look too bothered by the casualness of the insult.

They play 'Whatever', and Liam jumps off the stage to watch from the middle of the floor.

When they end, he shouts to Noel, 'Strings sound wrong.'

'Yeah?' Noel says, taking off his guitar.

'They do,' Liam insists.

'Sound all right to me,' Noel states. Then he is handed an acoustic guitar, sits on a stool and plays 'Wonderwall'. Liam kisses his teeth in frustration and walks off.

Halfway through 'Wonderwall' Noel stops and asks, 'Is there an effect on this, Jacko?'

Jacko confirms there is.

'Fucking typical,' Noel says. 'You ask for an effect and can't get it. When you don't want it, like right now, you get it. Take it off for fuck's sake. I sound like Syd Barrett.'

Backstage, as Noel's voice fills the arena with the words 'Maybe, you're going to be the one that saves me', the boys, except for Guigsy, clamber back on to the scooters and drive around. Guigsy meanwhile starts expertly juggling with a football.

The scooter boys pull up by a van whose radio is giving out that day's football results.

Liam clicks his fingers in triumph. Manchester City have beaten Bolton Wanderers. No doubt about it, this is going to be a perfect day.

Here is the news.

'They may have the capacity to backfire at will and possess the on-stage demeanour of a group permanently caught in the rigor mortis of a soundcheck, but Earls Court, proved among other things, Oasis have got the trust and the belief of the nation in their hands like no other group in the country.'
Paul Moody, *New Musical Express.*

'They began by churning up "The Swamp Song". Next "Acquiesce". Who else would start Britain's biggest-ever shows with two B-sides?'
Nicholas Barber, *Independent On Sunday.*

'We file out, touched by something sublime. It's like a world-class gig from antiquity . . . The kids outside are of one voice. "They kicked shit out of Blur's Mile End!" ventures a sweaty youth with a wide grin. "I was at Spike Island and tonight was *better*." argues another.'
Ian Harrison, *Select.*

'Because if Oasis are "just" about reminding people why they fell in love with rock 'n' roll in the first place, they do their job better than anyone for twenty years . . . When Liam goes walkabout behind a wall of yellow T-shirt-clad bouncers during a cover of "I Am The Walrus" to shake hands with the kids at the front of the stage, he really does look like a man who could topple governments.'
Paul Lester, *Melody Maker.*

'But in the end it all comes down to three things: tunes, tunes and tunes, and Oasis have them coming out of their ears.'
David Cheal, *Daily Telegraph.*

'Gig Of The Year Potential: Extremely high. Even hardened Oasis-haters were heard to mumble reluctant sentences about how fantastic it all was.'
John Harris, *Raw* magazine.

'Parts of West London have just suffered an earthquake – thanks to the rock group Oasis. Candlesticks rattled, chandeliers swung and buildings wobbled, accordint to dozens of reports received at Scotland yard from Fulham, Kensington and Chelsea

. . . There are about 300 earthquakes a year in Britain. This is the second believed to have been caused by a concert.'
Geraint Smith, *Evening Standard*.

Liam Gallagher and the band photographer Jill Furmanovsky stand in Earls Court Arena watching the huge screens either side of the stage replay the concert from the night before. Today, Liam wears a woollen hat, a leather fur-collared jacket and jeans that stretch past his ankles and part hide his trainers. He is slightly unshaven.

'I didn't go to that party last night,' he reveals. 'Couldn't risk my voice. But I'm fucking having it tonight.'

Much to Meg's chagrin, none of the band had gone to the party except Noel. He walked in, walked around and was home within the hour.

'Do you ever get nervous?' Jill enquires, as the screen now features a close-up of the singer.

Liam looks at her with a knowing smile. 'Nah,' he says, 'You front it, don't you? Don't get nervous. You get wound up and then you give it front.'

'Did you see Bono after the show?'

'Yeah, mad cunt. He reminds me of me dad. Same height, same face only when he was younger. I told Bono that. He said, "I am your dad." I said, "No, you're not." He said, "I am your dad and I am your son." Mad cunt. He keeps giving us presents. First one was a cactus.'

'A cactus?'

'Oasis. Desert,' Liam explains. 'We were on tour in America and he sent us this huge cactus. Then he gave us these rings. Last night, he said, "I've got a present for you." I said, "Well, give us a Rolls-Royce, you cunt." What did you think of the show, like?'

'Really good, but I wish you'd sing "Wonderwall".'

'Everyone says that,' Liam wistfully noted. 'I know it'd be top but Our Kid won't let me, the cunt. He wants his moment of glory. Here, John Squire is coming tonight.'

'I saw Paul Simonon here last night,' Jill noted.

'Yeah, I've met him before. He's cool.'

'He's been painting for the last eight years.'

'Mad, isn't it? Go from The Clash to painting. I'd like to do that. I can draw a bit myself. Did a top peacock once. All the bits and everything. It was good.'

The screen now shows the band leaving the stage, waving to the audience. Liam stares at himself on a screen that is twenty feet high and forty foot across, raises his arms in the air, stretches his body and says, 'I'm off for a beer. See ya.'

As he walks towards the exit, Jill looks at him, her face an expression of love, and says, 'I do like him. He's such a sweet boy.'

Later, Noel sits on his scooter and is interviewed by MTV. It is the usual thing and he gives no surprising answers. Once again, he never directly looks at his interviewer for more than five seconds, his eyes dart everywhere as if to say, everyone's got something to hide except me and my guitar.

Then he goes into his dressing-room and an hour later walks out on-stage with Oasis to deliver their best performance at Earls Court. For the finale The Bootleg Beatles joined them.

'I Am The Walrus'.

Afterwards in the dressing-room, Noel said, 'When we were doing, "Walrus", I looked up and just for a minute, I was at a microphone with George Harrison in front of 20,000 people.'

It takes a lot to drag it out of him but that beatific smile creased his mouth at the memory.

Later, at the party, the band scattered to the corners. Liam sat with Alan McGee singing old unrecorded Oasis songs into the Scotsman's ear. McGee later said, 'It's something to tell your grandchildren, isn't it? Liam Gallagher sang me songs at the party.'

Noel walked around looking far more comfortable. There were far less celebrities here, many more of his friends.

Alan White and Bonehead got extremely drunk and abused the dancefloor and the DJs. Guigsy rolled himself a massive spliff and talked football to those who would listen.

That night, no doubt about it, Oasis were the tightest and the happiest band in the land. Nothing was gonna change their world.

The day after Earls Court, Noel Gallagher staggered into Capital Radio after staying up all night and fumbled his way through an interview.

Asked about the success of Robson and Jerome, he sneered,

'Robson and Jerome, more like Robson and Go Home.' He was still buzzing off the Ecstasy and cocaine he had ingested the night before.

The following morning he and Liam attended the Q Awards held at the Park Lane Hotel. Oasis had won the award for Best Live Act. Ronnie Wood of The Rolling Stones presented them with their prize and asked them what they were doing later.

'We're off to Paris now, for a gig,' Noel told him.

'Really? Fuck it, I'll give Keith a bell and we'll come over.' Then he staggered off and was never seen again.

Noel went back to his table wondering how Blur's *The Great Escape* had won the Best Album award.

Later that day, Oasis travelled to Paris to play to 8,000 people. It was an impressive number. France is considered the hardest European country to succeed in. It's not unusual to release a record there and then wait a year for it to chart. In 365 days, Oasis had made the kind of progress which takes other bands years to gain.

At soundcheck time in the big hall, still buzzing after Earl's Court, Oasis looked around and said, 'Fucking hell, it's like a club gig.'

The day after, Marcus left the band and caught the train back to London. When he took his seat, he vaguely recognised the guy sitting opposite him. It was Andy Ross of Food Records, Blur's label which signed through EMI.

The two men exchanged greetings. Obviously, both had firm loyalties but, like two football managers meeting in a bar after a Cup Final, they could now afford to be open with each other.

According to Marcus, Ross told him that he had tried his best to dissuade Damon Albarn from going head to head with Oasis. In the long term, he had argued it would gain them nothing. He also asserted that it was Steve Sutherland, the *NME* editor, who had put the singer up to it.

'I wish I could say it was,' Sutherland now says, 'but it's untrue. All I know is that when I was playing football with Damon once, I asked him, "Come on, was it you that switched the single date?" He said it was. But I certainly never put him up to it.'

The next day, *NME* and *Melody Maker* both made 'Wonderwall' their Single Of The Week. 'A mesmeric declaration of love,' Michael Bonner wrote in the *Melody Maker*. 'Haunting, beautiful and effortlessly simple.'

NME's John Robinson wrote, ' "Wonderwall" is one of Oasis's best records because it manages to be immensely robust while still being one of Noel's most lyrically personal songs.' He went on to add that it was 'nearly a "Penny Lane" for the 1990s'.

Radio One had proved equally supportive. In the month leading up to its release they had aired it sixty-seven times. By the time it finally slipped from the charts, it had been given 187 plays by Britain's biggest national radio station.

But that Sunday, Robson and Jerome stood firm and 'Wonderwall' bounced off their record and into the number two slot. The bookmakers did make Oasis a good bet for the Christmas number one, but in the end Robson and Jerome would maintain pole position until Michael Jackson released 'Earth Song' and won the coveted end-of-year position.

By that time, everyone in the country knew about Mike Flowers. He was a singer who had emerged from London's Easy Listening club scene and had covered 'Wonderwall' in his particular retro style. After a furious bidding war, Flowers was now signed to London Records.

A week before the single's release, Chris Evans played the song on his show. He informed his listeners that the record was an obscure 1950s original which Noel had callously ripped off, note for note. For that day, Britain believed him.

'Wonderwall' by The Mike Flowers Pops entered the top ten and started competing in sales with the Oasis original. Marcus told Noel that he could expect to make round about a quarter of a million pounds in royalties from that song alone.

That was also the amount of money that Sony had now given Noel to start up his own record label, which he named Helter Skelter Records.

'After a gig,' he revealed, 'the top Sony people came backstage and said they had this big present for me. I thought, top, it's a huge fuck-off bag of coke. But they gave me this cheque and said, "Here are, have a record label." It's good, isn't it?'

After Marcus's departure from Paris, the band had gone to an in-store signing session. One fan said to Noel, 'Do you regret being a junkie?'

For once, Noel was speechless.

Another informed him that his uncle was Alan Williams, the

manager who relinquished The Beatles to Brian Epstein.

Noel retorted, 'I bet he's a miserable cunt.'

On 14 November, after playing the Live Music Hall in Koln two days previously, Oasis travelled back for a show in Nantes, France. The next night they were in Lille and then they came home.

On the morning of Friday, 17 November, Noel and Maggie caught the train to Leicester for that night's gig at the Granby Hall.

On the journey, the conversation moved from The Beatles on to the subject of UFOs and space travel. Noel said, 'I'm going to be the first person to play on Mars and when I play there I am going to tell those extra terrestrials, "Look, sooner or later you're going to hear about this group, The Beatles. But don't take any notice. They were all right – but Oasis, that's the ones you want."'

At the train station they hopped into a couple of cars and before travelling to the hall made a detour to the nearby massive Donnington festival site. They were thinking of playing here the following summer. Noel was shown the field and how the set-up would work. Such was their current popularity, he had already been informed that Oasis could play two nights here if they so chose.

'Fuck it,' Noel told Marcus, 'let's do a third and not tell anyone. Surprise even ourselves.'

Later at the soundcheck, with Liam having not yet arrived, Noel started playing a new riff he had come up with. It would later grow into a song entitled 'Me and My Big Mouth'.

He also played another new tune. This time it was on acoustic guitar and was somewhat reminiscent of Ray Davies's work. Then he and Jason were interviewed for *Total Guitar* magazine. Noel revealed that Ephiphone had asked him to design a guitar. It would be called The Noel Gallagher Ephiphone.

Talking about the Oasis sound, Noel said, 'I've told Bonehead that if he ever plays open chords, that's it, I'm sacking him. He's out of the band.'

Then he went off to get ready in a dressing-room where some of the staff had hung defaced pictures of Blur on the wall.

The gig was well up to standard and about two hours after, Noel was on his way home.

In the van driving back to London that night, he said, 'This year, we've won the league. But in 1996 I think we should put our foot on the brakes a bit and slow down. I told the band that but all they said was, "Fuck off, let's go and record the next album as soon as possible." '

He took a drag of his cigarette and stared at the white lines flashing beneath him.

'Fuck knows,' he said.

When he got home, he played Meg the new songs that had been taped at the soundcheck. She then asked him if he would get involved with a charity club night they were planning for an A&R guy who had broken his back diving. Meg started explaining what she wanted to do but Noel's attention soon drifted towards the TV.

'Are you listening to me?' Meg suddenly demanded.

Noel jerked his head back. 'Sorry,' he said, 'You lost me round about the time you said A&R guy.'

On the Sunday, Oasis flew to Stockholm, Sweden. That night, most of the band and road crew went out for a drink but Noel headed out by himself. He didn't look too happy.

Some days that would happen. You would see him walking through the plush corridors of the hotels they now stayed in or walking alone through the vast empty arenas that his music would draw thousands of people to, and, with his head down and shoulders scrunched up, he could look like the unhappiest man on earth.

That night, as Liam went from bar to bar, and girls gathered round to have their names put on the guest-list, Noel stayed in his room and watched Earle Sebastian's documentary on Marvin Gaye, the genius singer who could never, whatever his triumphs, win his father's love or approval.

The next day at lunchtime, while Noel gave interviews, a representative of their record company secured the video for The Beatles' new single 'Free As A Bird', as well as a tape of their just released *Anthology 1*. Then she hurried to the hotel and organised a screening of the film in the room put aside for business conferences and the like.

Bonehead, Guigsy, Whitey and Liam eagerly sat down to watch the video. It was the first time they had heard the song which the three remaining Beatles had put together using a John

Lennon demo-tape from the 1970s.

'Fucking mad to hear this song,' Bonehead said.

After watching the video twice, the band applauded. It was a major relief. The new Beatles' single was fab, not sad.

As he walked out of the small auditorium, Liam said, 'If that single goes in at number two because of fucking Jerome and Robson and I meet them, I'm going to go up to them and say, "You daft cunts, how dare you." Then I'll do this,.' And he spat twice at the wall.

'Fucking right,' Guigsy said.

In the dressing-room before the show, Noel sat by himself replaying 'Free As A Bird' several times. He also listened to the *Anthology* tape, especially the songs The Beatles had once unsuccessfully and famously auditioned for Decca with.

'Fucking hell,' Noel said. 'All those years that everyone's been slagging that guy off for turning The Beatles down, and then you found out, he was right. If I heard that tape I wouldn't have gone near them.'

(This was probably the impetus for Noel's later comment that his first two albums were much better than anybody's first two albums. This included his beloved Beatles, but Noel failed to take into account one small matter. Noel had twenty-five years of pop to fall back on. The Beatles didn't.)

The gig was a ragged affair. The band played okay but never really connected with the Swedish audience. The crowd, in turn, seemed very aware of the presence of a section of football supporters who had an infamous reputation for violence.

They came to gigs now because the team they supported had been ordered to ban everyone from all their home games and play to an empty ground. This followed an incident when someone had run on to the pitch and beaten up the referee.

Concerts were one of the few places in which this mob could now congregate, and no doubt it was one of them who hurled a coin at Liam halfway through the show, eliciting the response, as it flew past his head, 'You cheeky cunt. I'll fucking have you.'

There was a party later at a club which Liam arrived at, walked inside and then said, "Fuck it, this is shit." He got back into the taxi, still raging about the coin incident.

Slumped in the back seat, he bitterly stated, 'I'd rather be a fucking taxi-driver with two eyes than in Oasis with one. I'd rather be a butcher. This fame game, I understand it, but I'm not in it for that, me. I could have lost a fucking eye tonight and then there wouldn't be an Oasis.'

At the hotel, he ignored everyone in the bar and headed for his room on the eighth floor. A minute after he had slammed his door, the drinks machine in his corridor lay on the floor, ice cubes everywhere, Coca-Cola slowly seeping into the carpet.

Noel meanwhile had gone to a small party in Frank, the lighting man's, room and then left to see Alan White. They sat talking until they heard the sound of men shouting outside.

Noel and Alan put their heads around the door to see what was happening. A drunken Irishman was swaying outside the room Noel had just been in and was being told to fuck off by Bear, one of the road crew. But the man kept trying to push his way back into the room.

'See that Bear guy,' Noel said to Alan.

But before Alan could answer, Bear suddenly pulled back his fist and unleashed a wicked punch to the man's head. The man staggered backwards and Bear followed up with about ten more punches in five seconds. Roadie Roger then stepped in to pull him off.

'Well,' Noel calmly continued, 'he was the ABA welterweight champion and the boxer Dennis Andries is his cousin. But I suppose you know that now, don't you.'

The boys went back inside and Noel switched on the TV and started changing the channels. The video for 'Wonderwall' appeared. Directed by Nigel Dick, this, along with, 'Cigarettes and Alcohol', was their best film yet.

As Noel watched himself, he said, 'You know that record that has come out of me and our kid fighting? It's gone in at forty-two. And guess how many Oasis singles are in the top hundred?'

'Ten,' Alan guessed.

Noel screwed up his face in disgust and looked over at him like a teacher whose star pupil has just said something unbelievably stupid. 'We've only made eight, you dickhead.'

But Alan was razor sharp. 'Yeah, but the fighting record has got two sides so that makes it ten. All right?' Then he breathed a sigh at getting away with his joke.

'It's fucking top,' Noel said turning back to the TV. The next week, under the name The Smokin' Mojo Filters, the version of

'Come Together' that had been cut at Abbey Road, would also enter the charts, ensuring Noel Gallagher's presence on ten singles in the top hundred. His brother Liam would be on nine of them, the remaining three members each on eight.

The next day, Oasis flew to Paris for the MTV awards. A very drunk Liam was interviewed at the party afterwards by one of their girl presenters.

'Everyone says that Liam Gallagher is hard to interview but he is with me now,' she said, 'so let's see what he's really like. Hello Liam.'

'He-ll-o. My na-me i-s L-i-am an-d I h-a-ve be-een told to sp-eak slo-w be-cau-use Ma-ncs spe-ak ve-ry fa-st and no-one und-er-st-and-s wh-at we'-re say-ing,' he slurred. Then he slipped his arm up the girl's back and started rubbing it. The interview finished a minute later.

After the MTV show, Oasis travelled to Copenhagen for a gig on 24 November, and two days later played their triumphant homecoming show in Manchester's NYMEX arena on the 26th.

The next day they arrived at the BBC studios in Wood Lane, London, to record three numbers for the *Later* show which would be transmitted the following week.

On the second day in London, Liam, who had been staying up most nights recently, walked out claiming his voice wasn't up to it. Noel flew into a rage, accusing him of unprofessionalism. Liam told him to fuck off, and Noel nearly hit him.

When the show was aired, presenter Jools Holland tactfully explained that Liam had called off 'with a sore throat'.

Noel now assumed vocal duties and the band opened with a fiery version of 'Cum On Feel The Noize'. The song, with its loud guitars and call-to-hedonism lyrics, perfectly suited Oasis. Indeed, their version betters the original. Noddy Holder's slightly jokey vocal is stripped away, and both Gallaghers sing it with a real passion.

Noel was then interviewed by Holland.

'I hope I haven't given Liam my cold,' Holland said.

'I'll give him something when I see him,' Noel snapped back.

Noel then went on to talk about his despised school music teacher ('I've got one thing to say to him,' Noel looks directly at camera, 'do you want to borrow a tenner?'), and as ever, found it hard to look directly at Jools, his eyes darting here, there and everywhere but the man.

After being shown a clip of Slade performing 'Cum On' Noel went back to what he felt most comfortable doing, and performed 'Wonderwall' with a string section. The programme ended with a roaring 'Round Are Way' complete with horn section.

The next night, Noel showed up at the third night of Paul Weller's four-night stay at the Brixton Academy. He watched for the first time Simon Fowler perform his acoustic ballad version of 'Live Forever', and was entranced by how the singer had totally transformed his song.

Then, much to the crowd's delight, Noel walked out with an acoustic guitar and delivered six songs: 'Wonderwall', 'Whatever', 'Cast No Shadow', 'Talk Tonight', 'Don't Look Back In Anger' and The Beatles' 'You've Got To Hide Your Love Away', which he had exclusively donated to radio for World Aids Day on 1 December.

Noel returned the following night to play again, and the next day he and Oasis departed for the US.

The band had also found time to record two new B-sides for their forthcoming single 'Don't Look Back In Anger'. These were Noel's song 'Underneath The Sky', and a cover of Slade's 'Cum On Feel The Noize', which would end with Tim Abbot babbling away in a Brummy accent.

'Don't Look Back In Anger' had been aimed at a Christmas release, but as the weeks passed that plan of action seemed more and more unlikely.

'Wonderwall' refused to leave the charts.

Every week more and more people were walking into record shops and purchasing it, as well as the *Morning Glory* album, pushing the band to a level of popularity that not even they, the proud, determined new Mancunians, had ever dreamt about. No one had. Creation, the management, the band, they all thought at the start they would equal The Stone Roses's success. Now their records really were starting to approach Beatles-like sales.

To stop themselves pondering on the implications of such worldwide success, the band kept working harder and harder. And, of course, the more they hid away through their work, the more their records sold, until finally the following September, the band would again snap in two before regaining its balance.

The American tour wasn't the usual round of venues that they were now getting used to playing in the States. This time the tour had a difference. At Christmas, many radio stations who place themselves in the 'alternative rock' bracket, hold festivals which are then broadcast live in their area.

Marcus had booked the band on to such a tour. 'It's the Trojan Horse theory,' he explains. 'Ostensibly we weren't doing gigs advertised as Oasis gigs. We were doing gigs advertised by radio stations, but the reason you do it is to demonstrate to American radio that you're up for it and you want it.

'And it worked. It was very significant. I mean, some hardcore Oasis fans were saying, "What the fuck are Oasis doing playing with these grunge bands like White Zombie or Jaw Breaker?"

'And I was like, "Why not?" We've got every right to play the game, we've got every right to say to radio, "Why are you playing this shit? You should be playing us." Unless you get in there and announce it, nothing's going to change.

'I knew the bills we were on would be the last bunch of bands you'd choose to play with. But that's why I call it the Trojan Horse theory. You get in there and then before they know it, you've started to break down a lot of American barriers and, more importantly, their preconceptions of British guitar music.'

The band played radio festivals in Seattle, Washington, Chicago, Minneapolis, Toronto, San Francisco, San Jose, finishing up in Los Angeles and playing a festival and Johnny Depp's Viper Room on the same day.

While there, they also shot a video for 'Don't Look Back In Anger', again directed by Nigel Dick, and featuring the famous British actor Patrick Macnee who had shot to fame in the 1960s TV show, *The Avengers*.

Macnee wouldn't be the only famous name from their past that Oasis would meet that day. That evening, back at their hotel, John Lydon, accompanied by his brother Jimmy, also paid them a visit.

Liam and Noel sat with the Pistols' singer, and a lot of the talk centered around football, Lydon being an Arsenal fan. Halfway through the conversation, Lydon made a quiet comment about Liam's vocals.

'What the fuck do you mean by that?' Liam challenged and maybe then the forty-year-old Lydon suddenly saw himself as he was twenty years ago. Lydon now had wisdom but Liam had youth on his side.

Rotten told Liam to calm down a bit, and he in turn started to make fun of Rotten's haircut. Rotten then kept referring to Liam as 'the singer', before revealing that The Sex Pistols would be reforming in 1996 and touring the States.

'Perhaps you could support us?' he offered.

'Yeah, mad for it,' Liam replied, knowing full well that if such an event took place it would be Oasis topping the bill.

Simon Halfon, a British sleeve designer living in the US was present at the table and reported that it was 'weird'. 'The conversation would be going all right and then Rotten would say something a bit off and it would all go a bit tense. Then it'd go back to being all right. At the end, I remember Rotten saying things like, "What do I know? I'm just a poxy Pistol."'

Rotten later invited Noel down to a recording session and then left.

On 19 December Oasis flew home, landing on the morning of the 20th and that night Noel went to see Mike Flowers play at London's LA2 venue. The press, meanwhile, had published their Best Records Of 1995 lists.

Typical was the *NME*, who made Tricky's trip-hop album *Maxinquaye* the number one placing, *Morning Glory* in second place. In the singles chart 'Some Might Say' was fourth, 'Wonderwall' sixth.

On the 22nd, the band assembled at *The White Room*'s TV studios in West London to make their seasonal appearance on the Channel Four programme.

For this show, which was televised on New Year's Eve, Oasis delivered excellent versions of 'Don't Look Back In Anger', 'Wonderwall', 'Roll With It', 'Round Are Way' and 'Some Might Say'. Channel Four's final and fitting image of 1995 was Noel performing 'Wonderwall'. But backstage the mood wasn't good. Tiredness had crept in now and they all just wanted to go home.

After the show, Oasis took a short ride to the Halycon Hotel in Holland Park where Creation had hired out a room. All the band were given major presents, but the centrepiece was when Alan McGee handed Noel a set of car keys and told him to go outside.

There a chocolate brown and white Rolls-Royce awaited Noel, who can't drive.

Liam, meanwhile, stayed inside.

*

That year, Noel had made appearances in three separate music documentaries. In the summer, he turned up on Granada's *My Generation* documentary on The Small Faces and spoke enthusiastically about Steve Marriott's vocal power. And over Christmas, he popped up twice. He was featured in a Carlton TV special on The Beatles and said that when he first met Paul McCartney, the songwriter told him that he looked like a Beatle.

'I hope so,' Noel shot back, 'I've spent enough money trying to.'

Noel also appeared on a Burt Bacharach documentary, where he revealed to the nation the 'inspiration' behind 'Half A World Away'.

By then he and Meg were in Manchester spending time with Peggy and Paul, while Liam flitted in and out.

On New Year's Eve, they, along with Jess and Fran, went to the Sunday Social where the same good-looking kid who had spoken to Noel precisely a year ago approached him and asked, 'So what's the best thing to have happened to you in 1995?'

'Meeting Paul McCartney,' Noel instantly replied.

Soon after, Noel, Meg and a few others returned to their Camden flat. At about six in the morning, one of the party, in front of Noel, started quizzing Jess about the Oasis songwriter.

'Do you think that Noel is honest in interviews?' she was asked.

'I think,' Jess replied, 'that Noel Gallagher gives out a series of truths and half-truths so that in twenty years time, when they come to look at his career, they'll never really know who he was.'

Eighteen

On Monday 8 January 1996 Noel got into his Rolls-Royce and was driven by Les to Garry Blackburn's offices in Stamford Brook, West London.

Blackburn is a plugger who runs his own company, Anglo Plugging. The company is responsible for securing TV and radio appearances for acts such as Oasis, Portishead and The Beautiful South.

Today, they have booked Noel on to Channel Four's *Hotel Babylon*. The show is hosted by Dani Behr who will interview Noel. Afterwards, he is scheduled to perform an acoustic version of the new single, 'Don't Look Back In Anger'.

The single has already been put back a month because 'Wonderwall', both by Oasis and The Mike Flowers Pops, is still high in the charts.

As the band will be away touring on the day of the single's release, Blackburn is keen for Noel to make at least one TV appearance in support of 'Anger'. The fact that it will undoubtedly be a major hit isn't an issue. But Blackburn is wary of taking any chances. There have been too many incidents in the past of successful groups shunning all promotion only to see their new records falter.

For Blackburn, there was also a nice little knock-on effect. By securing a high-profile artist such as Noel for the show, Blackburn was now in credit with the show's producers. Therefore, the next time he had a new band to promote, traditionally the hardest to get on TV, he could then cash in his chips. I got you Noel that time, he would remind them. Scratch mine, I'll scratch yours. It is the law that the music business was built on.

Noel enjoyed going on TV. In interviews, he was always witty and charming and, of course, he relished playing anywhere.

The fact that the show was hosted in a large country house that he had been led to believe had been bought by George Harrison for the Natural Law party, was an extra bonus for Noel. Plus, he had good news. 'We've got Maine Road,' he told Blackburn as they drove out of London.

'What?'

'Yeah, it was firmed up last week. It's in April of this year.'

'Christ,' Blackburn said, 'How many does it hold?'

'40,000,' Noel said, trying to sound matter of fact. 'Probably get more than they do at their home games. How's Karen by the way?'

'Recovering in Sri Lanka,' Blackburn replied. Karen was the girl who accompanied Oasis to all their TV and radio shows. Her reputation was that of a tough negotiator, a perfectionist. It was her job to see that everything ran smoothly: that the band were on time, the show went according to plan.

Blackburn, who was sitting in the front seat, turned to Noel. 'See, to be quite honest with you, we've never had a band like yours, one that's gone . . . shoosh!' He made a motion with his hands of a plane quickly taking off. 'So for her it's been mad.'

'It has been for us as well,' Noel quickly reminded him.

'I killed her the other day,' Blackburn said laughing. 'I phoned her up in Sri Lanka and said, "By the way do you know the Oasis single has been put back a month? That's your first job when you get back." ' He laughed and turned back to face the road. 'She loves it really.'

'What's the worst band you've ever worked with?' Noel asked.

'There's not one band,' Blackburn said carefully, 'but the worst incident was with Primal Scream. They'd put out the follow-up to "Rocks" and it wasn't doing that well. So I went to *Top Of The Pops* and begged them to do something special.

'They were in Ireland at the time and I persuaded Ric Blaxill, the show's producer, to build them a special set for the show. It was a really big deal. They don't often put themselves out like that.

'Come the day, I get this phone call from Jeff Barrett. The band can't make it. I thought he was joking. He wasn't. I couldn't believe it. At three in the afternoon I had to call the show up and say, "Look lads, the Scream can't make it but I have got this other band . . ." It put me in so much shit, I dropped them after that. Nightmare, absolute nightmare.'

'What was up with them?' Noel asked.

'I think they were too out of it to get on the plane. I wouldn't have minded but it was a private jet. All they had to do was pour themselves on it.'

Noel burst out laughing. He had been grinning throughout the whole story. 'Proper,' he said, mimicking one of Andrew Innes's, the Scream's guitarist, most quoted phrases, 'fucking proper.' Noel settled back in his seat. The story had cheered him up no end.

The car pulled up by the stately home. Noel got out wearing his fake-fur coat, a paisley shirt, jeans and Gucci shoes. The producer met him and led him to his own caravan.

'I don't suppose you'll be wanting make up.'

'I don't suppose I will. But I'd love some scran.'

'Sorry?'

'Food. Something to eat.'

The producer laughed self-consciously. 'Oh, right. What do you want? We've got things like bacon sandwiches . . .'

'Ah, bacon butty, yeah.'

Dani Behr then made her entrance. She had interviewed Noel once before on *The Big Breakfast Show*. It was when Noel was on tour in Japan and they spoke by phone. At the time, Behr was secretly seeing the Newcastle player Les Ferdinand. Noel didn't know the relationship was meant to be hush-hush.

Halfway through the interview, Noel started dropping hints about the pair of them. Behr kept trying to change the subject but Noel wasn't having that. He kept on about Ferdinand. After their chat was over, Noel put down the phone in his Japanese bedroom. Then it rang again. It was Meg calling from their Camden home.

'What the fuck are you doing?' she cried. 'You've just told the whole of the country about Les Ferdinand and Dani Behr and no one is meant to know.'

Today Behr was bearing no grudges. She was all sweetness and light, long boots and short skirt.

As no bacon butty was immediately forthcoming, Noel was taken into the huge house. The owners had allowed the show three of their main rooms. The rest of the house was cut off. Noel would be filmed checking into the hotel. Then he would be interviewed by Behr before performing in the show's bar to an assembled audience.

The interview came first. It was all frivolous stuff. How much money have you made? Who does your mum love more, you or Liam? What's it like being a star? Throughout it all, Noel answered as best he could. He put on his difident manner and struggled to make wisecracks in the face of such anodyne probing. After the second question, you could see Noel turning on to auto-pilot.

Nearby, a young girl, sixteen, no more, watched the proceedings with growing disgust. She was an extra on the show, employed to sit around and look pretty.

'They always do these stupid interviews,' she said. 'It's all right if it's crap like Boyzone, but that's Noel Gallagher.'

The only interesting moment came when Behr asked Noel about the Maine Road shows. They had only been known about within the Oasis camp for less than a week and already the word was out. The question caught Noel on the hop.

'I'll take the fifth amendment on that one,' he said, thereby confirming the shows. Mentally, he was making a note to find the leak.

Afterwards, he was placed on a stool by the bar. As the cameras and lights were prepared, Noel absent-mindedly strummed his guitar. He played 'Hung Up' by Paul Weller and 'A Day In The Life' by The Beatles.

Finally, they were ready. Noel positioned himself on his stool and then performed 'Don't Look Back In Anger' three times. The crowd cheered loudly after each performance.

And then, as soon as they said go, he was off to his caravan. There, at last, was his bacon butty. He wolfed it down and in between mouthfuls, said to Blackburn, 'This is a crap show.'

Blackburn grimaced, caught between a hard rock star and a soft-headed TV show he would have to do future business with.

'I know, Noel, but the viewing figures are good. By the way,' he said swiftly, changing the subject, 'Channel Four have got this new show starting. It's called *The Girlie Show*. The idea is that it's presented by kind of laddish women. They want you to go on it.'

At this news, Noel brightened up considerably. 'I'll have some of that,' he said, wolfing down the rest of his butty.

In the Rolls on the way back, the talk turned to politics.

'I can't think of any politicians I like,' Noel said. 'Tony Blair. And Tony Benn, maybe.'

'Yeah, but he was the one who banned pirate radios in the 1960s,' Blackburn pointed out.

'Did he? Right, he can fuck right off. I know. Dennis Skinner, the Beast of Bolsover. One day, I reckon he's going to get up and go to some Tory bastard, "Right, you cunt I've been meaning to say this for years . . ." '

Blackburn said his goodbyes and got out at Chiswick. Noel moved into the vacant front-seat. The car moved off. As Les was driving, Noel started to inspect the car's walnut dashboard.

'They sculpt that out of one piece of wood,' Les told him. 'It's not like in other cars where they put it together from all different parts. They actually take one huge piece of wood and sculpt it out of that.'

'What, this is wood?'

'Of course it is, you divvy,' Les replied. 'Fucking Rolls-Royce, isn't it? You got it all, mate. Wood, leather, the lot.'

'Look mate,' Noel said, opening up the dashboard and feeling the leather interior, 'I'm from the 1970s and 1980s. If it ain't Formica I'm confused.'

In central London, the car got caught up in traffic. At one point, it stopped by a huge advert for Blur's *The Great Escape* album.

Noel looked over at it and said, 'I heard the other day that the album isn't selling as well as they want it to. Serves their record company right, fucking around with the *Help* album like that. It's their karma.'

Noel was referring to EMI's bid to have the *Help* album registered in the charts as a compilation album and not as a proper LP. EMI had lodged a complaint with the BPI three days before the album's release. A storm of criticism hit them within hours of the news. EMI then withdrew their complaint. But it was too late. The BPI had voted in EMI's favour and wouldn't rescind their decision.

The album would now only show in the compilation charts and not the more influential main LP chart. As *Help* was being released the same week as Blur's record, many people had been putting two and two together.

Noel looked at the poster and kissed his teeth in disgust. The Rolls silently moved away.

The next day, for the first time, it was reported in one of the tabloids that Liam had been seen on a night out with Patsy Kensit.

A few days later, the band travelled to Germany for four gigs. Marcus stayed behind to arrange the Maine Road shows and further negotiate another concert, Oasis headlining at Slane Castle in Ireland.

The next day the *NME* carried this information in their news pages and Channel Four's Teletext service reported that seven Oasis singles were in the Irish top forty and that *Morning Glory* had re-entered their LP chart at number one. The magic showed no sign of weakening.

At their first German concert, the Music Centre in Utrecht, the band were forced to cut short the set when Liam's voice started to fade. A section of the crowd reacted badly and started to smash up the hall. The band, now safely ensconced in their dressing-room, watched the proceedings on closed-circuit TV.

'Go on, my son,' Noel said, watching a fan hurl a chair in the air.

'You want to watch out, Noel,' Guigsy said. 'That's your amp that geezer's going for.'

'Give a shit,' Noel replied.

The band then travelled to Munich. Much to Noel's, Liam's and Guigsy's delight, the aircraft hangar they were playing in was situated on the same runway that the aeroplane carrying the 1958 Manchester United squad had crashed on, wiping out eight players.

At the gig that night, Liam came on-stage and kept shouting 'Muu-nich, Muu-nich, Muu-nich' into his microphone for about two minutes. The crowd roared back thinking he was saluting them. Not so. This was the chant used by City fans to seriously distress their hated United rivals and Liam couldn't resist the opportunity.

The band also bought a pile of postcards that depicted the airport and sent them back to Mark Coyle, a fervent United fan.

When Coyley received the first card, he thought, that's cool, the band sending me a card. Nice. When the fourth one came through the wind-up became apparent. He was left to grind his teeth in fury.

The band moved on. They played Huxley's in Berlin, where

Liam and Bonehead were interviewed by MTV. Noel gave his security guys the slip and visited Berlin Zoo. He figured he wouldn't be recognised and could relax for a couple of hours. Wrong. A group of visiting British school-children spotted him. He spent the next half-hour signing autographs.

The next day they travelled back to Britain by coach and ferry. Noel had stayed up all night and was comatose by the time they reached the border.

Roger, Bonehead's and Whitey's roadie, woke him up. 'Noel, have you got any drugs on you?'

'Sure,' Noel sleepily replied, fiddling in his pocket. 'Rack me out a line as well.'

'No, you idiot, get rid of them. We're at the border.'

They arrived back in London late afternoon. Noel picked up Meg and then they travelled over to Julie's restaurant in Holland Park for Kate Moss's birthday party.

A gaggle of reporters were waiting outside, having been tipped off to the event. Noel and Meg breezed past them and into the restaurant where everyone had just finished eating.

They ordered Jack Daniels and coke and fell into conversation with Kate and her boyfriend, actor Johnny Depp, about the last time they had met. This had been about a month earlier when the band played a surprise concert at his LA club, The Viper Room.

'What did people think of the gig we did?' Noel asked Johnny.

'Ah, man, people were buzzing after that show.'

'Do you remember,' Noel said, 'how we'd been up all night and you asked us to play and we were all, "Yeah, we'll have some of that?" Well, when I went to bed, about ten in the morning, I thought, nah, everyone's too smashed to remember when we wake up. There'll be no gig.

'So I go to sleep, wake up, turn on the radio and there's this geezer going, "And tonight at The Viper Room, Oasis will be playing a special concert." I thought, oh shit.'

Depp smiled. 'That was your brother. I said to him, "We can keep this a dead secret or we can advertise it in which case there will be chaos." Liam just went, "Chaos, let's have some chaos."'

'Tell me about it,' Noel said. 'I turned up and it took me about half an hour to get in. I was going to the bouncer on the door,

"I'm in the band," and he was going, "Yeah, you and million others, mate. Now get to the back." '

After the party Kate, Jess, Meg, Noel and a few others went back to Paul Simonon's flat. Simonon, once the bassist in The Clash, and his wife Tricia had a child and a spacious apartment in Ladbroke Grove.

As they played old Dubliners' records, Noel sang along to all of them. Then he and Meg gave Kate her present, an exclusive four-CD set of Burt Bacharach songs. They had been released to influential music figures only and just a few sets had been pressed up.

They put the CDs on. When 'This Guy's In Love With You' came on, Noel with his arm around Meg and sitting on the sofa, sang the song to her.

Nineteen

There had to be some bad news soon. Just had to be. It couldn't last like this. Life in the world of Oasis could never be smooth. If it was, then that's when you'd have to seriously start thinking about jacking it in.

In January, it was announced that Tony McCarroll would be suing the band for half a million pounds. His dismissal, he claimed, wasn't due to his lack of ability but simply because Noel Gallagher disliked him. When Oasis's lawyer looked into the matter he discovered some bad news. When McCarroll left the band, the record contract that he had signed with the other four members hadn't been re-negotiated or the partnership dissolved. Therefore, the claim couldn't be ignored.

Meanwhile, Oasis were in Germany, playing Utrecht on the 10th, Munich ('Muu-nich!') on the 12th, Berlin on the 14th, Bielefeld on the 15th. They were annoyed that McCarroll was still haunting them, but any anger was softened by the news from America.

'Wonderwall' had started selling and that in turn had massively boosted the sales for *Morning Glory*. Both records now looked like entering their respective US charts. The band's forth-coming US tour, starting in late February, could only help matters.

Oasis now returned to play three UK gigs, one at Whitley Bay and two at Edinburgh's Ingeleston Exhibition Centre. On the second night, after support band Ocean Colour Scene's set, the PA piped through producer Brendan Lynch's remix of 'Champagne Supernova', another one-off twelve-inch record designed for the clubs.

Liam, the purist, was standing on-stage with Guigsy and Bonehead at the time and when he heard the mix he started shouting at them, 'I fucking hate these records. It's not Oasis, it doesn't suit us. They're shit.

Lynch, who had worked on all of Paul Weller's solo material, had, on Noel's request, completed and delivered three versions of the song. The one he most liked, Noel rejected. The one he thought too obvious, Noel okayed. Brendan was very aware of Liam's dislike of such records. The singer had told him so in no uncertain words.

After the gig, in the hotel bar, Lynch regretfully said, 'I wish I had never agreed to do it. It's been absolute mad.'

As he spoke, *News Of The World* reporters were casually sat around, watching the band's every move. Ocean Colour Scene were also present that night. They had recently been signed to MCA and were now excitedly getting ready for their first record in years to be released.

Noel sat with Meg and Jefferson Hack, the editor of *Dazed and Confused*, a new magazine that wanted to interview him. Noel wasn't interested.

'I'll tell you what,' he told the editor, 'you'll get far better stuff if you get fifty Oasis fans together in a room and interview them. They'll tell you much more than I ever could.'

This was a regular trait of Noel's, to dismiss breezily his work and refuse to analyse it. It was as if he believed that by putting his mind to explanations it would somehow kill the magic. Often, he would laugh off his work.

'People go on about "Cigarettes and Alcohol", being a great insight into Thatcher's children,' he'd say with a pretend laugh, 'But I was taking the piss when I wrote it.' Or 'that "Live Forever" song, wrote it in ten minutes, mate'.

It was his defence mechanism, another way of warding people who wanted to get too close, who desired answers.

The next morning Noel woke up to find Liam and Ocean Colour Scene's vocalist, Simon Fowler, still drinking at the bar. He and Meg then flew back to London, and that night attended the *NME* Brat awards.

Vic Reeves and Bob Mortimer hosted the ceremony. Among the winners, which were decided on a mixture of the writers' choice and readers' voting, Pulp and Black Grape were both honoured.

The hosts then announced that there were no more bands to

talk about as one band had totally swept the board. They were, of course, Oasis, who this year had won the awards for Best Act, Best Album, Best Single and Best Band.

Noel slowly walked to the stage and holding his four trophies, he told the audience, 'It's really hard to come up here and be humble. So I won't. You're all shit.'

Later, he had his photo taken for the *NME*, backstage with Jarvis Cocker and Shaun Ryder. 'It was funny,' he later reported. 'Ryder was going to Jarvis, "I know what you're like, you're like one of those kids who always sat at the back of the class but was a real perv and had loads of girls and that." I don't think Jarvis knew what was going on.'

In February Noel went down to a London studio to sing on a Chemical Brothers' track. The idea had first come about because of the Chemicals regularly playing the Beatles' 'Tomorrow Never Knows' within their breakbeat-fuelled sets at the Social. Noel had expressed an interest in singing on a cover of it with them. Instead, that idea was dumped and Noel came up with a set of lyrics, which he entitled 'Setting Son' (he had now renamed his own song of that title, 'D'Ya Know What I Mean'), and then sang over a new Chemicals' track. It took him about an hour. Then he was gone. In October 1996 it would enter the charts at number one.

Later that month, Noel travelled to Rome with Marcus and Meg to do radio and press interviews and take a long wekend break.

Oasis were highly popular now in Italy and Spain, and this was a chance to promote Oasis through various foreign media.

On Thursday, he booked into one of Rome's top hotels on the Via Sistina. On Friday, a newspaper reported where he was staying and by Friday afternoon literally hundreds of fans had gathered outside the entrance.

Noel undertook interviews for both Italian and Spanish radio. The Spanish interviewer told him that *Morning Glory* was the number-one album, having sold some 85,000 copies.

'To give you a perspective on that number,' he told Noel, 'Blur have sold about 25,000 copies. That's the average sales for my country.'

Noel smiled at that news. On the Saturday, he and Meg visited the Vatican and then went shopping. Meg left him to go back to the hotel, and when he and Marcus finally arrived back, a sea of fans rushed him and he was literally lifted off his feet as carried to the door. As he sailed into the entrance on a sea of shouting, cheering kids, that beatific smile crossed his face once more.

On Sunday, he returned to London and made his way to the BBC studios in Wood Lane where Paul Weller was recording a special show for *Later*.

Noel watched Weller keenly and then afterwards at the party danced with Paul's mum, Ann. 'Fucking hell,' he said, 'I kept going to Paul's dad, John, "Is this all right? I don't want you whacking me". Ann was going, "Oh, don't worry about him." '

The next day Noel travelled up to Manchester to meet the Manchester City chairman Francis Lee, spend time with Peggy and Paul, and also visit Mark Coyle and Phil Smith.

Then it was back to London for the Brit Awards and to start rehearsals for their most important US tour to date. *Morning Glory* was now nestling in America's top-ten. The only British group to achieve that status in 1995 was The Beatles. And 'Wonderwall' had entered the singles charts at twenty-one. The hard work was finally paying off.

Oasis were now firmly embedded in Britain's consciousness. Every week either the tabloids or the quality papers were running stories on them.

Girls regularly appeared on cheap front-pages dishing the dirt on their flings with Liam. For Noel, it was normally stories such as his father trying to sell a scrap of paper containing the lyrics for one of the first songs he ever wrote (apparently called 'Sunday', and which read in part, 'You said yes on Monday/ Wednesday we were wed/ You left me on Friday/ If it's Sunday, am I dead?' Consciously or not, this recalls the old traditional song 'Solomon Grundy', which runs 'Born on a Monday/ Married on a Tuesday, etc'). Other articles would examine the band's US success.

The real proof of their celebrity status was when the popular satirical TV programme *Spitting Image* started to run sketches on the band. Their funniest shot concerned the brother's well-documented liking of cocaine, with Liam saying to Noel, 'There's eighteen inches of snow in Scotland,' and Noel replying, 'Oh, *that*'s where I left it.'

On the day that Creation released the ninth Oasis single, 'Don't Look Back In Anger', c/w 'Step Out', 'Underneath The Sky' and

'Cum On Feel The Noize' (it came wrapped in one of Cannon's best sleeves, the image being that of a drum kit covered in colourful tulips. It was a tribute to the time when Ringo Starr rejoined The Beatles, after briefly quitting in 1968, and George Harrison had the studio decked out in flower to welcome him back) Oasis arrived at Earls Court on the night of 19 February to attend the Brit Awards.

The band sat at a table with their girlfriends (Liam and Patsy were now a public item), management and record company, and were called three times to the stage to accept awards for Best Video with 'Wonderwall' (Guigsy commenting, 'I'm not even in it'), Best Group and Best Album.

During their speeches, they swore profusely, insulting INXS singer Michael Hutchence (an E'd up Noel Gallagher telling him that 'Has beens shouldn't give prizes to going-to-be's'), Chris Evans (Liam stating, 'No ginger-haired bastard can throw Oasis off-stage'), and took their revenge on Blur by singing the 'All the people, so many people' refrain from 'Country House', and 'Shite Life' to the tune of 'Parklife', and ended with Noel stating that there were only seven people in the hall who could help young British people, and that was Oasis, Alan McGee and Labour leader Tony Blair, who was also present. The music business quietly seethed at their tables.

There were live performance from Pulp, Simply Red, David Bowie, and Take That put in their final appearance before splitting up.

But it was Michael Jackson, dressed in Jesus-like white robes and surrounded on-stage by hundreds of children, that prompted the night's more memorable act when Pulp's Jarvis Cocker tried to invade the stage to register his disgust. He was later taken to a nearby police station for questioning.

Noel remained in the arena and told every interviewer who approached him that he didn't give a shit what 'fat cats earning £450,000 a year' thought of his band, the only prizes worth having were the ones voted for by fans'.

Later on, Oasis partied until the early hours at the Landmark Hotel and then crawled into their hotel rooms or houses to watch the show on television that night. Carlton TV edited out all the swearing and Jarvis Cocker's actions. But at a later date, in a late-night slot, the TV station screened the whole affair. The bands that had upstaged, upset and insulted the entire music industry establishment were now so popular that TV programmers were willing to run the show at the risk of the undoubted 'public outrage' the newspapers would then whip up.

If anything, Oasis and Pulp gained even more support when their behaviour was made public in the next day's papers.

And the industry should care. Record sales, after a slump in the early 1990s, were now, thanks mainly to the new breed, standing at an all-time high.

Music was now outselling computer games.

At about one-thirty in the morning, as the coach travelled towards St. Louis, Noel Gallagher stepped into the front area where Guigsy, Bonehead, Liam and Alan White were sitting, and said, 'Have I got a tape to play you.'

'What?' Liam quickly demanded. 'What you got? What is it?'

'Ah, ah,' Noel said, bending down to slot the tape into the machine. He pressed the play button and then sat down with an all-knowing smile on his lips.

'Come on,' Liam demanded. 'What the fuck is it?'

Suddenly, the old Oasis number 'Colour My Life' started up through the speakers.

'Fucking hell,' Bonehead exclaimed, 'it's us!'

'Where do you get it? Where do you get it?' Liam demanded.

'Bootleg CD that's just come out,' Noel informed him. 'No prizes guessing who's put it out.'

'Who?' Liam asked.

'Well, who else apart from us and Coyley would have access to rehearsal tapes or a gig from the Boardwalk?' Noel replied.

For the next hour the band settled down, delighted to hear themselves and their music from four years ago. Songs such as 'Tape Me', 'See The Sun', 'Must Be The Music', 'Better Let You Know', 'Snakebit', 'I Will Show You' and the acoustic number 'Life In Vain', took them straight back to the Boardwalk, to rehearsing and dreaming, of Liam being regularly thrown out of the club, of Noel bouncing cheques to pay their way.

Part of the CD also featured an early gig at the Boardwalk.

'There were four people at that gig,' Liam remembered, 'and we were fucking giving it to them. Come on, Oasis!'

'You know,' Noel commented as the last song died away,

'that's better than the Beatles' demo tape. Some of those lyrics aren't too bad. I think I'll use some of them.'

Then he paused to think.

'How top would that be? I've ripped everybody else off. Now I'm ripping myself off.'

The American tour had started in Kansas City on 23 February, moved to St. Louis (a gig they had cancelled two times previously) on the 24th. Journalists from the British music press and the nationals followed them everywhere.

Backstage, after the St. Louis show, a fan told the newly-bearded Liam, 'You know, you really remind me of Charlie Manson with that beard.'

'Fuck off, you dickhead,' Liam shot back, 'Did you ever see Charlie Manson singing on-stage?' and then he walked off.

They played Minneapolis on the 26th and afterwards Noel sloped off as usual to the production room. Liam stayed alone in another room, ruminating on the subject of fame.

'Fame,' he sneered, 'you keep it at one pace behind you all the time. You never let it walk in front of you because if you do then it totally blocks your view, gets right in the way of your goal. The reason I'm in a band is to get the music over to people. That's it. I can't be arsed with anything else.

'The music. Simple. But you get all these people who read about you and stuff. They think they know you. But they don't. How could they? They've never spoken to me. They've only read about me.'

Liam was talking in the week when over 400,000 Oasis records were bought by the British public. A quarter of a million of them were accounted for by the new single 'Don't Look Back In Anger', which had smashed its way in at number one.

On the coach that night they watched their appearance on *Top Of The Pops*. The video started as Blur were finishing off a frenetic performance of their new single, 'Stereotypes'.

The camera then moved across to Noel, standing coolly at the mike. He was wearing shades, a white button-down shirt and playing his Union Jack guitar. It was a stately performance.

Then, for one the very few times in the show's history, Oasis performed a second number, this time Slades's 'Cum On Feel The Noize', with Liam deliberately singing out of sync on the line

'So you think my singing's out of time'.

The band replayed the video at least twenty times, Noel pointing with real pride in his voice, 'That's us, The Jam and The Beatles who have been given two numbers on the show.'

It hardly needed saying, but the war with Blur was finally over.

On 27 February, having stayed up until one-thirty that afternoon and then slept for just an hour, Noel Gallagher walked out on-stage with Oasis and delivered a show in Chicago's, Aragon Ballroom that Marcus later said was 'frighteningly good'.

In the major American cities, 'the music towns', as roadcrew manager Trigger called them, Oasis thrived. In the smaller towns, a significant section of the audience had only come to hear 'Wonderwall' ('that's so cool, that song,' the band were often told), and would often leave straight after hearing it in Noel's acoustic section.

In Minneapolis, the band were photographed for the prestigious cover shot of *Rolling Stone* magazine, Noel and Liam attending a separate session the next day. They walked out after an hour. They were bored and as they told the protesting photographer, '*Rolling Stone* need us more than we need them.'

At the next gig in Milwaukee they played in a hall that had also booked a Mexican band for the club next-door, causing huge confusion as each set of roadies entered the hall with their equipment. Noel stayed on the coach, watching the farce and using his now-favourite expression, 'I've got one of the biggest selling albums in America and this happens to me.'

It was Cleveland on 3 March, Detroit the next night, Indianapolis two nights later, and then shows in Fairfax and Philadelphia.

Prior to the latter show, Noel sat down with Ben Stud of the *Melody Maker* and in the course of the interview, confessed to having been involved in burglaries and car radio theft.

When the paper ran the article over two weeks in April, they pulled out and highlighted Noel's statement. The Easter holiday is traditionally a barren time for news, so it wasn't too long before an enterprising journalist rang up Dr. Adrian Rogers of the Conservative Family Institute for a reaction. Predictably,

Rogers went public, demanding a full police enquiry and asking British fans to boycott the band.

The story quickly became a lead news item over Easter, and Chief Superintendant David James of the CID informally interviewed the writer Ben Stud. He was then asked to provide police with a written statement regarding the interview.

Stud did so, defending Noel and stating that the band were well known for their fanciful statements.

'Had I believed he was remotely serious,' Stud wrote, 'as a professional journalist of some ten years' standing I would have pursued him on the point.'

Even so, the row continued with, at one point, some MPs claiming that they would raise the matter in the Houses of Parliament.

Meanwhile, back in the US, Noel, not Liam, succumbed to a sore throat and the band cancelled gigs in Phoenix and Los Angeles. It was while recuperating there that Noel finally met his hero, Burt Bacharach.

They had breakfast together and Burt arranged for Noel to see his own personal physician. The half-hour visit cost Noel $1,000. Bacharach also revealed that he was booked to perform two shows in London in June. He asked Noel to make a guest appearance on the song 'This Guy's In Love With You'.

At Oasis's Providence gig, as a result of objects being thrown at them in previous dates, tickets were printed with the warning that if anyone should throw anything on-stage the band would discontinue the gig.

Predictably, someone threw a boot at Noel during his acoustic set, and the band refused to return to the stage. The next day, Noel travelled to perform a solo acoustic set at a Snowasis show that was to take place in a mountain resort. There were other acts booked to play that afternoon.

Noel walked on-stage in the bitter cold air, played two songs and then quit. His hands had frozen up and he couldn't play his guitar.

The band then travelled to New York.

On their first night there, they all gathered in a nearby Irish bar. Robbie Williams was also in attendance, having flown in with his girlfriend after holidaying in the Caribbean.

Patsy Kensit had also arrived, as had Tim and Chris Abbot,

Johnny Hopkins and Jill Furmanovsky. Noel left the Irish bar early and walked up to Motown's new bar opposite Central Park. He ordered drinks and was chuffed to fuck when the barman refused his money. Even Motown Records took Oasis seriously.

There was a party that night in Liam and Patsy's room where Bonehead's brother, Martin, who lived in America and was now clearly worse for wear, kept trying to talk to Noel about Oasis. Finally, Noel took a lamp off the bedside cabinet, crouched in the corner holding it up to his face and said, 'Go away. I've got the biggest selling album in the . . .'

Richard Ashcroft, formerly of The Verve, was also present. He was supporting Oasis at their gig in the Paramount Theatre.

Later on, Noel sat in his bedroom, confessing to real nerves about recording the next Oasis album. 'I'm a fucking millionaire,' he said. 'Most of my songs were written when I was on the dole. What do I write about now?'

It was a smokescreen. In the red-and-black-covered exercise book he carried everywhere with him, there sat some forty sets of lyrics, many of them already set to music in his mind.

The next morning, Noel travelled to JFK airport at the invitation of Johnny Depp, who was shooting his new movie *Donnie Brasco* with Al Pacino. Noel waited on-set for about an hour, hoping to meet Pacino. But at two he had to leave for a photo session with Jill in Central Park.

When Noel got back to the hotel, all the band minus Liam were in the bar waiting for the shoot. Finally, Kevin came over and said, 'Liam doesn't want to do it.'

Jill said, 'Well, we could always do individual shots,' and Noel looked up and said, pointing to the other three members, 'Who the fuck would want to look at pictures of him, him and him? Fuck it, I'm going shopping.'

He stood up and said, 'Liam's a wanker. I could be meeting Al Pacino now, going to him, "Now Al, don't do it like that, try this."'

Oasis sounchecked at five that afternoon. The gig was actually in the same complex that housed Madison Square Gardens. According to Marcus the band could have played there. 'But where do we go when we come back?' he rhetorically asked.

Meanwhile, tickets outside were selling for $250; Epic were

forced to buy some off the touts so that their staff could get in to see this top-ten act of theirs.

The next day the band flew back into London for a brief rest before resuming with gigs in Wales, two in Cardiff on 18 and 19 of March and two in Dublin.

As the papers speculated on Liam and Patsy, Oasis flew to Germany for three dates, one in Offenbach on the 26th, two in Munich on the 27th and 29th, before taking in gigs in Milan on the 29th, Grenoble on the 31st, Barcelona on 2 April and Bordeaux on the 4th.

Then it was back to the States for three shows in Vancouver, Seattle and San Francisco on the 10th, 11th and 13th.

On their arrival home, the Noel's robbery story had now broken large. At Manchester Airport, Liam was asked for a reaction from the crowd of photographers and journalists who awaited him.

'Yeah, I did it,' he shot back, 'and your house is next.'

Noel meanwhile had travelled to Chris Evans's new TV show, *TFI Friday* on Channel Four and delivered, in the circumstances, a very relaxed and humorous interview.

He applauded Jarvis Cocker's actions at the Brits, and said of Michael Jackson, 'He comes to our country and comes on-stage thinking he's God. I mean who does he think he is. Me?'

But that night in his Camden flat, Noel locked all the doors and said to Meg, 'I can't believe it. They're going to ask fucking questions in the Huse [Parliament] and all I've ever done is write some songs and swear on TV.'

For most people present, it was the most worried anyone had ever seen him. He was also fuming about McCarroll's legal action.

'It's costing us thousands of pounds in lawyers,' he fiercely stated, 'and he's claiming royalties on an album that is selling because Alan White, who doesn't get any royalties from it, is flogging his arse around the world promoting. That can't be right.'

The only thing Noel had to look forward to now was the two massive open-air shows at Manchester City's Maine Road ground.

The day after they began a three-month break.

*

Liam finally gave in and moved out of Manchester to stay with Patsy in London. He was still wary of the capital, but he couldn't take a step in Manchester without someone being upon him. Reluctantly, he packed his bags and moved out of his mum's house where just about everybody knew the address.

'Sometimes,' Peggy would say, 'I'd see him just sitting there on his own, thinking away. I'd say, "Liam, what are you doing?" And he'd say, "I'm getting my head together, Mam. This is the only place I can do it." '

Now he wanted to spend as much time as he could with the girl that was now dominating his mind. That summer he and Patsy would holiday in privacy in the Caribbean and fall further in love. The relationship was a new experience for Liam, he'd never felt this way for anybody in his whole life.

In his first week in London, he and Noel went to see the first of two Ocean Colour Scene gigs at London's Electric Ballroom. The band's album *Moseley Shoals* had now been released and was outselling *Morning Glory*, which was still a top-ten album.

'You fuckers,' Noel told the band in their dressing-room, 'Help you out all these years and now you're selling more records than me.'

After the show, he and Liam went to a Creation party organised by meg to launch The Super Furry Animals album *Fuzzy Logic*.

The pair of them then turned up again at the Ballroom the next night and played a short acoustic set for the audience. They came back on later to join Ocean Colour Scene for their encore, delivering a blistering version of 'Ticket To Ride'.

On 24 May Noel arrived at the Hit Factory Studio to visit Paul Weller, who was busy recording his new single 'Peacock Suit'.

The next day he and Meg took off for a month's holiday on the island of Mustique. Kate Moss and Johnny Depp joined the couple, as did Fran and Jess.

Two weeks into the holiday, part of which was spent at Mick Jagger's house (they blew his stereo's speakers), Owen Morris arrived. On the first night, Noel threatened to send him home when he expressed his doubts about the Ocean Colour Scene album. The next day they began recording demos for the next Oasis album, provisionally entitled *Be Here Now*.

On his return home, Noel would play the tape to trusted

friends and the like although he rarely mentioned the existence of another tape he had also cut with Owen. This featured seven more songs, written in the earlier part of the year, that he claimed were the best he had ever come up with. He would deposit them in his songwriting account for future use.

He and Meg had moved from Albert Street and were now residing in St. John's Wood. The papers soon got hold of the new address and started turning up at all hours of the day and night, looking for pictures and a story.

The fans also cottoned on. One day Noel plugged in his electric guitar and played it for about forty-five minutes, working out various ideas. When he finished, he received a round of applause from the fans listening outside.

This fame game was seriously getting to him now. It wasn't so much the constant attention, although that was bad enough, it was the fact that the sheer volume of publicity was now detracting from the music.

Oasis weren't a serious musical force to many newspaper readers, they were a band known for everything but that.

Of course, sometimes this did have its uses. One Sunday he and Meg went to Ronnie Scott's to see Paul Weller deliver a surprise support slot for the singer Gabrielle.

After the show, along with Simon Halfon, Keren and Sarah from Bananarama and Brendan Lynch, they headed back to Halfon's flat in St. John's Wood.

Halfon and Lynch managed to wave a taxi down but as there were too many to fit in the car, the others let them go. Standing on Tottenham Court Road, a dustcart pulled up, the drivers instantly recognising Noel.

'Give us a lift to St. John's Wood, mate' Noel asked.

'Sure thing, jump in.'

As Simon and Brendan got out of their taxi, they were amazed to see a dustcart pull up behind them and deposit their celebrated friends. Halfon then invited the dustmen up to his flat where they stayed for an hour, drinking and grabbing pictures and autographs.

'You better send us the pictures,' one of them said as they went back to work, 'no cunt will ever believe this.'

*

On 27 June. Noel sat on a stool on the stage of the Royal Festival Hall, and with Burt Bacharach at the piano, he sang the song that had inspired and affected him so much, 'This Guy's In Love With You'.

Of course, he had invited Coyley and Phil Smith down to stay at his house and finally meet the man whose records meant so much to them all.

Liam and Guigsy were also in the audience, the latter in the process of buying a new house and starting work on a book about a footballer called Robin Friday, an extremely talented player from the 1970s whose predilection for the good life had sadly curtailed both his career and his life.

'He could have been in Oasis,' Guigsy once remarked.

Bonehead, Kate and Lucy had finally moved out of the *Definitely Maybe* flat and into much larger premises.

Bonehead spent his summer having his teeth fixed and spending as much time as he could with his family.

Alan White had also moved to new premises with his new girlfriend, and took a month's holiday in Thailand. But brother Steve was still on his case. 'Look at your beer gut,' he'd say. So now Alan went running.

And then in late July they began rehearsals at Birmingham's NEC complex for six huge festival dates. Two in Loch Lomond on 3 and 4 August, two in Knebworth Park, on the 10th and 11th, for which a staggering two million ticket applications had been made, and two in Cork the following week.

Tragedy struck at the Loch Lomond festival when a worker was accidentally crushed to death the night before the first show. Tragedy had also struck The Charlatans who were scheduled to support, when their keyboard player Rob Collins was killed in a car accident while the band recorded at the Rockfield Studio in Wales. At the Knebworth Festival Meg organised a raffle for a scooter that was placed by the Creation tent and thousands of pounds were raised for Rob's family.

The bill for each day was changed and mirrored Noel's passion for British music in 1996. Ocean Colour Scene, Kula Shaker, The Charlatans, The Prodigy and Manic Street Preachers were some of the bands featured.

Oasis's first night at Knebworth was fine but as usual with these events, the band always took time acclimatising themselves. By the second night, they were ready.

Noel walked on-stage, grabbed the mike and shouted to the 125,000 strong crowd, 'This is history.'

Liam then butted in. 'No it's not,' he said, 'it's Knebworth.'

It was the kind of thinking that Noel loved about his brother. 'No one else in the world,' he would later say, 'could come out with that. No one.'

Oasis that night, in front of a much louder crowd, worked the set with an evident energy and passion. They began with the song that had first introduced them to a nation, 'Columbia'; inserted two new songs, 'Me and My Big Mouth' and 'It's Getting Better, Man'; played 'Don't Look Back In Anger' and 'The Masterplan' back-to-back;' and finished with the final track from *Morning Glory*, 'Champagne Supernova', with John Squire, who had now left The Stone Roses, the band that had so inspired Noel and Liam back in Manchester, coming on both nights to play guitar.

After the show, as their friends partied backstage and the demos for the next album blasted into the night air, Noel and Marcus stood outside and wondered where on earth they could now take Oasis. And keep it interesting. And keep it vibrant.

It was the biggest problem facing the band. And Liam, of course, would be the first to display it publicly.

This is what the third Oasis album might have been. The cover portrays them standing on rostrums in tracksuits, their heads are bowed but their right arms are raised high in the sky, giving the two-finger salute.

Possible track listing: 'Listen Up', '(It's Good) To Be Free', 'Take Me Away', 'Headshrinker', 'D'Yer Wanna Be A Spaceman', 'Cloudburst', 'Up In The Sky (Acoustic)', 'Half The World Away', 'Fade Away (original version)', 'Talk Tonight', 'Acquiesce', 'Round Are Way', 'It's Better People', 'Swamp Song', 'Rockin' Chair' and 'The Masterplan'.

Title?

B-Side Ourselves.

After the shows in Cork, the band, under the tightest security, went into rehearsals for a special MTV *Unplugged* show.

During that week, Noel and Liam came to blows, and the

result was the singer refusing to take part in the show at London's Royal Festival Hall.

On the Thursday, Noel rehearsed the band and sang all the songs himself. Liam sat in the front row, a pint of Guinness in hand, mock applauding and making various loud comments.

He did leap up on-stage to sing 'Round Are Way', but that was all. Noel studiously avoided him. The next night, after keeping the audience waiting outside for at least an hour and a half, the doors finally opened and the crowd were seated.

Oasis, minus Liam walked on-stage, Noel briefly explaining that his brother had 'a sore throat'. In the boxes to his right, Liam watched as Noel led the band through a selection of songs, including a welcome airing of 'Listen Up', that Noel introduced 'as a brand new song'.

At the end, with the crowd asking for more, Liam descended from the box, went into the auditorium and walked across the stage toward the dressing-room.

The word from the aggrieved MTV was that the show was likely to be broadcast in Europe but that American transmission looked doubtful.

On 27 August the band arrived at heathrow airport to set out once more for a three-week American tour. Ten minutes before they were due to fly, Liam suddenly ordered his bags to be taken off the plane and, as the band took off without him, he explained to reporters that he needed to sort out his housing arrangements, and then headed back home to St. John's Wood.

In the Oasis scheme of things this was business as usual, but now the eyes of the world were upon them the following day's avalanche of publicity blew the incident up into an orgy of speculation as to the band's future.

As reporters and TV cameras waited outside Patsy's house, the band began their US tour in Chicago, Noel handling the vocals. He also agreed to be interviewed by Carlton's breakfast show *GMTV*.

'I suppose,' the reporter asked, 'you'll be giving your brother a slap around the head when you see him.'

Whatever Noel's feelings, he was quick to defuse the situation and defend Liam. He said that his brother obviously needed to get himself together and threats weren't going to help him do so. Liam obviously needed some space to put himself right and when he did that, then they'd be more than happy to see him back on-stage. But Liam's mind was obviously elsewhere. He emerged from his house on the Friday, fiercely defending his actions by saying that he couldn't let his fans run his life.

He wore a smart black reefer coat with epaulettes on the shoulders, and when the interviewer asked him about Patsy being the Yoko Ono of the band, he replied, 'She can't be, Yoko's this tall,' he explained raising his hand, 'and Patsy is taller.'

Then he got in a car to take him to the airport. When he landed in America, he hurled a load of swearwords at waiting reporters and then hopped in a cab to meet the band.

The following week, at the MTV Awards in New York the band soundchecked with the lights off so that no one could film them. The organisers then interviewed every band who arrived to perform, bar Oasis. Liam reacted by spitting and swearing on-stage.

At their Philadelphia show, one onlooker thought that Liam's on-stage behaviour was now in danger of turning into a parody.

Friends of the support group Manic Street Preachers reported that at the two shows in Jones Beach, when he wasn't singing, Liam either took the mickey out of the crowd or adopted a totally disinterested pose, ending the gig sitting on a riser, smoking a cigarette and swigging on a bottle like a bored workman in his lunchbreak.

The crunch came in Buffalo, when hours before the show Noel and Liam exchanged punches, cancelled the gig and then returned to their hotel for a serious talk.

The next day Noel returned to London on Thursday 12 September. This was the third time America had witnessed Oasis going to an edge that would destroy most other bands. But, as in Las Vegas, when Noel found himself previously in a time of trouble, The Beatles once again made an appearance.

Sitting right behind Noel as he flew home was none other than the head of Apple and the man they sometimes referred to as the fifth Beatle, Neil Aspinall.

He told Noel, 'Listen mate, don't worry abut splitting Oasis up. At least you're not the man who split The Beatles up.'

Thanks a lot, Noel thought, as he pondered on his and the band's future.

*

The rest of the band arrived home the next morning.

Liam said nothing as he marched through the airport, only pausing to shout out, 'Whitey!' at his drummer before getting into a cab.

The cancellation of the tour made front-pages everywhere. While America readied itself to bomb Iraq, the Oasis story superseded even this conflict to become the lead item on most news stories.

It had taken just three years of their recording career to do so.

There was only one definite plan now. On 7 October, Oasis were booked to enter studio two in Abbey Road Studios to start recording their new album. This is the studio that The Beatles wrote and recorded a series of songs that would later embed themselves in the minds of Noel and Liam Gallagher, and inspire them to go out and shake the world.

The last song The Beatles recorded there before they split up was called 'I Me Mine'.

Outro

Always at it. Always the pair of them. Noel and Liam, Liam and Noel. The Gallagher brothers. Will it ever stop this struggle for control? Probably not. Probably never. Tonight, of course, is no exception.

It is 27 April 1996, and Oasis are on-stage at Maine Road. They have just started playing 'Whatever'.

Liam is at the mike, hands, as usual, firmly clasped behind his back. He starts singing but the 40,000-strong crowd roar out the first lines so loudly that he backs away from the mike to allow them to continue.

But the crowd aren't too sure of the next lines. Their singing quickly fades out and Liam is caught unawares. He quickly leans forward to sing but the music is in front of him now. So he simply walks off-stage, kicking a tambourine in frustration. The band grind to a half. Noel says, 'Thanks bruv,' and then he starts the song up again and sings it himself. Oasis finish to great applause, and as it splashes all over them in great sheets of sound, Noel looks around at the place he finds himself in.

To the right of him is the Kippax Stand where he stood all those years ago with his dad, watching Manchester City. Noel has cut all ties with his father now and in doing so has sworn himself to surpass Thomas Gallagher in everything.

Tonight it is he, Noel, who stands on the hallowed turf, the crowd roaring out his name. It took years to achieve, but as a friend once told him, revenge is a dish best served cold.

Now his gaze goes up to the box above the stand where his mother Peggy and Meg stand watching him, pure love in their eyes, the two women in the world that he has allowed beyond the barriers in his heart.

Present in that box also is Alan McGee, the man who stumbled across him and recognised instantly the talent raging before him.

Watching too is Marcus, the man who has helped him so carefully to plot the amazing path that Oasis have travelled.

Surround the stage are the road crew he has journeyed the world with. Maggie, Jason, Jacko, Pic, and in front of him the lighting and sound men, Hugh, Frank, and somewhere too, he can't see where, stand his close friends Coyley, who helped to start it all, and Phil Smith.

Close by are the band, Alan White, Guigsy and Bonehead, loyal to the last, waiting now for him to play another song that they are yet to tire of playing.

And there, lurking in the wings, stands his brother, the man he will be tied to forever. If Oasis was just Liam, they would never have been signed, they would have threatened to self destruct. If Oasis was just Noel, they would never have reached the heights they have. That is the truth they have arrived at, that is the truth that keeps them battling for the soul of this thing called, Oasis.

Bound by love and hate, trust and admiration, they will see this through together. Let no one stand in their way.

'This is called "Masterplan",' Noel announces, and he strums a chord that then rises high above the crowd and floats across Manchester, the town that helped shape him, the town he had to leave.

As Noel sings, 'Take some time to make some sense of what you want to say / And cast your words', the chord continues its journey, over Liverpool where they first recorded, and then high above the Irish sea, floating softly over the waves until Ireland is beneath.

It travels South, heading towards a little girl who sits by a river in County Mayo gazing into the water, searching for signs of her future. The chord reaches her and momentarily hangs above her head before descending and enveloping her body. The little girl gives a slight shiver and then looks up to the sky, knowing she has been touched.

Then she stands and walks away, whistling her song into the cool evening air, heading towards a future that nobody ever knows.

Bibliography

Lou Reed: The Biography, Victor Bokris
The Neophiliacs, Christopher Booker
The True Adventures of the Rolling Stones, Stanley Booth
Love Me Do: The Beatles Progress, Michael Braun
Parallel Lives, Peter Burton
And God Created Manchester, Sarah Champion
Awopbopaloobop, Nik Cohn
Untouchable: Robert de Niro, Andy Dougan
Last Train to Memphis, Peter Guralnick
Sweet Soul Music, Peter Guralnick
The Dark Stuff, Nick Kent
The Complete Beatles Chronicle, Mark Lewisohn
Revolution in the Head: The Beatles Records and the Sixties, Ian MacDonald
He's a Rebel: Phil Spector, Mark Ribosky
Morrissey and Marr: The Severed Alliance, Johnny Rogan
The Lonely Londoners, Sam Selvon
Red Dirt Marijuana, Terry Southern
Dino: Living High in the Dirty Business of Dreams, Nick Tosches
Ecstasy, Irvine Welsh
The Sound of Phil Spector, Richard Williams
Wired, by Bob Woodward
You Send Me: The Life and Times of Sam Cooke, Daniel Woolf, S.R. Crain, Clifton White and G. David Tenenbaum

Many of these books were purchased at the Helter Skelter Bookshop, Denmark Street, London. Thanks to Sean and all the staff there: Books Forever.